T0213003

Lecture Notes in Business Information Processing   **261**

More information about this series at http://www.springer.com/series/7911

Václav Řepa · Tomáš Bruckner (Eds.)

Perspectives in Business Informatics Research

15th International Conference, BIR 2016
Prague, Czech Republic, September 15–16, 2016
Proceedings

 Springer

Editors
Václav Řepa
Department of Information Technology
University of Economics
Prague 3
Czech Republic

Tomáš Bruckner
Department of Information Technology
University of Economics
Prague 3, Praha
Czech Republic

ISSN 1865-1348   ISSN 1865-1356   (electronic)
Lecture Notes in Business Information Processing
ISBN 978-3-319-45320-0   ISBN 978-3-319-45321-7   (eBook)
DOI 10.1007/978-3-319-45321-7

Library of Congress Control Number: 2016948608

Printed on acid-free paper

This Springer imprint is published by Springer Nature
The registered company is Springer International Publishing AG Switzerland

Preface

Business informatics is a discipline that combines information and communication technology (ICT) with the knowledge of management. It is concerned with the development, use, application, and the role of management information systems and all other possible ways of using ICT in the field of management. It is also an important interdisciplinary academic and research discipline. The Perspectives in Business Informatics Research (BIR) conference series was established 16 years ago as a result of a collaboration of researchers from Swedish and German universities in order to create a forum where researchers in business informatics, both senior and junior, could meet and hold discussions. The conference series is led by the Steering Committee, to which one or two persons from every appointed organizer are invited. To date, BIR conferences were held in: Rostock (Germany – in 2000, 2004, 2010), Berlin (Germany – 2003), Skövde (Sweden – 2005), Kaunas (Lithuania – 2006), Tampere (Finland – 2007), Gdańsk (Poland – 2008), Kristianstad (Sweden – 2009), Riga (Latvia – 2011), Nizhny Novgorod (Russia – 2012), Warsaw (Poland – 2013), Lund (Sweden – 2014), and Tartu (Estonia – 2015). This year's 15th International Conference on Perspectives in Business Informatics Research (BIR) was held during September 14–16, 2016, at the University of Economics, Prague (PUE), the biggest and most prestigious Czech university of economics and business.

This year the BIR conference attracted 61 submissions from 16 countries. They were precisely reviewed by 42 members of the Program Committee representing 21 countries. As the result, 22 full papers and two short papers from nine countries were selected for presentation at the conference and publication in this volume together with abstracts of invited talks by Dimitris Karagiannis and Giancarlo Guizzardi. The papers presented at the conference cover many important aspects of business informatics research. This year there was a particular emphasis on business processes and enterprise modeling, information systems development, information systems management, learning, capability, and data analysis issues. The main conference was also accompanied with satellite events: three workshops and a doctoral consortium took place during the first day of the conference.

We would like to thank everyone who contributed to the BIR 2016 conference. First of all, we thank the authors for presenting their papers, we appreciate the invaluable contributions from the members of the Program Committee and the external reviewers, and we thank all the members of the local organization team from the University of Economics, Prague, for their help in organizing the conference. We acknowledge the EasyChair development team for providing a valuable tool for preparing the proceedings and the Springer publishing team for their excellent collaboration. Last but not the least, we thank the Steering Committee for directing the BIR conference series.

July 2016

Václav Řepa
Tomáš Bruckner

Organization

Program Co-chairs

Václav Řepa   University of Economics, Czech Republic
Tomáš Bruckner   University of Economics, Czech Republic

Program Committee

Eduard Babkin   State University Higher School of Economics (Nizhny
                       Novgorod), Russia
Per Backlund   University of Skövde, Sweden
Ilia Bider   Stockholm University/IbisSoft, Sweden
Daniel Braunnagel   Universität Regensburg, Germany
Rimantas Butleris   Kaunas University of Technology, Lithuania
Cristina Cabanillas   Vienna University of Economics and Business, Austria
Sven Carlsson   Lund University, Sweden
Raffaele Conforti   Queensland University of Technology, Australia
Massimiliano de Leoni Eindhoven University of Technology, The Netherlands
Marlon Dumas   University of Tartu, Estonia
Peter Forbrig   University of Rostock, Germany
Bogdan Ghilic-Micu   Bucharest University of Economic Studies, Romania
Jānis Grabis   Riga Technical University, Latvia
Giancarlo Guizzardi   Federal University of Espirito Santo, Brazil
Markus Helfert   Dublin City University, Ireland
Björn Johansson   Lund University, Sweden
Anna Kalenkova   National Research University Higher School of
                       Economics, Russia
Marite Kirikova   Riga Technical University, Latvia
John Krogstie   Norwegian University of Science and Technology,
                       Norway
Michael Le Duc   Mälardalen University, Sweden
Barbara Livieri   University of Salento, Italy
Irina Lomazova   National Research University Higher School of
                       Economics, Russia
Raimundas Matulevicius University of Tartu, Estonia
Charles Møller   Aalborg University, Denmark
Jacob Nørbjerg   Aalborg University, Denmark
Grzegorz J. Nalepa   AGH University of Science and Technology, Poland
Alexander Norta   Tallinn University of Technology, Estonia
Boris Novikov   St. Petersburg University, Russia

Michael Petit	University of Namur, Belgium
Tomáš Pitner	Masaryk University, Czech Republic
Manuel Resinas	University of Seville, Spain
Kurt Sandkuhl	University of Rostock, Germany
Flavia Santoro	UNIRIO, Brazil
Pnina Soffer	University of Haifa, Israel
Chris Stary	Johannes Kepler University of Linz, Austria
Janis Stirna	Stockholm University, Sweden
Bernhard Thalheim	Christian Albrechts University Kiel, Germany
Peter Trkman	University of Ljubljana, Slovenia
Anna Wingkvist	Linnaeus University, Sweden
Stanislaw Wrycza	University of Gdansk, Poland
Jelena Zdravkovic	Stockholm University, Sweden
Iryna Zolotaryova	Kharkiv National University of Economics, Ukraine

External Reviewers

Hassan Adelyar, Estonia	Giovanni Maccani, Ireland
Anis Ben Othman, Estonia	Aleksas Mamkaitis, Ireland
Szymon Bobek, Poland	Alfonso Marquez-Chamorro, Spain
Mario Bochicchio, Italy	Mirella Muhic, Sweden
Thomas Falk, Germany	Karima Qayumee, Estonia
Owen Foley, Ireland	Salim Saay, Estonia
Nicklas Holmberg, Sweden	Eriks Sneiders, Sweden
Amin Jalali, Sweden	Olgerta Tona, Sweden
Miranda Kajtazi, Sweden	Filip Vencovsky, Czech Republic
Krzysztof Kluza, Poland	Benjamin Wehner, Germany
Alexandr Kormiltsym, Estonia	

BIR Series Steering Committee

Mārīte Kirikova	Riga Technical University, Latvia (Chair)
Kurt Sandkuhl	Rostock University, Germany (Co-chair)
Eduard Babkin	State University – HSE, Russia
Rimantas Butleris	Kaunas Technical University, Lithuania
Sven Carlsson	Lund University, Sweden
Peter Forbrig	Rostock University, Germany
Björn Johansson	Lund University, Sweden
Andrzej Kobyliñski	Warsaw School of Economics, Poland
Raimundas Matulevičius	University of Tartu, Estonia
Lina Nemuraitė	Kaunas Technical University, Lithuania
Jyrki Nummenmaa	University of Tampere, Finland
Václav Řepa	University of Economics Prague, Czech Republic
Benkt Wangler	University of Skövde, Sweden
Stanislaw Wrycza	University of Gdansk, Poland

Sponsoring Institutions

Česká spořitelna, a.s., Czech Republic

BIR2016_Keynotes

Agile Modelling Method Engineering - AMME

Dimitris Karagiannis

University of Vienna, Vienna, Austria
dimitris.karagiannis@univie.ac.at

In this context, the foundations of a "conceptual-model"-awareness approach for next generation Enterprise Information Systems will be presented. This novel approach makes use of semantic networks to extend model-awareness towards arbitrary types of models that are developed for specialized communities aiming for domain-specificity (or even case-specificity) in their modeling language, therefore favoring productivity at the expense of reusability across domains. The technological space for capturing and bridging knowledge through model semantics is primarily based on diagrammatic models. Two categories of models are employed in this context: (1) Models of Concepts – for describing a common understanding of a domain through its concepts and relations; (2) Models that use Concepts – typically domain-specific models based on some already established understanding of the domain.

The hereby introduced Agile Modeling Method Engineering – AMME- concept aims to apply the principle of agility established in Software Engineering (e.g., evolutionary development, flexible response to change) to the practice of Modeling Method Engineering. The main assumption is that a modeling method may evolve iteratively based on changing modeling requirements and feedback loops.

Within the context of AMME, a full methodological life cycle is established by the OMiLab Laboratory (http://www.omilab.org), with encompassing five phases: (1) create, (2) design, (3) formalize, (4), develop and (5) deploy/validate. The approach is supported, in its prototyping stage, by the meta modeling domain-specific language MM-DSL and within the academic version of the meta-modeling platform ADOxx (http://www.adoxx.org).

Formal Ontology, Patterns and Anti-Patterns for Next-Generation Conceptual Modeling

Giancarlo Guizzardi

Federal University of Espírito Santo, Vitória, Espírito Santo, Brazil
gguizzardi@inf.ufes.br

In his ACM Turing Award Lecture entitled "The Humble Programmer", E.W. Dijkstra discusses the sheer complexity one has to deal with when programming large computer systems. His article represented an open call for an acknowledgement of the complexity at hand and for the need of more sophisticated techniques to master this complexity. This talk advocates the view that we are now in an analogous situation with respect to Conceptual Modeling. We will experience an increasing demand for building Reference Conceptual Models in subject domains in reality, as well as employing them to address classes of problems, for which sophisticated ontological distinctions are demanded. One of these key problems is Semantic Interoperability. Effective semantic interoperability requires an alignment between worldviews or, to put it more accurately, it requires the precise understanding of the relation between the (inevitable) ontological commitments assumed by different conceptual models and the systems based on them (including sociotechnical systems). This talk advocates the view that an approach that neglects true ontological distinctions (i.e., Ontology in the philosophical sense) cannot meet these requirements. The talk discusses the importance of foundational axiomatic theories and principles in the design of conceptual modeling languages and models. Moreover, it discusses the role played by three types of complexity management tools: Ontological Design Patterns (ODPs) as methodological mechanisms for encoding these ontological theories; Ontology Pattern Languages (OPLs) as systems of representation that take ODPs as higher-granularity modeling primitives; and Ontological Anti-Patterns (OAPs) as structures that can be used to systematically identify possible deviations between the set of valid state of affairs admitted by a model (the actual ontological commitment) and the set of state of affairs actually intended by the stakeholders (the intended ontological commitment). Finally, the talk elaborates on the need for proper computational tools to support a process of pattern-based conceptual model creation, analysis, transformation and validation (via model simulation).

Contents

Business Processes
and Enterprise Modeling

A Conceptual View of Enterprise Resource Planning Systems as Services

Nicklas Holmberg and Björn Johansson(⊠)

Department of Informatics, School of Economics and Management,
Lund University, Ole Römers Väg 6, Lund, Sweden
{nicklas.holmberg,bjorn.johansson}@ics.lu.se

Abstract. This paper brings forward a conceptual view, based on practical experiences from designing information systems as services. Viewing information systems (IS) as services is beneficial but still an unexplored approach in organizations. The aim of this exercise is to contribute to the knowledge base of IS designers and modelers. In the paper, we present an analysis of Enterprise Resource Planning (ERPs) systems through a conceptual lens of Service Oriented Architecture (SOA). This paper contributes to the debate on viewing ISs as services by presenting a view of SOA-architected ERPs as facilitating to fulfill business needs. This paper is influenced by systems and design thinking, and service oriented IS design. Based on shared promises between SOA and ERP we discuss the question whether SOA or ERP fulfills business needs? The analysis of ERPs from a SOA perspective provides us with the conclusion that the question is not about SOA or ERP but rather to provide SOA architected ERPs. It can be said that by viewing ERPs as services it is clear that the combination of ERPs and SOA could be seen as one way forward when designing ISs that aims at bridging gaps between IS and business e.g., processes and, allowing the business to fuse with IS forming servitized SOA based ERPs.

Keywords: Enterprise Resource Planning · Service Oriented Architecture · Business processes · Business rules

1 Introduction

At the end of 1990's there were a big hype among organizations to implement standardized software packages named Enterprise Resource Planning (ERPs) systems. Implementation of ERP systems was the prize organizations had to pay to compete in a constant emerging market. Despite the fact that a service dominant economy emerged and influenced organizations to be recognized as goods or service dominant, not much was done by dominant providers to design Information Systems (ISs) as services [1, 2].

ERP systems must reflect "reality" because they have profound influence on business processes, the inner workings of a business and thus on the way business runs. Manifesting the idea about; business and IS fusion forming a business oriented IS [3], captures much of the essence in the prerequisite for such reflection. Similar directions are discussed by Hirschheim and Klein [4] and Taylor and Raden [5]. Business owners have limited influence on ERPs design thus, vendor specific standardized software packages emerged as embedded business actors [6, 7].

© Springer International Publishing Switzerland 2016
V. Řepa and T. Bruckner (Eds.): BIR 2016, LNBIP 261, pp. 3–15, 2016.
DOI: 10.1007/978-3-319-45321-7_1

Implemented ERPs, to some extent, do not fulfill the promises that were indicated by vendors making organizations searching for other solutions. One solution presented is Service Oriented Architecture (SOA), and according to Forrester Research SOA penetration is stronger than ever [8].

Viewing IS as services is beneficial but still an unexplored approach for IS in organizations [1]. In addition, thinking of systems as services enables new systems design methods to emerge [1]. Indeed, new IS Development (ISD) methods aim to improve business communication and provide practical routes toward increased relevance of IS in business and society [1].

This paper is influenced from practical experiences of a national research project named VacSam. VacSam is a set of composed digital services shaping a servitized IS as a SOA architected Enterprise System (ES).

VacSam provides unique vaccination recommendations to any foreign child entering Sweden with a purpose to decrease child deaths due to preventable infectious diseases. VacSam exemplifies one of many applicable contexts for the suggested view of ISs e.g., decision support, diagnosis, predictive analytics.

From glancing at SOA it can be said that the conceptual architecture promises to service orient a business by bridging the gaps between IS and business processes permitting business to shape IS, automated through services [9, 10]. From a quick overview of the promises of ERPs it is indicated that ERPs promise to deliver a similar solution. However, if ERPs aim at bridging gaps through service-orientation is not clear. That brought us to explore ERPs from a service perspective, - a conceptual view of ERPs as services.

SOA is used as a lens for the conceptualization and as the architecture providing a service with properties and the suggested view with a concrete ground for explanation of what SOA services are. Because SOA shares promises expressed by ERPs we question whether SOA or ERP fulfills business needs? The view of ERPs and SOA as separate but related entities is more carefully discussed in future sections of this paper organized accordingly:

First, we present and define SOA and the concept of services in SOA. The section thereafter defines ERPs and discusses problematic issues with ERP implementation. The reason for doing so; is to be able to provide an exploration of designing ERPs as services, which is done in Sect. 4. In the final section concluding thoughts on what it means to design ERPs as services as well as giving some directions for future studies in this area is presented.

2   Service Oriented Architecture (SOA)

The presented approach to SOA departs from a none-technical point of view; (1) SOA as a conceptual architecture, (2) SOA manifesto and the basic principles of SOA and, (3) SOA realizing technologies. The purpose is to decrease the risk of putting SOA on a par with e.g., Web-services, one of many SOA realizing technologies [10].

SOA is a conceptual architecture functioning independent from choice of realizing technology [9]. During the last decade, SOA received criticism as an ambiguous buzzword only realizing obsolete application platforms e.g., standardized software packages. In 2007 Gartner [11] predicted less than 25 percent of large companies to manage their SOA projects by 2010.

This paper therefore argues that only realizing obsolete application platforms is not the intention of SOA [9, 10, 12]. Just as different designers have different understandings of different material and its respectively properties, SOA means different "things" depending on whom you ask [13].

Sincere efforts to operationalize SOA have been made. In 2005, Erl [10] established the basic principles for SOA. Eight basic principles could now intrinsically express Separation of Concerns (SoC) and properties for a SOA service. However, it was still unclear how SOA managed SoC in terms of which logic to encapsulate. A few years later in 2009, Arsanjani et al. [9] established the SOA Manifesto. Fourteen guiding principles stressed the importance of maintaining a business perspective in any SOA initiative [9]. To consider shared services therefore became more important than specific purpose implementations.

In 2009, the SOA manifesto, an extended abstract level of SOA, expressing high level business modeling guidelines was set e.g., 'to respect the social and power structure of the organization' [9]. To achieve architecture supporting the SOA manifesto the basic principles for SOA became of profound importance. The eight principles express properties that a SOA service must possess to be recognized as eligible and responsible. Supporting SoC, the basic principles express modularization and encapsulation realized through information hiding, also, commonly known in Object Oriented Programming (OOP).

"Conceptual", -a property of SOA, dates back to the origin of "service". At the time, the non-defined term "service" was and, sometime still is, the reason to the intrinsic confusion of what SOA is.

In the 1930's, the U.S. Department of Commerce's Standard Industrial Classification (SIC) provided a service a code of classification. In the late 1970's Hill [14] provided "service" a definition [2]: "[…] a service is a change in the condition of a person, or a good belonging to some economic entity, brought about as the result of the activity of some other economic entity, with the approval of the first person or economic entity." [14].

Thus, a SOA service changes a condition of a Service Provider (SP), because of an activity, corresponding to a request made by a Service Requestor (SR) to a SP through a transport medium e.g., Internet, with the approval of a SP.

Arsanjani et al. [9] suggests that service-orientation, a term encapsulating: service, frames what "one does". Service-orientation of SOA is then interaction between a SR, requesting a service from a SP, providing a service from a Service Directory (SD). That is similar to how Gustiené [15] stressed the importance of interaction as the base for service orientation which must support principles of SoC.

Then, "[…] Service-oriented architecture (SOA) is a type of architecture that results from applying service orientation." [9]. While, interaction is "[…] Related mutual actions occurring within a shared space of time or place." [16]. Interaction occurs through a transport medium and its direction is no simplistic association but guideposts indicating orientation of interaction in "reality". Then, an SD-listed-service permits peer-to-peer communication between SR and SD with approval of SP. It can therefore be said that service-orientation based on interaction permits a service to become a unit of communication enabling a SR, a SP and a SD, to interact within a shared space on a share time in a known real world direction i.e., SOA depicted in conceptual and data level in Fig. 1 accordingly:

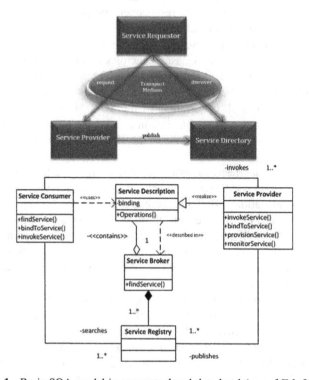

Fig. 1. Basic SOA model in conceptual and data level (use of Erl, 2005)

Industry bodies and e.g., OASIS Group and Open Group created formal definitions of SOA with intentions to facilitate SOA's implicit terminology and reduce its different meanings to: "A paradigm for organizing and utilizing distributed capabilities [...]" [17]. According to the SOA manifesto SOA is realized with varying technologies and standards and functions independent from choice of realizing technology [9].

Based on this we define SOA accordingly: SOA is a paradigm that shapes a conceptual architecture, functioning independent from choice of realizing technology, providing abilities to describe a service, its properties and its orientation, for conscious change or design of a service-oriented business.

2.1 SOA Services

Addressing SOA services addresses SOA realizing technology. SOA realizing technology is used for designing a SOA service as a unit of communication realizing interaction. Services responsible for functional components, together shaping a SOA based

ES, could thus be viewed as components equipped with logical boundaries forming composable subject matters. Hence, a service is responsible for the logic it encapsulates independently existing, as an entity of its own right, from other services and ISs.

SOA realizing technologies are: e.g., Simple Object Access Protocol (SOAP), Universal Description, Discovery and Integration (UDDI), Web Service Description Language (WSDL) etc. Such technologies are architectural styles or patterns solving reoccurring known design problems quite contrary to conceptual SOA [10, 13] which rather benefits from being thought of in Alexandrian terms e.g.; design methodology applicable when suitable. Based on that, there is a plethora of SOA realizing technologies putting the basic principles of SOA into use and thereby supporting SoC.

Then the basic principles of SOA are: (1) Services are reusable, (2) Services share a formal contract, (3) Services are loosely coupled, (4) Services abstract underlying logic, (5) Services are composable, (6) Services are autonomous, (7) Services are stateless, (8) Services are discoverable [10] are what shape SOA services representing a part of the physical form of a SOA. Based on the same conditions we argue that functional areas shaping components of ERPs can be designed as services. That is better discussed and explained in Chap. 4.

3 Enterprise Resource Planning Systems

The ERP concept is broad and the market of ERP is dominated by a number of few companies including SAP, Oracle, and Microsoft. However, there are a number of key characteristics that more or less all ERP systems have making them a unique subtype of IS: (1) ERPs are standardized packaged software [18] designed with the aim of integrating an entire organization [19–21]. (2) The ERP ought to cover all information processing needs and to integrate the internal value chain with an organization's external value chain through Business Process (BP) integration [19] and (3) Provide the entire organization with common master data [22]. From this it can be stated that ERPs have a high impact on organization's business processes, but as argued by Millman [23] there exist problems, such as, it is either not used or is implemented in the wrong way.

The main problem presented is the misfit between ERP functionality and business requirements. Soh, Kien and Tay-Yap [24] describe this as a common problem when adopting software packages. The problem of "misfit" means that e.g., "Many people feel that the current ERP system has taken (or been given) a role that hinders or does not support the business processes to the extent desire" [7]. Then, ERPs are process-based or at least attempt to be process-based. According to Koch [25] the basic architecture building on a department/stab model as for instance SAP'R/3 makes ERPs not supporting the idea of BPs and thereby not the integration between different departments in an organization. It does not help that the ERP vendor attached some words about BPs onto their ERP if the basic architecture does not support BPs [25].

3.1   Functional Areas of ERP Systems Architecture

ERPs are often described from a functional perspective meaning that the systems architecture mimics a functional organizational description. That implies that each department has its own ERP component. However, the basic architecture of an ERP follows the master data thoughts [22]. Then, functional ERP areas use a unified database. Different ERP vendors describes this in different ways, however, the most common description is to discuss *modules*. Thus, the implementing organization implements a core module and then selects what modules to implement on top of the core module(s). The ERP architecture therefore builds on a vertical organizational description. The implication of that is that horizontal work tasks involving different departments are not clearly described in ERP architecture. Resulting in that users of ERPs could understand the ERPs as not supporting the business process they work with, resulting in a misfit between ERP and users interpretation of how the system fulfill their needs.

4   Designing ERP Systems as Services

ERPs as described above, builds to a high extent on functional areas e.g.; (1) Inventory, (2) Production, (3) Accounting, (4) HR, (5) Delivery, (6) BI, (7) Sales, (8) Engineering, (9) Production Planning, and (10) Purchase. However, the volatile nature of business makes it complex to implement the same ERP in all organizations. Based on the basic principles of SOA, functional areas of an ERP system could be designed as independent components, separated by logical boundaries, designed with the same accuracy as a single class or entity is [10, 26]. That view is based on modularization realized through information hiding and to learn ISD by "doing".

From the description of ERPs it can be stated that it is hard to see if its promises - bridging the gaps between IS and business processes - have been fulfilled. The same can be said about SOA promises. However, it seems that if combing the ideas of SOA when designing an ERP that may be a way forward to fulfill promises from both ERP and SOA.

From this it could be claimed that the desired result is to bridge the gap between BPs and IS so that business shapes IS into what could be described as a SOA architected ERP. The question is then how can SOA improve the design of ERPs? A tentative answer to that question could be that the focus moves from a functional view to a conceptual holistic view, meaning that functions in the ERP, if designed as services, could be seen and provided as applications that could be used in different BPs. In practice this could imply that an organization is permitted to deal with the problem of organizational support with a horizontal supportive IS.

On those conditions, functional areas of an ERP could form components shaped by services eligible to execute in SOA. Based on practical experiences from VacSam, it is shown that by composing digital services a SOA architected IS can be shaped.

Through the design science research initiative it can be said that this conceptual view of ERPs as services became even more evident.

Through the Enterprise Model (EM) (see, [27]) of the VacSam project it can be seen that Fig. 4 depicts that the five sub models of the EM express how business rules integrate in a business and how the business vision model casts the ground for the business strategy and common business goal; *fully vaccinated according to the Swedish vaccination schedule.*

Moreover, the EM depicts that (1) The business rules model (a) triggers the business process model, (b) defines the business concepts model, (c) uses the business resource and actor model and, (d) supports the business vision model. (2) The business process model in turn, requires the business rules model. (3) The business concepts model (a) defines the business rules models. (4) The business vision model motivates and requires the business rules model [27].

In addition, (5) the business resource and actors model, including General Practitioners (GPs), Subject Matter Experts (SMEs) and Vaccination Experts (VEs), is, responsible for the business rules model [27].

Based on that it can be said that Fig. 4 depicts the business models that were digitally transformed and automated through digital services forming applications that could be used in different BPs and shaping the servitized IS named VacSam:

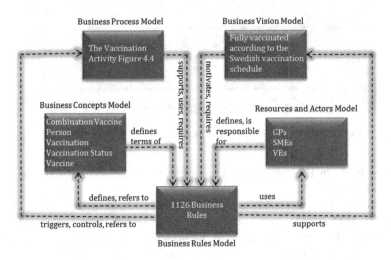

Fig. 2. The business model of VacSam (use of, [27])

If applying this view on the design of ERPs with the aim of integrating an entire organization, a noteworthy detail is that the five models of the business model in Fig. 2 fits e.g., the Zachman framework for Enterprise Architecture (EA) as integrals accordingly:

Hence, the business model of VacSam indicates the desired level of service-orientation and the desired result in the form of a SOA based ES. This is further exemplified through the BRs model and the BP model of VacSam. With the business concepts model in hand BRs it is possible to design well-formed business rules. The business rules model was thus

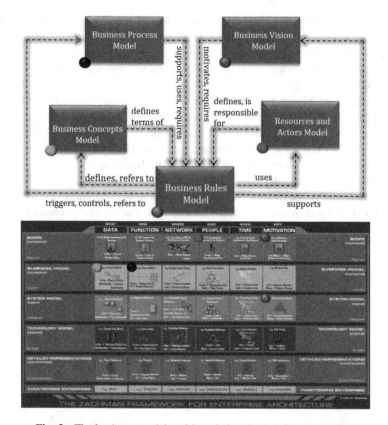

Fig. 3. The business model and its relation the EA framework [27]

constituted by 1126 BRs all designed according to the principles of Business rules approach (BRA) (Fig. 3).

Together the BRs forms business rules packages which in turn shapes decision logic centric SOA services expressing a businesses' "what", only exposing a WSDL according to the basic principles for SOA. Implementing the process logic centric SOA services in imperative JAVA results in an expression of a businesses' "how"

This means that all rule projects including a number of BRs is automated through digital services of their own right. Those decision logic centric services are meant for governing the business process presented in Fig. 4. The business process model in Fig. 4 depicts the process logic explored, extracted and implemented in VacSam:

Together the businesses' "what" and "how" implemented as SOA services support the inner functioning of the business process of Fig. 4. However, the business models per se, could be viewed as archetypes in terms of well-known "standard" ISD models. Thus, it is not the models that are of interest but their combination and service-orientation.

Through SOA, these models are service-oriented and automated hence modular and encapsulated realized through separate digital services kept by the service directory of

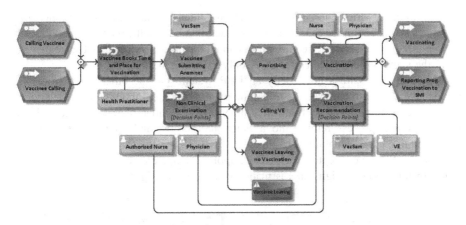

Fig. 4. The Business Process for VacSam's Process Logic

Fig. 5 below. As a result, each service reflects part of a reality and together the services reflect a reality, a holism i.e., the Swedish vaccination recommendation activity. As a result business processes and IS merges to the servitized ES named VacSam through this SOA perspective:

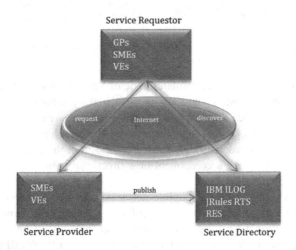

Fig. 5. The Intuitive SOA Orientation Model of VacSam (instance of Fig. 1) (use of, [10])

Figure 5 depicts that SOA has been realized both technically and conceptually. This means that in the VacSam-project SOA was implemented as:

The paradigm informing the design of models and frameworks for a conceptual architecture for interaction, functioning independent from realizing technology, providing abilities to describe a service, its properties and its orientation, for conscious change or design for business service orientation.

The intuitive orientation model, permitting inter-organizational communication, illustrates key actors in the SOA based on the actors-model of the business model. Each service listed in the service directory knows about the other services listed since they all share the same basic principles for SOA only exposing WSDL.

However, VacSam is not strictly an ERP system. On the other hand, from this perspective, VacSam corresponds to a component shaped by about 60 digital services used by GPs for diagnosis. Logically, diagnosis is similar to any Business Rules (BR) governed process reified into a functional IS-area and could most likely be compared to e.g., an accounting-module of a ERP. That is the foremost reason to why we consider SOA a conceptual architecture applicable in a plethora of contexts and not a pattern for routine design. This is made even clearer in Fig. 6.

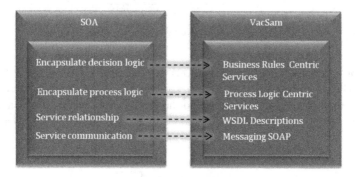

Fig. 6. How SOA Encapsulates Logic in VacSam (use of, [10])

Figure 6 depicts how SOA encapsulates logic of VacSam. It is clear from the figure that process logic and decision logic are encapsulated by separate species of digital services. However our idea draws on that each functional area of an ERP could be analyzed for extracting its process logic respectively decision logic for implementation into separate digital services. Through service composition the collection of different services could easily replace a component or a functional area of an ERP shaping a truly flexible IS.

Thus, SOA permits to design eligible services and thereby service orienting a business regardless of its character. With profound influence on "how" and "what" business runs, functional areas of any IS must reflect reality to be able to support business processes as a whole thus, bridging the gap between IS and BPs. Therefore it is crucial for the purpose, entitling the being, of an ERP to support decision points in a BP permitting or constraining its execution. Such decision points require business rules why the decision per se could be viewed as the connection between business processes and business rules. Moreover, any ERP must have such business rules as a ground for decisions.

This SOA approach also facilitates managerial IS capabilities in terms of e.g., a shared service repository and the fact that changing one SOA service will not affect the other services because a service is responsible for the logic it encapsulates. This ought to provide better chances for bridging the gap between business processes and IS and the chances for the IS to continue to function in the businesses' active equilibrium through managing change in an organized way.

From research on ERPs we recognize a lack of transparency regarding logic responsibility. What logic that shapes a functional area of an ERP component, is not clear. According to Morgan, [28], Graham, [29] and Von Halle [30] part of business logic shapes decision logic. The other part of business logic is shaped by BPs i.e., process logic [31]. Logic separation through SoC then has profound influence on foundational e.g., alethic logic, and is crucial for IS and ISD success [31]. Tentative results of such SoC is consistent automated business logic [30] -a promise made by Business Rules Approach (BRA) familiar as a support to SOA nowadays [28, 29], but, still an unrecognized approach for native ERP design.

BRs of BRA renounce from expressing "who", "when", "where" or "how" a business rule executes [28, 30, 32] or any temporal aspects managed by operational process logic of an IS [31] as can be seen above. Thus BRs express "what" [32]. BRs then either constrain BP activities from executing or permit them to execute attaining a state why BRs triggers BPs [27]. A BR could therefore be viewed as a definition or a delineation of an aspect of a business [28, 29, 33]. Then, BRs govern BPs [34]. And, BRs are recognized as the operational decision logic of an IS.

Quite contrary, BPs are recognized as the operational process logic of an IS [31]. With that distinction a business's "what" i.e., decision logic expressed by BRs and, "how" i.e., process logic expressed by BPs, becomes transparent and manageable as separate but interrelated components shaped by business objects advocating IS and business alignment [27, 31].

Without separation of logic, decision logic is scattered with process logic and application specific code in the same object, in plural forming components or modules, commonly known as obsolete legacy IS. That makes it hard to recognize what a functional area of an ERP is and which logic each component shaping a functional area of an ERP is encapsulating. Moreover, that would renounce SoC, SOA and BRA by being solely one track minded [26, 28, 29, 34, 35]. Even if there has been some progress, ERPs could be seen as quite far from supporting SoC, since it implies to "consume an elephant" rather than trying to break down problems into smaller manageable pieces, similar to objectification or break down of connections. That directs us to the conclusion that it would be beneficial viewing ERPs as services to a higher extent.

5 Conclusion

We have learnt that, ERP since it is a standardized software package demands adopting organizations to change BPs. However, if viewing ERPs as services, that would not be the case. The view would rather force BPs or their process logic to shape composable services forming one part of an ERP expressing "how", to achieve goals. The other part is shaped by BRs or their decision logic as services expressing "what", to achieve goals. When the two types of services are composed, they can be viewed as a component reflecting a functional area of an ERP providing a desired result similar to those provided by components for e.g., diagnosis or accounting. That would then correspond to a SOA-architected ERP.

Viewing ERPs as services explicitly renounce from any "silver bullet approach" but implies to break down problems into smaller pieces, supporting principles of SoC, and systematically design responsible services, supporting SOA, shaping components reflecting functional areas of an ERP in turn supporting business needs, one at a time. The analysis of ERPs from a SOA perspective provides us with the conclusion that the question is not about SOA or ERP but rather to provide SOA-architected ERPs. By viewing ERPs as services it is clear that the combination of ERPs and SOA could be seen as one way forward when developing software that aims at bridging the gaps between supporting IS and business processes. However, additional empirical research e.g., DSR on designing functional areas as components, shaped by SOA services, supporting important business problems, followed by evaluation, would cast a better ground for interesting future research on the suggested perspective of ERPs. To the best of our knowledge, this perspective of ERPs, BRs and BPs, is an important area for IS research providing more knowledge on how business and IS are independent but intrinsically related entities of today.

References

1. Alter, S.: Viewing systems as services: a fresh approach in the is field. Commun. Assoc. Inf. Syst. **26**(11), 195–224 (2010)
2. Chesbrough, H., Spohrer, J.: A research manifesto for services science. Commun. ACM **49** (7), 35–40 (2006)
3. El Sawy, O.A.: The IS core ix: the 3 faces of is identity: connection, immersion, and fusion. Commun. Assoc. Inf. Syst. **12**(1), 588–598 (2003)
4. Hirschheim, R., Klein, H.K.: Four paradigms of information systems development. Commun. ACM **32**(10), 1199–1216 (1989)
5. Taylor, J., Raden, N.: Smart (Enough) Systems, How to Deliver Competitive Advantage by Automating Hidden Decisions. Prentice Hall, Pearson Education, USA (2007)
6. Melin, U.: The ERP system as a part of an organization's administrative paradox. In: 11th European Conference on Information Systems, Naples, Italy (2003)
7. Askenäs, L., Westelius, A.: Five roles of an information system: a social constructionist approach to analyzing the use of ERP systems, In: Twenty First International Conference on Information Systems, pp. 426–434. Association for Information Systems, Brisbane (2000)
8. Robinson, J.: SOA still kicking, says Forrester (2009). http://www.information-age.com/channels/development-and-integration/perspectives-and-trends/1053022/soa-still-kicking-says-forrester.thtml. (Cited 22 Nov 2011)
9. Arsanjani, A., et al. The SOA Manifesto (2009). http://www.soa-manifesto.org/. (30 September 2010)
10. Erl, T.: Service-oriented architecture: concepts, technology, and design. Prentice Hall PTR, Pearson Education, Upper Saddle River (2005)
11. Gartner. Bad Technical Implementations and Lack of Governance Increase Risks of Failure in SOA Projects. Gartner Newsroom. Press Release (2007). http://www.gartner.com/it/page.jsp?id=508397. (21 October 2011)
12. Erl, T.: SOA Principles, The Service-Orientation Design Paradigm (2008). http://www.soaprinciples.com/p3.php. (04 March 2010)

13. Holley, K., Arsanjani, A.: 100 SOA questions asked and answered. Pearson Education, Inc., (2011)
14. Hill, P.T.: On goods and services. Rev. Income Wealth **23**(4), 314–339 (1977)
15. Gustiené, P.: Development of a New Service-Oriented Modelling Method for Information Systems Analysis and Design. Karlstad University, Karlstad (2010)
16. Alexanderson, P.: Adding Audibility, in Department of Informatics. Lund University, Lund (2007)
17. OASIS Group. Reference Model for Service Oriented Architecture 1.0. (2006). http://docs. oasis-open.org/soa-rm/v1.0/soa-rm.pdf. (06 October 2011)
18. Wieder, B., et al.: The impact of ERP systems on firm and business process performance. J. Enterp. Inf. Manag. **19**(1), 13–29 (2006)
19. Lengnick-Hall, C.A., Lengnick-Hall, M.L., Abdinnour-Helm, S.: The role of social and intellectual capital in achieving competitive advantage through enterprise resource planning (ERP) systems. J. Eng. Technol. Manag. **21**(4), 307–330 (2004)
20. Rolland, C., Prakash, N.: Bridging the gap between organisational needs and ERP functionality. Requirements Eng. **5**(3), 180–193 (2000)
21. Wier, B., Hunton, J., HassabElnaby, H.R.: Enterprise resource planning systems and non-financial performance incentives: the joint impact on corporate performance. Int. J. Acc. Inf. Syst. **8**(3), 165–190 (2007)
22. Hedman, J., Borell, A.: ERP systems impact on organizations. In: Grant, G. (ed.) ERP & Data Warehousing in Organizations: Issues and Challenges, pp. 1–21. Idea Group Publishing, Hershey (2003)
23. Millman, G.J.: What did you get from ERP, and what can you get? Financ. Executives Int. **5**, 15–24 (2004)
24. Soh, C., Kien, S.S., Tay-Yap, J.: Cultural fits and misfits: is ERP a universal solution? Commun. ACM **43**(4), 47–51 (2000)
25. Koch, C.: BPR and ERP: Realising a vision of process with IT. Bus. Process Manag. J. **7**(3), 258 (2001)
26. Dijkstra, E.W.: On the role of scientific thought. In: Selected Writings on Computing: A Personal Perspective, pp. 60–66. Springer-Verlag New York, Inc., New York (1982)
27. Bajec, M., Krisper, M.: A methodology and tool support for managing business rules in organisations. Inf. Syst. **30**(6), 423–443 (2005)
28. Morgan, T.: Business rules and information systems: aligning IT with business goals. Addison-Wesley, Boston (2002)
29. Graham, I.: Business rules management and service oriented architecture: a pattern language. Wiley, Chichester (2006)
30. Von Halle, B.: Business Rules Applied: Building Better Systems Using the Business Rules Approach. John Wiley & Sons, Inc., Computer Publishing, New York (2001)
31. Holmberg, N., Steen, O.: Business process and business rules modelling in concert for e-service design and business alignment. In: 1st International Conference on Cloud Computing and Services Science (CLOSER), Noordwijkerhout, The Netherlands (2011)
32. Date, C.J.: What Not How: The Business Rules Approach to Application Development. Addison-Wesley, Reading (2000)
33. Van Eijndhoven, T., Iacob, M.E., Ponisio, M.L.: Achieving business process flexibility with business rules. In: 12th International IEEE Enterprise Distributed Object Computing Conference, pp. 95–104 (2008)
34. BRG. The Business Rules Manifesto Version 2.0., November 1, 2003 (2003). http://www. businessrulesgroup.org/brmanifesto.htm. (04 January 2011)
35. Ross, R.G.: Principles of the Business Rule Approach. Addison-Wesley, Boston (2003)

Supporting Social Network Analysis Using Chord Diagram in Process Mining

Amin Jalali[✉]

Department of Computer and Systems Sciences,
Stockholm University, Stockholm, Sweden
aj@dsv.su.se

Abstract. Data visualization is an important area of research aims to empower people to discover information from data through visual artefacts. The huge volume of data can result in abundance of elements in data visualization, which can make the information discovery challenging. Chord diagrams is a sort of visual representation that has been recently introduced to increase the level of abstraction. Although this diagram is widely used and adapted in many disciplines, it is not currently implemented in Business Process Management (BPM). Thus, this paper extends the social network visualization approaches in BPM area using chord diagram. This paper defines the formal definitions of elements and elaborates on how the visual representation can be compiled from them. The visualization is supported by implementing a plug-in in ProM. The plug-in is used to demonstrate social networks discovered from real log files in compare with those discovered by current visualization techniques. The result shows that this technique can complement previous ones to discover more social network patterns in BPM area.

Keywords: Business process · Visualization · Social network · Process mining

1 Introduction

Visualization is an important area of research investigating how to increase the capability of people to capture information from data. This area has been investigated for a long time resulting in many visual artifacts and methods that are adapted to be used in many research areas, which makes the data visualization area multidisciplinary. The development of information systems changed the scale of recordable data, and the emergence of big data in recent years has increased the volume of data rapidly. The large volume of data is considered as a major challenge in data visualization because it results in the abundance of visual elements in a visual representation.

A large number of elements in a visual representation can hinder the capability of people to understand it, so representing information in different levels of details is considered as an effective approach to make the visual artefacts more useful. Different techniques support data visualization at different levels of

© Springer International Publishing Switzerland 2016
V. Řepa and T. Bruckner (Eds.): BIR 2016, LNBIP 261, pp. 16–32, 2016.
DOI: 10.1007/978-3-319-45321-7_2

abstraction. Some techniques aggregate data and present information in a higher level of abstraction, so they enable people to discover general trends based on data. Therefore, people can identify and select a slice of data that is relevant for their analysis. This capability enables people to focus on a particular set of data and employ relevant techniques to discover more information, which is known as slicing and dicing operations in data analysis area.

A chord diagram is a sort of visual representation that has been recently introduced to increase the level of abstraction in visualizing relations among nodes in networks. It is widely used and adapted in many disciplines to investigate and analyse patterns in different sort of networks including social networks, biological networks etc [7,10,12,18,26]. BPM supports managing business processes using different artefacts, and the interaction among people while enacting business processes play an important role in managing processes. Thus, discovering social networks from enacted processes data can facilitate managing business processes to be more efficient and effective. Our previous study also shows potential benefits in employing and adopting this technique in Business Process Management (BPM) area, which can increase the level of abstraction in visualizing social networks [9].

Despite different works that investigate how this technique should be applied, configure and adapted in different research areas, it is not clear how this technique can be employed in Business Process Management (BPM). Thus, this paper extends the social network visualization approaches in BPM area using chord diagram. It defines the formal definitions of elements and elaborates on how the visual representation can be compiled from them. The visualization is supported by implementing a plug-in in ProM - an open source framework for process mining. The plug-in is used to demonstrate social networks discovered from real log files in compare with those discovered by current visualization techniques. The result shows that this technique can complement previous artefacts to discover more social network patterns in BPM area.

The remainder of this paper is organized as follows. Section 2 introduces social network analysis in BPM area. Section 3 elaborates on how the chord diagram can be used to visualize social networks in BPM area. Section 4 introduces the implemented artifact that supports visualization of social networks in BPM using chord diagram. Section 5 demonstrates and discusses cases in which both this artifact and traditional techniques are used to visualize the social network. Section 6 discusses some related work. Finally, Sect. 7 concludes the paper and introduces future works.

2   Background

In this section, we explain terms and concepts of social network analysis in BPM area briefly.

Process models play an important role based on which people can design, understand, discuss, analyze, configure, enact, run and adjust business processes. Thus, different business process modelling technique are developed to support designing process models, e.g. Business Process Model and Notation

(BPMN) [14], Yet Another Workflow Language (YAWL) [1], Petri nets [16], Unified Modeling Language (UML) [20], etc.

There are different perspectives based on which a business process can be defined to function effectively and efficiently like control-flow, data, resource, etc. The control-flow perspective is the dominant one in BPM area, and it focuses on the definition of the order of activities that should be performed when enacting a business process. The resource perspective focuses on definition of people and resources who are involved in a business process. The data perspective defines the information aspects of a business process. These perspectives are not entirely separated, and their combination specifies how a business process should be enacted. The model reflecting the combination of these perspectives that defines how a business process should function is called business process model.

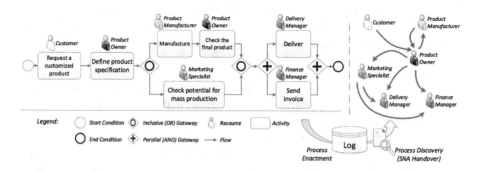

Fig. 1. The handover of works in the selling process

The left side of Fig. 1 shows a fictitious process model using BPMN notation. This process aims to support the selling of customized products. In BPMN, the resource perspective is demonstrated through segmentation of a process model based on resources. This segmentation is done through artifacts called pools and swim-lanes. For the sake of simplicity, we demonstrate this perspective only through annotating each activity by the name of the role that is responsible for executing it.

A process model can be configured/implemented and enacted in different ways. The business process can be supported by Business Process Management Systems, or it can be supported by various software systems that their coordination supports the enactment of the process model. An instance of a business process model is called a case. Regardless of how a process is implemented, the enactment result can produce a log file recording how the process participants execute activities in different cases. The log file can be used to investigate different aspects of a business process.

Process Mining [21] is the area of research that aims to investigate insights from the enactment result of business processes. There are different techniques which are defined in this area to support such investigation, known as process discovery, process conformance, and process enhancement [21]. The process discovery techniques aim to extract insight about different aspects of business processes from the log files. The social interactions among process participants is also one of the important aspects that can be discovered from the process log in the presence of resource information.

There are different social network discovery metrics that are defined in process mining area, i.e. Handover of work, Subcontracting, Working together, Similar tasks and Reassignment [22]. These metrics are defined based on relations that can be identified among activities based on the order of events in the log file. For example, activity A can have a causal relation with activity B (shown by $A \rightarrow B$) iff for all events in the log, the events of activity A has followed at least for one case by the event of activity B, but the event of activity B has never followed directly by the event of activity A. For example, Manufacture has causal relation with Check the final product, but Deliver and Send invoice has not such a relation (since the are parallel). The casual relation can be considered as a direct succession relation. There is also indirect succession relation. For example, if $A \rightarrow B \rightarrow C$, we can consider A has an indirect succession relation with C. There are different metrics that are defined to discover different social networks in business processes [22]:

- *Handover of work* metric enables us to identify the resources who passed the work to another resource in general. There are different variations of the definition of the handover of work metric [22]. For example, this metric can be defined with/without considering the causal relations in a process model. The right side of Fig. 1 shows the social network graph discovered based on a variation of this metric based on the causal relation and direct succession. The nodes in this graph represent the roles of people, and the edges represent handover of works. This is an unweighted graph that does not take into account the amount of interaction between people. The weighted graph can represent the number of the handover of works through the thickness of the edges.
- A subcontractor is defined as a person who performs a work based on a contract for another party. In process mining, the discovery of potential *subcontracting* patterns is identified if a resource handed over work to another one and receive it back directly. This metric also has different variants.
- *Working together* metrics help us to identify the resources which used to work together. It ignores causal dependencies and focuses on resources who work together for the same case.
- *Similar tasks* metric enables identifying people who used to work more on specific tasks together. It assumes that those people have stronger relations in compare to others. This metric also ignores the causal relationships among event, but it focuses on activities instead of cases. The metric for example can support the discovery of roles for a process model since activities in a business process can be executed by people with similar roles.
- *Reassignment* metric investigates if the work has been reassigned among different resources in a process instance for an activity, so we can improve the process by avoiding such extra reassignments. By presence of a log file with the status of instances of activities, we can discover those interactions in the social

network through reassignment metric. This metric can also be used to identify the potential power relations among resources, e.g. a boss may reassign the work to his or her employees.

There are some other works like discovering of handover of roles that aims to discover more insight from organizational perspective from event logs [3].

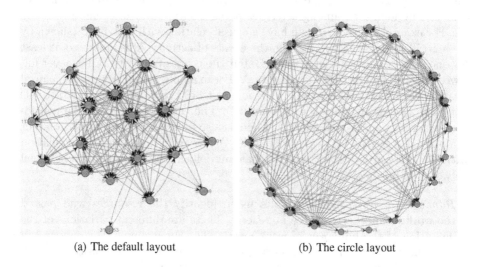

(a) The default layout   (b) The circle layout

Fig. 2. Social network models mined from a real log file

The introduced metrics can result in models that can be represented by the usual graph visualization techniques using nodes and arcs. The representation of these model in process mining is supported by social networks plugins in ProM [25]. The size of the graph increases when the number of nodes and interactions increases, so it can be very difficult and inefficient to use such visualization technique in real applications.

Figure 2 shows two graphs that represent the handover of works among participants in a business process mined from a real log file. As it can be seen, it is very difficult to discover the interactions among participants based on these visualizations. The next section introduces our technique that can facilitate identifying some aspects of social networks for these cases.

3   Approach

This section introduces our approach to visualize dense social networks using chord diagram. Here, we introduce basic definitions which are used to explain the approach.

3.1 Definitions

Definition 1 (Social Network Graphs). *A social network graph is a tuple* $G = (N, E, w)$, *where:*

- N *is the set of nodes,*
- $E \subseteq N \times N$ *is the set of edges connecting nodes together, and*
- $w : E \rightarrow \mathbb{R}^+$ *is a function that assigns a non-negative and non-zero real number to each edge.*

The weight of an edge $e \in E$ can be retrieved by $w(e)$. In addition, we define two other operations retrieving the incoming and outgoing edges of a node:

- The set of incoming edges of a node $n \in N$ can be retrieved by $\bullet n = \{\forall(x, y) \in E | y = n\}$.
- The set of outgoing edges of a node $n \in N$ can be retrieved by $n\bullet = \{\forall(x, y) \in E | x = n\}$.

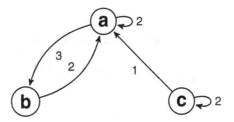

Fig. 3. An example graph

For example, the graph represented in Fig. 3 can be defined as:

$$(N = \{a, b, c\}, E = \{(a, a), (a, b), (b, a), (c, c), (c, a)\}, w = \{((a, a), 2), ((a, b), 3), ((b, a), 2), ((c, c), 2), ((c, a), 1)\}).$$

In this graph, we exemplify the following operations to clarify definitions:

- $w((a, a)) = 2$ that retrieves the weight of the edge that connects the nore a to itself, i.e. (a, a),
- $\bullet a = \{(a, a), (b, a), (c, a)\}$ that retrieves the incoming edges to node a, and
- $a\bullet = \{(a, a), (a, b)\}$ that retrieves the outgoing edges from node a.

A chord diagram consists of *Arcs* and *Chords*.

- An arc is a segment of the circumference of the circle that is mapped to a node in a social network graph. Figure 4(a) shows an example of arcs in a chord diagram that represents nodes in given example.

– A chord is an area of the circle that connects two arcs together. It is possible that a chord connects an arc to itself. Figure 4(b) shows an example of a chord that connects two arcs (a and b) together. The details for computation are explained later.

Figure 4 (c) shows a complete version of the chord diagram that represents the given graph. We define how the elements in this diagram is computed as follow.

Definition 2 (Chord Diagrams). *A chord diagram is a tuple* $(G = (N, E, w), r, \phi, \chi)$, *where*

– *G is a social network graph,*
– *r is the radius of the graph,*
– *$\phi : N \rightarrow (N, \mathbb{R}^+)$ is a function that returns the set of arcs of the chord diagram based on graph $G = (N, E, w)$, where:*

$$\phi(n) = (n, \frac{2\pi r \sum_{e \in n\bullet} w(e)}{\sum_{e \in E} w(e)})$$

– *$\chi : (n \in N, m \in N) \rightarrow (N, N, \mathbb{R}^+)$ is a function that returns the set of chords of the chord diagram for each pairs of nodes from graph $G = (N, E, w)$, where:*

$$\chi(n, m) = (n, m, \frac{2\pi r w(n, m)}{\sum_{e \in E} w(e)})$$

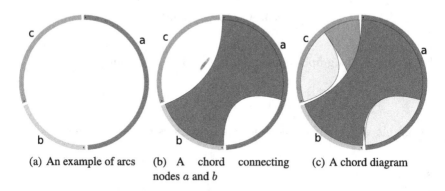

(a) An example of arcs   (b) A chord connecting nodes a and b (c) A chord diagram

Fig. 4. A Chord diagram and its elements

It should be highlighted that for every two nodes a and b, it is important to compute both $\chi(a, b)$ and $\chi(b, a)$. We explain this definition through the given graph as an example. The chord diagram for our graph is a tuple including a graph, a variable r that define the radius of the circle, and two functions that compute the length of arcs and chords, i.e. ϕ and χ respectively.

$$\phi(a) = (a, \frac{2\pi r \sum_{e \in a\bullet} w(e)}{\sum_{e \in E} w(e)}) = (a, \frac{2\pi r \sum_{e \in \{(a,a),(a,b)\}} w(e)}{\sum_{e \in \{(a,a),(a,b),(b,a),(c,c),(c,a)\}} w(e)}) =$$

$$(a, \frac{2\pi r(2+3)}{2+3+2+2+1}) = (a, \pi r)$$

This means that the corresponding arc of the node a is $(a, \pi r)$, which is half of the circumference of the graph. The rest of the arc in Fig. 4 (c) is computed accordingly.

As mentioned earlier, a chord connects two arcs together. The χ function computes the length of each side of a chord. For example, $\chi(a, b)$ and $\chi(b, a)$ computes the length of the chord that connects nodes a and b in each side respectively.

$$\chi(a,b) = \frac{2\pi r \times w(a,b)}{\sum_{e \in E} w(e)} = \frac{2\pi r \times 3}{\sum_{e \in \{(a,a),(a,b),(b,a),(c,c),(c,a)\}} w(e)} =$$

$$\frac{2\pi r \times 3}{2+3+2+2+1} = \frac{2\pi r \times 3}{10} = 0.6\pi r$$

The length of the other side of the chord ($\chi(b, a)$) and the rest of the chords can also be computed accordingly. It should be mentioned that $\chi(a, b)$ and $\chi(b, a)$ can have different values because the first one is calculated based on the total outgoing weight of node a to b while the second one is based on the total outgoing weight of node b to a.

The calculation of χ for all nodes enables visualization of the chord diagram, shown in Fig. 4(c). As it can be seen, the visualization of chords overlaps each other. Therefore, different configurations can be applied to enhance the capability of people to understand this diagram. Some possible configurations are explained in the next section.

3.2 Visualization Properties

The effective visualization of dense networks does not only depend on quantitative aspects but also qualitative [27]. Different qualitative aspects can enhance the usefulness of a visualization artifact, which are used in different approaches. Wills G.J. enumerates some of these aspects like the "ability to show or hide parts of a graph", "color[ing] nodes and edges", "selective labeling of nodes under user control" and supporting user interactions e.g. through mouse [27]. In this section, we explain how some of these aspects can be considered when illustrating a social network model using a chord diagram.

Interactivity. The nodes in social networks are represented as arcs in chord diagrams. The weight of relations of a node to other nodes is represented by the length of the arc. Thus, arcs and their length provide support to compare the weight of relations among different nodes in a social network. However, it is difficult for people to investigate these relations when there is a lot of chords in a social network. Therefore, the relations among nodes can be a good subject to be shown/hid to/from users based on the user interaction, e.g. when the mouse is moved over an arc. Therefore, our artifact only shows the relations of a node when a user moves the mouse over the corresponding arc.

Selective Hints. The name of arcs in the diagram can be specified explicitly. However, it is not a good idea to annotate the diagram with detailed information. Thus, our artifact shows the labels of the chords as hints of a mouse when a user moves the mouse over a chord. In this way, the user can receive the information about the particular chord that interests him/her.

Colors. Colors can play a significant role in visualization. In this artifact, we considered two design choices in regards to coloring the diagram. The first decision is to color arcs differently to facilitate their recognition by users. The second decision is to color a chord as the same color of the arc in which the chord has wider length. In the case of the equal length, we color the chord white. In this way, more aspects of relations among nodes can be visualized without making the diagram unreadable.

4   Implementation

This section specifies the architecture and the functionalities of the plug-in that we implemented to support visualization of social networks using chord diagram for business processes.

4.1   Architecture

Prom framework [25] has been selected as the framework to implement the artifact that can support visualization of the chord diagram. This framework is chosen because it is open-source, and there is social network analysis plug-ins that are already implemented there. Figure 5 shows the adapted version of the ProM architecture that explains how our plug-in supports visualization of social networks using chord diagram.

The ProM framework has a log filter component that supports importing log files with a specific format to the framework. Different social network plug-ins are implemented in this framework that produces various social network models based on imported log file. Despite the different semantics behind these plug-ins, the models have the same structure, i.e. it is a weighted network graph. The social network model can be visualized through the visualization engine.

Although the ProM engine supports different sort of interactions, it does not provide the intractability feature that we require to fulfil the mentioned qualitative criteria in the previous section. Therefore, We define our plug-in as an export plug-in that produces a chord diagram based on HTML and

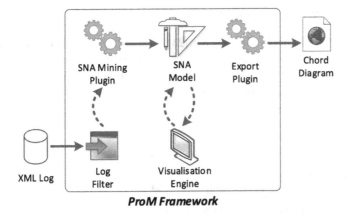

Fig. 5. The Architecture, adapted from [25]

D3 library [2]. D3 is a JavaScript based library that supports the development of graphical representation on the web using HTML and JavaScript. In this way, we support visualization of all social network analysis algorithm with the chord diagram because all of them produces the same social analysis model from the log file.

5   Demonstration and Discussion

We conducted a preliminary evaluation of our artifacts applicability using a real log file. We compare the visualization result of our approach with traditional ones. We selected real log files to investigate and analyze the results, i.e. logs from Fifth International Business Process Intelligence Challenge (BPIC15). The logs record all building permit applications for around four years in five Dutch municipalities. The processes in these municipalities are very similar, yet they have their own differences due to variations that are required to be applied in each municipality.

In this paper, we do not aim to evaluate the usefulness of the visualization result, and we only focus on showing the potential of our artifact that can produce visualizations that reveal more aspects of social networks. Thus, we present the visualization results of our approach and traditional ones. In addition, we compare them based on information that we can infer based on the visualization result.

We consider four cases to discover social networks for working together, the handover of works, subcontracting and similar task metrics. The reassignment metrics is not considered since the log files do not contain enough information to discover it.

5.1   Case 1: Working Together

We used the first municipality log file [23] to investigate and compare the visualization results of our approach with previous ones. We used the "Mine for a Working-Together Social Network" plug-in to discover the social network of resources who works together. Figure 2(a) shows the discovered social network model using the default layout.

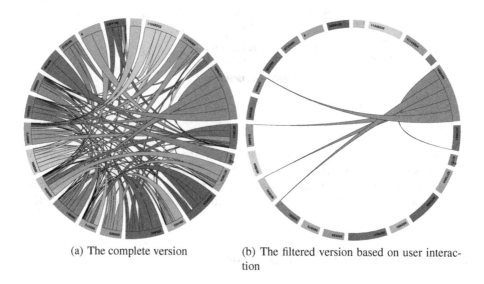

(a) The complete version

(b) The filtered version based on user interaction

Fig. 6. Chord diagram for the working together metric (Color figure online)

There are also other layouts that sometimes organizes nodes and arcs in a better way, but we could not find a more meaningful layout for this model. Figure 2(b) shows another layout of the same model, i.e. circle layout. This layout organizes nodes on a circle and draws interactions among them. In these two layouts, we can identify two nodes that have one incoming and one outgoing arc. These networks are dense, and it is very difficult to get more useful insights from them.

Figure 6 shows the chord diagram that is generated by our plug-in. Figure 6(a) shows the complete version of the diagram. Figure 6(b) shows only a part of the diagram that is filtered based on the user interaction. The diagram is filtered based on the node that the mouse is moved over it. We list our findings as follow.

- *Resource involvement*: It is possible to compare how much each resource is contributed to the semantics of the social network based on the length of its arc, e.g. it can easily be recognized that node "1898401" has a higher involvement.
- *Association direction*: It is possible to identify the dominant direction in a relation between two nodes. This feature is supported by colouring the arcs,

e.g. the relations from the selected node ("1898401") to other nodes have the same colour as the selected node, which means that the relation from the selected node to others are stronger than the relations from others to this node (see Fig. 6(b)).

– *Association contributions*: It is possible to identify and compare the degree of contribution of each node in a relation, e.g. the contribution of the selected node ("1898401") in its relation with the node "2670601" is higher that other nodes. The contributions can be compared using the length of the chord at the end points, i.e. involved arcs.

– *Special nodes*: The association direction and contributions support identification of special nodes that e.g. *only initiate the work* (e.g. nodes "1898401" and "6") or *is related to only one node* ("3175153").

5.2   Case 2: Handover of Works

We also used the first municipality log file [23] to investigate handover of works using the "Mine for a Handover-of-Work Social Network" plug-in. Figure 7 shows the visualization of discovered social network model using the chord diagram and the traditional approach.

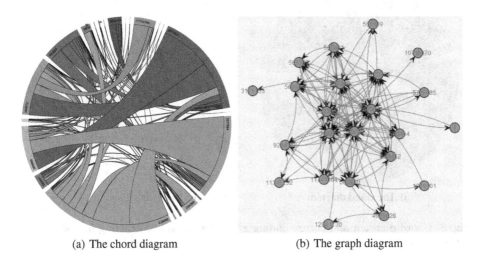

(a) The chord diagram   (b) The graph diagram

Fig. 7. Chord diagram and corresponding graph for the handover of works metric (Color figure online)

The introduced patterns in previous case can also be identified here, i.e. *Resource involvement, Association direction, Association contributions* and *Special nodes*. In this case, there are some relations that can be identified in traditional visualization technique easier. For example, there is only one incoming arc to the node "3175153" from node "560925". The traditional visualization

technique shows this relation more clearly; while this relation is harder to identified through the chord diagram. The reason is that the chord diagram shows
the relationships on a more abstract level, and the relations of resources with
very tiny contributions are difficult to discover.

– *Resource abstraction*: Chord diagram facilitates identifications of resources
  with higher contribution degree in compare to those who has very small contributions to others.

5.3   Case 3: Subcontracting

We used the fourth municipality log file [24] to investigate and compare the
visualization results of our approach with previous ones. We used the "Mine
for a Subcontracting Social Network" plug-in to discover the social network of
resources who may subcontract works to others. Figure 8 shows the visualization
of discovered social network model using the chord diagram and the traditional
approach.

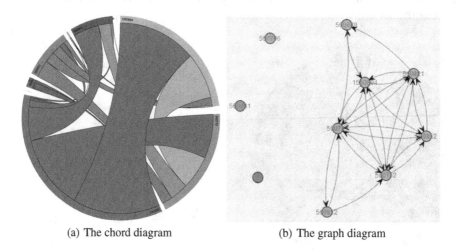

(a) The chord diagram   (b) The graph diagram

Fig. 8. Chord diagram and corresponding graph for the subcontracting metric (Color
figure online)

As it can be seen in Fig. 8(b), there are some nodes in the traditional visualization technique which are completely isolated from others. These nodes do not
have any relations to or from other nodes. These nodes are not demonstrated
in the chord diagram as can be seen in Fig. 8(a). However, it can show other
perspectives that we mentioned previously.

– *Isolation limit*: Chord diagram does not show nodes which do not have any
  relation to others.

5.4 Case 4: Similar Task

We used the fourth municipality log file [24] to investigate and compare the
visualization results of our approach with previous ones. We used the "Mine
for a Similar-Task Social Network" plug-in to discover the social network of
resources who subcontract works to others. For this case, we filtered the log file
based on "date decision for inspection" event. Figure 9 shows the visualization
of discovered social network model using the chord diagram and the traditional
approach.

In this metrics, the weight of relations among every two nodes is the same.
Thus, all chords are white (see Fig. 9(a)). As it can be seen in Fig. 9(b), all
nodes are related to each other. The traditional approach does not reveal more
information; while the chord diagram enables comparison of each chord to others.
For example, the relation between nodes "560821" and "560752" is stronger than
nodes "560821" and "1550894".

– *Association strength*: Chord diagram enables comparison of relations between
  nodes.

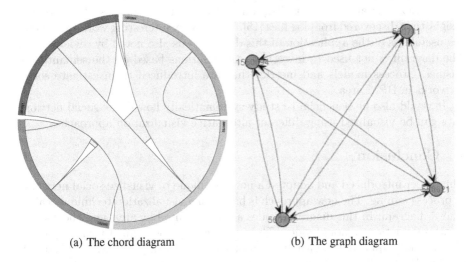

(a) The chord diagram   (b) The graph diagram

Fig. 9. Chord diagram and corresponding graph for the similar task metric (Color
figure online)

6 Related Work

The identification and analysis of similarities and differences in a large amount
of data have been addressed by developing a tool called Circos [11]. This tool
introduces a diagram, which is later called chord diagram. The diagram is used
to display large volumes of genomic data, and it is then inspired the data visualization paradigm to increase the level of abstraction in the visualization of a

large number of data. This diagram has been applied in other areas like finance to analyze trade data with monetary values [13]. D3 is the framework that supports the development of such diagram [2]. This diagram has been used widely in different areas to support identification and analysis of a large amount of data.

Henneman S. investigates several approaches representing information-rich visualization of dense geographical networks. He also describes this diagram as "very impressive due to its high information density" to visualize dense networks [8]. As another example of the application of this diagram in another area, we can refer to the visualization of mapped security standards for analysis and use optimisation [19]. The authors mention that "A big number of links between nodes are grouped to increase the abstraction level. However more detailed information can be extracted including interactive explanations, highlights, etc". They also mention that the lack of standard structure for displaying more information can be considered as a disadvantage of this diagram, which is addressed through the qualitative aspects in our paper. This diagram is also used to analyze multidimensional astronomical datasets to represent the correlations among the galaxy properties [5]. There are many other applications of this diagram in different areas, e.g. [4, 17].

In BPM area, we only found one application of using this diagram so far. Paszkiewicz Z. et al. utilize this diagram to investigate a hypothesis based on the insight they discovered from log files [15]. This is very interesting work that shows the usefulness of the application of this diagram - as also noted by reviewers [6]. The diagram is not used to investigate the relations based on the semantics of business process models and metrics that are introduced to investigate social networks in BPM area.

It would also be beneficial to study systematically how dense social network data can be visualized using different alternative visualization approaches.

7   Conclusion

This paper introduced and adapted a new technique to visualize social networks in process mining. The new approach is based on a visualization technique, called Chord diagram. In this diagram, nodes are represented by arcs, and chords represent interactions among nodes. The new technique is defined formally, and a plug-in that supports the visualization of social networks in BPM area is developed in ProM. The plug-in is used to visualize social networks in real scenarios using both chord diagram and traditional graph visualization technique.

The result shows that the new artifact can support investigation of new insights from the social network, such as resource involvement, association direction, association contributions, special nodes, and resource abstraction. It also reveals that this approach cannot show nodes which are isolated from others.

The approach can be further evaluated in future. The evaluation can be performed based on the investigation of usability of the visualization technique. It can also be evaluated in an organization in which a researcher has access to both stakeholders to interview and log files of processes that contains resource information.

References

1. van der Aalst, W.M.P., Aldred, L., Dumas, M., ter Hofstede, A.H.M.: Design and implementation of the YAWL system. In: Persson, A., Stirna, J. (eds.) CAiSE 2004. LNCS, vol. 3084, pp. 142–159. Springer, Heidelberg (2004)
2. Bostock, M., Ogievetsky, V., Heer, J.: D^3 data-driven documents. IEEE Trans. Visual. Comput. Graphics **17**(12), 2301–2309 (2011)
3. Burattin, A., Sperduti, A., Veluscek, M.: Business models enhancement through discovery of roles. In: IEEE Symposium on Computational Intelligence and Data Mining (CIDM), pp. 103–110. IEEE (2013)
4. Comai, A.: Decision-making support the role of data visualization in analyzing complex systems. World Future Rev. **6**(4), 477–484 (2014)
5. Souza, R.S., Ciardi, B., COIN collaboration, et al.: AMADA-Analysis of multidimensional astronomical datasets. Astron. Comput. **12**, 100–108 (2015)
6. van Dongen, B.F., Weber, B., Ferreira, D.R., De Weerdt, J.: Report: business process intelligence challenge 2013. In: Lohmann, N., Song, M., Wohed, P. (eds.) BPM 2013 Workshops. LNBIP, vol. 171, pp. 79–88. Springer, Heidelberg (2014)
7. Heim, D., Budczies, J., Stenzinger, A., Treue, D., Hufnagl, P., Denkert, C., Dietel, M., Klauschen, F.: Cancer beyond organ and tissue specificity: next-generation-sequencing gene mutation data reveal complex genetic similarities across major cancers. Int. J. Cancer **135**(10), 2362–2369 (2014)
8. Hennemann, S.: Information-rich visualisation of dense geographical networks. J. Maps **9**(1), 68–75 (2013)
9. Jalali, A.: Reflections on the use of chord diagrams in social network visualization in process mining. In: Research Challenges in Information Science (RCIS). IEEE (2016)
10. Keahey, T.A.: Using visualization to understand big data. IBM Bus. Analytics Adv. Visual. (2013)
11. Krzywinski, M., Schein, J., Birol, I., Connors, J., Gascoyne, R., Horsman, D., Jones, S.J., Marra, M.A.: Circos: an information aesthetic for comparative genomics. Genome Res. **19**(9), 1639–1645 (2009)
12. Mazel, J., Fontugne, R., Fukuda, K.: Visual comparison of network anomaly detectors with chord diagrams. In: Proceedings of the 29th Annual ACM Symposium on Applied Computing, SAC 2014, pp. 473–480. ACM, New York (2014)
13. Myers, R.: Using circos data visualizer to analyze trade data a review and how to guide. Soc. Sci. Comput. Rev., 0894439314561735 (2014)
14. I. O. Object Management Group: Business Process Model and Notation (BPMN). Technical report, Object Management Group, Inc. (OMG) (2013)
15. Z. Paszkiewicz and W. Picard. Analysis of the Volvo IT incident and problem handling processes using process mining and social network analysis. In: BPIC@ BPM (2013)
16. Petri, C.A.: Introduction to general net theory. In: Brauer, W. (ed.) Net Theory and Applications. LNCS, vol. 84, pp. 1–19. Springer, Heidelberg (1980)
17. Prasetyo, P.K., Achananuparp, P., Lim, E.-P.: On analyzing geotagged tweets for location-based patterns. In: Proceedings of the 17th International Conference on Distributed Computing and Networking, p. 45. ACM (2016)
18. Ramanauskaitė, S., Olifer, D., Goranin, N., Čenys, A., Radvilavičius, L.: Visualization of mapped security standards for analysis and use optimisation. Int. J. Comput. Theor. Eng. **6**(5), 372–376 (2014)

19. Ramanauskaitė, S., Olifer, D., Goranin, N., Čenys, A., Radvilavičius, L.: Visualization of mapped security standards for analysis and use optimisation. Int. J. Comput. Theor. Eng. **6**(5) (2014)
20. Rumbaugh, J., Jacobson, I., Booch. G.: The unified modeling language reference manual (1999)
21. van der Aalst, W.: Process mining: discovery, conformance and enhancement of business processes. Springer Science & Business Media, Heidelberg (2011)
22. Aalst, W.M., Reijers, H.A., Song, M.: Discovering social networks from event logs. Comput. Support. Coop. Work (CSCW) **14**(6), 549–593 (2005)
23. van Dongen, B.: BPI challenge 2015 municipality 1 (2015). http://dx.doi.org/10.4121/uuid:a0addfda-2044-4541-a450-fdcc9fe16d17
24. van Dongen, B.: BPI challenge 2015 municipality 4 (2015). http://dx.doi.org/10.4121/uuid:679b11cf-47cd-459e-a6de-9ca614e25985
25. van Dongen, B.F., de Medeiros, A.K.A., Verbeek, H.M.W.E., Weijters, A.J.M.M.T., van der Aalst, W.M.P.: The ProM framework: a new era in process mining tool support. In: Ciardo, G., Darondeau, P. (eds.) ICATPN 2005. LNCS, vol. 3536, pp. 444–454. Springer, Heidelberg (2005)
26. Wang, L., Liu, S., Pan, L., Wu, L., Meng, X.: Enterprise relationship network: build foundation for social business. In: 2014 IEEE International Congress on Big Data (BigData Congress), pp. 347–354, June 2014
27. Wills, G.J.: NicheWorks—interactive visualization of very large graphs. J. Comput. Graphical Stat. **8**(2), 190–212 (1999)

Crowdsourcing in Business Process Outsourcing: An Exploratory Study on Factors Influencing Decision Making

Kurt Sandkuhl[1,3(✉)], Alexander Smirnov[2,3], and Andrew Ponomarev[2]

[1] Institute of Computer Science, Rostock University, 18059 Rostock, Germany
kurt.sandkuhl@uni-rostock.de
[2] SPIIRAS, 14-th line, 199178 St.Petersburg, Russia
{smir,ponomarev}@iias.spb.su
[3] ITMO University, Kronverksky pr. 47, 197101 St.Petersburg, Russia

Abstract. Cloud computing architectures and outsourcing of business processes into the cloud are potential candidates to increase flexibility on the enterprise side when it comes to service delivery. In this paper, we focus on a specific aspect of cloud computing and outsourcing: The use of concepts from crowdsourcing in business process outsourcing (BPO). More concrete, the question addressed in this paper is, whether crowdsourcing is a feasible approach for supporting BPO. Based on a literature study in the areas of BPO, cloud computing and crowdsourcing, this paper identifies potential factors relevant for decision making in favour or against using crowdsourcing in BPO scenarios. The factors identified are investigated in a case study from BPO, which confirms many of the factors and gives reason to believe that the work contributes to a better understanding of outsourcing decisions in BPO and the relevant factors. However, just one case study will not give a conclusive picture whether the identified factors can be assumed to be relevant for the majority of BPO cases.

Keywords: Cloud computing · Crowdsourcing · Business process outsourcing

1 Introduction

In many industrial sectors efficient service delivery is considered as the key factor to competitiveness in a globalized market environment and information technology (IT) is an enabler and strategic instrument. Quick adaptation of the IT to new business situations affecting service delivery is often considered as serious challenge in enterprises since the business environment and the IT in an enterprise continuously change, but the pace of change and the time frames needed to implement changes are different in both areas. This is due to the fact that factors influencing the development in both areas are different and largely independent. In the business environment, changes regarding legal aspects, regulations, business requirements, economic factors, etc., play an important role [14]. In the IT area, technological trends such as virtualization, cloud computing or service-oriented architectures are changing the way IT services are provided [21].

V. Řepa and T. Bruckner (Eds.): BIR 2016, LNBIP 261, pp. 33–49, 2016.
DOI: 10.1007/978-3-319-45321-7_3

Cloud computing architectures and outsourcing of business processes into the cloud are potential candidates to increase flexibility on the enterprise side when it comes to service delivery [7]. But these approaches often are criticized for being not sufficiently scalable or flexible as soon as automatable and manual tasks have to be combined. In this paper, we focus on a specific aspect of cloud computing and outsourcing: The use of concepts from crowdsourcing or crowd computing in business process outsourcing (BPO).

More concrete, the question addressed in this paper is, whether crowdsourcing is a feasible approach for supporting BPO. If so, what application scenarios are possible and what characteristics do they have? The main contributions of the paper are identification of factors to be taken into account when deciding in favor or against use of crowdsourcing in BPO and a case study from utility industry investigating BPO and relevance of the identified factors in a real-world context.

The remainder of the paper is structured as follows: Sect. 2 will discuss the research method used during work presented in this paper. Section 3 identifies and analyses relevant literature in the fields of business process outsourcing and crowd computing. From this analysis factors to be taken into account are derived. Section 4 describes an industrial case study from utility industries which was performed in order to explore the pertinence of the factors. Section 5 summarizes the findings, discusses threats to validity and outlines future work.

2   Research Method

Research work in this paper started from the following research question which is based on the motivation presented in Sect. 1: *In business process outsourcing, what factors influence decision making in favor or against the use of crowdsourcing for the whole business process or parts thereof?*

The research method used for working on this research question is a combination of literature study and descriptive case study. Based on the research question defined, we started identifying research areas relevant for this question and analyzed literature in these areas. The purpose was to find existing theories, approaches or technologies which help explaining or investigating what factors affect decision making regarding the use of crowdsourcing in BPO. Due to the focus on cloud computing, one research area to investigate is how business process outsourcing is implemented with or supported by cloud computing approaches. Existing work in crowdsourcing obviously also is an area of interest in the analysis of existing work.

Since the literature study returned only "candidates" for factors to be investigated rather than proven theories (see Sect. 3), we decided to perform a case study in order to gather information pertinent for the subject area. Qualitative case study is an approach to research that facilitates exploration of a phenomenon within its context using a variety of data sources. This ensures that the subject under consideration is not explored from only one perspective, but rather from a variety of perspectives which allows for multiple facets of the phenomenon to be revealed and understood. Within the case study, we used three different perspectives, which at the same time represent sources of data: We observed the activities during business service provision, we examined the business process models used for execution of the outsourcing and we interviewed different roles involved in BPO services (cf. Sect. 4.1).

Yin differentiates various kinds of case studies [23]: explanatory, exploratory and descriptive. The case study presented in Sect. 4 has to be considered as descriptive, as it is used to describe the phenomenon of process outsourcing and the real-life context in which it occurs. Based on the case study results, we conclude that there is a potential of using crowdsourcing in business process outsourcing if certain characteristics are given. This argumentative-deductive part is discussed in Sects. 4.3 and 5.

3   Results of the Literature Study

This section presents the results of the literature study on cloud computing (Sect. 3.1) and crowd sourcing (Sect. 3.2). The purpose of the analysis was to identify factors which potentially could influence the decision whether or not to use crowdsourcing in BPO. Section 3.3 summarizes the factors identified.

3.1   BPO in Cloud Computing

When analyzing literature on business process outsourcing in cloud computing, many publications were found on architectures, security [6], business models and challenges [10] of cloud computing. Although these publications are not addressing the subject of business process outsourcing, we identified two areas of relevance for BPO and cloud computing: The architecture of cloud services and deployment models of cloud computing. Furthermore, there is also work on factors influencing the decision of business process outsourcing, but this is not specifically targeted to cloud computing. This section summarizes the relevant findings regarding architectures, deployment models and decision factors.

The basic aim of cloud computing is to make better use of distributed resources, orchestrate them to achieve a higher throughput scalability. Cloud computing architectures often are described with layers or categories of cloud services (see, e.g., [11]), which also include layers relevant for implementing business process outsourcing. A selection of frequently used service layers provided to the service user (consumer) is:

- Infrastructure-as-a-Service (IaaS) provides hardware which allows for consumer to deploy and run operating systems and applications on the provisioned resources.
- Platform-as-a-Service (PaaS) adds to IaaS operating systems and platforms or tools, and gives the consumer the possibility to deploy and run own applications.
- Software-as-a-Services (SaaS) extends PaaS by providing software applications (e.g., business applications or enterprise information systems).
- Business process-as-a-Service (BPaaS) allowed providers to provision horizontal or vertical business process services on top of using SaaS.
- Business-as-a-Service (BaaS) aims at providing an integrated set of transactional services, business processes and collaborative work support to accomplish organizational goals. BaaS usually builds upon SaaS and BPaaS concepts.

The actual architecture of a cloud service for business process outsourcing is expected to influence the decision for or against use of a hybrid cloud. The use of several software systems in the SaaS layer or various platforms as basis for SaaS in the PaaS layer will increase complexity of the overall BPaaS service. The more complex the overall architecture the more efforts will have to spent on providing the basis for BPaaS "on demand" for every crowd members to be involved.

The most well-known deployment models are the use of public clouds, private clouds or hybrid clouds. Cloud services for offered for public use (e.g., those provided by Amazon, Google or Microsoft) are called public clouds. Private clouds use virtualization and other cloud computing techniques based on enterprise-internal resources in order to achieve a better utilization of these resources. These cloud solutions are not offered for public use. Some enterprises use hybrid clouds with mission-critical application in the private cloud and publicly accessible applications in the public cloud. In many context, there will also be other hybrid models with components in different private clouds or in private and public clouds. The use of public clouds only is expected to ease the use of crowdsourcing since the access to the public cloud requires less complex security mechanisms.

Factors influencing the decision of business process outsourcing were investigated by Lacity et al. [8, 9] and Yang et al. [22] who based their work on literature analysis and two sets of expert interviews. They concluded that three factor groups influence decisions most: expectation, risk and environment:

- Three factors were identified in the group "expectations": (a) Cost savings: Outsourcing is only desirable when the expected costs for coordinating the relationship of the prospective supplier are lower than the production cost advantage that this supplier may provide. (b) core competence: Activities which a company considers as part of their competitive advantage should not be outsourced whereas activities, which can be provided with higher quality by suppliers are candidates for outsourcing. (c) flexibility: Outsourcing in general is expected to increase flexibility since internal resources can be used for core competences and decreases financial risks by reducing capital investments. Furthermore, enterprises expect service providers to flexibly adapt to new requirements of their clients' markets quickly.
- The most significant factor for decision making and the only relevant one in the factor group "environment" is the service quality provided by the service provider. Enterprises consider outsourcing when they believe that the quality provided by an external actor is significantly better than the quality internal resources could achieve. Good quality is one of the most important success factors of outsourcing.
- Risk refers to an *"undesirable outcome or the factors leading to an undesirable outcome"* ([22], p. 3772). The most prominent risks in outsourcing are information security concerns and loss of management control.

All factors above can also be expected to contribute to decisions on BPO to crowds.

3.2 Crowdsourcing

Crowdsourcing is an emerging research area and it is usually understood (e.g., [4, 5, 13]) as a form of outsourcing, in which tasks traditionally performed by organizational employees or other companies are sent through the internet to the members of an undefined large group people (called "crowd"). Business process crowdsourcing has already been paid some attention in literature. It was originally introduced by Vecchia and Cisternino [18] as a model allowing organizations to crowdsource their internal business processes. However, currently, it is still at an early stage of development [16].

Attempts to analyse factors influencing the decision to crowdsource were already made and are discussed in this subsection. It was recognised that making an informed decision whether to crowdsource or not requires a comprehensive analysis in which multiple factors should be examined in a systematic way [12, 24]. By examining the characteristics of crowdsourcing in practice, Schenk and Guittard [13] have stressed task complexity as the first important dimension. They proposed the classification of tasks to simple, complex or creative. Simple tasks are jobs that can be accomplished with generic skills. Complex and creative tasks require expertise and problem solving skills. They also analysed the difference between the integrative and selective nature of the crowd computing process as another dimension, distinguishing between performing tasks individually or competitively.

Crowdsourcing in the form of contests was analysed by Afuah and Tucci in [1]. Four organizational factors that positively influence the probability of crowdsourcing are: Characteristics of the problem (ease of delineation and transmission, and modularizability), characteristics of knowledge required for the solution (effective distance, and tacitness and complexity), characteristics of the crowd (pervasiveness of problem solving know-how, and motivation), and characteristics of solutions to be evaluated and of evaluators (experience-good orientation, and number of solution evaluators required). The external factor includes the pervasiveness and cost of IT, which positively moderate the relationship between aforementioned variables and the probability of crowdsourcing.

Theoretical framework by Thuan, Antunes and Johnstone [17] adapted the various layers of a complex sociotechnical system from Vicente's work [19] and classified the identified factors to these layers: (1) the task an organization wants to crowdsource, (2) the people who perform the task, (3) the management which plans how the task can be coordinated, (4) the environment. Task properties: Can be delivered and collected through the internet, interaction between organization and members during activity, presence of sensitive information, ease of partitioning. People properties: presence of enough human resources to accomplish task, availability of crowd members able to perform a particular task. Management: Budget of crowdsourcing, ability to handle the coordination of crowd workers, risk and risk management. Environment: Availability of crowdsourcing platform (and pool of members).

Buecheler et al. [3] examined collective intelligence in scientific method. They suggested a framework of three factors (environment, agent, and task) to determine the viability of crowdsourcing. Although each constituent principle has detailed variables, the authors did not specify how these variables influence the crowdsourcing decision. More importantly, the framework cannot be fully validated as the authors themselves stated "the data collection was not thorough enough to analyse all the variables mentioned in our framework".

Rouse in [12] advises the decision to crowdsource should "only be made" after examining four factors: production, costs, coordination and risks. Sharma [15] provided a framework of several success factors associated with crowdsourcing initiatives, which are necessarily involved in the decision to crowdsource. In this framework, motive alignment of the crowd is the central factor influencing crowdsourcing success since it is "aligned to long term objectives of the crowdsourcing initiative". This factor is affected by five peripheral factors: vision and strategy, human capital, infrastructure, linkages and trust, and the external environment. However, many factors in this framework need to be detailed before the framework can be used to support managers to make informed decision [24].

3.3 Conclusion: Factors to Be Investigated

The literature analysis presented in the previous sections revealed that there are no established theories, approaches or models for decisions on crowdsourcing in the context of BPO. But it resulted in a number of factors which are expected to be relevant for this purpose, since they originate from either decision making on BPO in general, cloud computing or crowd sourcing. Some factors from decision making on BPO and crowd sourcing have a large overlap and therefore were integrated. Table 1 summarizes the identified "candidate" factors. In the case study in Sect. 4, we investigate the pertinence and relevance of these factors.

Table 1. Factors identified in the literature study

Origin	Factor	Description	Lit.
Cloud computing (Sect. 3.1)	Complexity of cloud service architecture CPLX	Indicator: number of different components required on SaaS and PaaS level in order to provide the BPaaS for the BPO under consideration The more components on SaaS and/or PaaS architecture level, the more efforts have to be spent to provide IT system for crowd members	[11]
	Deployment model DEPL	Indicator: Kind of deployment [public, private, hybrid] cloud Private and hybrid cloud deployment require more access security for crowd members than public cloud deployment	[11]

(Continued)

Table 1. (*Continued*)

Origin	Factor	Description	Lit.
Decision on BPO in general (Sect. 3.1)	Core Competence COMP	Indicator: Is the task to be outsourced a core competence of the enterprise? [Yes, No] Core competence should not be outsourced	[8, 9, 23]
	High service quality QUAL	Indicator: Is the expected service quality provided by outsourcing higher than the quality achieved internally? [Yes, No] Significantly better service results motivate outsourcing	[8, 9, 23]
	Loss of management control CTRL	Indicator: Does outsourcing lead to a not-acceptable loss of management control? [Yes, No] The business process has to be on an acceptable level under management control, both within the enterprise or when outsourced	[8, 9, 23]
Decision on BPO in general (Sect. 3.1) and Crowdsourcing (Sect. 3.2)	Cost savings/budget COST	Indicators: Saving per time period; availability of budget Outsourcing makes only sense of it leads to cost savings and is only possible if the organization has fund to pay for it	[8, 9, 23]
	Security risk/sensitive information SECU	Indicator: Is either data related to the service, the resources used or the process applied subject to confidentiality? [Data, Resource, Process, None] Confidential data, resources, processes should not be exposed to actors outside the enterprise	[8, 9, 23]
	Flexibility, Availability of internal HR FLEX	Indicator: Are enough human resources available in-house? Does outsourcing increase the flexibility of internal resource use? [Yes, No] In case of (temporary) shortage of capacity, outsourcing can provide higher flexibility than increasing internal resources	[8, 9, 23]

(*Continued*)

Table 1. (*Continued*)

Origin	Factor	Description	Lit.
Crowdsourcing (Sect. 3.2)	Ease of task decomposition DECO	Indicator: Can the task be easily decomposed into subtasks that could be solved independently? [Yes, No] Decomposition is important to speed up task execution by parallelizing it	[1, 13, 17]
	Possibility to deliver task through the internet; INTN	Indicator: Whether this task and its expected result can be delivered through the internet Crowd computing uses network interaction as its primary information channel	[1, 17]
	Interaction between organization and members INTA	Indicator: A number of people in organization that usually influence task completion or the number of inner organization resources and instructions that need to be used for task completion Tasks that are relatively independent of the organization's information infrastructure are easier to crowdsource	[15, 17]
	Availability of crowd members needed for task CMAV	Indicator: Is the estimated number of crowd members (of a particular crowd provider) able to complete the task sufficiently large? Some tasks require special skills that are incompatible with a usual demographics of crowd members	[1, 15, 17]
	Coordination COOR	Indicator: Ability to handle coordination of crowd workers The presence of management staff able (from the skill perspective as well as from the working schedule perspective) to coordinate crowd computing effort can result in better performance	[1, 12, 17]

(*Continued*)

Table 1. (*Continued*)

Origin	Factor	Description	Lit.
	Risk RISK	Indicator: Can the organization embed the risk of low quality crowdsourcing result to its risk management scheme? The result of crowdsourced task can be of relatively low quality, and if it is critical for the organization, then crowdsourcing probably should be avoided, or engineered in a more careful way	[12, 17]
	Platform PLAT	Indicator: Does the organization possess its own crowd platform/typical pool of crowd members The availability of crowdsourcing platform can decrease cost	[1, 15, 17]

4 Case Study: BPO in Energy Sector

This section summarizes the design, content and results of a case study on business process outsourcing which was performed in the utilities industry. The purpose of the case study was twofold: On the one hand we intended to study business process outsourcing and the options to use crowd sourcing in a real-world context in order to understand the specifics of this area. On the other hand, we wanted to analyze the factors identified in the literature study in the context of the case study data. The question to investigate is whether the case study indicates that the factors really can be considered as affecting the decision on business process outsourcing into the crowd.

4.1 Case Study Design

In order to investigate the field of business process outsourcing, we had the possibility to study a business services provider from the energy sector. Within this business service provider (BSP), we collected information about BPO in several ways:

- One researcher worked during 3 months two or three working days every week at the BSP's facilities. The researcher was part of the team operating the business service and maintaining the SaaS platform used for provisioning the services to the service provider's clients. The researcher maintained a work diary and collected information about the work processes, technologies used and practices by observing the co-workers and taking notes. The management of the BSP agreed to this procedure and the co-workers were informed about the purpose of the data collection.

- The BSP specifies the services to be provided to the clients by defining business process models. These models have to be kept accurate and up-to-date since they are used to create executable workflows. Some of the models were accessible to the researchers and could be analyzed.
- The internal business processes at the BSP, which were performed for delivering the business process service to the clients, were captured by interviewing different roles in the BSP. The roles interviewed were the service owner (responsible for the features of the service and the flow of activities in it), knowledge worker (performing manual activities in the process), system operator (responsible for configuring and managing the infrastructure platform) and the BSP manager (responsible for acquisition of clients, analyzing their demands and setting up the service level agreements). In total six interviews were performed as expert interviews [2] guided by a list of questions related to the propositions (see below).

The main subject to investigate was "How are BPO services delivered by a BSP to its clients in terms of processes performed, organization structure used, technology applied and information used". As already indicated in Sect. 2, the character of the case study is descriptive. Furthermore, we defined two propositions P1 and P2.

- P1: The case shows the potential for outsourcing some of the tasks performed within the BPO services to the crowd.
- P2: Factors identified in the literature study can be observed in the case study.

To set clear boundaries for the case we defined that only data collected during the three months work of the researcher (see above) at the BSP's facilities (including the process models and interviews) in the organization units responsible for service provision to clients in the energy sector and for SaaS maintenance shall be taken into account. Not subject of the case study are other organization units of the BSP, BPO services provided to other utility industries (water, gas, etc.), the clients of the BSP and sub-suppliers used for BPO by the BSP.

4.2 Summary of Case Study Data

Due to the space limitations only a summary of the data collected in the case study can be presented in this paper. In this summary, we inserted the codes defined for the factors (see Table 1), e.g., [FLEX] for the factor "flexibility", if the information collected can be linked to the factors. This "linking to codes" will be used in Sect. 4.3 when evaluating the case study data.

The BSP studied in the case study is a medium-sized enterprise from Germany which offers more than 20 different BPO services to their clients. The target group for these services is medium-sized utility providers and other market roles of the energy sector in Germany and several other European countries. Many energy distribution companies are outsourcing some business functions and business processes connected to these functions. Examples are meter readings, meter data evaluation, automatic billing, processing and examination of invoices, customer relationship management and order management. The motivation of these companies for outsourcing business processes is twofold: Some companies use BSP is to temporarily increase the capacity for performing the processes, as they do not have sufficient internal resources for certain high capacity periods [FLEX]; others want to minimize efforts for adaptation to market or legal changes [COST]. Energy companies in Germany are facing a continuously changing business environment due to new regulations and due to competitors implementing innovative technical solutions, like intelligent metering or grid utilization management. In this context, both the business processes in organizations and information systems supporting these processes need to be quickly adaptive to changing organizational needs [FLEX].

The BSP offers the performance of a complete business process for a business function or only of selected tasks of a business process. In this context, the BSP has to offer and implement solutions for different variations of these business processes or tasks. One variation is inherent in the business process as such. Even though core processes can be defined and implemented in standard software systems, configurations and adjustments for the organization in question are needed. The second cause of variation is the configuration for the country of use, i.e., the implementation of the actual regulations and bylaws. The third variation is related to the resource use for implementing the actual business process for the customer, i.e., the provision of technical and organizational capabilities.

The IT-basis for these services in our case study is a software product which was developed and is maintained by the BSP. Integrated with a workflow engine and business activity monitoring, this software product provides the business logic for the energy sector, which is implemented using a database-centric approach. In addition to this software product, other cloud-based services for information exchange, document management and security are integrated [CPLX]. Different deployment models are used including a provider-centric model (the software product and the business processes are run at the BSP's computing center), a client-centric model (the software product is installed at the client site and the manual work of the business process is performed at the BSP) and mixed models (e.g., the software product is offered in the cloud, work and process are performed partly at the client and partly at the BSP) [DEPL] [INTN].

An example business process, which is offered as BPO service and consists of various activities [DECO], is to process information about energy consumption based on meter readings. This information is exchanged between different market roles in the energy sector using EDIFACT-like messages. Each file exchanged between the market roles might contain thousands of messages which in turn follow a defined syntax with a multitude of constraints and rules regarding the semantics of the information included. The processing of the files and messages is only a small part of the process. More efforts and activities are caused when errors are detected in the messages or exceptions are discovered due to violation of constraints and rules. In these cases, the automatic processing is interrupted and human intervention required. The competence required from the "knowledge workers" ranges from simple correction of syntax errors or substitution of faulty codes to remedy of so far unknown exceptions which requires expert knowledge from the energy sector and the IT services used. This expert knowledge is considered as one of the most important competitive advantages [COMP].

BSP and client have an agreement which defines the capacity to be provided, the cost model, levels of confidentiality [SECU] and service quality. The BSP is responsible for providing the contractually agreed capacity and quality. Sub-suppliers will only be integrated if the agreement with the client does not exclude this option [SECU] and if they provide the required quality of the service [QUAL] [RISK]. So far, no experience with crowdsourcing exists. The BSP can imagine evaluating crowdsourcing techniques for specific, isolated tasks [INTA] with low training efforts, like the correction of error codes, when there is a lack of own capacity [FLEX]. Precondition would be the availability of a defined group of people with known competences [COMP] [CMAV] who flexibly could be integrated into service provision. Furthermore, the status of the contributions from the crowd should be transparent [CTRL] and it should be economically rewarding [COST].

The maintenance process encompasses steps for designing, developing, deploying and operating the software systems used for BPO. The case showed three different phases in the maintenance process:

- The conceptual solution addresses the development of business services which fit to the strategic objectives and meet the practical demands of the customer under consideration. Focus here is on the business logic, not on the technical implementation [COMP].
- The technical solution prepares the conceptual solution for execution. This usually requires an enhancement or refinement of the conceptual solution when adapting it for a specific technical platform for execution [CPLX],
- The executable solution represents the technical solution deployed on a specific platform. This "running system" is managed by the customer that uses it or by a service provider [DEPL].

The technology stack encompasses all IT-tools and platforms requires for the above phases of the engineering process. This includes tools and notations or languages for modeling the conceptual solution, like process modeling, business process management or enterprise modeling tools, workflow engines and process execution environments as well as software development environments in case services or software components have to be integrated, and operating platforms and monitoring tools used during execution of the solution [CPLX].

4.3   Case Study Analysis

The main technique for analyzing the case study data was to link the data to the propositions. Thus, we will discuss both propositions in the light of the case study data. As both propositions are related to the factors identified in Sect. 3 and summarized in Sect. 3.3, we will start the analysis by providing an overview what information is visible in case study data regarding the factors. This summarized in Table 2.

For some factors, there was no or not enough information available in the case study to decide on their relevance: ability to handle coordination of crowd workers, availability of an own crowd platform to the organization and the required number of knowledge workers to handle a given case.

Table 2. Factors and their presence in case study data

Factor	Description
Factors whose relevance for decision making about crowdsourcing in the case study was **confirmed**	
Complexity of cloud service architecture	The architecture in the case study consists of the BSP's software product and – depending on the client – of potentially additional software service. In case of additional software, outsourcing to the crowd is considered more difficult.
Core Competence	Tasks requiring expert knowledge will not be outsourced, since this is considered as competitive advantage which the BSP protects
High service quality	Precondition for considering crowdsourcing for certain activities is that the service level agreement with the client can be kept
Loss of management control	The responsible persons for service management require transparency regarding status and performance of the crowd-members
Cost savings/budget	Crowd sourcing would only be considered if it is economically rewarding
Security/sensitive information	If the contract with the client excludes an outsourcing option, the BSP will not include any kind of sub-supplier
Flexibility, HR availability	Precondition for considering crowdsourcing would be a lack of internal capacity
Deliver task with Internet	In the case study, all parts of the outsourcing are provided using Internet technology
Availability of crowd members	Crowdsourcing would require a defined group of people with known competences
Interaction of organization and crowd members	Only specific and isolated tasks will be considered for outsourcing
Risk	Precondition for considering crowdsourcing is that the service level agreement with the client can be kept, i.e., no risk of too low quality
Required level of adaptation	If an exception requires special adaptation of the case handling it will not be considered for outsourcing
Factors whose relevance was **not confirmed** by the case study	
Deployment model	In the case study, deployment in one or several private clouds was possible. Crowd members would be awarded access right to specific private cloud
Ease of task decomposition	In the case study, the overall business process is already decomposed into single tasks. Decomposition was not considered.

P1: The case shows potential for outsourcing some of the tasks performed within the BPO services to the crowd. Both the case study data and the evaluation of factors in Table 2 show that the case shows the possibility for involving crowd-members in provisioning the BPO service. The potential for crowdsourcing seems quite limited since it is only for "simple" tasks in exception handling which require limited training efforts for a known group of crowd-members. Furthermore, the BSP does not have experience with crowdsourcing and will consider this as an "experiment", which indicates that the subject so far is given low priority. However, for the research work presented in this paper it is important to notice that due to the potential for using crowdsourcing it was a suitable case study for investigating the factors identified in the literature study.

P2: Factors identified in the literature study can be observed in the case study. Table 2 shows that most of the factors actually could be observed in the case study and most of them were confirmed relevant. Only two factors were not confirmed: deployment model and ease of task decomposition. For these two factors, which intuitively make sense, we will need to investigate further cases in order to decide on their pertinence.

5   Summary and Future Work

Based on a literature study in the areas of BPO and cloud computing and crowd-sourcing, this paper identified potential factors relevant for decision making in favor or against using crowdsourcing in BPO scenarios. The factors identified were investigated in a case study from business process outsourcing, which confirmed many of the factors and gives reason to believe that the work contributes to a better understanding of outsourcing decisions in BPO and the relevant factors. However, just one case study will not give a conclusive picture whether the identified factors can be assumed to be relevant for the majority of BPO cases. Future work will have to investigate more cases. The factors identified have to be considered as a theory contribution grounded in literature and one case study.

Research including empirical studies has threats regarding its validity, and so has the case study performed in this paper for investigating the decision factors for crowd sourcing. However, to early identify such threats and to take actions to mitigate the threats can minimize the effect on the findings. Common threats to empirical studies are discussed, for example in [20] and [23]. The threats to validity can be divided into four categories: construct validity, internal validity, external validity and conclusion validity. Construct validity is concerned with obtaining the right indicators and measures for the concept being studied. Internal validity primarily is important for explanatory studies with the objective to identify causal relationships. External validity is addressing the question about to which extent the findings in a study can be generalized. Conclusion validity addresses repetition or replication, i.e., that the same result would be found if performing the study again in the same setting.

With respect to *construct validity*, the following threats were identified and actions taken: (a) Selection of employees from the BSP interviewed and observed in the case study. The results are highly dependent on the people being interviewed and observed. Only persons experienced in business process outsourcing and the application domain under consideration will be able to contribute to judging the importance of factors. To obtain the best possible sample, only people having worked in this area for a long time and hence having the required background were interviewed or observed during the case study. (b) Reactive bias: A common risk in studies is that the presence of a researcher influences the outcome. Since the selected participants in the study and the researcher performing the study have been collaborating for a long time, this is not perceived as a large risk. However, as the crowdsourcing idea was proposed by the researcher there is the risk that the interviews are biased towards this idea and to find evidence for the relevance of factors. In order to reduce this threat, the interviewees were informed that crowdsourcing can be used in different ways and the purpose of the study was to investigate feasibility. (c) Correct interview data: There is a risk that the questions of the interviewer may be misunderstood or the data may be misinterpreted. In order to minimize this risk, the data collected during the interviews was presented afterwards to the interviewees to allow for verification. Furthermore, the interviews were documented, which allowed the researcher to check certain parts of the interview again if portions seemed unclear.

From the perspective of *external validity*, a potential threat of the study is of course that the actual interviews and observations have been conducted with members of only one BSP. It will be part of the future work, to conduct a study with other BSPs. *Conclusion validity* mainly concerns the interpretation of data: The outcome of the study potentially could be affected by the interpretation of the researcher. To minimize this threat, the study design includes capturing the relevant aspects by different data, i.e., to conduct triangulation to check the correctness of the findings. Furthermore, another risk could be that the interpretation of the data depends on the researcher and is not traceable. To reduce the risk the data interpretation was discussed with other researchers and validated by them.

In addition to more case studies and the collection of additional data regarding the identified factors, future work has to contribute a deeper conceptualization of the different factors. We identified factors and confirmed their pertinence in one case, but we did not fully operationalize them. For factors like architecture of cloud service, we will need to spend more work on finding indicators which show, when the factor under consideration has substantial influence and when the influence is negligible. For the example of the factor "cloud service architecture" this would mean to determine, with which indicator to measure this factor and what indicator values would have to be considered too high for a decision in favor of outsourcing. Another direction of the future work is to separately evaluate each factor's influence for different crowdsourcing models, as the employed model (e.g., microtask markets, solution contests) may affect factor's relevance.

Acknowledgements. Parts of the research were supported by the EU FP7-project CaaS (project # 611351). Other parts were partially supported by grants # 14-07-00345, # 16-07-00466 of the Russian Foundation for Basic Research, and by Government of Russian Federation, Grant 074-U01.

References

1. Afuah, A., Tucci, C.L.: Crowdsourcing as a solution to distant search. Acad. Manag. Rev. **37**(3), 355–375 (2012)
2. Bogner, A., Menz, W.: The theory-generating expert interview: epistemological interest, forms of knowledge, interaction. In: Bogner, A., Littig, B., Menz, W. (eds.) Interviewing Experts, pp. 43–80. Palgrave Macmillan UK, London (2009)
3. Buecheler, T., et al.: Crowdsourcing, open innovation and collective intelligence in the scientific method: a research agenda and operational framework. In: Artificial life XII. Proceedings of the twelfth international conference on the synthesis and simulation of living systems, Odense, Denmark (2010)
4. Howe, J.: The rise of crowdsourcing. In: Wired magazine, pp. 1–4. Dorsey Press (2006)
5. Howe, J.: Crowdsourcing: a definition (2006). http://crowdsourcing.typepad.com/cs/-2006/06/crowdsourcing_a.html. Accessed 27 Nov 2014
6. Jansen, W., Grance, T.: Guidelines on security and privacy in public cloud computing. NIST special publication SP 800-144 (2011)
7. Krogstie, J.: Model-Based Development and Evolution of Information Systems - A Quality Approach. Springer, London (2012)
8. Lacity, M.C., Willcocks, L.P.: An empirical investigation of information technology sourcing practices: lessons from experience. MIS Q. **22**(3), 363–408 (1998)
9. Lacity, M., Willcocks, L.P.: Information Systems and Outsourcing: Studies in Theory and Practice. Palgrave, London (2009)
10. Motahari-Nezhad, H.R., Stephenson, B., Singhal, S.: Outsourcing business to cloud computing services: opportunities and challenges. IEEE Internet Comput. **10**(4), 1–17 (2009)
11. Rimal, B.P., Choi, E., Lumb, I.: A taxonomy and survey of cloud computing systems. In: NCM 2009, Fifth International Joint Conference on INC, IMS and IDC, pp. 44–51 (2009)
12. Rouse, A.C.: A preliminary taxonomy of crowdsourcing. In: ACIS 2010: Information Systems: Defining and Establishing a High Impact Discipline: Proceedings of the 21st Australasian Conference on Information Systems. ACIS (2010)
13. Schenk, E., Guittard, C.: Towards a characterization of crowdsourcing practices. J. Innov. Econ. **2011**(1), 93–107 (2011)
14. Seigerroth, U.: Enterprise modeling and enterprise architecture: the constituents of transformation and alignment of business and IT. IJITBAG **2**(1), 16–34 (2011)
15. Sharma, A.: Crowdsourcing Critical Success Factor Model: Strategies to Harness the Collective Intelligence of the Crowd. Working paper (2010)
16. Thuan, N.H.: To establish crowdsourcing as an organizational business process: an exploratory study. Phd Research Proposal, School of Information Management, Victoria University of Wellington, New Zealand (2013)
17. Thuan, N.H., Antunes, P., Johnstone, D.: Factors influencing the decision to crowdsource. In: Antunes, P., Gerosa, M.A., Sylvester, A., Vassileva, J., Vreede, G.-J. (eds.) CRIWG 2013. LNCS, vol. 8224, pp. 110–125. Springer, Heidelberg (2013)
18. La Vecchia, G., Cisternino, A.: Collaborative workforce, business process crowdsourcing as an alternative of BPO. In: Daniel, F., Facca, F.M. (eds.) ICWE 2010. LNCS, vol. 6385, pp. 425–430. Springer, Heidelberg (2010)
19. Vicente, K.J.: Cognitive Work Analysis: Toward Safe, Productive, and Healthy Computer-Based Work. CRC PressI LLC, Boca Raton (1999)
20. Wohlin, C., Runeson, P., Host, M., Ohlsson, C., Regnell, B., Wesslèn, A.: Experimentation in Software Engineering: An Introduction. Kluver Academic Publishers, Norwell (2000)

21. Woitsch, R., Karagiannis, D., Plexousakis, D., Hinkelmann, K.: Business and IT alignment: the IT-Socket. e & i Elektrotechnik und Informationstechnik **126**(7–8), 308–321 (2009)
22. Yang, D.H., Kim, S., Nam, C., Min, J.W.: Developing a decision model for business process outsourcing. Comput. Oper. Res. **34**(12), 3769–3778 (2007)
23. Yin, R.K.: Case Study Research: Design and Methods. Applied Social Research Methods Series, vol. 5, 3rd edn. Sage Publications Inc, Thousand Oaks (2002)
24. Zhao, Y., Zhu, Q.: Evaluation on crowdsourcing research: current status and future direction. Inf. Syst. Front. **2012**, 1–18 (2012)

On the Role of Enterprise Modelling in Engineering Cyber-Physical Systems

Kurt Sandkuhl[1,2(✉)]

[1] University of Rostock, Albert-Einstein-Str. 22, 18059 Rostock, Germany
[2] School of Engineering at Jönköping University, 55111 Jönköping, Sweden
kurt.sandkuhl@uni-rostock.de

Abstract. Cyber-Physical Systems (CPS) are considered as key elements of the next industrial revolution which have an enormous innovation potential. However, the existing gap between methods, modelling approaches and viewpoints of the disciplines involved in CPS development creates significant difficulties for creating viable CPS solutions. In this paper we investigate the potential of using enterprise modelling as an integrative method for large parts of CPS development projects. The work is based on a case study from transportation industry. The main contributions of this paper are (1) a case study from transportation illustrating CPS development with business and technical aspects, (2) a discussion of enterprise modelling potential in different development phases of CPS, and (3) a proposal for a CPS development process integrating technical and business aspects.

Keywords: Cyber-Physical Systems · Enterprise modelling · Case study · Transportation industries

1 Introduction

Cyber-Physical Systems (CPS) are considered as key elements of the next industrial revolution which have an enormous innovation potential. CPS are expected to be the key to higher efficiency and flexibility in many industrial domains [5]. From a technical perspective CPS tightly integrate physical and IT (cyber) systems based on interactions between these systems in real time [11]. Such systems rely on communication, computation and control infrastructures commonly consisting of several levels with different resources, such as sensors, actuators, computational resources, services, humans, etc. From an enterprise perspective CPS have the potential for initiating product innovation (see [6] for an example from health industries), process innovation (see [8] for an example from manufacturing) or business model innovation (see [18]).

A challenge frequently experienced in the development of CPS is the gap between methods, modelling approaches and viewpoints of the involved disciplines. In order to create viable CPS solutions from business and technical viewpoint, stakeholders from different enterprise functions should be involved as the services and products depending on CPS will have to be integrated in the enterprise's business processes, need qualified

© Springer International Publishing Switzerland 2016
V. Řepa and T. Bruckner (Eds.): BIR 2016, LNBIP 261, pp. 50–64, 2016.
DOI: 10.1007/978-3-319-45321-7_4

personnel, are part of the enterprise service structure. This gap has been addressed by some research projects but is not fully covered yet.

This paper addresses the above challenge by discussing the potential of enterprise modelling as an integrative method for large parts of CPS development projects. More concrete, we investigate based on a case study from CPS development in transportation, which development steps of CPS could be supported by enterprise modelling methods and how an integrated development method including business and technical aspects would have to look like. The main contributions of this paper are (1) a case study from transportation illustrating CPS development with business and technical aspects, (2) a discussion of enterprise modelling potential in different development phases of CPS, and (3) a proposal for CPS development process integrating technical and business aspects.

The remaining part of the paper is structured as follows: Sect. 2 will give a brief overview to background for this work in enterprise modelling and CPS development. Section 3 gives an overview to the research method used. Section 4 presents the case study from transportation industry with its design and analysis approach. Section 5 discusses the role of enterprise modelling in CPS development as a result of analysing the industrial case. As a conclusion from the industrial case, Sect. 6 proposes an enterprise modelling-based CPS development approach. A summary and description of future work is subject of Sect. 7.

2   Background

This section summarizes the conceptual background for our work with focus on enterprise modelling (Sect. 2.1), Cyber-Physical Systems (Sect. 2.2) and development methods of CPS (Sect. 2.3).

2.1   Enterprise Modelling

In general terms, enterprise modelling is addressing the systematic analysis and modelling of processes, organization structures, products structures, IT-systems or any other perspective relevant for the modelling purpose [22]. Sandkuhl et al. [16] provide a detailed account of enterprise modelling approaches. Enterprise models can be applied for various purposes, such as visualization of current processes and structures in an enterprise, process improvement and optimization, introduction of new IT solutions or analysis purposes. Enterprise knowledge modelling combines and extends approaches and techniques from enterprise modelling. The knowledge needed for performing a certain task in an enterprise or for acting in a certain role has to include the context of the individual, which requires including all relevant perspectives in the same model [13]. A practice for identifying these perspectives is the so-called "POPS*"-approach proposed by [12]. POPS* is an abbreviation for the perspective of an enterprise to be included in an enterprise model: process (P), organization structure (O), product (P), systems & resources (S) and other aspects required for the modelling purpose (*). The practice basically recommends to always include the four POPS perspectives in a model because they are mutually reflective: process are performed by the roles captured in the organisation structure, the roles are using systems and resources which at the same time capture information about products; manufacturing and design of products is done in processes by roles using systems, etc. [12].

2.2 Cyber-Physical Systems

As already mentioned, CPS tightly integrate heterogeneous resources of the physical world and IT world. This term is tightly related to such terms as Industry 4.0 and Internet of Things. Currently, there is a significant amount of research efforts in the area of cyber-physical networks and their applications, e.g., in production [8], transportation [23], and many other. Such systems rely on communication, computation and control infrastructures commonly consisting of several levels for the two worlds with various resources [20] as sensors, actuators, computational resources, services, etc. CPS belong to the class of variable systems with dynamic structures.

Having analysed the state-of-the-art of different CPS approaches and supporting technologies, among other conclusions, Horvath and Gerritsen conclude that "the next-generation of CPSs will not emerge by aggregating many un-coordinated ideas and technologies in an incremental fashion. Instead, they will require a more organized and coordinated attack on the synergy problem, driven by an overarching view of what the future outcome should be" [7]. Although recent research approaches start to address this issue, e.g. for the design of interoperable Internet-of-Things manufacturing systems [9], the statement by Horvath and Gerritsen continues to be valid. This means that the whole structure of a CPS under development has to be built in advance based on the analysis of the required CPS functionality. Enterprise models can be a valuable information source in this case since they describe various aspects of an enterprise, acting units, their competences and relationships.

2.3 Development Methods of Cyber-Physical Systems

As part of the background work for the paper, we performed a literature study in order to identify development methods for cyber-physical systems. This study followed an explorative approach using Google Scholar, IEEE Xplore and SpringerLink as primary sources for literature search. In the first stage, we looked for methods dedicated to CPS development or engineering. The literature search in this field revealed that there is a workshop on the topic of engineering CPS, but no dedicated method for CPS development or engineering could be identified [14]. The literature search showed the use of systems engineering methods (see, e.g. [21, 23]), pragmatic approaches (e.g. [1]) or iterative incremental developments like in software engineering (e.g. [15]).

In the next stage we checked the existing methods in related areas. As CPS integrates physical systems and IT-systems, these areas primarily were systems engineering and software engineering. Software engineering methods usually integrate the business perspective as part of requirements engineering but focus on use cases or process modelling [19]. If hardware has to be integrated, hardware/software co-design methods have to be applied which do not include the business aspects [4]. Systems engineering methods [3] focus on identifying interdependent parts of systems and in designing the internal environment, functions and interface of these parts. This neglects both the user and business perspective [2].

The result of the analysis was that there is no method covering all steps from business model development to system engineering.

3   Research Method

Research work in this paper started from the following research question which is based on the motivation presented in Sect. 1: *In CPS development projects, how to use enterprise modelling for the integration of business and technology aspects?*

The research method used for working on this research question is a combination of literature study and descriptive case study. Based on the research question defined, we started to identify existing CPS development approaches. The purpose was to find existing theories or approaches that integrate business aspects of CPS and technology/ engineering aspects during the CPS development. Since the literature study returned no such theories or approaches (see Sect. 2.3), we decided to perform a case study in order to gather information pertinent for the subject area. Qualitative case study is an approach to research that facilitates exploration of a phenomenon within its context using a variety of data sources [25]. This ensures that the subject under consideration is explored from different perspectives which allows for multiple facets of the phenomenon to be revealed and understood. Within the case study, we used two different perspectives, which at the same time represent sources of data: We observed the activities during CPS development and we analyzed documents from different phases of the development process, including the early phases dedicated to business model definition, the phase of specifying business and operation processes, and the engineering phases of the technology (cf. Sect. 4.1).

Yin differentiates various kinds of case studies [25]: explanatory, exploratory and descriptive. The case study presented in Sect. 4 has to be considered as descriptive, as it is used to describe the phenomenon of CPS development and the real-life context in which it occurs. Based on the case study results, we conclude that there is a potential of using enterprise modeling for integrating the business and technology aspects of CPS development. This argumentative-deductive part is discussed in Sect. 5.

4   Case Study: CPS Development in Transportation

This section summarizes design and content of a case study on CPS development in transportation industries. The purpose of the case study was twofold: On the one hand, we intended to study integration of business and technology aspects during CPS development in a real-world context in order to understand the specifics of the underlying procedure. On the other hand, we analyzed the potential for using enterprise modeling as integrative approach between business and technology.

Table 1. Available documents for qualitative case analysis in the industrial case

Document	Main Purpose	Format	Development Phase
Funding application, Stage A	Market study for innovative products	Text document	Business objectives development
Meeting notes	Notes from meetings of researchers and founders of the company about idea and basic concepts	Handwritten notes	Business objectives development
Project Report A	Result report from funding application, stage A	Text document	Business model dev.
Funding application, Stage B	Feasibility study of integrated IT and physical components	Text document	Specification of CPS
Business Plan (excerpt)	Description of services to be offered with key features and target groups	Text document	Business model dev.
Architecture sketch	Identify main components and basic information flow between components	Drawing	Specification of CPS
Report from Project B	Result report from feasibility study project, stage B	Text document	Business model dev., Specification of CPS
Funding application, Stage C	Development of high risk products	Text document	Specification of CPS
Work Process	Define work processes from end user and back-office perspective	Process model	Integration into enterprise processes
Project Report C	Result report from project, stage C, describing the actual services, implementation status	Text document	Enterprise architecture modelling
Software and systems architecture	Architecture model with different views on components, information, hardware and infrastructure	Drawing	Specification of CPS
Dependency chart	Visualize the dependencies of back-office systems and software components	Drawing	Specification of CPS
Design specification	Specify interaction sequence, message exchange and implementation requirements	Text + UML diagrams	CPS implementation

4.1   Case Study Design

In order to investigate the development of CPS, we had the possibility to study a case from transportation industries. This CPS development originated from a cooperation between industry and academia which started already in a very early phase of developing the business idea, i.e. the feasibility of developing the underlying technology for the CPS was confirmed and the idea for new kinds of business services was existing, but there were no defined business plans, architecture descriptions, service specification, economic models or similar. This resulted in the rare opportunity to accompany the development process of a CPS from idea to implementation.

As already stated in Sect. 3, the main subject to investigate was *"In CPS development projects, how to use enterprise modelling (EM) for the integration of business and technology aspects?"* For this research question, we identified three sub-questions:

- What are the steps in developing CPS?
- For which steps are EM methods applicable as they are?
- What extensions of EM would be required or advisable?

From a method perspective, we followed the recommendations of [10] for performing qualitative case analysis. The unit of analysis in the case study is a single project of CPS development, i.e. our work does not address businesses developing a portfolio of CPS or CPS product families. The actual project we analysed is described in Sect. 4.2. This project includes one technological solution and several business services offered to the clients on basis of this technological solution. Since our objective is to study applicability of enterprise modelling in practice of CPS development, our focus had to be on data sources containing very detailed information. The data sources used are original project documentation and notes taken by the personnel involved in the project. Table 1 shows the list of documents analysed and indicates in the column "development phase" from what phase of CPS engineering the document originates. The analysis of the data sources was performed based on the research question with its sub-questions, i.e. a qualitative content analysis of all documents shown in Table 1 was performed in order to link the documents to the research (sub-)question(s).

4.2   Case Study Summary

Due to the space limitations only a summary of the data collected in the case study can be presented in this paper (see also Sect. 5). The work reported in this paper was performed in an industrial project in transport and logistics industries. The logistics industry makes intensive use of modern information technology and CPS for achieving high efficiency of processes and solutions in a globalized market. One of the world's largest truck manufacturers designed and implemented new transport related services based on a CPS consisting of electronics in truck-trailers and an IT system using the information from the trailers for information logistics services. The trailers have a wireless sensor network (WSN) installed in the position lights. Each light carries a sensor node able to network with neighbouring nodes and furnished with a radar sensor. This sensor can be used for various purposes, including protection of the goods on the trailer against theft or surveillance of the trailer or its different compartments (e.g. by electronically sealing them). A gateway in the trailer is controlling the WSN in the position lights and communicates with the back-office of the owner of the trailer. Several services were developed within the project, which exploit the possibilities of combining sensor information and IT services. One of these services is additional protection of the trailer when parked against theft, also called secure trailer access control (STAC) (see [17] for more details).

The development of STAC and the other new services started in 2009 and continued until 2012. Everything started with the idea of creating new transportation-oriented services based on wireless sensor networks built into truck-trailers. The Swedish innovation agency VINNOVA funded in 2009 a market study in this area and 2010 a feasibility study for technical solutions. In parallel to these projects, business plan development and investigation of different service scenarios and potential technical designs took place. End of 2010, it was decided to enter actual product development which financially was supported by investors from transportation industry and project funding from the "Research & Grow" program of VINNOVA. The development included design of the business model, the systems architecture, the devices to be built into the trailers, the software infrastructure, back-office and usage process and the overall system architecture. Furthermore, integration into existing service systems had to be taken into account. In 2012 the development was moved to another organizational context as the developing company was bought by another enterprise.

5   How to Use EM for the Integration of Business and Technology Aspects in CPS Development?

During the case analysis described in Sect. 4, we discovered a number of work steps or phases of the CPS development which would be suitable for enterprise modelling use. This section will provide information from the analysed documents and discuss these phases from three perspectives: (a) what has been done in the industrial case using enterprise modelling methods, (b) what could have been done if the possibilities of enterprise modelling would have been fully exploited, and (c) implications for enterprise modelling (if any) in terms of required extensions or changes in methods or w.r.t. integration with other methods.

5.1   Definition of Business Objectives

Before the start of the actual system development, the business objectives to be reached were discussed among the founders and defined. In the industrial case, business objectives were seen as a means to prioritize between the different possible services and customer groups and as a way to focus the business model development (see Sect. 5.2). The result of this step was a list of business objectives. One of the business objects defined was *"To establish the service of 'secure transport access (STAC)' for medium-sized and large haulers with at least 250 trailer installations and 50 % cost coverage during the first two years"*.

What has been done with EM use? – Definition of business objectives was performed without using EM techniques. Most of this step was supported by brainstorming and (unstructured) discussions.

What could have been done with EM? – Goal modelling is part of several EM techniques and would have been a suitable way to support systematic development of goal hierarchies and agreeing on priorities. 4EM goal modelling (see [12]) would be a suitable technique for this.

Implications for EM? – None.

5.2 STAC Business Model (Excerpt)

Business model development did not only cover the business objective shown in Sect. 5.1, but also business objectives for other services. The development was guided by the approach of partial business models proposed by Wirtz [24]. Five partial business models were used: The *procurement model* describes production factors and their sources, i.e. identification of suppliers is an important aspect. The *manufacturing model* covers the combination of input factors to the service under consideration. Demand structures as well as the competitive situation are described by the respective sub-models of the *market model*. The *service offer model* defines which IT services are provided to the customers, and the *distribution model* focuses on the channels used to make the IT services available to the specific customer groups. Table 2 shows an excerpt from the business model description as an illustration.

Table 2. Excerpt from business model from "secure trailer access (STAC)"

Partial models of business model	Business model of trailer theft control
Procurement model	Different elements of the services are contracted to service providers:
	• authentication of the truck driver: provided by trust centre • communication between gateway and back-office: provided by telco • security service in case of security incident, e.g. attempt of theft: provided by security provider
Manufacturing model	The general administration services, operational services and control services all are provided from the own back-office of the enterprise (i.e. service operator, infrastructure operator, project manager, help desk, etc.) using own IT hardware and software systems (fleet management, contract management, configuration environment).
Service offer model	The transport access control service is offered as stand-alone IT service or as "security bundle" with the services "electronic fence" and "electronic seal".

What has been done with EM use? – EM was not used in this stage; the approach proposed by Wirtz was applied (see above).

What could have been done with EM? – Procurement model, manufacturing model and service offer model basically consist of very rough identification of stakeholders and process groups within and outside the enterprise. In principal, most enterprise modelling method offer possibilities to capture such organisational elements and "process maps" as starting point for process modelling.

Implications for EM? – Enterprise modelling methods should be extended in order to explicitly support business model development, i.e., EM methods should include methods components or procedures describing what steps to take in business model identification. We consider such an extension more as a matter of defining an appropriate procedure than of actually extending notations or meta-models.

5.3   Business Processes for CPS Operation and Use

The business model excerpt shown in Sect. 5.2 can be used to identify where integration of the new service into the existing structure of the enterprise is needed. The manufacturing model defines what parts of the service are implemented in-house, i.e. from here we identify the existing roles and organization units (e.g. i.e. service operator, infrastructure operator, project manager) and resources involved (e.g. contract management, configuration environment). Procurement model and service offer model help to identify external roles, external processes and product structure elements.

What has been done with EM use? – As the business model was neither precise enough for specifying the exact integration in the enterprise nor meant for this purpose, we used EM for this development step. We developed an enterprise model capturing the POPS perspectives (see Sect. 2.1) for the relevant part of the case company from Sect. 3 and extended this model for the new services, which also visualizes how the CPS is integrated into business processes.

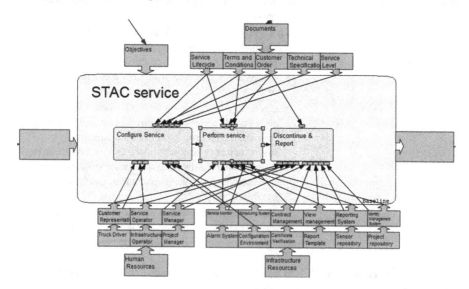

Fig. 1. Enterprise model excerpt for STAC with focus on process/role/resource

Figure 1 shows an excerpt from the enterprise model for STAC. In the middle of the figure, the high level business process "STAC service" is depicted. On the lower left of the process container, the roles involved are modelled (including internal and external roles); on the lower right of the process container, the systems and infrastructure resources are shown. Above the process container, important documents (e.g. contractual elements, like terms and conditions) are modelled. The arrows in the figure are typed relations between the model elements, which for example show which role "is_responsible" for what activity in the process. Both, human resources and infrastructure resources are part of specific sub-models for the overall enterprise not shown in the figure.

What could have been done with EM? – see above.

Implications for EM? – None.

5.4   CPS Integration into Product and Service Structure

When defining the business processes (see Sect. 5.3) and system architecture it became obvious that the CPS uses components of already existing products or services in the enterprise. An example is the technical maintenance service for trailers which currently is supposed to fix technical problems of the trailer's electricity or chassis but can be extended to also take care of the troubleshooting for the sensor network or trailer gateway. Another example is the power supply component in trailers which normally is installed in case refrigeration functionality is added to the trailer but within the CPS system can provide additional power supply for the trailer gateway. The dependencies and relationships to such existing products or services was in the industrial case captured by diagrams using feature model-like notations.

What has been done with EM use? – EM was not used in this stage.

What could have been done with EM? – Some enterprise modelling techniques, such as Active Knowledge Modelling, explicitly include capturing product knowledge and product structures. This approach could have been used in this development stage with the advantage that dependencies between processes, organisation structure and product/service component would have become more clear.

Implications for EM? – An enterprise modelling method used for CPS development has to provide the possibility of modelling product structures and inter-relationships to other modelling perspectives, like processes and organisation structures.

5.5   CPS Integration into Application and Information Architecture

When elaborating the software and system architecture it became clear that the CPS operation requires a tight integration with existing enterprise-IT for performing back-office processes. Examples are the integration with the ERP system for managing client data, orders, transactions and accounting issues, or with the fleet management system for tracking trailers and managing assignments to trucks.

In the industrial case, these connections were captured in an architecture diagram and tackled either in small integration projects with existing systems or by providing new installations of the application in question dedicated to the CPS operation.

What has been done with EM use? – EM was not used in this stage.

What could have been done with EM? – Modelling approaches for enterprise architecture management (EAM), like ArchiMate or TOGAF, clearly contribute to enterprise modelling with a focus on architectural structures. They provide constructs to model architectural dependencies between, e.g. business, application, information and technology architecture, and also provide means to capture much of the process and organization perspective of an enterprise as part of the business architecture. However, enterprise architecture approaches are not prepared and not meant for in-depth modelling of processes, organization structures, products and goals.

For the task of integrating CPS into application and information architecture, EAM approaches in general clearly are a suitable tool. However, this requires that the enterprise under consideration already has established EAM in the organisation, i.e. that the established enterprise architecture is known and documented.

Implications for EM? – Enterprise modelling methods should at least provide basic features for modelling enterprise architectures which can be used if no established EAM exists in the enterprise under consideration. In case EAM is established, the results from Sects. 5.3 and 5.4 have to be analysed regarding their implications for the EA.

5.6   Software and Systems Development

The development of the actual CPS system and the back-office infrastructure required a specification of what use cases had to be supported and what existing systems, information sources and interfaces had to be integrated. Although the business processes were defined in an enterprise model (see Sect. 5.3), additional UML use case diagrams were defined, which basically contained the same information, but provided exactly the view on one specific use case desired by the software and systems engineers.

What has been done with EM use? – The processes for CPS use were included in the business process model, but not applied.

What could have been done with EM? – EM basically offers all information and features required for the purpose. The main shortcoming in this development step was that the tool support did not offer a powerful view concept which allowed to provide the developer-specific view on the business process required.

Implications for EM? – Enterprise modelling methods selected for CPS development have to provide tool support also prepared for the needs of software and systems engineers. Alternatively, software and systems engineers need to be acquainted with enterprise modelling techniques-

6   EM-Based CPS Development Process

During the literature analysis presented in Sect. 2.3 we made the observation that most CPS developments seem to assume that development of the technical CPS system (which consists of a physical and an IT-system) and the integration of this CPS system into the enterprise IT and the enterprise's business are different activities which can be supported by different methods. In contrast, we argue - based on the results of the case study in

Sect. 5 - that CPS System development should not be separated from the integration into enterprise IT and business because not only the internal communication between physical system and IT system is affected by real-time communication and coordination but also the related enterprise systems and possibly even actors in the enterprise other than the users and operators of the actual CPS. Thus, we need a much more integrated method support for system development, system integration into business and business model development. The design of a CPS is much more than the design of the actual physical and IT-system and has to include the "organizational" system. We also argue that enterprise modelling methods can support this although they need extension.

Based on this observation we propose a CPS development process based on enterprise modelling which consists of the following phases:

a. Business objectives development: The enterprise management defines the business objectives to achieve. This includes what actual services to offer in what priority, minimum number of customers, upper limit for investments into solution development and marketing, expected market share, and other general frame conditions. This step is supported by goal modelling.

b. Business model development: for each of the services supported by the envisioned CPS, which are part of the business objectives, a business model is developed. Conceptually, the business model is separated into partial models (see Sect. 5.2) and captured in process modelling and organisation structure modelling perspectives.

c. CPS integration into business processes and product/service structures: as the business model does not describe how the new services will be integrated into the existing processes and structures of the enterprise delivering theses services, the next step has to be to design and integrate such structures and processes. This step can be performed refining the process, organization structure and resource perspectives available in many enterprise modelling techniques. Product and service structure modelling is an essential part of it.

d. Enterprise Architecture Modelling: in addition to business process and product structure integration (previous step), the IT-infrastructure required for CPS needs to fit into the enterprise's architecture which has to be captured in architecture models.

e. Specification of CPS: the specification of the CPS has to include the architecture and functional/non-functional characteristics of the technical solution and the set of operational service for managing and operating the technical solution. Enterprise architecture model (step d.), business process and product structure model (step c.) form the requirements space for this step. The specification as such is not done using enterprise modelling. With this step, the use of an adequate systems modelling method starts

f. CPS implementation: based on the specification, the actual It and physical components for the CPS are developed and integrated into a running system

g. CPS testing can be supported by using the specified processes and interactions as basis for generating test data.

h. CPS deployment: the business process and product/service structure models usually indicate and specify organizational changes in the enterprise which have to be prepared and implemented independently of the CPS design. Within deployment of the CPS system, these changes have to be completed and introduced.

7 Summary and Future Work

Starting from an industrial case of a CPS for transportation industries, the paper investigated the CPS development process. The case study showed that different representations and methods were used for the process steps, e.g. partial business models, enterprise models and software architecture models or system specifications. This diversity confirms the gap between methods, modelling approaches and viewpoints often observed during CPS development. Furthermore, the potential for using enterprise modelling was investigated by analysing the original project documentation in the case study.

The case study analysis performed in the industrial case had the main objective to gain a better understanding of how enterprise modelling can be used in CPS development. Section 5 reported on the key findings of the analysis following the order of development phases visible in the case study documents. The main conclusion is that there are a number of candidate areas for the use of enterprise modelling which need further investigation. Future work will have to include an analysis of other CPS cases to confirm this conjecture and the development of a process for enterprise modelling use.

Another finding from the case study is that the development process used in the case can be improved by a better integration of the models produced in the different development phases (e.g. model of business model, model of operational process, model of software system). This potentially can be done using the enterprise modelling-based CPS development process proposed in Sect. 6. The underlying idea is that model-driven approaches are increasing the efficiency in information system development. However, this conjecture has to be investigated in future cases.

The main limitation of the paper is the focus on just one industrial case, i.e. the above development process has to be considered as a process hypothesis and not as a validated research result. The conclusions reached and the experiences presented obviously cannot be taken as valid for all CPS cases but need further validation. Another limitation of this paper is the focus is developing completely new CPS, i.e. we consider a situation where a CPS forms the basis for new customer services of an enterprise which did not exist before. These customer services need to be defined including the processes for implementing them, the roles involved in the enterprise, resources required and the way the CPS is used for delivering the customer services. The use of enterprise modeling in such a context probably is more promising than in existing service areas which are modified by CPS use or replacements of established technical solutions with CPS. Thus, future work will also have to investigate, whether our experiences can be transferred to these CPS development areas.

References

1. Bassi, L., Secchi, C., Bonfé, M., Fantuzzi, C.: A SysML-based methodology for manufacturing machinery modeling and design. IEEE/ASME Trans. Mechatron. **16**(6), 1049–1062 (2011)
2. Baxter, G., Sommerville, I.: Socio-technical systems: from design methods to systems engineering. Interact. Comput. **23**(1), 4–17 (2011)

3. Buede, D.M.: The Engineering Design of Systems: Models and Methods, vol. 55. Wiley, Hoboken (2011)
4. DeMicheli, G., Sami, M. (eds.): Hardware/Software Co-design, vol. 310. Springer Science & Business Media, Heidelberg (2013)
5. Deutsche Bank Research. http://www.dbresearch.de/PROD/DBR_INTERNET_EN-PROD/PROD0000000000333571/Industry+4_0%3A+Upgrading+of+Germany%E2%80%99s+industrial+capabilities+on+the+horizon.pdf. Accessed 15 June 2016
6. Hackmann, G., Guo, W., Yan, G., Sun, Z., Lu, C., Dyke, S.: Cyber-physical codesign of distributed structural health monitoring with wireless sensor networks. IEEE Trans. Parallel Distrib. Syst. **25**(1), 63–72 (2014)
7. Horvath, I., Gerritsen, B.H.M.: Cyber-physical systems: concepts, technologies and implementation principles. In: Horvath, I., Rusak, Z., Albers, A. Behrendt, M. (eds.) Proceedings of TMCE 2012, pp. 19–36 (2012)
8. Fisher, A., Jacobson, C.A., Lee, E.A., Murray, R.M., Sangiovanni-Vincentelli, A., Scholte, E.: Industrial cyber-physical systems – iCyPhy. In: Aiguier, M., Boulanger, F., Krob, D., Marchal, C. (eds.) Complex Systems Design & Management, pp. 21–37. Springer International Publishing, Switzerland (2014)
9. Kannengiesser, U., Weichhart, G.: Designing and executing interoperable IoT manufacturing systems. In: Enterprise Interoperability: Interoperability for Agility, Resilience and Plasticity of Collaborations (I-ESA 14) Proceedings. Wiley (2015)
10. Kitchenham, B., Pfleeger, S.M., Pickard, L.M., Jones, P.W., Hoaglin, D.C., El Eman, K., Rosenberg, J.: Preliminary guidelines for empirical research in software engineering. IEEE Trans. Softw. Eng. **28**(8), 721–734 (2002)
11. Lee I., Sokolsky O.: Medical cyber physical systems. In: Proceedings of IEEE Design Automation Conference, Proceedings of the 47th Design Automation Conference, Anaheim, CA, USA, pp. 743–748 (2010)
12. Lillehagen, F.: The foundations of AKM technology. In: 10th International Conference on Concurrent Engineering (CE) Conference, Madeira, Portugal (2003)
13. Lillehagen, F., Krogstie, J.: Active Knowledge Modelling of Enterprises. Springer, Heidelberg (2009). ISBN 978-3-540-79415-8
14. Muller, H., Mylopoulos, J., Litoiu, M.: Engineering cyber physical systems. In: Proceedings of the 25th Annual International Conference on Computer Science and Software Engineering, pp. 328–332. IBM Corp. (2015)
15. Ringert, J.O., Rumpe, B., Wortmann, A.: From Software Architecture Structure and Behavior Modeling to Implementations of Cyber-Physical Systems. arXiv preprint arXiv:1408.5690 (2014)
16. Sandkuhl, K., Stirna, J., Persson, A., Wißotzki, M.: Enterprise Modeling: Tackling Business Challenges with the 4EM Method. The Enterprise Engineering Series. Springer, Heidelberg (2014). ISBN 978-3662437247
17. Sandkuhl, K., Borchardt, U., Lantow, B., Stamer, D., Wißotzki, M.: Towards adaptive business models for intelligent information logistics in transportation. In: Aseeva, N., Babkin, E., Kozyrev, O. (eds.) Perspectives in Business Informatics Research - 11th International Conference, BIR 2012, Nizhny Novgorod, Russia, 24–26 September 2012. ISBN 978-5-502-00042-0
18. Smirnov, A., Sandkuhl, K., Shilov, N.: Multilevel self-organisation and context-based knowledge fusion for business model adaptability in cyber-physical systems. In: Bakhtadze, N. (ed.) Manufacturing Modelling, Management, and Control, Saint Petersburg, vol. 7. Elsevier, IFAC (IFAC proceedings volumes), pp. 609–613 (2013)
19. Sommerville, I.: Software Engineering, 8th edn. Addison-Wesley, Boston (2006)

20. Teslya, N., Smirnov, A., Levashova, T., Shilov, N.: Ontology for resource self-organisation in cyber-physical-social systems. In: Klinov, P., Mouromtsev, D. (eds.) KESW 2014. CCIS, vol. 468, pp. 184–195. Springer, Heidelberg (2014)

21. Thramboulidis, K.: A cyber–physical system-based approach for industrial automation systems. Comput. Ind. **72**, 92–102 (2015)

22. Vernadat, F.B.: Enterprise Modelling and Integration. Chapman & Hall, London (1996)

23. Wan, J., Zhang, D., Zhao, S., Yang, L.T., Lloret, J.: Context-aware vehicular cyber-physical systems with cloud support: architecture, challenges, and solutions. IEEE Commun. Mag. **52**(8), 106–113 (2014)

24. Wirtz, B.: Electronic Business. Gabler Verlag, Wiesbaden (2010)

25. Yin, R.K.: Case Study Research: Design and Methods. Applied Social Research Methods Series, vol. 5, 3rd edn. Sage Publications, Inc., Thousand Oaks (2002)

Working with Process Abstraction Levels

Oleg Svatoš[(✉)] and Václav Řepa

Faculty of Informatics and Statistics, Department of Information Technologies,
University of Economics, Prague, Czech Republic
{svatoso,repa}@vse.cz

Abstract. The hierarchical abstraction used in business process modeling is a strong feature which requires careful application by analysts in order to take the advantage of the benefits it brings. Failing in this case may not only bring headache to the analysts, when trying to manage the complexity of the created model, but also turn the whole created business process model useless. In this paper we look at research that has been done in the field of the business process abstraction level management according to which we review and extend the Methodology for Modeling and Analysis of Business Processes (MMABP). Eventually we discuss the benefits the extended MMABP brings compared to the current state-of-the-art.

Keywords: BPM · MMABP · Process levels · Abstraction

1 Introduction

Business process modeling languages allow us to work out the business process models into unlimited number of levels of abstraction. This possibility of limitless hierarchical abstraction is, no doubt, a strong feature but also very dangerous if used unwisely and its wrong application may eventually make the whole business process model either too complex and detailed or too abstract. Unfortunately in both cases the wrong application of the abstraction makes the use of the created business process model very hard or makes the model even unusable at all. Moreover, wrong use of the model hierarchy can even cause the conflict with basic principles of process-driven management. This is one of the challenges the business process modeling methodologies should provide a solution for and give the analysts guidelines how to keep the business process abstraction levels under control through bringing an order into the hierarchical abstraction.

In this paper we go by the hypothesis that there is no standard or dominant approach to the business process abstraction management. We expect the different approaches of different methodologies and frameworks to business process abstraction management to be close in number and granularity of business process abstraction levels, but to significantly differ in their understanding of the individual process abstraction levels as their purpose and the origin would differ. Further on we expect that just two process abstraction levels present in the MMABP are not sufficient for complete coverage of the complexity of the process abstraction and that there will be necessary an extension of the number of process abstraction levels accompanied by a methodological extension

© Springer International Publishing Switzerland 2016
V. Řepa and T. Bruckner (Eds.): BIR 2016, LNBIP 261, pp. 65–79, 2016.
DOI: 10.1007/978-3-319-45321-7_5

in order to have a complete set of rules for process abstraction level management incorporated in the MMABP.

In the following text we have shortened the term process abstraction level to a process level for the better clarity of the text.

2   Current Research Review

There is no standard or dominant approach in the current research to number of process levels or their definition. By contrast, we can say that there is a wide variety of approaches differentiating in the degree of formalization. As the most liberal we can consider the business process modeling standards such as BPMN [1] or IDEF3 [2] which allow an analyst to have unlimited number of process levels. They leave this completely up to the analysts with the idea behind that they are the ones who should consider the sensibility of each process level. In the same manner go along authors like [3, 4], who are aware of this issue but through their experience they came to only general recommendation that one should create as few levels as possible and as many as necessary keeping in consideration the sensibility and clarity when adding or removing a process level.

In opposition to this freedom without boundaries there are methodologies and frameworks which try to give rules to the process levels. The number of defined process levels ranges from three [5] over four [6–8] to five [9, 10]. Even though the number of suggested process levels differs, there is possible to map individual levels on each other according to the process level granularity [9].

Table 1. Different approaches to process abstraction levels

#	APQC PCF [6]	LEAD [9] process levels	SAP [10] process levels	[7] SCOR	Fundamentals of BPM [5]	Siebel [8]
1	Category	Process area	Business Area	Level 1		Process domain
2	Process group	Process group	Process group			
3	Process	Business process	Business process	Level 2	Process	Business process
4	Activity	Process step	Process step	Level 3	Process step	Process step
5		Process activity	Process activity	Level 4	Process activity	Task

We have put the different process hierarchy definitions from different methodologies and frameworks into the Table 1, which shows that the different definitions share most of the process levels in general. This does not mean that all definitions of the process levels are the same. They agree on granularity of the abstraction levels, but the definition how the process abstractions are defined differs as the basic principles of each methodology or framework differ. The difference is also in how well worked out the process level definitions and the guidelines are.

Looking at the Table 1 one can see that all process level hierarchy definitions have two process levels in common: a business process and a process step (not necessarily named the same way).

Business processes form the basic stones of process hierarchy definition and the way they are understood, forms the definitions of the other process levels. Probably the clearest example of this is the difference in understanding what a core process is and what a supporting process is. This is well illustrated in the Sect. 4. The two process levels above the business process constitute a form of summarization, which groups together business processes with common goals. Some process hierarchy definitions work with two levels of summarization others only with one or the [5] with even none. The top process level usually identifies enterprise functionality the business processes are part of. This process abstraction constitutes relatively independent process level, which can be then analyzed and discussed separately. This top level is present in most of the process hierarchy definitions in the Table 1, but the same cannot be said about the second process level – the process groups. This process abstraction is strongly dependent on the business processes level as it really represents only a form of summarization of business processes than a separate level of abstraction. This may be one of the reasons why this process level is present only in some process hierarchy definitions.

Looking the other direction from the business process level, the process step level splits a business process into steps with individual goals which are then implemented at the activity level. The process step level is generally agreed level but, again, the definitions of a process step do differ. Some see it as one actor activity which leads to production of one business object [9, 10]; some relate it only to production of one business object [7] no matter how many roles are involved and others like [5] see the process step level as an activity of organizational unit that is involved in the process. The process level beneath, which is present in most of the process hierarchy definitions, is the activity level. The activity represents concrete work that has to be done usually by one actor. The process hierarchy definitions share common understanding of the activity definition, although there is missing a clear definition where one activity ends and another starts, so that an analyst can be sure that all the activities in one's model are really at the same level of abstraction. Even though the activities are the lowest abstraction level, they are still an abstraction. The strength of the abstraction makes it very hard to be consistent at activity abstraction at this process level and one may end up mixing complex activities with very simple ones [4] when there are missing unambiguous rules for the activity abstraction.

No matter how perfect or imperfect the process hierarchy definitions discussed in this chapter are, they illustrate well the complexity and importance of the process abstraction level management and provide us with enough reasons and material to extend the MMABP. The most complex and worked out process hierarchy definition we have found in the [9] and we will often refer to it in the following MMABP extension.

3   MMABP

Behind the ideas expressed in this paper lays the Methodology for Modeling and Analysis of Business Processes – MMABP. The methodology is based on three principles (see Fig. 1):

- principle of modeling
- principle of abstraction
- principle of different (three) architectures

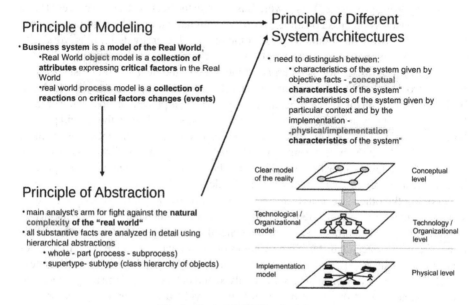

Fig. 1. Basic MMABP principles

The principle of modeling expresses the presumption that the objective basis for the implementation of the business system in the organization must be constituted by real facts existing outside of, and independently of, the organization. In other words, every organization as an implementation of some business system (business idea) is someway a model of the Real World.

The principle of abstraction expresses the fatal need for creating abstract concepts while modeling the Real World. Despite many possible classifications of abstractions very important kinds of abstraction are hierarchical abstractions.

The principle of different architectures then represents the way how to make abstractions with primary respect to the principle of modeling. According to this principle the highest abstraction level should be focused on the clear model of the Real World which is not influenced by any generally specific (i.e. technological or organizational) nor individually specific (i.e. implementational) aspects. Following lower level of abstraction should respect generally specific aspects of the business system implementation, i.e. used technology and organization. Only after that it is possible to respect other - individually specific – aspects like particular qualification of people, enterprise culture etc. (see Fig. 1). The lower-level the more complicated the model is because it contains everything from previous levels completed with the specific aspects of its level. This way the primary reason for abstraction directly follows from the Principle of Modeling. The Principle of Different Architectures thus can be regarded as a consequence of both Principle of Modeling and Principle of Abstraction (see Fig. 1).

Regarding modeling the Real World (on the conceptual level) the MMABP distinguishes between two basic dimensions of the Real World: structure and behavior. Structural (object-oriented) model describes the Real World as a system of objects and their mutual relationships while the behavioral (process-oriented) model describes the Real World as a system of processes and their substantial relationships. Basic dimensions of the Real World are not mutually substitutable: substance of the Real World cannot be expressed via describing behavior as well as behavior cannot be expressed via describing structure.

In both mentioned dimensions there are two basic types of model: global (system) view on the system as a whole and detailed (particular) view on just one element of the system. Similarly, like two basic dimensions also both basic views of the Real World are not mutually substitutable: system cannot be expressed via describing action details, and detail time dependencies cannot be expressed via describing the structure of the whole system.

The main general difference between the global (system) and the detailed (particular) views is in the factor of time. System (global) view always tries to abstract this factor and focus on stable, time independent aspects of the modeled system while the detailed model respects it anyway by focusing mainly on it. Global view then can be characterized as object-oriented while detailed view as process (algorithmic)-oriented.

If one combines two basic dimensions of the Real World (object/process) with two basic types of model (global (object-oriented)/detailed (process-oriented)) then four basic types of model can be seen (Fig. 2):

- Object-oriented (global) model of business processes usually called Process Map.
- Process-oriented (detailed) model of a single business process usually called Process Model.
- Object-oriented (global) model of business objects usually called Conceptual Model.
- Process-oriented (detailed) model of a single business object usually called Object Life Cycle Model.

Besides that, each of these four models brings its specific piece of information which is not present in any other model. Conceptual Model represents a generally independent view on the Real World in terms of objects and their mutual essential relationships while Process Map describes the intentionality in the Real World as a system of mutually communicating business processes including their functional classification to key and supporting ones which is a crucial condition for the process-driven way of enterprise management. Process Model describes the way of fulfilling the particular business goal while Object Life Cycle represents an algorithmic definition of general business rules in terms of events, actions and their possible consequences.

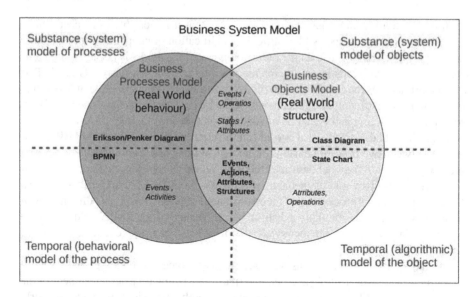

Fig. 2. Two times two dimensions of the Real World (Business System) Model

The tools used by the methodology are based on common standards BPMN [1], UML [11, 12], and Eriksson/Penker Notation [13]. The root of the methodology is defined in the formal meta-model [14] as a part of the development project OpenSoul [15]. The key ideas of the modeling method are described in [16], and [17]. Figure 3 illustrates how the above mentioned standards are used in the methodology for the global and detailed view on business processes:

Global view of all processes is represented by the Global process model of an organization (see Fig. 3). Global model is always complete which means that it identifies all important processes of the organization. In fact the Global process model represents the object view of processes; it describes the existence of processes and their mutual relationships. This means that the Class Diagram from UML would be the proper diagram for this model. Nevertheless, as all processes have attributes of the same type, all relationships are oriented and with the same meaning, and there are just small number of other complementing types of objects (goal, document, product,…) some specialization of the Class Diagram is more suitable. So that we use the Eriksson-Penker specialization of UML [13] for the Global Process Model.

Global view is complemented with possible detailed view of selected processes (usually all key processes, and some important supporting processes). This detailed view, compared with the global one, is partial only, it shows just one process. Nevertheless, it allows seeing the process details in the process manner. Unlike the global view it describes the run of the process. We use the Business Process Modelling Notation [1] for this model.

The important piece of knowledge of the presented methodology is the fact that it is necessary to view the process system from both: global and detailed perspectives where both perspectives are mutually incommutable. It is impossible to describe all processes in the organization including their mutual relationships using just the BPMN. It is

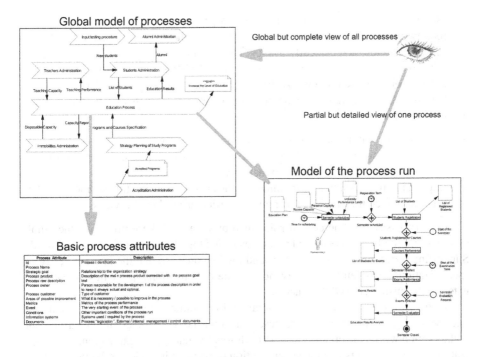

Fig. 3. Global versus detailed view on process

because BPMN is able to describe just the process run, but not the full context of the process (i.e. all its communication with other processes). So we always need to complement the process-oriented view of the process with the object-oriented view (represented here by the Eriksson-Penker Notation) describing the global context of processes[1].

4   MMABP Process Hierarchy and Its Extension

The current research review shows that, although, the various process hierarchy definitions generally agree on the types of process levels and their granularity, the definitions of particular process abstractions differ substantially. The main driver behind it is the different understanding of what business processes are and this difference then "multiplies" itself when projected into the whole process hierarchy. This sets the way how the MMABP extension is done. We work with the process levels identified in the current research review but the definitions of particular process abstractions have to be defined in accordance with MMABP's basic principles.

---

[1] In fact, there is the only way how to include all processes into one model using BPMN: to subordinate all the processes to the one of them as sub-processes. This idea however absolutely contradicts with the main idea of the Process Management, and thus it is not relevant anyway.

As we have shown above, the all reviewed process hierarchy definitions have in common two process levels: the business process and the process step. This holds true for the MMABP too as it currently has just these two levels.

The way a business process is understood in MMABP is significantly different from other methodologies and frameworks. Based on the main idea of process-driven management from [18] the MMABP's general classification of processes in the organization distinguishes mainly between:

- Key processes, i.e. those processes in the organization which are linked directly to the customer, covering the whole business cycle from expression of the customer need to its satisfaction with the product/service.
- Supporting processes, which are linked to the customer indirectly - by means of key processes which they are supporting with particular products/services.

Key processes play the crucial role since by means of these processes the whole system of mutually interconnected processes is tied together with the customers' needs. Supporting processes are organized around the key ones, so that the internal behavior, specialization, and even the effectiveness of the organizations' activities are subordinated to the customers and their needs.

Such a view of the behavior of the organization is quite different from the traditional one. Mainly, the key processes represent an unusual view of communications and collaboration within the organization. In traditionally managed organizations the organization structure reflects just the specialization of work; it is static and hierarchical.

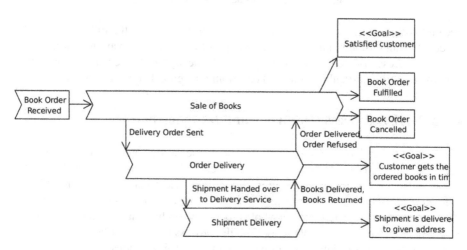

Fig. 4. Global process map – Book Selling

This is well visible in the way how business processes are captured in diagrams. For instance [8, 9] capture them in proprietary process maps as simple sequences of business processes while in MMABP there are captured business processes with their goals, possible outcomes and dependencies among core process and supporting processes. There are no sequences of processes at all. As a diagraming technique, there is used

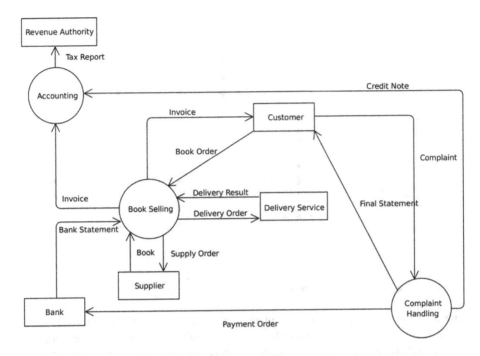

Fig. 5. Enterprise functionality map

adoption of standard Eriksson-Penker diagram (Fig. 4). This difference is caused by the different approach to key process definition and this is also the reason why it does not make sense to think about process groups in context of the MMABP. They are already there, formed by dependencies among the processes. What makes sense for the MMABP is to work with the top process level (Process area), but again, not in its grouping form presented in [9] but in the form we can find in [10] or [8] - a high level aggregation of company functionality or an enterprise domain which is a grouping of business processes from the perspective of an entire enterprise. This approach allows forming independent process level which can be mapped and analyzed separately from the lower levels. This process level is in MMABP missing and its addition would definitely extend its capabilities and make it not only even with the other methodologies and frameworks, but also add something new compared to them. For mapping this process level we find appropriate the data flow diagram (DFD) which in the MMABP would form the top process level diagram – the enterprise functionality map (Fig. 5). This diagram not only captures the enterprise functionalities but also external entities and information flows. Compared to other reviewed frameworks and methodologies, which do not work with such complex diagram, the DFD diagram allows more advanced analysis and review of this process level.

The process step level in MMABP is rather specific. Unlike the [9] or [10], which specify a process step as unit of work that is related to exactly one object and that is executed by one role, the MMABP process step represents work that has to be done between the event, which the process step responds to, and a process state, which is

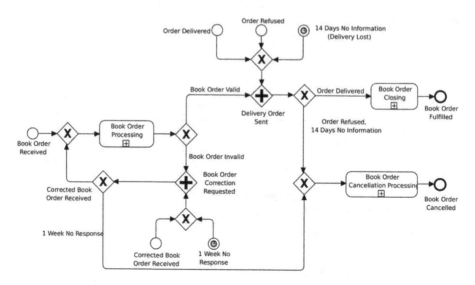

Fig. 6. Process step level in detailed process diagram - Sale of Books

result of the process step execution and also a place in the process where the process execution stops and, if not the final state, waits for occurrence of particular event outside the modeled process in order to continue the process execution. The not final process states are captured as logical ANDs with a text, describing the process state at which the execution stops (Fig. 6).

Looking into Table 1 one can see that the process level beneath the process step level, the activity level, is present in most of the process hierarchy definitions as the lowest process level. The shared definition in general is that the activity level represents complete set of actions required to produce an output from a process step [9]. Problem of this definition is that it is missing an unambiguous definition of the level of abstraction that should be applied at this process level. The hierarchical abstraction allows us to decompose the activities into great details like each movement of a hand, but models with such high level of detail would be unusable for the business process management. Even though we consider the activity level as the lowest, there has to be the level of abstraction clearly defined. Choice of the level of abstraction at this process level is left upon the individual analysts except those frameworks which work with the predefined activities. The case can be rather different in the MMABP due to its orientation at object life cycles.

Looking at the Fig. 2 one can see that the process model is in the MMABP in close relation to object model. The interconnection between these two worlds is captured in object life cycles (Fig. 7). As the level of abstraction of the process step and business process level is usually higher than the level of abstraction of object life cycles, they work only with the limited number of object states which are in processes present in form of process states. In the MMABP is the activity level currently missing, but it makes sense to include it and complete this way the interconnection between the process and the object model. The activity process level in the MMABP is then the level where the object life cycles meet the processes completely and it is the abstraction level of object life cycles, which sets the abstraction level of the activity. Thus, the activity is a unit of work that changes particular state of an important object to another and the changes of important objects' states define where one activity ends and another starts.

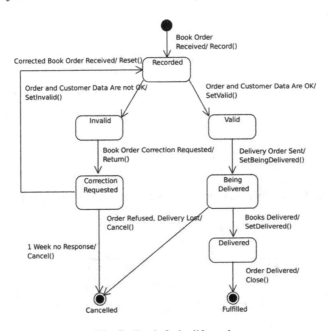

Fig. 7. Book Order life cycle

The adjective "important" has in this case its specific meaning. Object model usually contains great number of objects, but only the ones which influence the control flow of processes (i.e. entities which attribute values or changes of lifecycle state are referenced in the control flow of the process model) are the important from the perspective of the process model and are required to have the life cycles captured. The consistency inherent the interconnection of the process and object model then constitutes the basic rule that all life cycle states of important objects have to have a reference in a detailed process diagram and all object life cycle states referenced in the process model have to be part of particular objects' life cycles. Since the activities are part of the detailed process model the modeling notation is the same as for the process steps as illustrated in the Fig. 8.

Table 2. Extended MMABP process level hierarchy

#	Process abstraction level	Model	Diagram
1	Enterprise functionality	Enterprise Functionality Map	Data flow diagram
2	Business process	Global Process Map	Eriksson-Penker Extension
3	Process step	Detailed Process Diagram	BPMN
4	Activity	Detailed Process Diagram	BPMN

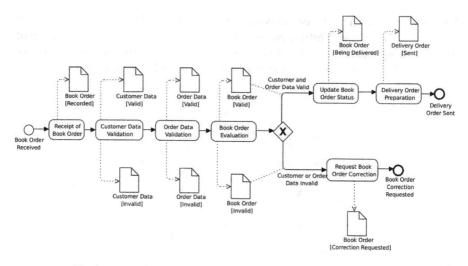

Fig. 8. Activity level in detailed process diagram - Order Processing

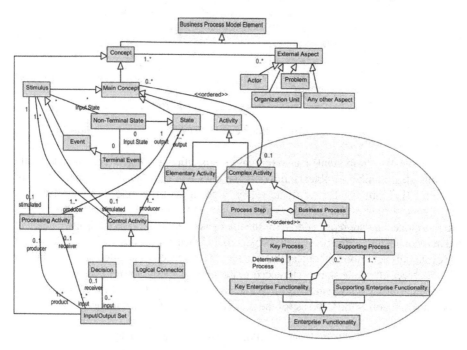

Fig. 9. MMABP Business Process Meta-Model – a fragment

The analysis and discussion done above, leads us to the following extension of the MMABP by two process levels – the enterprise functionality and the activity. The suggested MMABP process level hierarchy is summarized in the Table 2 and with it associated MMABP Business Process Meta-Model extension in Fig. 9.

How the process levels look like and relate to each other is illustrated in the figures above where one can see the all abstraction levels of the Sale of Books process, each captured in a standard notation. At the top level of abstraction the Sale of Books process is a part of the Book Selling enterprise functionality (Fig. 5), which is then at the lower abstraction layer presented as the set of processes captured in the Fig. 4. The Sale of Books process is then at the step process level decomposed into process steps (Fig. 6) and in the activity level into individual activities as illustrated in the Fig. 8 for the process step Order processing. In case of the process steps the level of abstraction is driven by synchronization with the events coming outside the Sale of Books process and in case of the activity level the level of abstraction is driven by the different objects' life cycle states, where one of them is the Book Order life cycle (Fig. 7).

The Fig. 9 describes a part of the MMABP Business Process Meta-Model where have been added the new concepts reflecting the process hierarchy levels. In this part the meta-model describes the internal structure of the detailed model of business process using the basic concepts and their relationships. The marked part in the right lower corner of the model defines the process levels hierarchy. There are two basic types of Activity: Elementary Activity (primitive, non-decomposable activity as a kind of the single Main Concept) and Complex Activity which consists of more Main Concepts. Process Step is a kind of Complex Activity. Another – more complex - kind of Complex Activity is the Business Process which is defined at the same time as an ordered set of Process Steps. To define the concept of Enterprise Functionality it is necessary to distinguish between two functionally different kinds of Business Process: Key Process and Supporting Process. Key Enterprise Functionality is than determined by one Key Process complemented with typically more Supporting Processes. This construction should be interpreted as follows: every key process (i.e. the process which completely covers the production of the value for the customer) together with all its supporting processes constitutes one key enterprise functionality. Supporting Enterprise Functionality than means just a set of (at least one) Supporting Processes. The concepts of key and supporting (process or functionality) is always relative to the whole (business or enterprise) which means that in the given field it is always clear what is key and what is supporting while in other fields it can be different. This way the MMABP concept of Enterprise Functionality is certainly consistent with the meaning of other MMABP concepts and consequently with the principles of process-driven management.

5   Conclusions

In this paper we have reviewed the current state-of-the-art in process abstraction management and introduced an extension of the Methodology for modeling and analysis of business processes (MMABP). Our research review has shown that there are various approaches to process abstraction management which, in general, share the number of the process abstraction levels and their granularity, but the process abstraction definitions are different.

When we compared them with the MMABP we had to conclude that the MMABP is missing some process abstraction levels and the theory bound with it, we could find at the other methodologies. This led us to extension of the MMABP. We have extended the MMABP with complete theory on the process abstraction level management so that it is now not only fully competitive with the other methodologies, but also, through the extension based on its basic principles, brings new perspective into this field. The original two process abstraction levels (Business process and Process step) were extended by two new levels: Enterprise functionality level and Activity level.

Enterprise functionality level represents new top level of process abstraction hierarchy in the MMABP. It is an independent process abstraction level which can be, thanks to the accompanied data flow diagram, mapped and analyzed separately from the lower levels. The wide possibility of analysis is unique as the other reviewed methodologies and frameworks use much more simple diagrams at this level of abstraction, if any.

Activity level on the other hand represents new bottom level of the process abstraction hierarchy in the MMABP. This level is the only level where the object life cycles meet the processes completely and it is the abstraction level of object life cycles, which sets the abstraction level of the activity. This interconnection of two points of view on real world behavior is again something unique compared to other methodologies and frameworks.

The field of process abstraction management is under constant development and, as we have shown, there are various approaches to this phenomenon. In general, our analysis has shown that the upcoming research has to focus on clarification and standardization of process abstractions especially on the activity level. The MMABP extension presented in this paper should be seen as our contribution to solution for these issues.

The extension introduced in this paper enriched the MMABP with complete theory on process abstraction level management, but there are areas within the MMABP, related to the introduced extension, the future research should focus on. Object life cycles, which are tightly connected with the activity level, deserve extension of theory on their abstraction level management and there would be also helpful normalization theory on correct process abstraction identification in order to have well-ordered process abstraction levels. All these aspects shall be further elaborated.

Acknowledgments. The paper was processed with contribution of long term institutional support of research activities by Faculty of Informatics and Statistics, University of Economics, Prague.

References

1. Object Management Group: Business Process Model and Notation (BPMN) Specification Version 2.0.2. http://www.omg.org/spec/BPMN/
2. Mayer, R. J., Menzel, C. P., Painter, M. K., Dewitte, P. S.: Information Integration for Concurrent Engineering (IICE) IDEF3 Process Description Capture Method Report. Knowledge Based Systems (1995)
3. Mertins, K., Jochem, R.: Quality-Oriented Design of Business Processes. Springer, New York (1999)
4. Davis, R.: Business Process Modelling with ARIS: a Practical Guide. Springer Science & Business Media, London (2001)

5. Dumas, M., La Rosa, M., Mendling, J., Reijers, H.A.: Fundamentals of Business Process Management. Springer, Heidelberg (2013)

6. Process Classification Framework | APQC. https://www.apqc.org/pcf

7. The Supply Chain Operations Reference model (SCOR). http://www.apics.org/sites/apics-supply-chain-council/frameworks/scor

8. Siebel Business Process Implementation Guide Version 7.5, Siebel Systems (2003)

9. von Rosing, M., von Scheel, H., Scheer, A.W.: The Complete Business Process Handbook: Body of Knowledge from Process Modeling to BPM. Elsevier Science, San Francisco (2015)

10. Rosenberg, A.: SAP Modeling Handbook - Modeling Standards. https://wiki.scn.sap.com/wiki/display/ModHandbook/

11. UML OMG Unified Modeling Language Specification, v. 1.5. document ad/03–03-01, Object Management Group, March 2003

12. UML Superstructure Specification, v2.0 document 05-07-04, Object Management Group (2004)

13. Eriksson, H.E., Penker, M.: Business Modeling with UML: Business Patterns at Work. Wiley, New York (2000)

14. Řepa, V.: Business System Modeling Specification. http://opensoul.panrepa.org/metamodel.html

15. Řepa, V.: OpenSoul Project. http://opensoul.panrepa.org

16. Řepa, V.: Process dimension of concepts. In: Jaakkola, H., Kiyoki, Y., Tokuda, T. (eds.) Information Modelling and Knowledge Bases XIX. pp. 322–329. IOS Press, Amsterdam (2008)

17. Řepa, V.: Modeling objects dynamics in conceptual models. In: Wojtkowski, W., Wojtkowski, W.G., Magyar, G., Knapp, G. (eds.) Advances in Information Systems Development, pp. 139–152. Springer, New York (2007)

18. Hammer, M., Champy, J.: Reengineering the Corporation: A Manifesto for Business Revolution. Nicholas Brealey Publishing, London (1993)

A Coarse-Grained Comparison of Modelling Languages for Business Motivation and Intentional Distribution

Rando Tõnisson and Raimundas Matulevičius[✉]

University of Tartu, Tartu, Estonia
randotonisson@gmail.com, rma@ut.ee

Abstract. Goal modelling is an important activity to reason *why* different software decisions are taken, or architecture solutions are implemented. Currently there exist a number of goal-oriented modelling approaches. In this paper, we apply the semiotic quality framework to compare quality of the business motivation model (BMM) and *i** modelling languages at the coarse-grained level. The study reports on the BMM and *i** language quality and model quality. The study also presents observations on how the BMM and *i** models could be used to reason on and support construction of the business process model expressed in business processes model and notation.

Keywords: BMM · The *i** framework · SEQUAL · Business process management · Language quality · Model quality

1 Introduction

Goal-oriented modelling is one of the most important research developments in the requirements engineering field. During goal modelling one needs to shift the focus from *what* and *how* (i.e., data and processes) as addressed by traditional analysis, to *who* and *why* (i.e., actors and goals). With recent increase of importance of business process management (BPM) and BPM modelling approaches it becomes necessary to understand the rationale of one or another business process decision or system architecture solution. Therefore, a combination of the goal-oriented approaches and business process modelling becomes rather a necessity than an option.

On one hand, *business motivation model* (BMM) supports identifying factors that (*i*) motivate business plans and (*ii*) define means of how these plans are related to each business goal [15]. On another hand traditional goal-oriented modelling addresses the early analysis of requirements. But they can also be applied to support and reason on decisions taken during the business process management. Among various goal-oriented approaches, such as GBRAM [2], KAOS [10], Lightswitch [17]), the *i* framework* [19] (and its multiples extensions, such as GRL [7], TROPOS [4], NRF [5]) is one of the most widely used goal modelling language [3]. The *i** framework supports systematic understanding of the system actors, their goals and reasoning of achieving these goals by the available means.

© Springer International Publishing Switzerland 2016
V. Řepa and T. Bruckner (Eds.): BIR 2016, LNBIP 261, pp. 80–95, 2016.
DOI: 10.1007/978-3-319-45321-7_6

In this paper, we apply the semiotic quality framework (SEQUAL) [9] to compare both modelling, i.e. BMM and *i**, languages. The goal of this study is threefold. It includes (*i*) comparison of BMM and *i** language quality, (*ii*) comparison of BMM and *i** model quality, and (*iii*) identification of the mappings of the BMM and *i** models to the business process model and notation [16].

The remaining of this paper is structured as follows: in Sect. 2 we will present the SEQUAL framework, BMM and *i** modelling languages. In Sect. 3 we compare both languages using the SEQUAL guidelines. Section 4 presents the related work. Finally, in Sect. 5 we conclude our study.

2 Background

This section introduces the SEQUAL framework. Next, the BMM and *i** languages are presented.

2.1 SEQUAL

The SEQUAL framework [9] argues for the constructivistic world-view that recognises model creation as part of a dialog between participants whose knowledge changes as the process takes place. It separates between several quality types to assess information systems models. For instance the *physical quality* addresses how tools are used for making the model. *Empirical quality* deals with error frequencies when reading or writing model, as well as coding and ergonomics when using modelling tools. *Semantic* and *syntactic quality* types are used to evaluate the semantic/syntactic correctness and completeness of the model. *Pragmatic* quality deals with model understandability and interpretation both by the modelling tools and the audience (i.e., users) of the model. Social quality seeks agreement among the participants' interpretation of the model. Finally, the *deontic* quality type focuses on the financial aspects and the goals of the model.

The SEQUAL framework also separates among the six appropriateness types [9] to evaluate quality of the modelling language. *Domain appropriateness* (*DA*) evaluates the basics of the modelling language and how useful they are to use. *Comprehensibility appropriateness* (*CA*) is used to understand the social interpretations. *Participant appropriateness* (*PA*) is used to evaluate the participants' knowledge on the language. *Modeller appropriateness* (*MA*) evaluates the knowledge of the modeller with the modelling languages. *Tool appropriateness* (*TA*) is used to evaluate the languages tools. Finally, *organisational appropriateness* (*OA*) shows the relations between the language and the organisation using it for work.

In Sect. 3 we will apply the SEQUAL framework to assess quality of BMM and *i** languages and models.

2.2 Business Motivation Model

Business motivation model (BMM, version 1.3, 2015) [15] contains a set of built-in concepts, which define the elements of business plans. All the elements of BMM are developed from a business perspective. The visual constructs are summarised in Fig. 1. The major constructs include *Ends*, *Means*, *Influencers*, and *Assessments* areas. The *Ends* characterise the goal that the business wants to succeed in, and the *Means* are the processes that are employed to achieve this goal. *Influencers* are the cause to do something in the business. They shape the elements in the business plan and also are the base for *Assessments* that impact both the *Ends* and the *Means*. All of those are related to each other by some fundamental questions, which the BMM user needs to answer – "what is needed to achieve in order to achieve what the business wants to achieve?" (answered by completing the *Means*) and "why does each element of the business plan exist?" (answered by analysing the *Ends*, i.e., business goals).

There are three concepts defined as external BMM references. Firstly, *organisation unit* participates in defining boundaries of the enterprise being modelled. This means, organisational unit is used to express *ends, means, assessments, influencers* and *strategies*. Secondly, *business process* is a part of *courses of action*. It provides the steps, sequences, structure, interactions, and connections to events that are part of the process. Hence the *organisational unit* is also responsible for the business processes. Finally, *business rules* provide a specific, practical way to implement *business policies*. Business rules are derived from *business policy* and they may guide the policy and may affect the *tactics*.

Figure 2 presents a simple BMM model. Here the *assessment* indicates that Warehouse is not suited for delivery. Therefore the Warehouse needs rework to support delivery as indicated by the *internal influencer* construct. Then, the argumentation is moved to the means section, where *mission* for warehouse reworked to support delivery contribute to *vision* (on the *ends* area) of warehouse suited for delivery. Similarly the *tactics* to hire a construction company and to plan the rework are defined to establish a *strategy* for reaching the goal of warehouse rework completed.

In the current example the *organisation unit* is the retail chains management. The *business process* is given in Fig. 6. Finally, the *business rules* are not explicitly defined, however, for example, the retail chain management will have to respect the country laws.

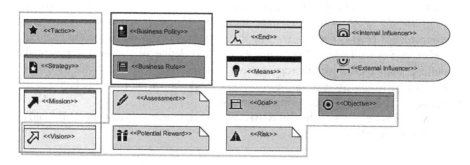

Fig. 1. BMM constructs

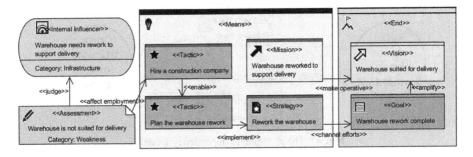

Fig. 2. BMM constructs

2.3 The *i** Framework

The *i** framework uses two diagram types to separate between two levels of abstractions [19]: (*i*) strategic dependency model (i.e., intentional level) to identify actors treating them as the "black boxes", and to define actor dependencies, and (*ii*) strategic rationale model (i.e., rational level) to define internal rationale and intentions of each actor. Language constructs are listed in Fig. 3.

In the strategic dependency model, an *actor* describes an entity that has strategic goals and intentions within the system or within the organisational setting. *Dependency* between two actors indicates that one actor (the *depender*) depends for some reason (*dependum*, expressed using goal, softgoal, task, or resource construct) on another actor (the *dependee*).

In the strategic rationale model, an *actor* is a holder of intentions and characterises active entities, who want goals to be achieved, tasks to be performed, resources to be available, and softgoals to be "satisficed". A *goal* is a condition or state of affairs that the stakeholders would like to achieve. Like a goal, a *softgoal* is a condition that the stakeholder wants to achieve, but there are no clear-cut criteria to determine whether this condition is achieved. A *task* describes a particular way of doing something. A *resource* is an entity for which the main concern is whether it is available. To combine constructs, relationships, like means-ends, decomposition, and contribution,

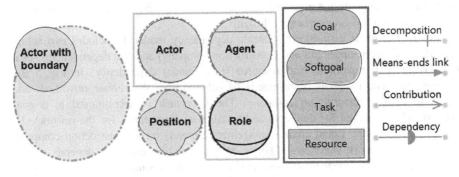

Fig. 3. The *i** constructs

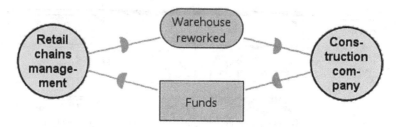

Fig. 4. The *i** strategic dependency model

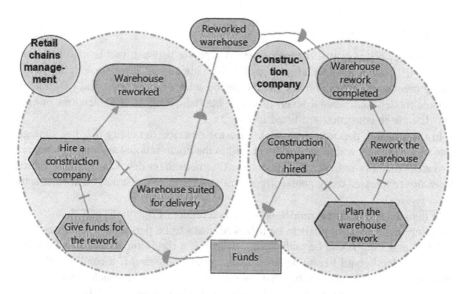

Fig. 5. The *i** strategic rationale model

are applied. *Means-ends* are used to describe how goals are achieved, typically through tasks. A *decomposition* link defines the subcomponents of a task, typically (but not limited to) the subgoals that must be accomplished. A *contribution* describes the impact that one element has on another by design.

Figure 4 presents a simple *i** strategic dependency model. It includes two actors (i.e., Retail chain management and Construction company) and two dependencies: goal (i.e., Warehouse reworked) and resource (i.e., Funds) dependency. In Fig. 5 the strategic rationale model is represented. To achieve goal Warehouse reworked, one needs to Hire a construction company. The later task is decomposed to a goal (i.e., Warehouse suited for delivery) and a task (i.e., Give funds for the rework). To achieve this goal the Retail chain management depends on a Construction company (for the goal Rework warehouse). However, Construction company depends on the Retail chains management for the Funds (i.e., resource dependency).

3 Comparison

In this section we define our research method and overview the validity threats. Then, the evaluation results received when comparing the BMM and i* languages and the BMM and i* models are presented. Next, the section is continued with the discussion on how the BMM and i* models are used to support preparation of the business process model.

3.1 Research Method

Our research method includes three steps resulting in the coarse-grained analysis of BMM and i*. Firstly, we analyse the language quality. This means that we select a set of evaluation criteria from [11] that allows comparing some characteristics of the language appropriateness to the *domain* (DA), *comprehensibility* (CA), and *participants* (PA). In the second step we evaluate the BMM and i* models. The list of evaluation criteria is defined following the SEQUAL framework [9] and contributes to the assessment of the *physical, empirical, semantic* and *syntactic* quality.

In the third step we map the BMM and i* models to the business process model. Hence we observe the language concepts and constructs used to reason on and support the construction of the business process model.

3.2 Threats to Validity

Before presenting our findings we will overview some validity threats. The following should be noted:

- *Subjective assessment.* Both language and model evaluation is performed by the authors of this paper. Potentially, the results could be different if a group of respondents were performing these assessments in the controlled experimental settings (e.g., like in [11]). However, to mitigate this threat, we were trying to deal with the evaluation criteria which were possible to measure objectively;
- *Few quality characteristics assessed.* This is direct impact from the above issue. We tend to assess a smaller amount of characteristics, but to base our assessment on the objectively measured ones;
- *Limited versions of the languages.* One could argue that in the comparison limited versions of the BMM and, especially, i* languages are taken. Potentially if comparing various extensions of these languages, the study could result in different observations. However, this is not included in the scope of our study;
- *Limited model size.* The size of the analysed models is limited. Potentially the models could be much larger if modelling some other problems. Our purpose was to provide the illustrative and yet targeted examples of the language constructs and models, thus, avoiding the unnecessary details (e.g., duplication of the usage principals) that might be brought by the larger scope cases.

3.3 Languages Evaluation

The evaluation of the BMM and *i** languages is performed along *number of constructs* (contributing to *DA, CA,* and *PA*), *construct semantic similarity* (*DA*), *modelling perspective* (*DA*), *expressive power* (*DA, CA*, and *PA*), *well-defined constructs* (*PA* and *CA*), *graphical representation* (*CA*), and *perceptual discriminability* (*CA*) criteria [11]. The summary of this evaluation is presented in Table 1 and discussed below.

Number of constructs. The BMM modelling language contains *15* graphical syntax elements, listed in Fig. 1 (only constructs are presented); the *i** language – *13* listed in Fig. 3 (9 constructs, e.g., *actor, goal, task* etc., and 4 relationships, e.g., *dependency, means-ends*, etc.).

Construct semantic similarity. Although both languages could be used to understand rationale for the business decisions and process management, there are only few semantic concepts, which have similar meaning (see Table 2). For instance, we observe sematic similarities between BMM *vision* and *i* goal*, BMM *goal* and *objective* and *i* softgoal*, BMM *course of action* and *i* task*, and BMM *influence* and *i* actor*. However, this makes only approx. *27 %* (received as similar constructs divided by the number of all considered language constructs) of BMM and *31 %* of *i** language similarity one to another.

At the same time it should be noted that there are few constructs, which have the same name, but has different semantics. For example, the BMM *end* is something that/where the enterprise wants to be; the *i* end* is something to be achieved (goal), performed (task) or produced (resource). Another example is *means:* in BMM they are

Table 1. Evaluation of BMM and *i** languages

Evaluation criteria		BMM language	*i** language
Number of constructs		15 (all constructs)	13 (9 constructs and 4 relationships
Construct similarity		27 % of similarity to *i**	31 % of similarity to BMM
Modelling perspective	Behavioural	Partially	Partially
	Goal and rule	Yes	Yes
	Actor and role	No	Yes
Expressive power	Behavioural	3	6
	Goal and rule	9	6
	Actor and role	0	12
Well-defined constructs		Partially	Partially
Graphical representation		79 %	65 %
Perceptual discriminability		Very low	Low

Table 2. BMM and *i** construct semantic similarity

BMM constructs		*i** constructs	
Construct	Definition	Construct	Definition
Vision	An image of the desired end	Goal	A specific condition that actor wants to achieve.
Goal	Narrow version of the vision to make it easier too follow	Softgoal	Narrow version of goal to make it easier to understand.
Objective	Shows the steps towards the goal		
Course of action	Action taken towards achieving the end	Task	Specific way of doing something to achieve the goal
Influencer	Somebody or something to cause the change	Actor	Somebody, who want to achieve the goal(s)

steps needed to get to the end, in *i** *mean-ends* is a link between two nodes to show how end node will be achieved.

Modelling perspectives. In [9] Krogstie separates between seven modelling perspectives: behavioural, functional, structural, goal and rule, object, communication, and actor and role. Four modelling perspectives – functional, structural, object, and communication – are not supported or their support is very minimal in BMM and *i**. Below we will discuss how the analysed languages support the behavioural, goal and rule, and actor and role perspectives.

In behavioural perspective the main phenomena are states and transition between states. In BMM the *tactics* and *strategies* (i.e., event element) are used to achieve the *mission* (i.e., the goal element representing state). Similarly, in *i** the performance of *task* contributes to satisfaction of *goal* or *softgoal* (thus expressing the desired change of the state). In general, although in both languages we could observe the implicit elements of the behavioural perspective, this perspective is not explicitly supported by the visual language constructs.

In the goal and rule perspective the main phenomenon are goals (i.e., a condition or state of affairs that is wanted to be achieved) and rules (i.e., something that influences the action of a set of actors). Both BMM and *i** belong to this perspective. For instance, using the BMM language, one needs to define *visions*, which are, then, divided to goals, and *business rules* and *policies*, which needs to be followed in the organisation. Hence the *means* will show how the defined *goals* are achieved. Similarly in *i**, *goals/ softgoals* can be decomposed to lower *goals/subgoals*. Here *tasks* are used to define the rules and conditions to achieve these *goals*.

In the actor and role perspective the main phenomena are actors (or agents) and their roles. BMM does not support this perspective. However, the major principle of the *i** framework is to understand the major system actors (potentially their roles, agents and positions) and to define their dependency relationships, as illustrated in Fig. 5.

Table 3. Expressive Power of the BMM and *i** constructs

Modelling perspective	BMM constructs		The *i ** constructs	
Behavioural	Tactics, strategy, mission	3	Goal, softgoal, task, decomposition, means-ends, contribution	6
Goal and rule	Means, tactics, strategy, mission, vision, goal objective, business policy, and business rule	9	Goal, softgoal, task, decomposition, means-ends, contribution	6
Actor and role	–	–	Actor (also agent, position, and role), goal, softgoal, task, resource, dependency, means-ends, decomposition, and contribution	12

Expressive power is defined as the relationship between the number of constructs and the number of modelling perspective [11]. Table 3 shows that BMM has 3 constructs and *i** 3 constructs for the behavioural perspective; and BMM - 9 and *i** - 6 appropriately for the goal and rule perspective. Expressive power also shows a limitation of the language constructs regarding the *well-defined constructs*.

Well-defined constructs mean that constructs have a clear (but possibly informal) semantics. As illustrated in Table 3 both BMM (e.g., *tactics*, *strategy*, and *mission*) and *i** (e.g., *goal*, softgoal, task, and others) constructs could be used for different purposes (i.e., they have various meaning), thus, they could be misinterpreted by various model readers.

Graphical representation means that modelling language should possess a graphical representation of each construct [9]. The graphical syntax was confronted to the language abstract syntax definitions found in the literature. For instance, the core BMM concepts are defined in [15]. Hence we observe that all graphical constructs listed in Fig. 1, have their corresponding definitions in the BMM abstract syntax (approx. 79 % of BMM concepts). However, in addition, there exist a number of abstract BMM concepts, such as *directive* (generalises *business policy* and *business rule*), *course of action* (generalises *strategy* and *tactics*), *desired result* (generalises *goal* and *objective*), and *potential impact* (generalises *reward* and *risk*), which do not have their explicit graphical representations.

A comprehensive representation of the *i** abstract syntax is given in [3]. Hence, the visual constructs, listed in Fig. 3, have their correspondences in the abstract syntax. This makes approx. 65 % of the defined *i** concepts. But, like in BMM, there exist a number of abstract concepts, such as *intentional elements*, (generalises *dependum* and *intentional elements*), *internal elements* and *dependum* (both generalises *goal, softgoal, task* and *resource*), *dependable node* (generalises *actor* and *internal element*), *relationship* (generalises *means-ends, decomposition*, and *contribution*), which are abstract and do not have graphical notations.

Perceptual discriminability. Refers to the ease and accuracy with which symbols can be differentiated from each other [13]. Both BMM and *i** constructs have discriminability limitations. As discussed in [14], the *i** language has similar construct shapes (e.g., actors, agents, and roles are of the same shape) and limitations in relationship discriminability (e.g., contribution are differentiated only by their labels, etc.). Similar limitations are observed regarding the BMM constructs. Basically, they all are rectangles, mostly differentiated only by colours and icons, placed on the top left corner of the rectangle (see Fig. 1).

3.4   Model Evaluation

Table 4 presents the evaluation of the BMM and *i** models. It adapts criteria [9] for *electronically stored* and *reusability* (contributes to *physical quality*), *use of colour*, *font size* and *construct size* (*empirical quality*), *syntactic invalidity* and *syntactic incompleteness* (*syntactic quality*), and *semantic completeness, semantic validity* and *consistency* (*semantic quality*). The model evaluations are discussed below.

Physical quality. The BMM model is stored electronically in the Visual Paradigm format. Use of the tool also enables reusability (e.g., opening, copying, adapting, etc.) of previous model components. The *i** model is also stored electronically using the OpenOME tool. Like BMM, the *i** model components can be reused from model to model (e.g., opening, copying, adapting, etc.).

Empirical quality is assessed though the number of colours, model size (number of constructs) font size, and size of objects in the model. As advised in [9], model

Table 4. Evaluation of BMM and *i** models

Evaluation criteria		BMM model	*i** model
Physical quality	Electronically stored	YES, Visual Paradigm	YES, OpenOME
	Reusability	Opening, copying, adapting, etc.	Opening, copying, adapting, etc.
Empirical quality	Number of colours	11	4
	Model size	10 constructs (2 compounds)	12 constructs (2 compounds)
	Font size	Arial, 12 size	Arial, 12 size
	Construct size	Different size constructs	Different size constructs
Syntactic quality	Syntactic invalidity	Links used to connect constructs	No errors
	Syntactic incompleteness	No errors	No errors
Semantic quality	Semantic validity	Valid	Valid
	Semantic completeness	Incomplete	Incomplete
	Consistency	Consistent	Consistent

should potentially include from four to seven *colours*. In addition same colours should not be used for different objects and same objects should not have different colours. In the BMM model 11 different colours are used. Also, some colours used are very similar to one to another (e.g., different shades of yellow are used for *objective, goal and risk and vision*, different shades of blue are used for *mission, strategy* and *business rules*). In the *i** model four different colours are used.

The *font style* and *size* should be easy to read for most people [9]. Both in the BMM model and in the *i** model we have applied the Arial style, 12 size font.

Finally, the *element size* and *orientation* of the elements placed in diagrams could be used to make emphasis or indicate reading start points. Also the objects in the middle are mostly noticed first by the model readers. In the BMM model the first two elements seen on the model are *means* and *end*. They are way bigger in size than other objects and even contain smaller objects inside. This can be both, good and bad. Good in the aspect that the goal of the model is in the end object and the way to achieve it is defined in the means. But the cause of the modelling is defined in the influencer nodes that are smaller and will not be seen at first. The cause or motivation to do something is the main aspect of the model and with such visuals, it may not look like it. In the *i** model the size of the different actors is almost the same. This is caused by the number of their internal elements, which is the same. This is considered to be good, as the actors have same amount of dependencies on each other and have equal responsibility to achieve the goals. The size for other elements is also quite similar, but smaller than the actors.

Syntactic quality is the correspondence between the language used in the model and the language defined in the concepts of the modelling language [9]. Two kinds of errors – syntactic invalidity and syntactic incompleteness – could be observed. *Syntactic invalidly* means that model includes elements that are not part of the modelling language. *Syntactic incompleteness* means that the model does not have constructs, which are required by the used language.

All the constructs used in the BMM model are a part of the BMM language, thus, this makes the model syntactically correct. Although the model includes the links between the constructs, these links are not the part of the BMM abstract syntax [15]. However, it is not possible to combine the language constructs without them. The model is also syntactically complete as it has all the four main concepts including *influencers, assessments, means*, and *end*.

All the constructs used in the *i** models are the part of the modelling language, thus making the model syntactically correct. The *i** model is also syntactically complete as it includes all syntactic constructs in the way as defined in its abstract syntax.

Semantic quality is the correspondence between the model and the modelling domain [9]. While a lot of properties can be defined for semantic quality, the two main ones are semantic validity and semantic completeness. To be valid, the statements in the model must be defined correctly and be relevant to the domain. To be complete, the model has to contain all the statements that are correct and relevant for the problem. To be valid and complete, the model has to be consistent. Consistence requires the objects not to conflict with each other.

The BMM and *i** models are semantically valid as their all the statements are correct and carry over information about the warehouse construction problem.

However, both models are not semantically complete, because additional information about the problem could potentially be introduced. For example, it is possible to define more business rules and policies about the working conditions, required worker expertise, etc. Both models do not contain inconsistences.

3.5   Creating Business Process Model

Figure 6 presents the business process model expressed in business process model and notation (BPMN, version 2) [16]. This BPMN model presents a process between two *pools* Retail chain management and Construction company. The process starts with the *start event*, which defines the need for warehouse reworked to support delivery. The retail chain management needs to hire a construction company. Once this is done (see *state* Construction company hired), construction company plans the warehouse rework, reworks the warehouse and hands it (see *task* hand over the warehouse) to the retail chain management. Once the warehouse suited for delivery is received at the retail chain management, the process is over.

The creation of the business process is supported by the BMM (see Fig. 2) and *i** (see Figs. 4 and 5) models. In other works the BMM and *i** models provide the rationale for different elements of the BPMN model. This relationship is illustrated in Table 5 and discussed below.

BMM and BPMN.   The closest similarity between the BMM and BPMN meaning is the mappings between:

- The BMM ends (goal and vision) and BPMN *events*. For instance the BMM *goal* (i.e., Warehouse rework completed) and *vision* (i.e. Warehouse suited for delivery) are mapped to the appropriate BPMN *events*.

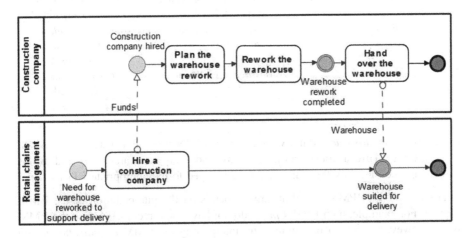

Fig. 6. The BPMN model

Table 5. Mappings among BMM, *i** and BPMN models

	BMM	BPMN	*i**
1	Deriving from *organisation unit* [Retail chains management]	*Pool* [Retail chains management]	*Actor* [Retail chains management]
2	Deriving from *tactic* [Hire a construction company]	*Pool* [Construction company]	*Actor* [Construction company]
3	*Influencer* [Warehouse needs rework to support delivery]	*Start event* [Need for warehouse reworked to support delivery]	*Goal* [Warehouse reworked]
4	*Goal* [Warehouse rework completed]	*Intermediate event* [Warehouse rework completed]	*Goal* [Warehouse rework completed]
5	*Vision* [Warehouse suited for delivery]	*Intermediate event* [Warehouse suited for delivery]	*Goal* [Warehouse suited for delivery]
6	*Tactic* [Hire a construction company]	*Task* [Hire a construction company]	*Task* [Hire a construction company]
7	*Tactic* [Plan the warehouse rework]	*Task* [Plan the warehouse rework]	*Task* [Plan the warehouse rework]
8	*Strategy* [Rework the warehouse]	*Task* [Rework the warehouse]	*Task* [Rework the warehouse]
9	*Not defined*	*Message flow* [Funds]	*Resource dependency* [Funds]
10	*Not defined*	*Start event* [Construction company hired]	*Goal* [Construction company hired]
11	*Not defined*	*Task [Hand over the warehouse]*	*Goal dependency* [Reworked warehouse]
12	*Not defined*	*Message flow* [Warehouse]	*Goal dependency* [Reworked warehouse]

- The BMM *means* (*tactics* and *strategy*) and BPMN *tasks*. For instance, the BMM *tactics* (i.e., Hire a construction company and Plan the warehouse) and BMM *strategy* (i.e., Rework the warehouse) are mapped to the appropriate BPMN *tasks*.

The rest of the BPMN model at large depends on the interpretation of the BMM element. For example, both BPMN *pools* do not have the direct mapping to the BMM model, however, they can be captured by interpreting the BMM *organisational unit* (i.e., Retail chains management) and, potentially, other BMM elements (i.e., *tactics* to capture Construction company). It is also important to note that some elements of the

BMM model are not captured in the BPMN model; for example, the meaning of *mission* and *assessment* are not expressed in the business process.

i* **and BPMN** models has rather very close meaning as illustrated in Table 5. For instance:

- BPMN *pools* (i.e., Retail chains management and Construction company) could be explained with the *i* actors*;
- BPMN *states* (i.e., Warehouse rework completed and Warehouse suited for delivery) are derived from the *i* goals*;
- BPMN *tasks* (i.e., Hire a construction company, Plan the warehouse and Rework the warehouse) has the correspondence to the *i* tasks*.

Finally, the *i** could reason the BPMN *message flows* between the pools. For instance the *i* dependency* relationships (i.e., *resource dependency* Funds and *goal dependency* Warehouse rework) helps to capture and explain why message flows of Funds and Warehouse are introduced in the BPMN model. Basically all the elements from the *i** model are mapped to or used to reason on the elements defined in the BPMN model.

4 Related Work

Literature includes a number of studies reporting the evaluation of the goal modelling languages. Ayala *et al.* have compared three languages (*i**, GRL and Tropos) to develop a reference model to conceptualise the *i**-based oriented languages [3]. Elsewhere, in [11] the experimental comparison of the *i** and KAOS languages indicated weak and strong characteristics of the goal oriented languages. In [6] it was studied how requirements engineering experts understand a language for modelling business goals and enterprise architectures (AMOR).

There exist few studies, which consider the fine-grained quality of goal modelling languages. For instance, in [14] the visual quality of the *i** notations is thoroughly studied according to the principles of language notation design [13]. The approach [1] of the unified enterprise modelling language (UEML) is used to understand and compare the ontological semantics of the GRL and KAOS languages [12]. Similarly, in [18] the ontological semantics of BMM and *i** is analysed using the UEML approach. Although the further model mapping between the BMM, *i**, and other modelling languages (e.g., GRL, KAOS, BPMN and other) could be performed using the UEML approach, this was left as the future study. In our study, however, we focus on the coarse-grained comparison of the BMM and *i** languages.

Koliadis *et al.* introduces the way to capture changes between the *i** and BPMN models [8]. Like observed in our study, they introduce the mapping relationships between the *i* actors* and BPMN *pool*, *i* dependencies* and BPMN *message flows*, *i* tasks* and BPMN *tasks*. Differently from our study, the authors argue on the link between the *i* goals* and BPMN *tasks*; in our case it is suggested to link *goals* to the BPMN *states*.

5 Conclusion

This paper presents a coarse-grained evaluation of two modelling languages – BMM and *i** and their models. Next, it considered how both languages could be used to reason on the preparation of the BPMN model. The study results in the following conclusion:

- BMM and *i** have similarities regarding the *ends* and *means*. This allows modellers to express phenomenon in the *goal and rule* perspective. However, the BMM *means* (i.e., *tactics, strategy,* potentially *business policy* and *business rule*) and *ends* (i.e., *vision, goal* and *objective*) extend the meaning of *i** *means* (i.e., *task*) and *ends* (i.e., *goal*). In addition the *i** language contains constructs to express organisational actors and relationships (in terms of the actor *dependencies*) between them. This means that modellers can represent phenomena in the *actor and rule* perspective using *i** but not BMM.
- Both models are rather of the equal quality. A slightly better quality could be observed for the *i** model, which uses less colors than the BMM model and contains no syntactic validity errors. However, one should also note that much also depends on the selected modelling tools.
- As observed the *i** framework suggests better means to support decision rationale when constructing the BPMN process model. It covers the complete set of the BPMN constructs, including such mappings as *i** *actor* and BPMN *pools*, *i** *goals* and BPMN *states*, *i** *tasks* and BPMN *tasks*. Also it provides guidelines to map and reason on the BPMN *message flows* through the *i** *dependencies*.

The study opens several future research directions. The further research is needed to understand how to use the *best* features of both languages; for instance, the *i** framework could be expanded with the additional constructs for *means* and *ends* taken from the BMM language. This would, also, lead to understanding of the new mappings to reason on the process models. However, these study directions also require the fine-grained investigation of the language quality.

References

1. Anaya, V., Berio, G., Harzallah, M., Heymans, P., Matulevičius, R., Opdahl, A.L., Panetto, H., Verdecho, M.J.: The unified enterprise modelling language – overview and further work. Comput. Ind. **61**(2), 99–111 (2010)
2. Anton, A.I.: Goal-based requirements analysis. In: Proceedings of the 2nd International Conference on Requirements Engineering (ICRE 1996), pp. 136–144. IEEE Computer Society (1996)
3. Ayala, C.P., Cares, C., Carvallo, J.P., Grau, G., Haya, M., Salazar, G., Franch, X., Mayol, E., Quer, C.: A comparative analysis of i*-based agent-oriented modeling languages. In: Proceedings of the International Workshop on Agent-Oriented Software Development Methodology (AOSDM 2005) (2005)

4. Bresciani, P., Perini, A., Giorgini, P., Giunchiglia, F., Mylopoulos, J.: Tropos: an agent-oriented software development methodology. Auton. Agent. Multi-Agent Syst. **8**(3), 203–236 (2005)

5. Chung, K.L., Nixon, B., Mylopoulos, J., Yu, E.: Non-Functional Requirements in Software Engineering. Kluwer Academic Publishers, Boston (2000)

6. Engelsman, W., Wieringa, R.: Understandability of goal concepts by requirements engineering experts. In: Indulska, M., Purao, S. (eds.) ER Workshops 2014. LNCS, vol. 8823, pp. 97–106. Springer, Heidelberg (2014)

7. ITU: Recommendation Z.151 (GRL) – Version 3.0, September 2003

8. Koliadis G., Vranesevic A., Bhuiyan M., Krishna A., Ghose A., Combining $i*$ and BPMN for Business Process Model Lifecycle Management, Business Process Management Workshops, 2006, pp 416–427

9. Krogstie, J.: Model-Based Development and Evolution of Information Systems. Springer, London (2012)

10. van Lamsweerde, A.: Requirements Engineering: From System Goals to UML Models to Software Specifications. Wiley (2009)

11. Matulevičius, R., Heymans, P.: Comparing goal modelling languages: an experiment. In: Sawyer, P., Heymans, P. (eds.) REFSQ 2007. LNCS, vol. 4542, pp. 18–32. Springer, Heidelberg (2007)

12. Matulevičius R., Heymans P., Opdahl A.L.: Comparing GRL and KAOS using the UEML approach. In: IESA 2007, pp. 77–88 (2007)

13. Moody, D.L.: The "Physics" of notations: towards a scientific basis for constructing visual notations in software engineering. IEEE Trans. Software Eng. **35**(5), 756–777 (2009)

14. Moody, D.L., Heymans, P., Matulevičius, R.: Visual syntax does matter: improving the cognitive effectiveness of the i* visual notation. In: Requirements Engineering, vol. 15, pp. 141–175 (2010)

15. OMG, Business Motivation Model (BMM, version 1.3) (2015). http://www.omg.org/spec/BMM/1.3/. (last check: 18 June 2016)

16. OMG, Business Process Model and Notation (BPMN, version 2.0) (2011). http://www.omg.org/spec/BPMN/2.0/. (last visited: 18 June 2016)

17. Regev, G.: A systemic paradigm for early it system requirements based on regulation principles: the lightswitch approach. Ph.D. thesis, Swiss Federal Institute of Technology (EPFL) (2003)

18. Tu, C.: Ontological evaluation of BMM and i* with the UEML approach. Master thesis, University of Namur (2007)

19. Yu, E.: Towards modelling and reasoning support for early-phase requirements engineering. In: Proceedings of the 3rd IEEE International Conference on Requirements Engineering (RE 1997) (1996)

Information Systems Development

The Novel Approach to Organization and Navigation by Using All Organization Schemes Simultaneously

Aneta Bartuskova[1(✉)] and Ivan Soukal[2]

[1] Faculty of Informatics and Management,
Center for Basic and Applied Research, University of Hradec Kralove,
Rokitanskeho 62, Hradec Kralove 500 03, Czech Republic
aneta.bartuskova@uhk.cz
[2] Faculty of Informatics and Management,
Department of Economics, University of Hradec Kralove,
Rokitanskeho 62, Hradec Kralove 500 03, Czech Republic
ivan.soukal@uhk.cz

Abstract. Traditional navigation of websites and web-based systems has a limited information value apart from text values of individual navigation items. We present a method for constructing an information-rich navigation, based on advantages of vertical menus, site maps and tag clouds. Our solution is theoretically grounded in classification of organization schemes and presents an arrangement by all organization schemes simultaneously. Layers of organization are distinguished by a combined use of textual, spatial and visual techniques. Proposed method utilizes combination of objective means of organization, increased information density and reduced interaction cost. This arrangement is expected to facilitate efficient browsing in web environment and is applicable also on learning or knowledge management systems.

Keywords: Organization schemes · Knowledge management · Website navigation · Site map · Tag cloud · Usability · Interaction cost

1 Introduction

Hierarchical menu is a traditional way for dealing with navigation on the Internet. It has however a limited information value apart from text values of navigation items. Tags in a form of tag clouds emerged as a new way of providing access to content. Tags facilitate higher information density [1], they are however not being used as a primary navigation, possibly because of their lack of any formal structure.

Our proposal is to combine high information density of tags with structural quality of hierarchical navigation. The presented method implements advantages of vertical menus, which prevent user disorientation [2], are more efficient and subjectively preferred over dynamic menus [3] and are more usable and easier to scan [4].

Navigation reflects the organization of information in any system. Several authors discussed classification of organization schemes, by which we can organize the information [5–8]. On this theoretical ground, we constructed a method which facilitates

© Springer International Publishing Switzerland 2016
V. Řepa and T. Bruckner (Eds.): BIR 2016, LNBIP 261, pp. 99–106, 2016.
DOI: 10.1007/978-3-319-45321-7_7

a spatial and visual arrangement by all organization schemes simultaneously. An arrangement by each scheme then presents one layer of organization and all layers can be seen simultaneously, which creates an information-rich navigation area. Presenting more information in one place is also presumed to reduce interaction cost and increase usability. The differentiation of each arrangement is ensured by combined use of textual, spatial and visual techniques.

2   Theoretical Background

2.1   Organization Schemes

Organization scheme can be described as a construct by which the information is organized. Morville and Rosenfeld [6] and later Kalbach [7] proposed primary division of schemes into exact/objective schemes, which divide information into well-defined and mutually exclusive sections, and ambiguous/subjective schemes, which divide information into categories that defy exact definition. Other authors suggested there are five ways to organize information. This approach is known as the LATCH, for Location, Alphabet, Time, Category and Hierarchy [5, 8] (Table 1).

Table 1. Organization schemes

Wurman [5]; Lidwell et al. [8]	Morville & Rosenfeld [6]; Kalbach [7]	
time (by chronological sequence)	chronological	exact
location (by geographical or spatial reference)	geographical	
alphabet (by alphabetical sequence)	alphabetical	
continuum or hierarchy (by magnitude)	-	-
category (by similarity or relatedness)	topic, task, audience	ambiguous

2.2   Organization Structures

Organization structures present different ways of structuring and visually organizing the information. Lidwell et al. proposed three types of non-linear organization: hierarchical, parallel and web [8]. This classification closely corresponds with the earlier division of spatial diagrams to hierarchy, matrix and network [9]. Similar organization structures were later proposed also by Morville and Rosenfeld [6]. They presented these organization types: hierarchy, database model and hypertext [6]. The three proposals can be mapped to each other (Table 2).

Table 2. Mapping organization structures by different authors

Novick et al. [9]	Morville & Rosenfeld [6]	Lidwell et al. [8]
hierarchy	hierarchy	hierarchical
matrix	database model	parallel
network	hypertext	web

2.3   Usable Navigation

Navigation is an important part of usability of any website or system [10]. The more negative the perceived navigability is, the less the perceived informativeness and entertainment are, which generate a negative attitude toward a web site [11]. Navigability is a complex construct, which depends on many design decisions. Structure, organization, labelling, browsing, and searching systems all contribute toward effective navigation [6]. A broad, shallow navigation structure with many visible links is usually more usable than a narrow, deep structure with just a few [4].

2.4   Social Navigation and Tag Clouds

Social interactions such as tagging, rating or commenting create collective intelligence, which can be described as the knowledge derived from the collaboration of many individuals [12]. Social navigation includes Amazon's collaborative filtering, recommendation systems or Flickr's tag clouds [6]. The important characteristics of tags is their higher information density. A higher information density along with fewer page revisits indicate that the use of tag clouds may lead to more focused page selection and better processing of the navigation compared to a hierarchical menu [1].

3   Issues Related to Navigation

3.1   Disorientation and Site Maps

Web users commonly experience disorientation while browsing, which has a negative effect on their performance [13]. One of the main contributors to this problem is confusing and disorganized navigation structure [14]. Danielson confirmed positive effects of constantly visible site maps used as a web navigation on user browsing [2]. Fowler and Stanwick suggested that it is easier to scan a large lists of organized possibilities than to pick one option that leads to another set of options and so on [4]. Leuthold et al. agreed to show as much navigation links as possible on the screen as vertical menus were also subjectively preferred by users [3].

3.2   Subjectivity in Creating Navigation

One issue with the navigation is the overall subjectivity. Subjective organization schemes divide information into categories that defy exact definition, they are difficult to design and maintain and can be difficult to use [6]. Problems with creating useful navigation according to subjective organization scheme include: broad vague categories, poor organization of menu options and poor grouping of categories [7].

3.3 Descriptive Potential of Navigation

Website navigation has a descriptive potential, which can be carried out e.g. by spatial arrangement and visual cues. However design and organization of navigation is mostly subjected to the desired appearance of the website or system and does not contain much information, only the text label, i.e. names of sections or pages, subjectively organized. Low information density can be characterized by minimal information at first sight, requiring user to click before seeing more information [15]. Descriptive characteristics of tag clouds were however appreciated [1]. Similarly visualization of article descriptors in the form of semantic networks was well accepted and positively evaluated [16]. Consequently, it can be assumed that higher information density of navigation area could be highly appreciated by users.

3.4 Cost in Human-Computer Interactions

Hong et al. identified two types of cost: interaction cost (mouse clicks, button presses, typing) and attention-switching cost (moving attention from one window to another) [17]. If the navigation area contained more information about the links themselves, users could make more elaborate choice without clicking forth and back. When site map was used as a web navigation (i.e. higher information density), users made less use of the Back button [2]. Similarly Walhout et al. confirmed fewer page revisits with use of tag clouds, which have higher information density [1]. Ware reviewed basic costs of some common modes of information access, where internal pattern comparison is much more efficient than mouse hovering, selecting or clicking [18]. Leuthold et al. confirmed that opening the dynamic menu needs an additional mouse movement and is thus more costly than just scanning the navigation items [3].

4 The Novel Approach to Navigation

4.1 Conceptual Proposal

Based on the evidence discussed in previous sections, in our solution we propose to provide web users with a constantly visible navigation area, which should diminish their disorientation. The next goal is to reduce subjectivity by objective means of organization. Because different organization schemes can be useful in different web browsing strategies, we propose to utilize several at the same time. Implementing arrangement by these organization schemes will create added information value to navigation items and increase information density of the navigation area (Table 3).

We can imagine individual arrangements as layers, stacked in a way that facilitate selective attention to each of them. Presenting more navigation links and more information about them in one place will also reduce interaction cost (users can better process links before clicking on them) and attention-switching cost (users will less likely click on the wrong link, followed by Back button).

Table 3. Summary of identified issues with possible solutions

Objective/benefit	Implementation
reduced disorientation of users	by providing constantly visible navigation area
reduced subjectivity	by using objective means of organization
increased information density	by utilising design elements for adding information value to navigation items
reduced interaction and attention-switching cost	by presenting more information about navigation items in one layout

4.2 Differentiation by Visual and Spatial Aspects

In this section we will discuss suitable design elements as the means for an arrangement by different organization schemes. E.g. Tversky [19] and Fowler and Stanwick [4] proposed using visual cues like colour, size and font to signify organization into groups. We should keep in mind that it is desirable to reduce complexity by reducing the number of elements needed to organize and communicate information [8]. Selected design aspects are summarized in (Table 4).

Table 4. Proposed aspects of design for differentiating items

Object	Design aspects	
	Visual	Spatial
text	colour, size, font	starting position (x,y)
shape	colour (or pattern), size	

Colour is used in design to group elements and indicate meaning [8]. The simplest solution would be to attach colour to the text of navigation item, however coloured text is often poorly legible due to thin lines of characters. Therefore it would be more usable to add solid coloured elements spatially associated with text items.

Size can be used to signify importance or magnitude. This technique is used in tag clouds, where the font size reflects the number of instances for each tag. It was confirmed that smaller fonts are often hardly legible on the computer screen [10]. Therefore to create a sufficient difference in font size for individual navigation items, we would have to use larger fonts, which would hardly fit on the screen.

Considering font, Lidwell et al. stated that a detectable difference between fonts is difficult to achieve without also disrupting the aesthetics of the typography [8]. Therefore differentiation neither by font size nor font type is suitable.

As for space, we are interested in the position of navigation items in the navigation area of the website. In a two-dimensional display, the element's position is defined by horizontal and vertical value, so the arrangement can be accordingly implemented either horizontally or vertically. As we have exhausted usable possibilities for design aspects applicable on navigation items themselves (i.e. on the text labels), additional design elements can be used for the arrangement by remaining organization schemes.

4.3 Mapping to an Arrangement by All Organization Schemes

Category can be best implemented by the principle of grouping or similarity. We propose its implementation by colour, because similarity of colour results in the strongest grouping effect [8]. Every category would be assigned a colour, and every item which belongs to this category will be marked with this colour.

Organization by alphabet can be done either horizontally, by sorting items as inline elements, or vertically like block elements. Tags are typically sorted as inline elements. We will choose the second approach to maintain better readability and to keep space for implementing other layers of organization.

Continuous organization schemes - continuum and time - can be best implemented by variable size or position (horizontal, vertical). Vertical arrangement was already taken by alphabet, so for continuous variables we propose as the first technique a horizontal arrangement. Arrangement by difference in size of text labels was rejected earlier in the text. Therefore as the second technique we propose adding a new element, with value given by its width. Finally, location can be represented by an associative link to the adjacent map. These conclusions are summarized in (Table 5).

Table 5. Proposal of individual methods for designing navigation

Org. scheme	Method	Explanation
alphabet	vertical arrangement	Items are sorted by alphabet in a traditional way
time	horizontal arrangement	Items are arranged by time using difference in horizontal starting position
category	square with dif. colour/pattern	Items are visually associated with a colour (or pattern), different for each category
subcategory	text label	Individual items are grouped into subcategories, represented by the displayed text labels
continuum	bar rating with different length	Items are visually associated with a bar of length reflecting the value
location	associative link	Items are linked to the adjacent map

Subcategory is not an elementary organization scheme. It is in fact a category on lower hierarchical level and is implemented only if the number of items is too high. By individual navigation item is meant single page, document or reference link with URL. To conclude, text labels represent either individual items or a collection of items grouped in a subcategory (in the case of a large number of items). The proposed solution is then applicable on both small and large websites and systems.

4.4 Spatial and Visual Design

This section brings a closer look on spatial and visual design of our proposal, illustrated in [Fig. 1]. To implement organization by categories, they have to be included in the

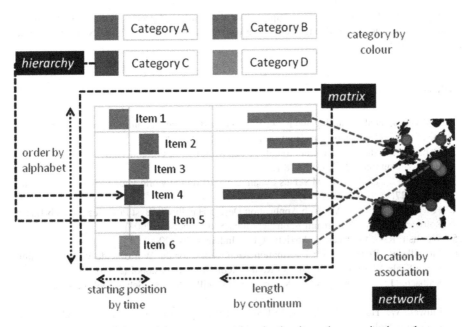

Fig. 1. Schema of the spatial arrangement of navigation items by organization schemes

navigation area, accessibly placed at the top. The rest of the schema corresponds with the proposals in previous sections with highlighted arrangements by individual organization schemes and in context with organization structures.

5 Conclusion and Discussion

In this paper we proposed a novel method for creating navigation as an alternative to the existing techniques. By implementing proposed method, we expect to achieve several major advantages over traditional navigation used on the Internet: (1) reduced disorientation of users, (2) reduced subjectivity, (3) increased information density, and (4) reduced interaction cost. The arrangement is expected to facilitate efficient browsing on web-based interfaces but also in other information or knowledge-based systems, as it can transform any static navigation list to a dynamic content overview.

Thorough testing would have to be performed before implementing this proposal, which is the objective of our future research. We have to take a learning curve into account, however we can expect both the performance and user satisfaction to improve in repeated visits. Santa-Maria and Dyson tested usage of online discussion forum in conventional and experimental design [19]. Users of the other version were disoriented and confused at first, however after short adaptation, the performance of both groups were almost equal, as well as the number of subsequent visits. Our proposal is then expected to be more useful on repeatedly visited websites, such as news websites, e-learning websites/systems, knowledge management systems etc.

Acknowledgment. The work was supported by the Students Specific Research Grant of the Faculty of Informatics and Management at the University of Hradec Kralove. (Students Specific Research FIM UHK No. 1/2016).

References

1. Walhout, J., et al.: Learning and navigating in hypertext: navigational support by hierarchical menu or tag cloud? Comput. Hum. Behav. **46**, 218–227 (2015)
2. Danielson, D.R.: Web navigation and the behavioral effects of constantly visible site maps. Interact. Comput. **14**(5), 601–618 (2002)
3. Leuthold, S., et al.: Vertical versus dynamic menus on the world wide web. Comput. Hum. Behav. **27**(1), 459–472 (2011)
4. Fowler, S., Stanwick, V.: Web Application Design Handbook: Best Practices for Web-Based Software. Morgan Kaufmann Publishers Inc., San Francisco (2004)
5. Wurman, R.S.: Information Anxiety. QUE, Indianapolis (2000)
6. Morville, P., Rosenfeld, L.: Information Architecture for the World Wide Web: Designing Large-Scale Web Sites, 3rd edn. O'Reilly Media, Inc., Sebastopol (2006)
7. Kalbach, J.: Designing Web Navigation. O'Reilly Media, Sebastopol (2007). ISBN: 978-0596528102
8. Lidwell, W., Holden, K., Butler, J.: Universal Principles of Design, Revised and Updated. Rockport Publishers (2010)
9. Novick, L.R., Hurley, S.M., Francis, M.: Evidence for abstract, schematic knowledge of three spatial diagram representations. Mem. Cogn. **27**, 290 (1999)
10. Bartuskova, A., Krejcar, O.: Design requirements of usability and aesthetics for e-learning purposes. In: Sobecki, J., Boonjing, V., Chittayasothorn, S. (eds.) Advanced Approaches to Intelligent Information and Database Systems. SCI, vol. 551, pp. 235–245. Springer, Heidelberg (2014)
11. Kang, Y.-S., Kim, Y.J.: Do visitors' interest level and perceived quantity of web page content matter in shaping the attitude toward a web site? Decis. Support Syst. **42**, 1187–1202 (2006)
12. Gruber, T.: Collective knowledge systems: where the social web meets the semantic web. In: Web Semantics: Science, Services and Agents on the World Wide Web (2008)
13. McDonald, S., Stevenson, R.J.: Navigation in hyperspace: an evaluation of the effects of navigational tools and subject matter expertise on browsing and information retrieval in hypertext. Interact. Comput. **10**(2), 129–142 (1998)
14. Fang, X., Holsapple, C.W.: An empirical study of web site navigation structures' impacts on web site usability. Decis. Support Syst. **43**(2), 476–491 (2007)
15. Reinecke, K., Bernstein, A.: Improving performance, perceived usability, and aesthetics with culturally adaptive user interfaces. ACM Trans. Comput. Hum. Interact. **18**(2), 1–29 (2011)
16. Pajić, D.: Browse to search, visualize to explore: who needs an alternative information retrieving model? Comput. Hum. Behav. **39**, 145–153 (2014). Hong, L., Chi, E.H., Budiu, R., Pirolli, P., Nelson, L.: SparTag.us: a low cost tagging system for foraging of web content. In: Advanced Visual Interfaces, AVI 2008, pp. 65–72 (2008)
17. Ware, C.: Visual Thinking for Design. Morgan Kaufmann Publishers Inc., Massachusetts (2008)
18. Tversky, B.: Spatial schemas in depictions. In: Spatial Schemas and Abstract Thought, pp. 79–111. MIT Press, Cambridge (2001)
19. Santa-Maria, L., Dyson, M.C.: The effect of violating visual conventions of a website on user performance and disorientation. How bad can it be? In: SIGDOC 2008 (2008)

When Do Projects End? – The Role of Continuous Software Engineering

Peter Forbrig[(⊠)]

University of Rostock, Albert-Einstein-Str. 22, 18051 Rostock, Germany
peter.forbrig@uni-rostock.de

Abstract. Agile development methods have been proven to increase the quality of interactive systems because they allow quick adaptation to continuously changing requirements that are enforced by a fast changing reality. Additionally, models are very helpful to specify the understanding of analysts; developers and users of the domain. If models can be animated, they provide very good basis for discussions. The engagement of all participants is often much higher in this case. Currently, a lot of specification languages like UML, BPMN, or S-BPM are used to document the results of the analysis of the domain in most projects. Additionally, it can be recognized that the focus on users increases. S-BPM is already an example for that. It provides a special view on business processes that is missing in BPMN. It focusses on subjects that often are users but could also be software systems. This shifting focus goes together with a trend from Technology-Driven Design to Human-Centered Design.

The paper discusses the combination of agile development methods with Continuous Software Engineering. It argues for an integration of Human-Centered Design methods with business process modeling and Continuous Requirements Engineering. The concepts of existing approaches of Continuous Software Engineering are extended accordingly. Therefore, classical maintenance does not exist anymore.

Keywords: Agile software development · Continuous Software Engineering · Continuous Requirements Engineering · Continuous Human-Centered Design · Continuous Business-Process Modeling · Subject-oriented BPM

1 Introduction

Traditionally, software development ends and maintenance starts. While a lot of attention is paid on methods and life cycle models of software development, maintenance stays unstructured in some way. While agile software development methods became more and more popular because of their advantages for rapid changing application domains, agile methods for maintenance are less discussed. However, problems are very similar. New requirements result on a changing domain. Because of these changed requirements, a further development of the interactive system is necessary. Continuous Requirements Engineering is extended to the usage phase of software. It should be combined with the Human-Centered Design approach that focusses on the user's needs. It is combined with evaluations and monitoring of running systems.

V. Řepa and T. Bruckner (Eds.): BIR 2016, LNBIP 261, pp. 107–121, 2016.
DOI: 10.1007/978-3-319-45321-7_8

The agile approach supports very much the communication between developers, users, and other stakeholders, because running results are produced in relatively short cycles. The twelve main principles of the agile idea were presented in [1]. They were characterized as the agile manifesto and argues for continuous delivery of valuable software. Additionally, changing requirements should be welcomed. The manifesto promotes already a sustainable software development. However, in a lot of projects maintenance is considered to be outside of the development process. Recent scientific discussions suggest to apply agile principles to maintenance as well. Terms like continuous requirements engineering and continuous software engineering were created.

Astonishingly, already several years ago in 1998 the idea of continuously engineering software systems was discussed in the Dagstuhl seminar 98092 [31]. The motivation for the organizers was the fact that "Information and organizers Systems are going together to long living Information and Communication Infrastructures that are mission critical to organizations, businesses, and whole society". Two years later a component concept for continuous software engineering was presented [22]. Recently further papers like [5, 13, 17, 20] were published.

The 1st workshop on continuous requirements engineering [21] was organized by us in 2015. Several ideas for facing the problem of continuously changing requirements were discussed during the event. Including the discussed ideas there was one presented by Fleischmann et al. [11]. Their paper discusses the idea of executing requirements that are expressed as subject-oriented S-BPM specifications. Users can express their idea directly to a system. Editors are provided that allow users to express their ideas or at least allow them to change existing running specifications.

This idea seems to be very attractive and inspired us to have a deeper look at the idea of continuous businesses process modeling in conjunction with continuous software engineering in general. From our point of view, even modeling without direct executions is very attractive and helps to create a common understanding of the domain. Based on or experience, this is true for all kinds of models. Additionally, we feel convinced by the agile development approach and human-centered design (ISO 9241-210). It seems to be helpful if the different approaches use joined models. Based on these ideas the integration of business process modeling, requirements engineering and human-centered design will be discussed and consequences for the development process will be shown.

The rest of the paper is structured in the following way. First, we recall and discuss some ideas of continuous software engineering. Based on these discussions three activities are identified that are worth to be mentioned explicitly. These activities are Continuous BPM, Continuous RE, and Continuous HCD. They are each discussed in a separate paragraph each and will be followed by a paragraph discussing the consequences for the project management. The paper will end with a summary and an outlook.

2   Continuous Software Engineering

With their paper, Fitzgerald and Stol [13] recently provided an interesting overview of ideas related to Continuous Software Engineering. They especially provided interesting arguments of trends and challenges in this domain.

The authors expressed that they identified three main sub-phases within the entire software development life cycle that they call Business Strategy & Planning, Development, and Operations. However, there is additionally a phase of Improvement and Innovation in their model that is summarized in Fig. 1.

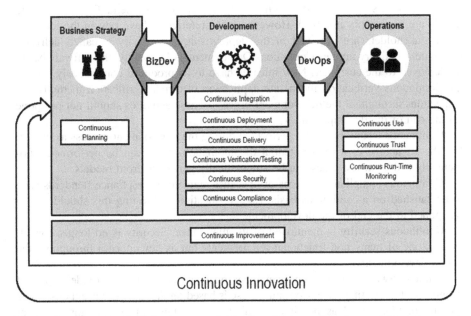

Fig. 1. Continuous*: A holistic view on activities from Business, Development, Operations, and Innovation (from [13]).

The main ideas of the concepts mentioned in Fig. 1 will be discussed in the following paragraphs before extensions will be provided.

2.1   Business Strategy and Planning

Continuous Planning was identified as the important activity of the first sub-phase. It is defined as a: "holistic endeavor involving multiple stakeholders from business and software functions whereby plans are dynamic open-ended artifacts that evolve in response to changes in the business environment, and thus involve a tighter integration between planning and execution" [13].

2.2   Development

Within the development sub-phase, certain activities are positioned. These activities are continuous integration, continuous verification & testing, continuous security and continuous compliance.

Continuous integration is already well known because it was identified an explicit practice in the Extreme Programming method. It consists of continuously building deployments package, running the code and test it for correctness and acceptance.

Agile methods focus on daily builds to allow quick feedback of the implementation under development from tests. Continuous deployment is the practice of continuously deploying good software builds automatically to some environment. The forthcoming user is not necessarily involved. However, it is preferred to have him in the loop.

If stakeholders are involved in the deployment, the activity is called delivery. Continuous delivery implies Continuous Deployment. Additionally, the software has to be deployed to the customer. New releases have to be produced continuously.

Continuous verification means the application of formal verification methods and inspections throughout the development process. These activities should not postpone till the end of the development.

Continuous testing has to be performed during the development process as well. It has the advantage of a high potential of automation. Tests can be performed automatically and even test cases can be automatically generated from models.

Continuous compliance is necessary because regulatory compliance standards have to be satisfied on a continuous basis. Like verification and testing this should not be postponed to the end of the development.

Continuous security is mentioned of its importance. Security is no longer considered as one of many non-functional requirements but as key concern throughout the whole development.

While software is in use one can focus on new customers or provide improved support for the existing once. Continuous use is based on the fact the current customers are supported as good as possible. It might be a better strategy to satisfy current customers and users than to attract new customers.

Focusing on existing customers is very much related to trust. Trust has to be developed over time. It is the result of interactions in the past. Customers must have the impression that developers act cooperatively. They must be sure that developers always try to do their best to meet the customer's expectations.

To fulfill the expectations of customers it is also very important to monitor applications during run-time and to provide immediate support if necessary. "As the historical boundary between design-time and run-time research in software engineering is blurring [2], in the context of continuously running cloud services, run-time behaviors of all kinds must be monitored to enable early detection of quality-of-service problems, such as performance degradation, and also the fulfilment of service level agreements (SLAs)" [13].

2.3 Improvement and Innovation

Continuous improvement is based on lean principles of smart decision-making and elimination of waste. It delivers small incremental quality improvements. These benefits allow to compete with competitors and can make the difference.

Continuous innovation is considered as a sustainable process that is responsive to evolving market conditions. It should be based on appropriate metrics across the entire lifecycle.

2.4 Summary of the Discussed Approaches of Continuous Software Engineering

The presented approach by Fitzgerald and Stol tries to close the gap between business and software development. They recognized that historically a gulf between business strategy and IT development has emerged. Software engineering has become a much broader domain from their perspective. We fully support the presented ideas of having a broader view on software engineering and believe that aspects of marketing and management of enterprises have to be considered in software engineering as well.

However, it seems to us that some aspects are underestimated in the presented approach. From our point of view modeling in general and especially business-process modeling should play an important role in software engineering in the future. Model-based and model-driven methods and techniques have been becoming popular in academic and industry. For business-process modeling, languages like BPMN or S-BPMN have proven to be useful.

For the business strategy, approved business processes are very important. They should be as precisely specified as possible. Process descriptions could be considered as one planning artefact. However, because of their importance they should be mentioned separately. From our point of view, business-process modeling is so important that it should be mentioned as a separate continuous activity. We will discuss more details in the following paragraph.

3 Continuous Business-Process Modeling

The idea of Continuous Business Process Improvement (CPI) has been discussed in several publications for several years. A book from the beginning 90th of the last century might be an example for that [8]. The topic is still important and can be characterized like the following content of a current webpage of Professional Business Solutions Inc. (PBSI): "To maintain their competitive advantage organizations must streamline their operations and processes. Continuous Process Improvement (CPI) is a strategic approach for developing a culture of continuous improvement in the areas of reliability, process cycle times, costs in terms of less total resource consumption, quality, and productivity. Deployed effectively, it increases quality and productivity, while reducing waste and cycle time. Since many business processes rely on information and participation from more than one department and even different organizations, CPI is designed to facilitate these processes by integrating the various components into one streamlined system that runs smoothly and efficiently on a partially or completely automated flow of steps."

Milewski et al. [23] discuss the technological process innovation from a life cycle perspective. They provide a framework and some related key results form case studies.

It seems to be common sense that Continuous Process Innovation is an integrated part of companies. This is supported by a lot of publications. Also searching in the internet for the term Continuous Process Innovation delivers a lot of references. Based on the knowledge about process innovation the need for Business Process Management arose. Bergener et al. [3] provide a nice explanation for that. They claim: "Business Process Management (BPM) has evolved as an integrated management discipline that aims to enable organizations to continuously innovate and improve their operations."

It is widely accepted that models of organizations in connection with business process models are very important for BPM and the corresponding IT support. According to Fleischmann et al. [10] play models an increasing role in adaptive process environments.

They argue that the modeling behavior relates to the quality of process models in several ways. This is based on argumentations provided by Claes et al. [6] "A modeler's structured modeling style, the frequency of moving existing objects over the modeling canvas, and the overall modeling speed is in any way connected to the ease with which the resulting process model can be understood." [10] Stakeholders have to build up communication skills to be able to understand and reflect models when shared along organizational learning steps. If such communication skills are missed, the development projects are likely to fail, as deficiencies in communication are in fact among the most frequent reasons for project failure [3].

Fleischmann et al. argue that BPM techniques have to be supported by tools and languages. Otherwise, the communication about processes is likely to require iterations until completely understood by involved stakeholders.

Fitzgerald and Stol [13] argue that "Enterprise Agile and Beyond Budgeting concepts have emerged as recognition that benefits of agile software development will be sub-optimal if not complemented with by an agile approach in related organizational functions such as finance and HR". They additionally argue: "that the link between business strategy and software development ought to be continuously assessed and improved".

This idea is fully supported by us. Additionally, the idea of modeling seems to be very attractive. Because we especially believe in the idea of modeling, we use the term Continuous Business Process Modeling to describe important activities as well in software engineering as in business administration. From our point of view, the activity of Continuous Business-Process Modeling should be integrated into the general approach of Continuous Software Engineering of business applications. Even that business-process models could be one type of the artifacts that are produced during planning. However, because of its importance business processes modeling should be mentioned explicitly. Therefore, Continuous Business-Process Modeling should be the second activity in the first phase. This idea was initiated by the discussions at the 1st Workshop on Continuous Requirements Engineering [21]. Bukša et al. [7] presented a method for integrated semi-automated business process and regulations compliance management. They especially referred to the changing business process models:

"However, there is a gap between continuously changing business process models that are maintained in a specific set of tools, and continuously changing regulatory requirements that usually are maintained outside organizations. There are tools that provide support for compliance management by means of Business Rules Engine, however, in most cases business rules must be entered manually and there is no live linkage with external legislative and regulative sources". They ask for specific tool support for Continuous Business Process Modeling.

Fleischmann et al. [11] even provided an approach that allows the rapid execution of business-process specification. It is called Subject-oriented Business Process Modeling is supported by a language that is calls S-BPMN [10]. This approach perfectly fits to the idea of Continuous Business-Process Modeling and the idea of Human-Centered Design. It models processes from the perspective of subjects involved. These subjects are most of the time humans. In this way, the approach is per se human oriented. However, subjects can be systems as well.

For S-BPM it is suggested that you start with modelling the communication of subjects via messages first. In this way, the big picture is specified. Later, the dynamic behavior of each subject is specified by finite automata. In Fig. 2 the approach is visualized. The available symbols of S-BPM are presented in Fig. 3.

Based on the requirements a communication model is specifies. In Fig. 2 there are only two subjects that are named as customer and supplier. There is only one message that is sent from subject customer to subject supplier.

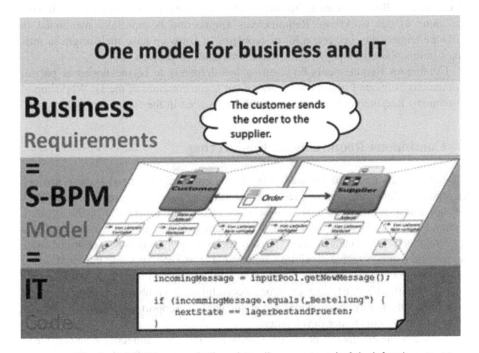

Fig. 2. S-BPMN approach (from https://www.metasonic.de/en/s-bpm)

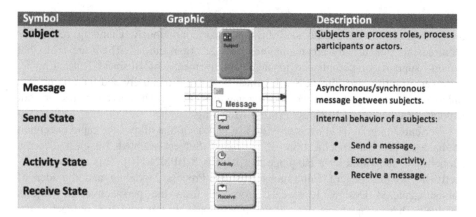

Symbol	Graphic	Description
Subject		Subjects are process roles, process participants or actors.
Message		Asynchronous/synchronous message between subjects.
Send State		Internal behavior of a subjects:
Activity State		• Send a message, • Execute an activity, • Receive a message.
Receive State		

Fig. 3. S-BPMN notation (taken from [12])

The subjects are refined by behavioral models that in detail specify under which condition subjects send messages and how they react on messages.

Fichtenbauer et al. [9, 12] report about using BPMN for the subject-oriented approach and make the specifications run. In this way, there is no need for a new language if BPMN is already known. However, in both cases using BPMN or S-BPM Continuous Business Modeling can be supported very well. This is very much related to Continuous Requirements Engineering. This was already mentioned earlier. It gave the name to our workshop. Requirements engineering is especially mentioned in software engineering because a lot of problems of software have their origin in mistakes in this phase of analyzing the needs and goals of projects.

Continuous Requirements Engineering has definitely to be mentioned as part of Continuous Software Engineering. Some of our argumentations of the 1st Workshop of Continuous Requirements Engineering will be recalled in the following paragraph.

4   Continuous Requirements Engineering

Current engineering-based approaches are rooted into well elaborated systems models, enterprise architectures, ontologies, and information logistics representations. They provide transparency, reliability, and security in the whole lifecycle of the sys-tem. Currently such approaches are designed and mainly applied for large enterprises that have relatively long change cycles. In case such changes have to be performed more frequently, a much higher flexibility is required. For such systems, the engineering processes grow into continuous engineering that requires continuous requirements engineering (CRE). CRE can only be successful if it combines rigid engineering principles with agility, emergence, and spontaneity to support sustainability and viability of the systems under development.

Smaller scale enterprises need new approaches, methods, and tools to be capable to embrace the growing variety of opportunities and challenges offered by fast changing and hardly predictable environment. In this type of systems continuous requirements engineering also can be a solution if it is integrated with management and design approaches applicable for smaller scale enterprises.

It is well known that wrong requirements cause a lot of problems. Some projects totally fail because of that, others waste a lot of money because the correction of resulted errors in the implementation is very time consuming and labor intensive. Therefore, new ideas in identifying the correct requirements are very important. Leah Goldin et al. [18] discuss the question whether in the development of large scale systems the institutionalized, proactive requirements reuse pays off. In their case study they found out that at least for the studied project it paid off to meet the moving target of requirements based on existing specifications.

Reuse of requirements specification might be one way to reduce time to market. However, there are still a lot of aspects to consider like the kind of specification languages for functional and non-function requirements. For the handling of BPMN and S-BPM specifications concepts for reusable components were presented in [14] and [15]. According tool support would very much support to quickly update requirements specifications. Workflow management systems can support the execution of business process specifications. Fleischmann et al. [11] follow this argumentation line by using S-BPM: "When agile project structures and active involvement of concerned stake-holders become part of organizational change, requirements to software development might change continuously. Hence, the effort for transforming representations from requirements specification to executable design models should be minimized. Ideally, requirement specifications support fine-grained modeling at a semantically precise level that enables the direct execution of these specifications. We have demonstrated such as an approach on the level of business processes utilizing the capabilities of Subject-oriented Business Process Management.

Its diagrammatic modeling language allows stakeholders continuously articulating their requirements and subsequently refining them to executable behavior components (subjects) ensuring utmost parallelism. However, it still has to be investigated how such a paradigmatic shift can be put to organizational development practice, namely maintaining an interaction perspective in parallel to the functional one on work and business structures".

Qureshi et al. [26] provide a framework CARE (Continuous Adaptive Require-ments Engineering) for building self-adapting systems that is goal- and user-oriented. They distinguish requirements engineering during design-time and run-time that is related to design-time reasoning and run-time reasoning for such specific systems.

However, monitoring of running systems might be useful for any kind of appli-cation. In this way, Continuous Requirements Engineering might find its way to general software systems.

5 Continuous Human-Centered Design

Agile development methods are currently very popular. However, they are often focused on customers. We would like to argue only with the first agility principle: "Our highest priority is to satisfy the customer through early and continuous delivery of valuable software." The focus is obviously not on the users.

In the same way as agile development methods are popular for software engineering experts Human-Centered Design (HCD) is popular for usability and user experience experts. It focusses on tasks users have to perform, usability and user experience, aspects that do not play their important role for software engineers in general. Software engineering focusses currently often on the technical aspects of an application only.

One of the main reasons for the success of HCD is that the context of use and the evaluation of design solutions play an important role. User requirements are more important than technical features that software engineers might like. Users get what they really want. The HCD process is standardized by ISO 9241-210. It consists of a planning phase and four phases that are performed in an iterative way.

Within the first phase analysts try to understand the context of use. Stakeholders are identified. Their roles and tasks are analyzed and typical application scenarios are specified. Additionally, artefacts and tools they work with are captured. Last but not least, the environment in which the application has to be performed is analyzed. This is done according to the location, the surrounding objects, and people. Sometimes the available services are important as well.

Based on this analysis user requirements are specified. Additionally to the goals of users, functional and nonfunctional requirements are collected. Domain specific requirements might be important as well. This is e.g. the case when domain specific standards exists that have to be fulfilled by the application. First design solutions are produced afterwards to fulfill the identified requirements. Such design solutions include first ideas of user interfaces.

The design solutions are evaluated in the last phase of the HCD process. If the requirements of the users are met, the development process comes to an end and the implementation of the application core can be performed. Otherwise, there are three possible continuations. If there are serious problems, one has to analyze the context of use again and has to proceed with the first phase. In case the general analysis of the context of use seems to be correct but some requirements were specified in the wrong way, one has to rewrite some requirements or identify some new ones. Finally, it can be possible that only new design solutions are necessary. In this case, requirements are specified in the right way but the design solutions have to be improved.

Figure 4 gives a visual impression of the discussed HCD process model. The figure provides a good overview of the main ideas of the HCD process. Unfortunately, the process model does not consider the integration of HCD into an agile development process.

Paelke et al. [24] published the process model of and called it Agile UCD-Process. (User-Centered Design was the predecessor of HCD.). The process model suggests to have a common initial phase for developers and HCI specialists. Afterwards there are activities of both groups. Unfortunately, it is not quite clear in which order these activities are performed. Additionally, the requirements elicitation is a little bit too much uncoupled from the software development process. A stronger coupling was suggested by Paul et al. [25]. It additionally provides the names of models like user or task model that have to be specified in the corresponding state of the software development.

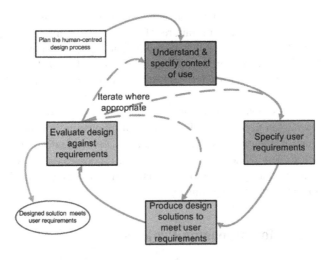

Fig. 4. The design process from ISO 9241-210– Human-centred design process (from https://thestandardinteractiondesignprocess.wordpress.com/).

In cycle two developers implement the design solutions from cycle one and in parallel their code from cycle one is tested by HCI experts. Additionally, they design for the next cycle and analyze for the cycle after the next cycle. This is the general development pattern. In some way, interaction designers work two cycles ahead to developers in analyzing customer data and one cycle ahead in developing design solutions.

A similar approach by separating the activities of analysts and developers was presented in [16] for the SCRUM approach. The development cycle of analysts is executed in parallel to the cycle of the developers. It runs at least one cycle ahead.

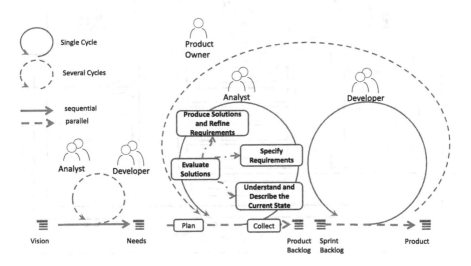

Fig. 5. Human-Centered Design Process for SCRUM

The human aspect becomes more and more important. Usability and user experience are key factors of success or failure of software systems. There are several attempts to integrate HCI aspects like usability into agile development processes. Examples of discussions of the process model are [28–30]. In [19] Kuusinen analyses the allocation of tasks between HCI specialists and developers in agile development projects.

As a result of these papers, one can conclude that innovation has always to be discussed from a human perspective. Technological innovation is important but it has to consider humans in their role as different stakeholders. Agile development methods often focus on customers while User-Centered Design focusses on users. Both aspects have to be considered during Continuous Human-Centered Design. This broader view is the reason for replacing user by human.

6   Consequences for Managing Projects

As a result, an extended holistic view was established. Its visual representation is presented by the graphics of Fig. 6. The development of companies and their IT infrastructure are intertwined and should be a continuous process. This means that the different stakeholders have to interact continuously.

Project teams have to adapt in their size to the current situation but should not stop their work by finalizing a project. Projects are long lasting with different focus during

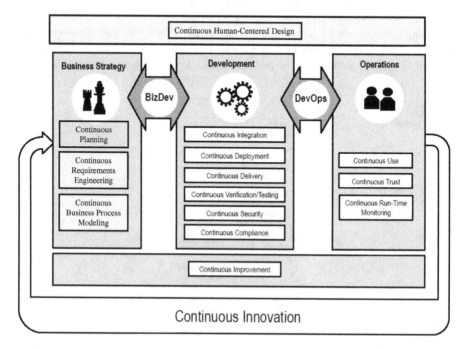

Fig. 6. Continuous*: An extended holistic view on activities in software engineering

usage time of the software [4]. At the beginning, a lot of manpower is necessary. Later the continuous adaptation can be managed by less people. It might be possible to merge several projects into one project on the long run. However, it is important that the activities of planning, requirements engineering, business process modeling and human-centered design never stop. This includes the monitoring of the running application.

Continuous Software Engineering can be characterized as combination of Software Engineering, Human-Centered Design and Business Administration, where adapting the business strategy is one crucial point.

7 Summary and Outlook

In this paper, the idea of extending the existing concept of Continuous Software Engineering was discussed. Within the existing concept, software engineering methods were already extended by activities from business administration. These activities adapt the business strategy to a changing environment. It was argued in this paper that an even broader view would be helpful. Three new terms were introduced to Continuous Software Engineering. These terms are Continuous Business Process Modeling, Continuous Requirements Engineering, and Continuous Human-Centered Design. This results in a really continuous development process that includes the current maintenance phase.

Case studies have to be performed and existing projects have to be studied to check how the suggested integrated approach works in industrial settings. It has to be analyzed how classical separated projects can be transformed into continuous projects. Additionally, it has to be analyzed how Continuous Software Engineering changes contracts and communication with external software companies. The future will show whether metrics of goals and needs can help to find prices for contracts with software developers.

It will be interesting to see whether a new kind of agility can be reached in the future that is based on analysis, planning, modeling and monitoring.

References

1. Agile Manifesto. http://agilemanifesto.org/. Accessed 4th June 2015
2. Baresi, L., Ghezzi, C.C.: The disappearing boundary between development-time and run-time. In: Future of Software Engineering Research (2010)
3. Bergener, K., Brocke, J.V., Hofmann, S., Stein, A., Brocke, C.V.: On the importance of agile communication skills in BPM education: design principles for international seminars. KM & E-Learn. 4(4), 415–434 (2012)
4. Bogsnes, B.: Implementing Beyond Budgeting: Unlocking the Performance Potential. Wiley, Hoboken (2008)
5. Bosch, J.: Continuous Software Engineering. Springer, Heidelberg (2014)

6. Claes, J., Vanderfeesten, I., Reijers, H.A., Pinggera, J., Weidlich, M., Zugal, S., Fahland, D., Weber, B., Mendling, J., Poels, G.: Tying process model quality to the modeling process: the impact of structuring, movement, and speed. In: Barros, A., Gal, A., Kindler, E. (eds.) BPM 2012. LNCS, vol. 7481, pp. 33–48. Springer, Heidelberg (2012)
7. Bukša, I., Darģis, M., Penicina, L.: Towards a method for integrated semi - automated business process and regulations compliance management for continuous requirements engineering. In: [21], pp. 25–33
8. Harrington, H.J.: Business Process Improvement: The Breakthrough Strategy for Total Quality, Productivity, and Competitiveness. McGraw Hill Inc., New York (1991)
9. Fichtenbauer, C., Fleischmann, A: Three dimensions of process models regarding their execution. In: Proceedings of the S-BPM ONE 2016, Erlangen (2016)
10. Fleischmann, A., Schmidt, W., Stary, C.: Open S-BPM = open innovation. In: Fischer, H., Schneeberger, J. (eds.) S-BPM ONE-Running Processes, pp. 295–320. Springer, Heidelberg (2013)
11. Fleischmann, A., Schmidt, W., Stary, C.: Requirements specification as executable software design – a behavior perspective. In: [21], pp. 9–18 (2015)
12. Fichtenbauer, C., Fleischmann, A.: Three dimensions of process models regarding their execution. In: Proceedings of the 8th International Conference on Subject-Oriented Business Process Management (S-BPM 2016), 8 pages, ACM, New York, Article 7. http://dx.doi.org/10.1145/2882879.2882892
13. Fitzgerald, B., Stol, K.-J.: Continuous software engineering and beyond: trends and challenges. In: Proceedings of the 1st International Workshop on Rapid Continuous Software Engineering – RcoSE 2014, pp. 1–9, ACM, New York (2014)
14. Forbrig, P.: Generic components for BPMN specifications. In: Johansson, B., Andersson, B., Holmberg, N. (eds.) BIR 2014. LNBIP, vol. 194, pp. 202–216. Springer, Heidelberg (2014)
15. Forbrig, P.: Reuse of models in S-BPM process specifications. In: Proceedings of the 7th International Conference on Subject-Oriented Business Process Management, S-BPM ONE 2015, Kiel, Germany, pp. 6–16. 23–24 April 2015
16. Forbrig, P., Herczeg, M.: Managing the agile process of human-centred design and software development. In: Beckmann C., Gross T., (eds.) INTERACT 2015 Adjunct Proceedings, pp. 223–232 (2015)
17. Forbrig, P.: Continuous software engineering with special emphasis on continuous business-process modeling and human-centered design. In: Proceedings of the S-BPM ONE (2016)
18. Goldin, L., Berry, D.M.: Reuse of requirements reduced time to market at one industrial shop: a case study. Requirements Eng. 20(1), 23–44 (2015)
19. Kuusinen, K.: Task allocation between UX specialists and developers in agile software development projects. In: Abascal, J., Barbosa, S., Fetter, M., Gross, T., Palanque, P., Winckler, M. (eds.) INTERACT 2015. LNCS, vol. 9298, pp. 27–44. Springer, Heidelberg (2015)
20. Lichter, H., Brügge, B., Riehle, D.: Workshop on Continuous Software Engineering. http://ceur-ws.org/Vol-1559/paper15.pdf
21. Matulevičius, R., et al. (eds.): REFSQ Workshop proceedings (2015). http://ceur-ws.org/Vol-1342/
22. Mann, S., Borusan, A., Ehrig, H., Große-Rhode, M., Mackenthun, R., Sünbül, A., Weber, H.: Towards a component concept for continuous software engineering, Technical report 55/00, FhG-ISST (2000)
23. Milewski, S.K., Fernandes, K.J., Mount, M.P.: Exploring technological process innovation from a lifecycle perspective. Int. J. Oper. Prod. Manag. 35(9), 1312–1331 (2015)

24. Paelke, V., Nebe, K.: Integrating agile methods for mixed reality design space exploration. In: Proceedings of the 7th ACM Conference on Designing Interactive Systems (DIS 2008), pp. 240–249, ACM, New York (2008)
25. Paul, M.: Systemgestützte Integration des Usability-Engineerings in den Software-Entwicklungsprozess, Ph.d. thesis, University of Lübeck (2015)
26. Qureshi, N.A., Perini, A., Ernst, N.A., Mylopoulos, J: Towards a continuous requirements engineering framework for self-adaptive systems. In: First International Workshop on RE @ Runtime at 18th IEEE International Requirements Engineering Conference (RE 2010), pp. 9–16, Sydney, September 2010
27. Rising, L., Janoff, S.N.: The Scrum software development process for small teams. IEEE Softw. **17**(4), 26–32 (2000)
28. Salah, D., Paige, R. Cairns, P.: A practitioner perspective on integrating agile and user centred design. In: Proceedings of the 28th International BCS Human Computer Interaction Conference (HCI 2014), pp. 100–109 (2014)
29. Singh, M.: U-SCRUM: an agile methodology for promoting usability, integrating usability engineering and agile software development: a literature review. In: Proceedings of the AGILE 2009, pp. 555–560, IEEE Press (2009)
30. Sy, D.: Adapting usability investigations for agile user-centered design. J. Usability Stud. **2** (3), 112–132 (2007)
31. Weber, H., Mueller, H. (eds.): Continuous Engineering for Industrial Scale Software Systems, Dagstuhl Seminar 98092 (1998). http://www.dagstuhl.de/de/programm/kalender/semhp/?semnr=98092

Business-Driven Open Source Software Development

Motivational Aspects of Collective Design

Birgit Großer[(⊠)] and Ulrike Baumöl

FernUniversitaet, Hagen, Germany
{Birgit.Grosser,Ulrike.Baumoel}@FernUni-Hagen.de

Abstract. Independence and a fancy company image are reasons why companies choose to use open source software instead of proprietary software. A challenge for companies outside the software domain arises if the desired software is not yet available. Established collective development models for such cases are missing. An important question in this context is how to motivate a collective of developers to pursue the goals of the company. In the present study a motivational system is outlined which can serve companies and other institutions in the process of how to coordinate such a collective. This collective becomes part of the resources used to implement the requirements of the business model, in this case the provision of the right software solution. Main insights are that the initiating company has to analyze and adhere to collective etiquette and should integrate a motivational context into their business model.

Keywords: Open Source Software · Incentive · Motivation · Business model

1 Open Source Software Development in a Business-Driven Context

The advent of the Open Source Software (OSS) movement radically changed the way, how a part of today's software has been and is developed. While all started with a nagging feeling that existing search engines and operating systems are somehow not adequate and the companies behind them have too much power over the user, OSS over time slowly became an alternative in many different application contexts. As a consequence, today there are many companies which use applications coming from an OSS background. There are various reasons for this, be it reducing costs or gaining a specific image [9].

The common procedure for introducing OSS into a business context is the search for the right piece of software and its integration into the existing application architecture. A much less common way, however, is the active driving of OSS development from inside a company. A first trigger for using the OSS approach in this context came from an international airline company which started to investigate the possibilities of developing a booking system not only as a mutual effort among airlines but also under the OSS paradigm. With this, also the opportunity for a new form of business model emerges. Participating companies and users could, e.g., form a virtual organization

© Springer International Publishing Switzerland 2016
V. Řepa and T. Bruckner (Eds.): BIR 2016, LNBIP 261, pp. 122–129, 2016.
DOI: 10.1007/978-3-319-45321-7_9

which has "fluid" boundaries. Based on the Business Model Canvas by [16], a business model can be conceptualized in nine "building blocks" (p. 15). The resource perspective taken in the present study affects the blocks regarding key resources, key partnerships and cost structure.

First analyses quickly revealed that adequate models that support the OSS development with focus on a business-driven context seem to be missing. A lot of research is performed concerning "pure" OSS development and the context in which people are willing to contribute to the development of an OSS seems to differ strongly from that of proprietary software (PS). Therefore, this is obviously one main aspect for creating and implementing an OSS development model that supports a business-driven context. Consequently, the focus of this paper is to analyze the incentives and motivations that make people participate in OSS development and to propose a first *motivational system for establishing and maintaining an OSS development community in a business-driven context* as compared to "pure" OSS development. The focus is especially on non-software companies that aim at OSS for their own needs. This is the main difference with respect to already common OSS development by software-companies as part of their core business.

In Sect. 2, theories concerning the analysis and structuration of motivations and incentives are researched and combined for the context of OSS development. A first survey among potential users was conducted (Sect. 3). The results are presented and finally, the incentives are mapped to a motivational context (Sect. 4).

2   Conceptual Foundations

First of all, the aspect of collective development has to be systematized. A research team of the MIT Center for Collective Intelligence studied collective intelligence (CI) from four perspectives: (1) what, (2) how, (3) who and (4) why [14, p. 22], [12, p. 245]. This system can be used as follows:

(1)   What is developed? The software required by a company presents the development subject. The focus is on open and free OSS.
(2)   How is the procedure? For this purpose, control mechanisms, tools for collaboration and communication as well as the existence of hierarchies and the distinction of phases are considered.
(3)   Who is responsible for which tasks? In the present context, the initiating company (business-driven development) and the external participants of the collective are responsible agents.
(4)   Why do subjects and units participate? This is the core aspect of this study. The observations are done with respect to the incentive system which is analyzed in the following.

2.1   Relevant Concepts

The concept "incentive system" as proposed in Fig. 1 refers to the perceived relationship between incentive, motivation, and action. Incentives can lead to extrinsic and intrinsic motivation; this classification is only one of many possible categorizations. For more alternatives see [4, 15].

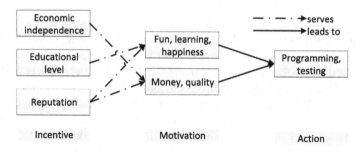

Fig. 1. Examples of relations between incentives, motivations, and corresponding actions

The term "motivation" is applied for the concept that covers possible answers to the question, why something is done. Synonyms, such as urge or motive are used to describe related dispositions, but differ in focus. Thus, motives represent a long term and socialized psychic property of an individual like curiosity, whereas motivations are formed through an interaction of an individual and confronting incentives [17]. Extrinsic motivation refers to external rewards for action that promise a satisfaction which the action itself would not generate. Intrinsic motivation however has a direct connection with its own intrinsic value [15, p. 215]. A motivation represents the effect created through an incentive and is followed by an action. The incentives as well as the motivations are not free of overlapping. E.g. can a higher reputation through participation in successful development projects facilitate networking with other participants; a stronger networking in turn, can enhance the possibility to get paid jobs leading to economic independence. For further examples of incentives and related motivations see the corresponding case study about idea competitions by [13].

To acknowledge the different perspectives of the collective and the initiating company the motivations are further split into micro and macro view. [7] connect the micro view to individuals and the macro view to organizations and communities (p. 137). This concept is here transferred to the collective (micro) and initiating company's view (macro). In Fig. 2 a few examples are shown.

	Micro	Macro
Extrinsic	Money Job	Lower costs Modern image
Intrinsic	Fun Learning Social	Purpose

Fig. 2. Discrimination of motivations into micro and macro view

However, these rationales do not fully explain why people decide to not participate in such projects, terminate their participation or are not willing to participate at all. Regarding these aspects, the concept of collective internal codes is analyzed in the following. The term "codes" conveys several aspects of certain etiquette. Codes can, e.g., be a specific use of language and the use of certain technologies. Moreover, the fact that the individuals within the collective cannot be assigned to specific tasks as paid employees usually can [3, pp. 34–36], leads to a different strategy for the initiating company. It has to be taken into account, that the individuals might reflect on given codes; separation of individuals and groups or a non-uniform use of terms and tools might occur (e.g. free vs. open, [8]). Once the process has started, the culture within an organizational unit and between companies can also adapt to the codes by gaining from learning effects by the members of the collective [18].

2.2   State of the Art

Many relevant aspects of the topics discussed here, have already been analyzed in existing literature and provide essential implications for the work at hand. The following presents a few results of a broad literature review.

[11] concludes that OSS development supports a normative character to follow collective goals which is also found in the present study. The use of OSS by companies and provision of self-developed OSS is investigated by [9]. Even though [9] analyzes the topic within the domain of software developing companies, his work provides profound discussion of motivations and incentives that support the assumptions made here. [17] analyze individual and group-related dynamics of motivations in a work-context from an organization-psychological perspective and provide substantial ideas about motivational theories and etiquette norms. [2, 22] support the findings about the motivations and incentives that are specific for the participation in OSS development in particular. The findings concerning the development platform and other infrastructure by [1] and [5] can be applied for a subsequent analysis of the influence of technical infrastructure on the design of a motivational context and vice versa. [20] focus on the initiation of OSS development projects and come up with a model of three phases. These findings lead to the hypothesis that the motivations might differ along the development process.

As shown by the examples above, a profound body of research concerning the single core aspects of the present study exists, especially from the 2000s. A research gap can be located in the combination of these specific aspects, which leads to the focus of this study: The combination of the aspects of OSS development, its initiation by a company, and especially the incentives and motivational aspects that need to be implemented in the development context.

3   Research Design

To obtain further information about motivational aspects in collective development, a survey among potential developers was conducted. The questionnaire including all answers and further information about the survey can be obtained from the authors.

The selection of participants for the survey was not a random sample, but a closed survey among all members of three networks that are affiliated with OSS development and use in business context. Thus, this can be considered a partial survey of consciously selected typical cases [19, p. 260]. At the time of the survey (11/24/2014) all 416 approached persons were listed as members of the networks Open Source Business Alliance, Open Source Business Foundation and Eclipse. The following possible relations and statements were the basis for questions in the questionnaire:

(a) The development of OSS differs from the development of PS. Answers could possibly point out the differences regarding voluntary vs. contracted participation, time span of development and structure of development.
(b) OSS development can be structured in phases. Since incentives and motivations might differ along the development process, a structuring of this process into phases could be convenient to structure the incentives and motivations [20].
(c) Companies and individuals need incentives for participating in software development.
(d) Collective work holds strong codes [6]. These codes differ depending on the considered collective and the use of a certain hard-/software, respectful behavior, etc.
(e) The participation of companies in OSS development can be in conflict with the collective codes.
(f) The choice of a suitable development platform can be crucial to the participation of individuals. An established, not project-specific platform could be favorable, as it might be more popular or users know how it works, respectively.

These questions are supported by related findings in research (see Sect. 2). All answers were read and corresponding categories were formed. The answers were then counted to determine the frequency according to these categories [19]. The results are thus to be interpreted as indicators, also due to a relatively small number of responses (in total 37).

4 Results and Discussion

The choice of participants proved to be beneficial, as most answers were very detailed. The tone of the answers was emotional. This leads to the interpretation that this survey tackled sensitive aspects of the assumed collective codes (statement d).

As differences between the development of PS and OSS (see statement a), the participants (number of mentions in brackets) listed the following aspects: transparency of the used programs (3), OSS is more secure (2), OSS makes more independent (3). (6) agreed with the structure of OSS development into private phase, transfer phase and public phase (statement b). (4) replied that the project should be publicly available as soon as possible. Concerning the question, which activities are located in which phases, answers with respect to the private phase are that a first operational version should be developed (4) and that the ideas and concepts should be documented (2). Concerning a transfer phase participants responded that the project would have to be advertised and other stakeholders should be sought (2). During the public phase, the initiators should be present and available for inquiries (2). The participation of a company in collective development is rejected by no participant (statement e). The answers regarding possible motivations for participating (statement c) are the direct benefit of the software, the associated feedback (5), reputation (2) as well as the motivation as a hobby and social interaction. In addition, the respondents name effectiveness and self-interest regarding software required for their own needs (4). To keep the participants active the initiators should be present and make informed decisions (2). Regarding the choice of platform participants uniformly stated that an established platform should be deployed (6), as this creates advertising and confidence (see statement f). It is mentioned (1) that an OSS platform like SourceForge should be used, since some, like GitHub are based on PS (statement d).

It can be concluded from the findings of the survey and the prior research that the sensitivities and emotions of the participants should be closely observed in order to avoid negative dynamics. To appreciate the "pro-social norms" ("prosoziale Normen", [15, p. 215]) and thereby achieve the acceptance of the collective, the company itself should be part of the collective. This can be considered as "generalized norm of reciprocity" ("generalisierte Reziprozitätsnorm", [15, p. 215]). Trust appears as a fundamental dynamic in the OS development [21]. If the intentions of the initiators or the motivation of those involved are not clear, this can also result in distrust and consequently the leaving of the collective [10].

The motivational system in Fig. 3 allows connecting motives, motivations, set incentives, and the motivational contexts. The motivational contexts are understood as the actual operationalization of the incentives by the initiating company, based on the incentives that are identified to trigger the perceived motivations.

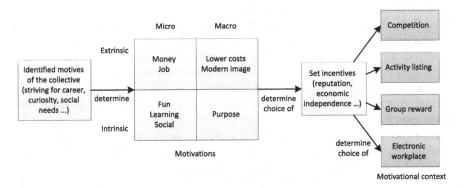

Fig. 3. Motivational system

As a first step when using the motivational system the motives of the participants of the targeted collective have to be analyzed, because the perceived motives determine the motivations. The identified motivations determine the setting of incentives, both from the micro and the macro view. Based on these insights, the initiating company can design and apply a fitting motivational context.

The following example may illustrate the theory proposed above. The motivation to lower costs from the macro view might determine the elimination of certain incentives that are high in costs, e.g. the free of charge provision of an electronic workplace to the developers as motivational context, serving the incentive of economic independence. Thus, the set incentives determine which motivational context fits. Competitions could be used as a context to address the extrinsic motivation [14, p. 29]. Any potential negative effects on intrinsic motivation should be considered, e.g., when triggering extrinsic motivation by offering paid jobs to the participants of the collective, for maintaining the artefact later on.

The motivational system should not only serve for attracting participants, but also support an active participation for the required duration. The design of the motivational context should therefore support the necessary activities in a prioritized structure and with respect to the different phases of the development process. The documentation should also be included in the motivational system. This still applies if self-determined onboarding and deboarding is a desired organizational property regarding the key partnerships.

5   Conclusion

There appears to be a strong interest in the collective development of OSS among different groups of stakeholders, e.g. scientists, companies as well as independent individuals. Since well-established OSS development models do not exist for the discussed context, there is room for research efforts. While both organizational and technical aspects of software development might be similar comparing traditional and OSS development, especially the cultural aspects seem to differ to a notable degree. Hence an important step was taken in this paper by providing indications for the design of a motivational context and system, respectively. When changing towards this more virtual form of organization, implementing a motivational system facilitates meeting new requirements for setting incentives. Connecting these ideas with scientific findings concerning leadership in virtual communities and mapping this to a Business Model Canvas [16] could improve the understanding of how to transform successfully into a, maybe partly, virtual organization. This promises to be interesting for future research.

Analyzing and respecting codes and etiquette of the targeted collective prove to be fundamental for successful business-driven OSS development. An example beyond the domain of software development is studied by [14], concerning the collective dynamics of the advertising campaign of ketchup manufacturer Heinz, who was blamed to exploit the unpaid collective work. To understand and avoid this failing of projects, the single aspects of the motivational system and their relationships as shown in Fig. 3 need to be validated. This will be further elicited through more extensive empirical research and related case studies of successful and failed cases.

References

1. Ågerfalk, P.J., Fitzgerald, B.: Outsourcing to an unknown workforce: exploring opensourcing as a global sourcing strategy. MIS Q. **32**(2), 385–409 (2008)

2. Benbya, H., Belbaly, N.: A multi-theoretical framework of motivation in open source. In: Mediterranean Conference on Information Systems Proceedings, Tel Aviv, Israel, paper 13. AISeL (2010)
3. Benkler, Y.: The Wealth of Networks. Yale University Press, New Haven (2006)
4. Bergquist, M., Ljungberg, J.: The power of gifts: organizing social relationships in open source communities. Inf. Syst. J. **11**(4), 305–320 (2001)
5. Brügge, B., Fiedler, M., Harhoff, D., Picot, A., Creighton, O., Henkel, J.: Open-Source-Software: Eine ökonomische und technische Analyse. Springer, Berlin (2008)
6. Eseryel, U.: Open innovation/open source leadership. In: Proceedings of the Americas Conference on Information Systems, AIS, Savannah, USA, pp. 1–10/2488–2499 (2014)
7. Feller, J., Fitzgerald, B.: Understanding Open Source Software Development. Addison-Wesley, Amsterdam (2002)
8. Fuggetta, A.: Open source software - an evaluation. J. Syst. Softw. **66**(1), 77–90 (2003)
9. Henkel, J.: Offene Innovationsprozesse - Die kommerzielle Entwicklung von Open-Source-Software. Habilitationsschrift University Munich. Deutscher Universitätsverlag, Wiesbaden (2007)
10. Lattemann, C., Stieglitz, S.: Framework for governance in open source communities. In: Proceedings of the 38th Hawaii International Conference on System Sciences, Hawai'I, USA, p. 192a. IEEE, New York (2005)
11. Lehmbach, J.: Vorgehensmodelle im Spannungsfeld traditioneller, agiler und Open-Source-Softwareentwicklung, Analyse, Vergleich, Bewertung. Dissertation. ibidem-Verlag, Marburg (2006)
12. Leimeister, J.M.: Collective Intelligence. Bus. Inf. Syst. Eng. **4**(2), 245–248 (2010)
13. Leimeister, J.M., Huber, M., Bretschneider, U., Krcmar, H.: Leveraging crowdsourcing: activation-supporting components for IT-based ideas competition. J. Manag. Inf. Syst. **26**(1), 197–224 (2009)
14. Malone, T., Laubacher, R., Dellarocas, C.: The collective intelligence genome. MIT Sloan Manag. Rev. **51**(3), 20–31 (2010)
15. Osterloh, M., Rota, S., Kuster, B.: Die kommerzielle Nutzung von open-source-software. Z. Führung + Organisation **71**(4), 211–217 (2002)
16. Osterwalder, A., Pigneur, Y.: Business Model Generation, A Handbook for Visionaries, Game Changers, and Challengers. John Wiley & Sons, New Jersey (2010)
17. von Rosenstiel, L., Nerdinger, F.: Grundlagen der Organisationspsychologie. Basiswissen und Anwendungshinweise, 7th edn. Schäffer-Poeschel, Stuttgart (2011)
18. Schlagwein, D., Bjørn-Andersen, N.: Organizational learning with crowdsourcing: the revelatory case of LEGO. J. Assoc. Inf. Syst. **15**(11), 754–778 (2014)
19. Schnell, R., Hill, P., Esser, E.: Methoden der empirischen Sozialforschung. Oldenburg Verlag, München (2013)
20. Senyard, A., Michlmayr, M.: How to have a successful free software project. In: Proceedings of the 11th Asia-Pacific Software Engineering Conference, Busan, Korea, pp. 84–91/1–8. ACM, New York (2004)
21. Sharma, S., Sugumaran, V., Rajagopalan, B.: A framework for creating hybrid-open source software communities. Inf. Syst. J. **12**, 7–25 (2002)
22. von Krogh, G., Haefliger, S., Spaeth, S., Wallin, M.W.: Carrots and rainbows: motivation and social practice in open source software. MIS Q. **36**(2), 649–676 (2012)

Attributes of User Engagement for Website Development

Jurgis Senbergs and Marite Kirikova[✉]

Department of Artificial Intelligence and Systems Engineering,
Riga Technical University, 1 Kalku, Riga 1568, Latvia
{marite.kirikova,jurgis.senbergs}@rtu.lv

Abstract. Recently, many webpage development companies have invested a lot of time and money into the user experience research. Together with the whole information technology industry, webpage development is moving in the direction of creating easy and useful solutions for their target audiences. It is important to understand what makes an enjoyable user experience and engages users into using webpages. While user engagement has been recognized as an important issue by scientists and practitioners, still, a systematic review of different aspects of user engagement and corresponding user experience enhancement practices is not available. Therefore, the goal of this paper is to link findings of research in user engagement with the best practices and trends in the user experience design and website development; and to propose recommendations for developing engaging websites.

Keywords: User engagement · Flow theory · User experience · Website development

1 Introduction

Availability of the internet has spread fast around the world; prices of technologies to access the internet are falling down, which makes the World Wide Web (WWW) very crowded. Just the presence of the companies on the Internet is not enough anymore; users have to have a pleasant and enjoyable experience while visiting the websites of the enterprises. Otherwise the enterprises might loose their customers or miss the opportunities to acquire new customers via their websites. Recently, many webpage development companies have invested time and money into the user experience (UX) research; now it is common that even a small website development companies hire UX specialists. Together with the whole information technology (IT) industry, WWW is moving towards easy and useful solutions for target audiences. It is important to understand what makes an enjoyable UX and consequently engages users into using the webpages.

While user engagement has been recognized as an important issue by scientists and practitioners, still a systematic review of different aspects of user engagement and corresponding UX enhancement practices is not available. Therefore, the goal of this paper is to link findings of research in user engagement with the best practices and trends of a nowadays UX design and website development. To achieve this goal the following research activities were performed: (1) to review the literature on user engagement;

© Springer International Publishing Switzerland 2016
V. Řepa and T. Bruckner (Eds.): BIR 2016, LNBIP 261, pp. 130–144, 2016.
DOI: 10.1007/978-3-319-45321-7_10

(2) to reveal the most important attributes of user engagement; (3) to propose links between the attributes of user engagement and website development best practices; (4) to propose the recommendations for engaging website development on the basis of the discovered linkage; (5) to build a website for testing the applicability of the recommendations.

The paper is organized as follows: Sect. 2 introduces the related work on user engagement and amalgamates and presents the list of relevant engagement attributes. Section 3 proposes links between attributes of user engagement and website development best practices. In Sect. 4, the recommendations for developing websites, taking into account findings from previous sections, are proposed and briefly discussed. Conclusions are provided in Sect. 5.

2   Related Work on User Engagement

The goal of this section is to find common attributes and properties among several theories and models, which describe user engagement.

Majority of research papers on user engagement mention or use as the basis the "flow theory" by Mihaly Csikszentmihalyi. Other papers for review were selected by relevance to the goal of this paper and the popularity in the field, which was determined by the number of citations.

Regarding the flow theory, the term "flow" describing the human experience is first defined in 1975 by Mihaly Csikszentmihalyi [1]. He describes that *"in the flow state, action follows upon action according to an internal logic that seems to need no conscious intervention by the actor. He experiences it as a unified flowing from one moment to the next, in which he is in control of his actions and in which there is little distinction between self and environment, between stimulus and response, or between past, present, and future."*

In flow state no goal is as important as the process, so even after a person has achieved the goal, s/he looks for the next one just to experience the flow again. However, the *"flow seems to occur only when tasks are within one's ability to perform. That is why one experiences flow most often in activities with clearly established rules for action."* Having right amount of skills to perform particular activity is very important. With the lack of skills the anxiety increases, while being overqualified makes one bored. Research also states that the attention of the person has to be concentrated on a limited stimulus field, or in other words – consciousness has to be narrowed. In the flow state the person receives unambiguous feedback to her/his actions making her/him aware of how is s/he doing – good or bad. *"But in flow, one does not stop to evaluate the feedback; action and reaction have become so well practiced as to be automatic."*

In 2004 M. Csikszentmihalyi in his TED Talk [2] summarized characteristics of the flow state in 7 items presented in the first column of Table 1: (1) completely involved in what we are doing – focused, concentrated; (2) a sense of ecstasy – of being outside everyday reality; (3) great inner clarity – knowing what needs to be done, and how well we are doing; (4) knowing that the activity is doable – that skills are adequate to the task; (5) a sense of serenity – no worries about oneself, and a feeling of growing beyond the boundaries of the ego; (6) timelessness – thoroughly focused on the present, hours seem to pass by in minutes; and (7) intrinsic motivation – whatever produces flow becomes its own reward. A more detailed Flow model [2] was also provided, which shows a total of 8 states. *Apathy* being the opposite of the *flow* is a negative feeling, when there is no challenge and one does not need to use one's skills, it can be experienced, e.g., while watching TV. *Worry* is the state when the person feels that her skills might not be enough to finish the task, while *anxiety* state is when the person knows for sure that s/he is not capable of finishing the task, because either challenge is too high or qualification is too low. *Boredom* is the state when one is overqualified for the given task, *relaxation* is a more challenging state, but still not very exciting. Then come the 3 most positive states – *control, arousal,* and *flow.* In the *arousal* area, the person is over challenged, the skill set is not sufficient, but it is quite easy to get in the flow state by improving the skills; this is the area where most people learn as they have been pushed out of their comfort zone. In *control* area the challenges are not very exciting, so in order to enter the flow, the level of challenges has to be raised. *Flow state* is the balance between challenges and skills; in the web development context, challenges can be associated with the goals or tasks the person has when visiting the page; - these can be finding information, buying a product or service, or having fun. The skills required to do such tasks can be: information searching, form filling, and website browsing. The balance between challenges and skills has to be considered when designing websites. It can be expected, that designing the website with *Flow state* attributes in mind (Table 1), the visitors might be able to enter the *Flow state* and become engaged with the webpage.

Table 1. Engagement attributes

Flow theory	Website attributes and web performance	Aesthetic experience	User engagement with technology
Focused, concentrated	Control	Unity/Wholeness	Aesthetic and sensory
A sense of ecstasy	Attention	Focused attention	appeal
Great inner clarity	Curiosity	Active discovery	Attention
Knowing that the	Intrinsic interest	Affect	Awareness
activity is doable		Intrinsic gratification	Control
No worries about		or felt freedom	Interactivity
oneself			Novelty
Timelessness			Challenge
Intrinsic motivation			Feedback
			Interest
			Positive affect

In early days of the WWW websites mostly were designed for practical goals. The main purpose was to provide the information to users. Since that time a lot has changed and now web developers are looking for ways to create websites that are both utilitarian and hedonic [3]. Therefore, it is interesting what is the role of web attributes in user engagement, i.e., in what way they can influence the web performance and whether correct use of them can provide users with *experiential flow.* "*Attributes are features or aspects of a website. Users see each website as a bundle of attributes with varying capacities to satisfy their needs.*" Attributes can be classified as user-oriented and technology-oriented; - the first ones are qualitative experiences of users, while the second ones are structural properties of the site. In [3], three main groups of website attributes were identified: complexity, novelty, and interactivity. *Complexity* is described as the amount of information provided by the website, if there is a vast amount of information, the website is considered complex. A good example of the complexity would be a website containing laws or standards with a large amount of text and paragraphs. *Novelty* can be novel experiences or information, or both at the same time. These are website elements that users find new, unexpected, or surprising. At some point these attributes become used to and are not novel any more, - a good example of such case is Google Maps. When they implemented Street View feature, it was something new and surprising, people used to browse the streets for no reason, just to see what the technology can do. *Interactivity* is an exchange of information between the user and the website. Interactivity is the main attribute, which distinguishes websites from other media types, although nowadays the smart TVs are providing similar features. Meaning of interactivity is further explained with following seven sub-attributes: Responsiveness - the ability of the website to provide the user with required information; Individualization - the ability of the website to provide the user with personalized information; Navigability - connectedness of the website, how well the information is connected among the parts of the website; Reciprocity - two-way information exchange between the user and the website; Synchronicity - the ability of website to provide real-time bidirectional feedback; Participation - the ability of the website to allow users create content; Demonstrability - the ability of the website to simulate or incorporate humanlike characteristics.

Huang [3] reduces *flow experience* to four main attributes (see Table 1): (1) Control, - sense of control over the website; (2) Attention, - how focused users are on the interaction; (3) Curiosity, - how aroused curiosity is during the interaction; and (4) Interest, - intrinsic interest in interaction of users. The author of [3] uses the concept of utilitarian and hedonic needs of users to better understand their experience. *Utilitarian* performance represents the practical goals of users, whether they have found what they looked for; *hedonic* web performance represents the emotional experiences when visiting the site, like amount of fun, pleasure, or playfulness. The model of how each of the attributes impact the UX is also proposed in [3]. The results of the research shows that complex sites are considered useful by users, but the main attribute that provides the hedonic and flow experience is interactivity. Novelty raises the flow experience, but undermines the hedonic performance.

Study [4] discusses the importance of fulfilling the customer needs to achieve business goals. Business processes must be aligned with the services provided by the website to create a good UX. It is important that business supports and responds promptly to user questions and feedback, as well as provides high quality services like fast shipping, easy refunding system and other services.

Theoretical background of *aesthetic experience* (AE) comes from centuries of philosophical discussions. The research in [5] studies both *flow experience* and *aesthetic experience* in the context of developing engaging and immersive websites. In their research the authors of [5] outline the main characteristics of AE (see also Table 1). *Unity/Wholeness* comes from the feeling of a high level of integration and coherence of all components related to the experience. *Focused attention* or *Object directedness* is intense absorption in an activity where our attention is "undivided". *Active discovery* is *"the excitement of meeting a cognitive challenge"* and *"insight into connections and organizations – the elation that comes from the apparent opening up of intelligibility"*. *Affect* is the spice that flavours experience and keeps us coming back for more. *"Emotion carries the experience forward, binding parts and moments together"*. *Intrinsic gratification* or *Felt freedom* is *"both a continuing enjoyment that is felt as part of the development of the experience and a final satisfaction or fulfilment that may linger after the experience has ended"*. *Intrinsic gratification* does not need external rewards: the focus is on the process, rather than the ultimate arrival. The authors of [5] provide also a comparison between AE and *Flow Experience* (FE). Based on interviews with professional developers *Aesthetic framework* is proposed which provides sub-attributes for each of main AE attributes [5].

The process of engagement can be described in four stages: point of engagement, period of engagement, disengagement, and reengagement, according to [6]. For each stage several attributes, which promote or demote engagement, are defined (see the last column in Table 1).

Above we have reviewed several research papers on user engagement. They all use some common attributes for describing engagement as a phenomenon. Some researches, [1, 3, 5], describe the required conditions to have positive UX and become engaged in the action, others - [4, 6], describe the process or steps required to engage someone into the activity.

The flow theory has a simple concept that has been linked with engagement. It is a ratio between the challenges, which are created by the action, and the skills required to fulfil the task. When the ratio is optimal one enters the flow state, which is described by seven attributes. Other researches, [3, 5], are constructed on the basis of these attributes or have similar attributes without linking them to the flow theory. Only [4] is not concerned with the engagement attributes, it has a wider scope and looks at the steps that a customer has to take to become engaged in a product, a service, or a company, so in this section we will not use this source for identifying main attributes of user engagement.

In Table 1 all the attributes from researches [1, 3, 5, 6] are listed.

For structuring the further discussion in this paper, the attributes represented in Table 1 are grouped in five groups. The grouping is based on attribute semantic similarity and the first author's years of experience in website development. The following groups of attributes will be used in the remainder of the paper (each group includes also the attribute with the same name as the group, i.e., the groups are named by the key attribute): (1) **Interest** – Interest, Intrinsic interest, Curiosity, Intrinsic motivation; (2) **Challenge** – Challenge, Active Discovery, Knowing that the activity is doable, Intrinsic Gratification or Felt Freedom, Unity/Wholeness; (3) **Focus** – Focused, concentrated, Focused attention, Attention; (4) **Control** – Control, Great inner clarity, Interactivity, Feedback, Awareness; (5) **Affect** – A sense of ecstasy, No worries about oneself, Timelessness, Affect, Aesthetic and Sensory Appeal, Novelty, Positive Affect.

The order of the groups has been chosen to match the website development process, but some activities and tasks will be discussed not strictly following this sequence, because the design and development process is not a linear activity. Majority of the above listed attributes are not technical ones. In the next sections we will link these attributes to practical and technical tools and methods to apply them to website development.

3   Mappings Between User Engagement Attributes and Possible Methods of Their Support

In the previous section we listed attributes of user engagement, which were found in four different research papers. In this section, for every group of attributes defined in Sect. 2, a way of how to apply them in the website development is proposed. In Figs. 1, 2, 3, 4 and 5 the attributes of each group are listed on the left side. The solutions that constitute the user engagement are on the right side. Based on the information sources indicated next to the solutions (in square brackets), the attributes are linked to certain solutions that are said to achieve engaging effects corresponding to these attributes.

In Fig. 1 the attributes of group Interest are shown.

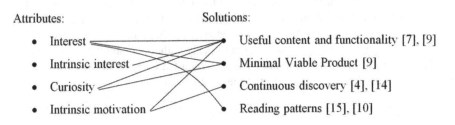

Fig. 1. Attributes of group Interest and corresponding solutions to meet them

In order to attract the interest of visitors, a website has to have a useful content or functionality. According to the article [7], *"Consumers are not interested in products and services. They are interested in problems and solutions."* Today the central role of defining requirements and outcomes of the website is shifted towards users' feedback [8]. *"Ultimately, the success or failure of your product isn't the team's decision—it's the customers'. They will have to click that "Buy Now" button you designed. The sooner you give them a voice, the sooner you'll learn whether you've got an idea that's ready to be built."* So getting out of the building or GOOB principle is proposed. It is based on the previous experience of requirements gathering process, where actual user needs will not be discovered sitting in the office and discussing them [9]. A website should not be developed for everybody, it is recommended to narrow the scope in the beginning, so that the website is targeted for a specific audience. When a solid amount of information about the users is gathered, customer personas (specific description of the customers) should be created [10, 11]. After the personas have been created, actions users take in order to accomplish their goals or tasks can be represented in user scenarios [10]. The user scenarios can be written in different forms – written narratives, visual storyboards, comic strips, or even videos [12]. Another method of representing scenarios is user scenario mapping – *"attempting to map out all the steps that a user will take to complete a task, with an initial focus on what your user will do, not necessarily how he or she will do it"* [12]. One more useful approach is so called *Minimum Viable Products*

(MVPs) [9]. It suggests to define the minimal functionality required to run the product, so it can be given to users as early as possible and learning process can start at the very early stage of software development. This greatly reduces "waste" – if the functionality or feature is not used or should be changed. It is easier to change or remove it in the early stages of development than after the website is fully finished and refined. Wireframing and prototyping can be used to test ideas before any development is done to save time and resources [13]. To establish *continuous discovery process*, the feedback from the users has to be collected. The good example of determining the usefulness of the content is a small feedback form provided in online support of Microsoft or Pinterest approach to allow users to mark/report pins that users consider unhelpful or any other way inappropriate. To determine usefulness of the functionality, the analytics can be set up to track the user interactions with the elements of the website [14].

Reading patterns can be taken into consideration to organize the information according to reading habits, e.g., for more dense texts, F shaped pattern can be used [15] and for simpler texts – Z shaped pattern [10].

Thus, in order to attract user interest, the following activities are advised: find out user needs; provide useful content and functionality; start small and reach users early; put the most important content in the places where users look; use analytics to determine usefulness of content or functionality; continuously gather and apply user feedback.

Figure 2 reflects engagement attributes of group Challenge and the corresponding solutions to satisfy users with respect to these attributes.

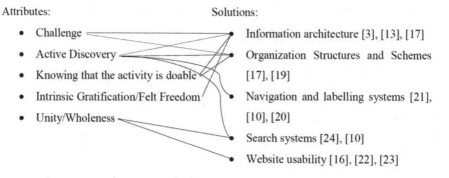

Fig. 2. Attributes of group Challenge and corresponding solutions to meet them

In Sect. 2 it was discussed that the challenge cannot be viewed separately from the skillset of the users. The websites with wide range of options might overwhelm visitors and make them feel that their skills are inadequate for challenges posed by the webpage [3]. Users get excited when they meet the cognitive challenge [5] and elation is felt when understanding how the website is structured. The website has to be developed in the way to give the visitors a clear way of discovering what they were looking for. This can be achieved with the help of *information architecture* [11] and by improving usability of the site [16]. The information architecture is defined as *"the structural design of an information space to facilitate task completion and intuitive access to content"* [13]. The information architecture for the WWW is concerned with the following main

Attributes: Solutions:

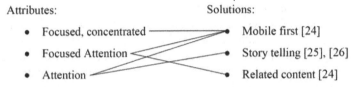

- Focused, concentrated
- Focused Attention
- Attention

- Mobile first [24]
- Story telling [25], [26]
- Related content [24]

Fig. 3. Attributes of group Focus and corresponding solutions to meet them

systems [17]: (1) organization structures and schemes: how the information is structured and categorized; (2) labelling systems: how the information is presented; (3) navigation systems: how the information is browsed by the users; (3) search systems: how the users look for information. In order to design such systems, the connection among the Users (audience, tasks, needs, information-seeking, experience), Context (business goals, funding, politics, culture, technology, resources, constraints), and Content (content objectives, document and data types, volume, existing structure, governance, and ownership) has to be understood [17].

Every website has a message it wants to clearly deliver to its visitors. But it is not easy to *organize and structure* the information in the way that users will find it easy to browse and find what they need. The ways how visitors seek for information [18] should be taken into account. Card sorting [19] is suggested as one of the methods for seeking the right structure and organization of the text [19]. In a larger website it is challenging to come up with a good navigation system and labels for it. Navigation of the website can be designed by main navigation with submenus or main navigation with drop down menus, and navigation with or without breadcrumbs. There have been studies showing that users do not like drop down menus, even worse, they find them annoying [20]. It is also important to know how many items should be put in the navigation. There have been studies researching the optimal number of items in navigation and have come up with contradictory results [21]. The reason of such results was found to be the quality of labeling the navigation items. The results of the research showed that target content was found much faster with high quality link labels than those with poor quality, regardless of the structure of the navigation. It can be concluded that the proper labeling of items is more important than the number of items in the navigation menu. To keep users informed about their current place in the site, navigation item highlighting, breadcrumbs, and the use of consistent headings are recommended [10].

Search systems can help to achieve unity (wholeness) of the website. *Website usability* is described by several elements – consistency of the interface, response time, mapping and metaphors, interaction styles and multimedia and audio-visuals [22], or ease-of-navigation, speed, and interactivity [16, 23].

Thus, to balance the challenges with skills of visitors, the following activities are advised: design the website with consistency in core of it; structure and organize the information in understandable way for visitors; provide clear labeling for information and navigation; provide clear feedback of the user's current location; improve performance of the website.

The attributes of group Focus and solutions suggested for user satisfaction with respect to them are shown in Fig. 3.

The goal of this group of attributes is to keep users' focus on the website. This is not an easy task, because of so many distractions around us today – mobile phones, radios, TVs, etc. Above we have already discussed some approaches that help to keep the users focused, namely, the interests of users taken into consideration and provided meaningful structure to find what they need, and trying to focus their attention on the content or functionality they are interested in. *Mobile first* [24] website development has almost become standard for every developer in recent years. When development process is started from the smallest screen, careful consideration has to be made of what is the goal of the website and what is the most valuable content that a page has to provide to visitors. *Story telling* is another popular approach of attracting the attention of users and keeping them focused on the content the website is providing. According to several research papers [25], a reader or a listener experiences the same sensations as the main character of the story [26]. According to Harvard Business Review article [8], it was found that e-commerce customers became more engaged when a wider scope of information related to products were provided. This shows that customers are more dedicated to buy products, when their imagination has created feelings or experiences from information and stories. Story telling then can also be linked to intrinsic motivation (group Interest) and intrinsic gratification (group Challenge). When there are multiple similar choices and visitors have not decided what to do next or they want to see more of a content [24], *related content* can help to keep users engaged with the website.

Thus, for keeping users focused on a website, the following approaches are suggested: develop mobile first to discover the most important content; tell the story in the content to induce feeling in visitors; and provide related content to keep users focused.

In Fig. 4, the attributes of group Control are presented. In the simple websites users usually are in control, thus, the main focus there is on usefulness of the content. But in more complex websites, e.g., hotel or flight booking websites, it is important to consider solutions presented in Fig. 4. *Input fields* and forms are among the most complex elements for both, developers and users. Over the last few years, the analytics of the websites has improved significantly and a lot of examples of online form optimization have appeared on the web. One of the most prominent examples was the Expedia removal of one input filed in their booking form which resulted in an extra $12 million profit for the company [24].

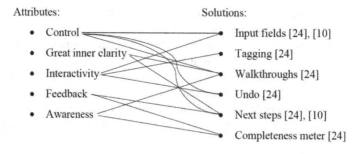

Fig. 4. Attributes of group Control and corresponding solutions to meet them

When a website has a large amount of data, *tagging* can help to organize the content in logical structures [24]. For complex websites like web applications that comprise many functions and features, *walkthroughs* are a very useful tool to give users the feeling of control. In a walkthrough it is possible to introduce users to the user interface, the basic usage and a workflow of the application, or some more advanced features that might be hidden in submenus. The possibility to *undo* also enables the users to feel as being in control [24]. Websites, that highly rely on user generated content and require the input from users, can apply thea list of *next steps* to take to finish an action or a task [10, 24]. This gives users a clear understanding of what to do next and makes them feel in control of the tasks. To give the user a feedback of the status of the task or activity a *completeness meter* is a good solution. It can show the completeness of the user's profile, asking her or him to add more information to reach the 100% in completeness meter. Also the multi-step forms are in use, where the user can see how many steps have been done and how many steps are still ahead [24].

Thus, for giving users a sense of control, the following activities are advised: simplify all inputs, provide tips or make them human language like; provide feedback when the user is filling forms or fulfilling the task; provide tips for next steps or actions; show the progress of the task.

In Fig. 5, the attributes and corresponding solutions of group Affect are shown.

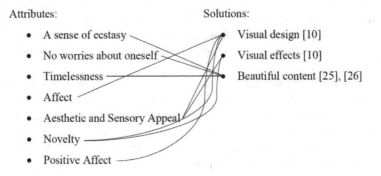

Fig. 5. Attributes of group Affect and corresponding solutions to meet them

The attributes of this group are rather subjective and the ways of achieving such properties will also be subjective. The goal is to be liked by the larger group of people. This can be achieved with a good *visual design* [10] and widely adopted and well know elements of the websites like navigation, media and inputs, which have been discussed in previous sections. Regarding *visual effects*, web technologies are progressing, equipping web developers with better and better tools, such as HTML5 and CSS3, that help making UX smoother. Aesthetically beautiful sites should not necessary have a beautiful design; they can even have a very ascetic design if the *content is beautiful*. Usually these are sites containing such artefacts as beautiful pictures, music, or videos.

Thus, to help to induce the positive affect, the following activities are suggested: use refined visual design; add visual effects to create sensation of continuity; use beautiful content and media to engage users.

4   Recommendations for Developing Engaging Websites

On the basis of information amalgamated in previous sections, the recommendations for designing engaging websites are proposed in this section. The purpose of the recommendations is to highlight, which engagement support methods have to be best considered at which functional areas of website development.

User research area. Websites should be designed for specific target audience and specific problem solving. To better understand the problem and how to solve it, the user research should be done. The following methods are recommended in this functional area of website development:

- *Define personas* [10, 11]. It is important to find the main customers first, – the people for whom the website will help to solve the problems. All the customers have some kind of problems, but not all problems or solutions have customers. Define several Personas and add good amount of details – age, gender, name, interests, to their description. Details will help to predict their problems and how to solve them. Visit and speak to people that are in the target audience, gather the data about them: what they like to do, what are their expectations. Then attach that data to Personas to make them conform to real life persons.
- *Write user scenarios* [10, 12]. Define realistic goals for Personas. Write the scenarios, where Personas try to resolve their problems with the help of the website. These can be written as steps required to achieve the goals of the customers. The scenarios will help to understand the structure of future website, as the steps will represent actions users have to take.
- *Test assumptions* [9]. When the target audience and their problems are defined, it is important to verify if they are true. This is again the time to go out and talk to people that match the target audience. The most difficult task in this activity is to know how to talk to the potential users. Questions have to be cleverly formulated otherwise interviews may lead to completely unusable data. It is because people are more optimistic and willing when there is no need for real action, but when they have to do it in real life, they are more reserved. Here are a few examples of how to talk to people: avoid asking if they would like to buy a product or service, but try to find out whether they use similar products or services; avoid asking if they have a specific kind of problems, but try to find out what they would do in the situation where the problem would occur; avoid giving them answer options to the question, let them give their own answers.

Feature selection area. When the target audience and their problems are researched, it is time to find the right solutions. Taking into account results from user research, the features of the website should be prioritized by the importance to the users. The following methods supporting user engagement are recommended for this functional area of website development:

- *Minimum Viable Product (MVP)* [9]. When defining MVP, it is important to understand what knowledge is to be learned. In most cases it is important to know is there a need for a solution to be designed, is there a value in the solution, and will users will be able to use it. After answering these questions respective features for MVP should be selected.

- *Select engaging features.* MVP is a good starting point, but alone will not provide engaging experience for website users. In Sect. 3 engaging attributes and activities to implement them in website development were described in detail. Here a summarized list of activities that help making website engaging is provided:
  - Put the most important content in the places where users look [10, 15]
  - Use analytics to determine usefulness of content or functionality [7, 14]
  - Provide easy means to submit feedback [14]
  - Design the website with consistency in core of it [16]
  - Structure and organize information in an understandable way for users [11]
  - Provide clear labelling for information and navigation [10, 21, 22]
  - Provide clear feedback of user's current location [24]
  - Improve performance of the website [23]
  - Develop mobile first to discover the most important content [24]
  - Use story telling in the content to induce feelings in visitors [25, 26]
  - Provide related content to keep users focused [24]
  - Simplify inputs, provide tips or make them human language like [10, 24]
  - Provide feedback when the user is filling forms or fulfilling a task [10, 24]
  - Provide tips for next steps or actions [10, 24]
  - Show the progress of the task [24]
  - Use refined visual design [10]
  - Add visual effects to create sensation of continuity [10]
  - Use beautiful content and media to engage users [25, 26].

Prototyping area. Prototyping [13] can save a lot of time in finding and testing the best solutions for user problems. There are several kinds of prototypes, each having advantages and disadvantages. The choice of the right kind of the prototype should be based on the available resources.

- *Low-Fidelity Prototypes.* These can be paper or digital prototypes. Paper prototypes are very easy to make, only basic skills are needed and it requires only paper, pencils or pens, and tape. This kind of prototyping allows easy collaboration among team members because everyone can participate and see the result. It is creative process and people, who spend the most of the time at computer screens, might enjoy spending time doing something non-digital.
- *Wireframes.* Wireframes are digital cousins of paper prototypes. Wireframes can be plain non-functional or with basic interactions (clickable). There are many tools that provide wireframe drawing, e.g., a well-known Microsoft Visio. This kind of prototype will give better insight on interactions with the website and the steps users will need to take to accomplish their goals.
- *Mid and High Fidelity Prototypes* [9]. Mid and high fidelity prototypes show a lot more resemblance to the final product, the level of detail for visual design; interactions and content design come close to the expected end result. For this kind of prototypes there are also several tools available, some provide lower other higher

level of interactivity, some tools have options for animations, transitions and other effects. Examples of such tools are inVision, Justinmind, and Moqups.

- *Coded prototypes* [9]. Coded prototypes offer the highest level of fidelity: people interacting with this kind of prototypes should not recognize that these are prototypes. These prototypes include all the elements of the final product – form fields, menus, buttons, and functions. The development of this kind of prototypes takes more time than all previously mentioned prototypes, but code from the prototype can later be used in production version of the website.

Ensuring high quality service across the whole organization area. It is not enough to provide *tools for giving the feedback* – contact form, online chat, and other tools. The organization has to have *the procedures how to process the information on feedbacks*, so the visitors get the feeling that their feedback matters. The same applies to other services like shipping goods or refunding money. If *organizational processes* do not support website functionality, it will not be possible to engage users [4].

Continuous improvement area. Even when a website is published, the work is not finished. There can be features that were not implemented, because they had low priority. Analytics might indicate weaknesses of the website. There can be many more reasons, why the website should be kept improved over the time. Not all websites generate enough income to be improved frequently; in these cases thorough analysis of analytical data from time to time and minor adjustments will be satisfactory. Improvements to published websites can be applied in the same way as described in above-discussed areas: by researching users and testing improvements before they are applied to the websites. At this point analytical data can help to find parts of the websites that should be improved. Such methods as *A/B testing* and *multivariate testing* can be used on published websites with real users to test new ideas or improvements.

Each functional area in the recommendations is related to at least one of the attributes discussed in the previous section. To test the recommendations, they were applied in the development of the website for water sports in Latvia. The developers perceived a bit unusually big effort required in the user research and feature selection. All four kinds of prototypes were developed and user feedback gathered using the interviewing technique. Also the expected procedures for ensuring high quality service across the whole organization and continuous improvement were envisioned. The perception was that, despite the application of the recommendations required more developer time, – the result was rewording, especially, when learning from user feedback that user engagement for the developed website was higher than for other thematically similar websites.

5   Conclusions

The purpose of this paper was to look closer to the attributes behind the user engagement which becomes one of the essential issues in information systems development. While there are many studies with respect to engagement, this paper fills the gap of the lack of their comprehensive survey. The survey is briefly represented in Sect. 2. Another contribution of the paper is mappings between the engagement attributes and different approaches, methods and techniques that can be used to achieve user engagement. On the basis of these mappings, the practical recommendations for website development are proposed, which can be applied using the given mappings and suggestions in literature sources presented in the solution side of the mappings. The recommendations were tested by the real-life experiment.

The mappings presented in Sect. 3 can be useful not only for website development. They may refer to information systems development in general. However, it has to be emphasized that the paper was targeted to website development and the literature for analysis was selected in this context. Therefore, additional research is needed to fully generalize the mappings presented in Sect. 3. The recommendations proposed in Sect. 4 can be used as a guideline in website development. They do not provide a breakthrough approach, however, they show, in which functional areas of webpage development which engagement issues have to be considered; and emphasize that the engagement cannot happen without appropriate "background" activities and continuous improvement. These recommendations might also help to reduce development and support costs, increase sales, and reduce staff costs for employers [27].

While the mappings, which are the basic contribution of the paper, are rather clear and can be useful in website development, further research would be beneficial to see whether it is possible to reduce the slight attribute overlapping and the solution overlapping that currently bit hinder straight-forward (supplementing recommendations free) application of the mappings.

References

1. Csikszentmihalyi, M.: Beyond Boredom and Anxiety, 231 p. Jossey-Bass Publishers, San Francisco (1975)
2. Csikszentmihalyi, M.: TED Conferences, LLC, Flow, the secret to happiness (2004). http://www.ted.com/talks/mihaly_csikszentmihalyi_on_flow?language=en
3. Huang, M.-H.: Designing website attributes to induce experiential encounters. Comput. Hum. Behav. 19(4), 425–442 (2003)
4. Sashi, C.M.: Customer engagement, buyer-seller relationships, and social media. Manag. Decis. 50(2), 253–272 (2012)
5. Jennings, M.: Theory and models for creating engaging and immersive ecommerce websites. In: Proceedings of the ACM SIGCPR Conference, pp. 77–85 (2000)
6. O'Brien, H.L., Toms, E.G.: What is user engagement? A conceptual framework for defining user engagement with technology. J. Am. Soc. Inf. Sci. Technol. 59(6), 938–955 (2008)
7. UX Booth, Content Marketing: You're Doing it Wrong (2014). http://www.uxbooth.com/articles/content-marketing-youre-wrong/
8. Eisingerich, A.B., Kretschmer, T.: In e-commerce, more is more. Harvard Bus. Rev. 86(3), 20–21 (2008)
9. Gothelf, J.: Lean UX: Applying Lean Principles to Improve User Experience, 152 p. O'Reilly Media, Sebastopol (2013)
10. Bank, C.: Web UI Design Best Practices. Web: UXPin, 109 p. (2014)
11. ConversionXL, Getting The Website Information Architecture Right: How to Structure Your Site for Optimal User Experiences (2013). http://conversionxl.com/website-information-architecture-optimal-user-experience/

12. UX for the masses, A step by step guide to scenario mapping (2010). http://www.uxforthemasses.com/scenario-mapping/

13. King, H.J., Jannik, C.M.: Redesigning for usability. Information architecture and usability testing for Georgia Tech Library's website. OCLC Syst. Serv. **21**(3), 235–243 (2005)

14. Kohavi, R., Henne, R.M., Sommerfield, D.: Practical guide to controlled experiments on the web: listen to your customers not to the hippo. In: Proceedings of the ACM SIGKDD International Conference on Knowledge Discovery and Data Mining, pp. 959–967 (2007)

15. Nielsen Norman Group, F-Shaped Pattern For Reading Web Content (2006). http://www.nngroup.com/articles/f-shaped-pattern-reading-web-content/

16. Wang, J., Senecal, S.: Measuring perceived website usability. J. Internet Commer. **6**(4), 97–112 (2008)

17. U.S. Department of Health & Human Services, Information Architecture Basics. http://www.usability.gov/what-and-why/information-architecture.html

18. Boxes and Arrows, Four Modes of Seeking Information and How to Design for Them (2006). http://boxesandarrows.com/four-modes-of-seeking-information-and-how-to-design-for-them/

19. Boxes and Arrows, Card sorting: a definitive guide (2004). http://boxesandarrows.com/card-sorting-a-definitive-guide/

20. KISSmetrics, Are You Making These Common Website Navigation Mistakes? (2013). https://blog.kissmetrics.com/common-website-navigation-mistakes/

21. Miller, C.S., Remington, R.W.: Modeling information navigation: implications for information architecture. Hum. Comput. Interact. **19**(3), 225–271 (2004)

22. Palmer, J.W.: Web site usability, design, and performance metrics. Inf. Syst. Res. **13**(2), 151–167 (2002)

23. Souders, S.: High Performance Web Sites: Essential Knowledge for Front-End Engineers, 170 p. O'Reilly Media, Sebastopol (2007)

24. Bank, C.: Web UI Design Patterns. Web: UXPin, 195 p. (2014)

25. The New York Times Company, The Neuroscience of Your Brain on Fiction (2012). http://www.nytimes.com/2012/03/18/opinion/sunday/the-neuroscience-of-your-brain-on-fiction.html

26. Maltz, M.: Psycho-Cybernetics: A New Way to Get More Living Out of Life, 288 p. Pocket Books, New York (1989)

27. Bias, R.G., Mayhew, D.J.: Cost-Justifying Usability: An Update for the Internet Age, 660 p. Morgan Kaufmann Publishers Inc., San Rafael (2005)

What Is a Framework? - A Systematic Literature Review in the Field of Information Systems

Dirk Stamer[(⊠)], Ole Zimmermann, and Kurt Sandkuhl

Chair of Business Information Systems, University of Rostock,
Albert-Einstein-Str. 22, 18059 Rostock, Germany
{Dirk.Stamer,Ole.Zimmermann,
Kurt.Sandkuhl}@uni-rostock.de

Abstract. The term 'framework' appears very often in scientific publications like journals and conferences. However, there is no universal definition of a framework. It seems that the term is not used in a consistent way by authors publishing on frameworks since they have very little in common compared to each other. The goal of this work is to analyse and show how frameworks in the fields of information systems are handled in the scientific literature over the past 10 years as well as giving a universal definition of the term 'framework' based on the relevant studies. The systematic literature review will serve to identify those studies and to categorize the identified frameworks. The contributions of this work are (1) a general overview about frameworks in the past 10 years, (2) a proposed categorization of frameworks and (3) a general definition of the term 'framework'.

Keywords: Framework · Systematic literature review · Definition

1 Motivation

The term 'framework' is frequently used in the field of information systems. In fact, there are many different kinds of frameworks to find in articles published in journals or conference proceedings. However, the term 'framework' itself is quite inconsistently used across the domain and interpreted very differently in these publications. For example, there are frameworks used to evaluate information systems, to describe information systems or to develop information systems. Despite being used so frequently, there is no clear and absolute definition what a framework actually is. There are no guidelines, rules or a consistency on how the term is used or should be used. Moreover, there are no basic studies that have dealt with this issue.

Johnson and Foote [6] describe a framework as a set of classes that contains an abstract design for solutions for a cluster of related problems which is reusable.

Johnson [5] described a framework in three different ways. First, a framework is the sum of components and patterns. Second, it is described as a reusable design of a whole system or parts of a system that is represented by a set of abstract classes and the interaction between the classes. Third, it is defined as a skeleton of an application that can be customized by the developer.

V. Řepa and T. Bruckner (Eds.): BIR 2016, LNBIP 261, pp. 145–158, 2016.
DOI: 10.1007/978-3-319-45321-7_11

The Oxford Dictionary [4] describes a framework as "an essential supporting structure of a building, vehicle, or object" or the "basic structure underlying a system, concept, or text".

These are only some existing approaches demonstrating that there is no accepted definition on the subject and explaining why the term is used in so many different ways.

The scope of this work is to give an overview about the usage and structure of frameworks in the scientific literature of the last 10 years. A systematic literature review helps to gain deep insight in the field. The structure of this work will mainly follow the systematic literature proposed by Kitchenham [8]. This procedure ensures traceability and a clear focus.

The systematic review is carried out to answer the given research question:

Research Question: How can frameworks be categorized in the field of information systems?

The contributions of this work are: (1) a general overview about the usage of the term 'framework' in the field of information systems, (2) a proposed categorization of identified frameworks and (3) a basic definition of the term 'framework'.

This work is structured as follows: Sect. 2 provides a general overview about our methodological approach in general. Section 3 describes the procedure used to conduct the systematic literature research. Section 4 discusses the results of this work. The last Sect. 5 summarizes and gives an outlook on further research.

2 Methodological Approach – Systematic Literature Review

This chapter describes the systematic literature review by Kitchenham. Furthermore, advantages and disadvantages of this method are discussed as well as the decision to use it.

Several discrete activities are part of a systematic review. According to Kitchenham, a systematic literature review consists of three parts [8]:

1. Planning the review.
2. Conducting the review.
3. Reporting the review.

However, the parts are not sequential. Most of them involve iteration. That means that predefined methods and guidelines in the review protocol can be refined and optimized when the actual review takes place. If the actual review process differs from the review protocol, it has to be documented. The instructions for each part are described in the following:

Planning the review. In this part, a check is performed to see if a systematic review is necessary to solve and look at a certain problem. It is necessary to gather all information about a problem in an unbiased, objective and rigorous manner. Also, a review protocol is required. This protocol is predefined before the research starts to avoid any bias on the part of the researcher. It serves as a guideline describing how the review is performed, what methods are used etc. In detail, the review protocol provides the following information:

- Reasons for performing the survey.
- Research questions the review wants to answer.
- The search strategy used to find primary studies (Search terms, resources).
- Inclusion and exclusion criteria for studies.
- Study quality assessment.
- Strategy on how relevant data is extracted from primary studies and what data should be extracted.
- How the data synthesis is performed?

Conducting the review. After the creation of the review protocol, the review process begins. However, the pre-defined steps in the protocol can still be refined and optimized when performing the review. The actual review consists of the following steps:

- *Research identification:* The goal of this step is to identify as many primary studies as possible which might be helpful to answer the research questions by using an unbiased search strategy. This process is then documented. Individual studies considered in the review are called primary studies while the systematic review is a secondary study.
- *Study selection:* After identification of the primary studies, the actual relevance of them is assessed by applying study selection criteria. Inclusion criteria are the criteria a study needs to meet in order to be relevant while exclusion criteria make a study irrelevant. Two or more researchers discuss whether or not a study is relevant.
- *Quality assessment of studies:* Not only the relevance is important, but also the quality of the included studies. Quality instruments are used to evaluate the quality of the studies.
- *Extraction of data and progress monitoring:* Relevant data to answer review questions is extracted from the primary studies. Data extraction forms are created to capture the relevant information. The forms should be defined in the review protocol. Two or more researchers should carry out the extraction of data independently.
- *Synthesis of data:* During this step, the results of the primary studies are summarized and collated in a way consistent with the research questions.

Reporting the review. In this part, the results of the systematic review are illustrated.

The systematic literature review offers a meticulous and fair approach in order to increase its scientific value and eliminate the risk of unbiased results. By creating a precise and detailed search strategy, it is possible to cover all necessary sources to gain the relevant information and thus answer the research questions comprehensively. It also allows to summarize existing evidence concerning the technology and to find new areas for further investigation, which is a part of this work, too. Another advantage is that the method is transparent and repeatable. If another researcher performs the same task again according to protocol, similar results should be obtained.

Nevertheless, the systematic literature review has also some disadvantages. It is possible that some relevant information is not found by using the search strategy because it does not cover the source, or the identified studies do not provide sufficient information.

3   Conducting the Research Search Process

In this chapter, the search process of the systematic literature review for relevant studies is documented and the execution of the systematic literature review will be described. The execution includes the presentation of the review protocol, the initial search for the primary study and the final selection of relevant primary studies considered in the review.

First, the time frame of the research has to be defined. We agreed on the past 10 years to cover recent trends and developments and to consider older works as well. Second, we had to agree on the sources for the research. Urbach et al. [15] already identified the relevant journals like MISQ, CACAM or BISE and conferences like ICIS, ECIS or AMCIS in the field of information systems in their work. Their choice will be adopted in the following.

The search is performed mainly by hand using the existing search engines. If possible, the search function offered by electronic libraries is used to search for search strings described below. Otherwise, all the titles and abstracts are read. Studies from certain journals and conferences in the time frame from 2005–2014 are searched through. During the initial search for primary studies, the abstracts are checked with one question in mind:

For English literature: Does the abstract or title contain a description or any information about frameworks used in the field of information systems? If yes, the study is selected and later checked thoroughly applying the inclusion and exclusion criteria. If not, the study is not relevant. Also, the synonym 'structure' is considered. The search term is formalized in a search string to increase traceability. The search string used to find studies is:

Title: 'Framework' or Abstract: 'Framework' in publication '[Name of source]'/ Title: 'Structure' or Abstract: 'Structure' in publication '[Name of source]' between 2005–2014.

For German literature: Same procedure with the exception that the abstracts and titles are searched through additionally with the German translation 'Rahmenwerk' and the German synonyms 'Plan' and 'Struktur'. The search string used to find studies is: *Title: 'Framework' or Abstract: 'Framework' in publication '[Name of source]'/Title: 'Rahmenwerk' or Abstract: 'Rahmenwerk' in publication '[Name of source]'/Title: 'Plan' or Abstract: 'Plan' in publication '[Name of source]'/Title: 'Struktur' or Abstract: 'Struktur' in publication '[Name of source]' between 2005–2014.*

The search strings are very general and not very specific on the purpose (e.g., it would have been an option to include 'IS', 'Information System' etc. in the search string to make it more specific). However, the goal is to capture as many primary studies as possible. The advantage of this decision is that more potentially relevant studies are detected and the whole research area is covered more extensively. Furthermore, when reading the title or abstract, the slightest hint that the study could contain information about frameworks in the field of information systems is sufficient to check the study later by using the inclusion/exclusion criteria. Only those studies which title or abstract are completely off topic are not considered. The overall goal is to reduce the risk of missing potentially relevant studies.

Conference proceedings and journals that are not open access or do not deal with information systems are not considered in this review. The exception is the BIS conference, where the years 2005–2006 were not accessible. These journals or conference proceedings are: MISQ, JMIS, JCIS ASQ, SMR, Omega, HBR, DSS, DSI, HCI, ISR, IJEC, AMJ, AMR, EJIS, IBMSJ, IEEESW, JACM, OS, and IEEETrans.

After a first study selection based on the title and the abstract, the studies are checked again in a more detailed manner. This means that the complete studies are read and then a decision is made whether or not a study is relevant. The following criteria are applied to make a study relevant or irrelevant:

Inclusion criteria:

- A study deals with a framework (or synonym of the word used during the initial search) related to information systems. The word information system or its abbreviation IS does not have to appear in the study if a software or system is described that fits the definition of information system given in the background chapter.

Exclusion criteria:

- The paper does not contain any relevant information about frameworks in the field of information systems.

Data Extraction/Data Synthesis: In this step, relevant data required to answer the research questions and general information about the study is extracted from the studies. The following data is identified as relevant and extracted from the studies: *Title; Author; Source; Purpose of the framework; Structure of the framework; Development approach; Framework implementation described in the study; Updates on existing Framework.*

The purpose, structure and development approach of the frameworks are used later in order to categorize them.

The extracted data is gathered in a table to show which study provides data to answer the research question. The table contains the above-mentioned data and is based on the data extracted from each study.

353 primary studies were identified during the first broad search for relevant studies using the search strings by checking the abstracts and titles whether or not they contain relevant information about frameworks in the field of information systems.

Selection of relevant studies: After selecting 353 primary studies based on their title and the content of their abstract, the inclusion and exclusion criteria were applied to identify primary studies to be included and evaluated in the final review. Through this procedure, it was possible to reduce 353 primary studies to 71 studies to be included in the final review. The following charts show the number of studies before and after the application of the inclusion and exclusion criteria sorted by source and publication year.

Figure 1 shows that most of the potentially relevant and the relevant studies originate from the conferences (ECIS, ICIS, HICSS, AMCIS, BIS, BIR). Exactly 226 out of 353 (64 %) studies before the application of the inclusion/exclusion criteria and 50 out of 71 (70 %) after the application make up the majority of the relevant studies.

The journals only make up 36 % (127 out of 353) of the relevant studies before the criteria application and 30 % (21 out of 71) after it.

Figure 2 shows that the occurrence of studies before and after the application of the criteria is not evenly distributed. For 2014, there are only two studies left after the criteria application compared to the years 2005 and 2011 with12 studies each.

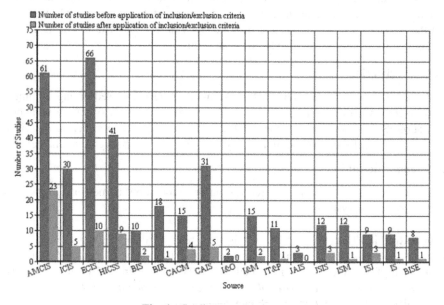

Fig. 1. Studies sorted by sources

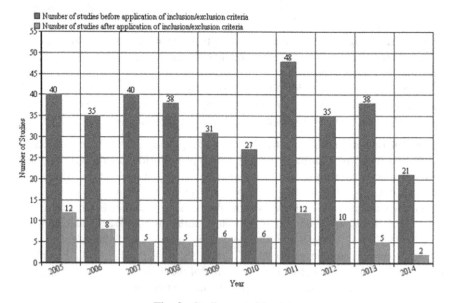

Fig. 2. Studies sorted by date

Another point to mention is that eight studies provide information about more than one framework. This explains why 93 frameworks were identified in the literature although there were only 71 studies in the field of information systems.

In this chapter, the relevant literature was identified through the systematic literature review. The next chapter outlines the results of the review based on the literature identified during the review.

4   Discussion of the Results

In this chapter, the research questions are considered in relation to the literature review. In addition, a definition of the term framework is given. This definition should fit all the identified frameworks in the studies. This chapter reports the review step of the systematic literature review. In this step, the results of the review are communicated.

4.1   Definition of the Term Framework

As already demonstrated, there is a variety of different definitions of the term 'framework' in the field of information systems. The focus is now on extracting information about the frameworks purpose, structure, development process, existing updates and implementations out of the systematic literature analysis.

It can be stated that the identified frameworks do not have many things in common. Out of the 71 identified studies, only one study defines the term 'framework'. The other studies employ the term without any given definition. According to the study by Kajan and Stoimenow [7], a framework is a middleware used to bridge problems with heterogeneity by putting in a generic template providing the desired functionality. However, this definition is very specific and does not cover the other identified frameworks. Based on all identified frameworks and the extracted information (purpose, structure, development process, implementations, and updates) about them and the definitions of framework proposed before, the following definition includes all identified frameworks in the field of information systems:

A framework is a structure underlying 'something' serving a specific purpose.

This definition is the lowest common denominator describing what all identified frameworks have in common. It is still very general but due to the fact that the identified frameworks vary strongly in all their aspects, finding a more specific definition is not possible and does not make sense. The definition is very close to the definitions given by the Oxford dictionary [4] describing a framework as 'basic structure underlying a system, concept, or text'. Basically, the notion of a framework as a structure of something is taken from these definitions and is then extended with the notion of solving a problem as the goal of a framework. It should be emphasized that only the structure part and not the basic structure part is taken from these definitions because a framework does not have to be necessarily only basic. The degree of detail describing the framework structure varies a lot between the identified frameworks. Some framework structures are described only generally while other framework structures are described very detailed.

A framework with a very simple structure is, e.g., the Clic framework [2]. In comparison to the Clic framework, the Zachman framework and its extension has a very complex structure [17]. Therefore, a definite degree of detail in frameworks cannot be included in the definition. Another point to mention is that a framework can provide the structure for anything. In the identified frameworks, the categorisation provided supports implementation processes, research agendas, green information systems etc. The fact that a framework has a purpose is added, implying that a framework is used to fulfil a purpose. These purposes can be very different. They can consist in describing an implementation, summing up existing research results on a topic, describing factors influencing the outcome of an activity and many more.

To sum up, a framework gives a structure to something. The goal is to fulfil a purpose by using the framework.

4.2   Answering the Research Question

RQ: How can frameworks be categorized in the field of information systems?

It seems useful to categorize the identified frameworks according to the extracted meta-data about them. These characteristics are the framework purpose, the development process of the framework and the structure of the framework. Figure 3 gives an overview by using percentages.

Categories based on framework purpose:

- *Green Information System Framework:* Green information systems frameworks focus on the environmental aspect of information system, e.g., the lifecycle assessment framework [13] for sustainable IS Management used to measure IS related environmental impact. Four frameworks are part of this category.
- *Test Framework:* The purpose of test frameworks is to examine the implementation of information systems, e.g., the distributed systems monitoring framework used to support unit component testing in distributed component-based systems [10]. Six frameworks are part of this category.
- *Development Framework:* These frameworks support the development of information systems or new information system features from two perspectives, the technical and general perspective. The technical perspective includes concrete parts of the implementation, e.g., the Gulliver framework [9] with the purpose to build smart speech based applications. The general perspective focuses on instructions for the development process, e.g., the Ethnorelative framework [11] which provides information system designers with information to understand their own cultural values relative to users of other national cultures. There are 27 development frameworks, 11 take the technical perspective and 16 the general perspective.
- *Research Framework:* Research frameworks focus on theoretical topics with little practical application, e.g., the Computer Security Research Framework [12] with the purpose to synthesize and summarize research done in the area of Information System Security. In total, 18 research frameworks belong to this category.
- *Evaluation Framework:* The purpose of evaluation frameworks is to evaluate information systems or certain aspects of information systems. Evaluated aspects are for example the systems compliance [3]. There are 16 evaluation frameworks.

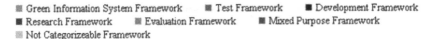

Fig. 3. Categories in percentage

- *Mixed Purpose Framework:* Frameworks in this class do not fit into only one of the categories. They are a combination of two or more framework categories based on the frameworks purpose. An example of a mixed purpose framework is the environmental impact framework that combines the green information system and development category. The purpose of this framework is to support IT system design based on the system environmental impact. It belongs to the green information system category because it deals with the environmental aspect of the information system. Also, it belongs to the development framework category because it supports the development of information systems [18]. Five frameworks are a combination of framework categories.
- *Not Categorizable Frameworks/ITSM:* The ITSM frameworks ITIL, the ITIL related HP ITSM, the Microsoft Operations Framework, and ISO/IEC 15504 are not categorizable and form a separate category.

Categories based on Framework Development Process: Only 50 frameworks contain a description of how they were developed. The development process of these frameworks can be divided into four categories. Also, there are four additional methods used to support the development of the frameworks. They are not used as the only method to create a framework but they support its development combined with one of the four framework development categories. The development of 17 out of the 50 frameworks is supported by these methods. These methods are:

- *Interviews:* Interviews with experts or practitioners (three frameworks).
- *Authors' experience:* Authors' personal experience (six frameworks).
- *Case Studies:* Research on a social phenomena (nine frameworks).
- *Field Studies:* This method supports the development of one framework.

The identified frameworks can be divided based on their development process into the following four categories:

- *Literature Review Developed Frameworks:* Frameworks in this category are developed through a literature review. 18 frameworks belong to this category. Case studies are used together with a literature review five times, field studies one time, interviews one time and the authors' own experience four times.
- *Research Developed Frameworks:* Frameworks of this category are based on existing research like models, theories, frameworks and so on. The research background of these frameworks varies a lot. 25 frameworks belong to this category. Case studies are used together with the existing research three times and interviews two times.
- *Requirements Developed Frameworks:* Frameworks of this category are developed based on the identified requirements the frameworks needs to fulfil. The framework is built on these requirements. Four frameworks belong to this category. In one case, a case study is combined with the framework requirements during the development process.
- *Mixed Developed Frameworks:* Frameworks of this category are developed based on multiple categories. There are three mixed developed frameworks. The three mixed developed frameworks combine the literature review approach and the use of the existing research for the development of a framework. Two times, the process is supported by the authors' personal experiences.

The following Fig. 4 shows the distribution of categories based on the development process in percentages.

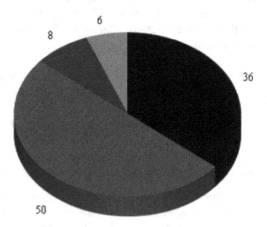

Fig. 4. Development process in percentage

Half of the frameworks are research-based frameworks presenting the knowledge used to develop the framework. The process of obtaining the knowledge is not shown like in the literature review developed framework which is also a method often used to develop frameworks (36 %). Frameworks developed based on their requirements and mixed developed frameworks are a minority.

It is noticeable that case studies are used to verify, improve and test the developed frameworks five times. An example for this is the IS flexibility framework. The initial framework is developed through a literature review. After that, the framework is tested with a case study. The case study uses data collected from interviews with managers [1]. Another observation is that there are only six frameworks where the authors' personal experience with the topic plays a significant role to develop the framework. In most cases (44 frameworks), the author relies on knowledge of other people.

Categorization based on framework structure: In 69 cases, the structure of the framework is described in detail. There exist eight framework structures building the categories. A combination of two categories is also possible. The following categories for the structures of frameworks were identified:

- *Layered Structured Frameworks:* Frameworks in this category have a layered structure, e.g., the Architect framework which consists of four layers [16]. A layer describes system features on different abstraction levels. Every layer is implemented based on the next lower layer. Six frameworks are part of this category.
- *Technical Structured Frameworks:* Frameworks in this category contain a description of the technical components they consist of. Technical components are e.g. include used protocols like HTTP and SOAP in the B2B Ontology-Driven Framework [7]. 12 frameworks are part of this category.
- *Sequence Structured Frameworks:* Frameworks in this category consist of activities performed in a sequential order and partly at the same time. There are frameworks which sequence has defined beginning and end cycle [2]. Four frameworks are part of this category.
- *Category Structured Frameworks:* Frameworks in this category structure a study phenomenon into different categories which can have different characteristics in each category, e.g., the cultural dimensions from Hofstede and their characteristics in different countries to help information system developers understand the people they deal with [11]. There are 10 frameworks in this category.
- *Factors-outcome Structured Frameworks:* Frameworks in this category take relevant factors into account and determine how these factors influence the outcome of a phenomenon, e.g., the IS flexibility framework shows which factors influence IS flexibility and how they influence this phenomenon [1]. 15 frameworks belong to this category.
- *Component Structured Frameworks:* Frameworks in this category have a component-based structure. The components describe the framework and the relationships between the components are shown, e.g., the conceptual framework linking Enterprise Systems to organizational agility which consists of enterprise systems related components and how they are connected to organizational agility [14]. However, the difference to sequenced and technical structured frameworks is

that the components are not technical and there is no sequence of activities between the components. Six frameworks belong to this category.

- *Mixed Structured Frameworks:* Frameworks in this category have structural attributes from multiple categories. Seven frameworks belong to this category.
- *Not Categorizable Frameworks:* These frameworks do not fit into any of the above-mentioned categories. Thus, nine frameworks are not categorizable by their structure. Each of the nine framework has its own structure category because their structure is unique compared to the frameworks being categorized.

The following Fig. 5 shows the distribution of categories based on the framework structure in percentages. The frameworks are relatively even distributed compared to the other two categories. Most frameworks are factors-outcome frameworks that make up the majority of identified frameworks (22 %).

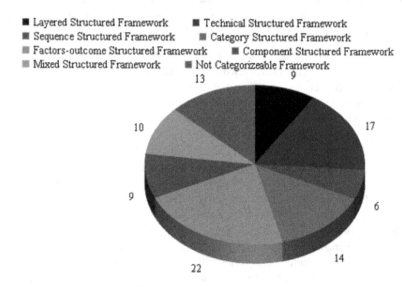

Fig. 5. Structure in percentage

5   Summary

The term 'framework' is frequently used in the field of information research. We could show that there are many different definitions of the term focusing mainly on the purpose of the framework and that many different frameworks were published.

The purpose of the performed research was to find out how frameworks in the field of information systems are handled in the scientific literature, i.e., in the most important journals and conferences of the field of information systems of the last ten years. To get an objective overview, a systematic literature review according to Kitchenham was used. First, 353 studies appeared relevant for this analysis. After a refinement, 71 papers with 93 frameworks were identified. Afterwards, relevant information about the frameworks was extracted and analysed to answer the research question. In the introduction, we stated that there is no consistency or any rules whatsoever in the usage of the term framework. There is also no accepted definition of what a framework is. Therefore, we proposed a definition of the term 'framework' extending the Oxford Dictionary version. This definition of a framework has to be very broad due to the many different kinds of identified frameworks.

The identified frameworks vary considerably in all their aspects as shown by the categorization of frameworks. It seems to be useful to categorize framework according to purpose, development process and structure.

It has to be noticed that only a few frameworks were implemented. In total, 10 frameworks were implemented in the studies. However, most of the implementations are prototypes. Only one framework was fully implemented in a real world application. It can be observed that only frameworks classified as test frameworks and development framework with the focus on technical aspects have been implemented.

It seems that frameworks are rarely updated. Only nine studies dealt with frameworks being updated and released in a new version. It should also be noted that no framework category is more likely to be updated than other classes.

Unfortunately, some sources were not open access. This might be the main shortcoming of this research. Nevertheless, all of the high-ranked journals and conference proceedings were freely available and included in our research.

References

1. Byrd, T.A., et al.: An examination of an information systems flexibility framework. Presented at the 2010 43rd Hawaii International Conference on System Sciences (2010)
2. Champion, D., et al.: Client-led information system creation (CLIC): navigating the gap. Inf. Syst. J. **15**(3), 213–231 (2005)
3. Chang, S.-I., et al.: Internal control framework for a compliant ERP system. Inf. Manag. **51** (2), 187–205 (2014)
4. Dictionary, O.: Framework definition
5. Gómez-Albarrán, M., González Calero, P.A.: Knowledge intensive case-based assistance for framework reuse*. In: Monostori, L., Váncza, J., Ali, M. (eds.) IEA/AIE 2001. LNCS (LNAI), vol. 2070, pp. 891–900. Springer, Heidelberg (2001)
6. Johnson, R.E., Foote, B.: Designing reusable classes. J. Object-Oriented. Program. **1**(2), 22–35 (1988)
7. Kajan, E., Stoimenov, L.: Toward an ontology-driven architectural framework for B2B. Commun. ACM **48**(12), 60–66 (2005)
8. Kitchenham, B.: Procedures for performing systematic reviews. Keele, UK, Keele Univ. **33**, 1–26 (2004)
9. Kurschl, W., et al.: Gulliver-A framework for building smart speech-based applications. In: 40th Annual Hawaii International Conference on System Sciences, HICSS 2007 (2007)
10. Li, J., Moore, K.: A runtime and analysis framework support for unit component testing in distributed systems. In: 40th Annual Hawaii International Conference on System Sciences, HICSS 2007 (2007)
11. Saab, D.J.: An ethnorelative framework for information systems design. In: Proceedings of the AMCIS 2008 (2008)

12. Schuessler, J.: An information systems security framework. In: Proceedings of the AMCIS 2007 (2007)
13. Stiel, F., Teuteberg, F.: Towards a conceptual framework for life cycle assessment in sustainable information systems management. In: ECIS (2013)
14. Trinh, P., et al.: Enterprise systems and organizational agility: a review of the literature and conceptual framework. Commun. Assoc. Inf. Syst. 31(1), 167–193 (2012)
15. Urbach, N., et al.: The state of research on information systems success. Bus. Inf. Syst. Eng. 1(4), 315–325 (2009)
16. Voisard, A., Ziekow, H.: ARCHITECT: a layered framework for classifying technologies of event-based systems. Inf. Syst. 36(6), 937–957 (2011)
17. Zachman, J.A.: A framework for information systems architecture. IBM Syst. J. 26(3), 276–292 (1987)
18. Zhang, H., et al.: Designing IT systems according to environmental settings: a strategic analysis framework. J. Strateg. Inf. Syst. 20(1), 80–95 (2011)

Combination of DSL and DCSP for Decision Support in Dynamic Contexts

Boris Ulitin[✉], Eduard Babkin, and Tatiana Babkina

National Research University Higher School of Economics,
Nizhny Novgorod, Russia
{bulitin, eababkin, tbabkina}@hse.ru

Abstract. The article is related to the problem of decision support in dynamic business contexts where conditions, values and goals frequently change over time, and users should participate continuously in the problem definition. In our research we explore an opportunity to organize and simplify decision support during complex resource allocation processes by combining domain specific languages (DSL) and distributed constraint satisfaction techniques (DCSP). We describe a particular domain-specific language and the corresponding semantic model in terms of a newly proposed DSL&DCSP framework. Applicability of the framework is demonstrated using a real-life example of resource allocation process in the railway transportation.

Keywords: Domain-specific language · Constraints satisfaction · Railway transportation · Decision support

1 Introduction

Currently in many domains continuous changes of the problem context require repeatable identification and reformulation of the models, used during the process of problems solving. Correspondingly, decision support in dynamic contexts becomes one of the most significant research challenges.

The resource allocation problem represents a business-relevant example of decision support in dynamic contexts. There are many well-known methods for resource allocation [1], however most of them require a stable context of the problem being solved. As a result, they are not applicable in the cases when frequent changes are possible in the solving procedure and conditions, as well as participation of stakeholders is required. To overcome such a drawback Hodgson, Fernandez-Lopez and Gomez-Perez offer to separate the model, which is responsible for the solving procedure, and a mechanism, which allows controlling this model [2–4].

Hodgson and Fernandez-Lopez [2, 3] define the trees and different kinds of state machines as the best choice for the specification of the solving model. Other researchers [4, 5, 7] offer special languages as the most effective choice for that task. We support the second direction, because in our opinion domain-specific languages (DSL) represent the most convenient, organic and clear method for controlling the dynamically changed context.

Our research presupposes a new approach to connect a user-defined specification in terms of DSL and a mathematical specification of the problem for automated constraints

© Springer International Publishing Switzerland 2016
V. Řepa and T. Bruckner (Eds.): BIR 2016, LNBIP 261, pp. 159–173, 2016.
DOI: 10.1007/978-3-319-45321-7_12

solvers. Following that approach, we propose a DSL&DCSP framework, which automatically translates DSL specifications of a certain resource allocation problem to a specification of a distributed constraint satisfaction problem (DCSP) [8]. For demonstration of our approach current research contained implementation of a software prototype based on the multi-agent DCSP-solver Choco [9] and evaluation the prototype in a real case of railways allocation.

There was an attempt by Prud'homme [18] to use a similar structure of the framework for translations of DSL specifications to constraints. But in contrast to our research, that example uses DSL for specialization of CSP from a general class of mathematical problems. That DSL does not correspond to the already existing, defined CSP model, moreover it is not oriented toward any specific practical application.

The article describes our results as follows. In Sect. 2 we give some facts from the theory of design of domain-specific languages and its using in the course of the solving constraint satisfaction problems. Section 3 describes a high level design and technologies of the proposed DSL&DCSP framework. Section 4 demonstrates in the case of the railway allocation problem how our approach is applied in the real-life situations. In Sect. 5 we discuss the results obtained. We conclude the article with analysis of the results and specification of the future researches.

2   Background

2.1   Definition and the Classification of the DSL

A domain-specific language (DSL) is a computer language specialized to a particular application domain. This is in contrast to a general-purpose language, which is broadly applicable across domains, and lacks specialized features for a particular domain [5].

Any DSL satisfies a number of conditions. The first one addresses the structure of the language. In this context it means that DSL includes not only some amount of commands, but their dependences also. The same command, paired with another language element, can carry a different meaning. The second condition specifies that DSLs should be designed as an equivalent to the natural domain language for users and experts of the target domain. Final condition reflects a limited expressive capacity of DSLs and specifies that DSL is only a new way to represent some part of the whole target domain.

DSLs are always associated with some other and more general language, which is named as a base language [6]. A manner of association divides all DSLs to two classes: external and internal DSLs. The external DSLs have domain-oriented syntaxes and therefore have to be translated into commands of the base language. In contrast, internal DSLs represent a non-typical use of the base language. A scenario in this DSL contains only a subset of the features of the base language [6].

In [6] two parts of the DSL are identified: (1) a syntactic part, which defines the constructions of DSL; and (2) a semantic part, which manifests itself in the semantic model. The first part allows defining the context for working with the second one, which defines the solving procedure for the problems of the target domain. Such a structure has several advantages [5]. Firstly, DSL developers can test and develop syntax of DSL and the model independently. Secondly, many different DSLs can be designed for the same model. Finally, developers can reuse the code of the model multiple times [7]. In such conditions, DSL represents only some additional component to the model. DSL simplifies the control procedure for the model, but it does not define it.

During design and application of DSLs developers face the challenge of syntactic analysis, which is always seems to be a resource-intensive process. Fortunately, in the case of DSL design a primitive syntactic analysis for translation DSL commands into the commands of the base language can be used. In that case compilation and correctness checking can be skipped. Kosar gives example of such DSL implementation in [16]. There are also many instruments for semi-automated developing DSLs in practice. For example, such workbench as MetaEdit [10] uses state machines for achieving this goal, which represent a native way to understand and analyze DSL syntax and its semantic model. If developers create DSL commands without a model inside, more simple analyzers cane used, such as ANTLR [11]. In our own research we selected the later tool, because we connect DSL with an external model solver. As a result, we need an instrument for translating and checking the correctness of DSL scenarios.

2.2 Constraint Satisfaction Problems

The paradigm of constraint satisfaction problems (CSPs) provides a generic method for declarative description of complex constrained or optimization problems in terms of variables and constraints [1, 2, 13–15]. Formally, CSP is a triple (V, D, C) where: $V = \{v_1, ..., v_n\}$ is a set of n variables, $D = \{D(v_1), ..., D(v_n)\}$ a corresponding set of n domains from which each variable can take its values from, and $C = \{c_1, ..., c_m\}$ is a set of m constraints over the values of the variables in V. Each constraint $c_i = C(V_i)$ is a logical predicate over subset of variables $V_i \subseteq V$ with an arbitrary arity k: $c_i (v_a, ..., v_k)$ that maps the Cartesian product $D(v_a) \times ... \times D(v_k)$ to $\{0, 1\}$. As usual the value 1 means that the value combination for $v_a, ..., v_k$ is allowed, and 0 otherwise. A solution for a CSP is an assignment of values for each variable in V such that all the constraints in C are satisfied.

A Distributed Constraint Satisfaction Problem (DCSP) is a CSP where the variables are distributed among agents in a Multi-Agent System and the agents are connected by relationships that represent constraints. DCSP is a suitable abstraction to solve constrained problems without global control during peer-to-peer agent communication and cooperation [16]. A DCSP can be formalized as a combination of (V, D, C, A, ∂) described as follows: V, D, C are the same as explained for an original CSP, $A = \{a_1, ..., a_p\}$ is a set of p agents, and $\partial : V \rightarrow A$ is a function used to map each variable v_j to its owner agent a_i. Each variable belongs to only one agent, i.e. $\forall v_1, ..., v_k \in V_i \Leftrightarrow \partial (v_1) = ... = \partial (v_k)$ where $V_i \subset V$ represents the subset of variables that belong to agent a_i. These subsets are distinct, i.e. $V_1 \cap ... \cap V_p = \varnothing$ and the union of all subsets represents the set of all variables, i.e. $V_1 \cup ... \cup V_p = V$. The distribution of variables among agents divides the set of constraints C into two subsets according to the variables involved within the constraint. The first set is the one of intra-agent constraints C_{intra} that represent the constraints over the variables owned by the same agent $C_{intra} = \{C(V_i) \mid \partial (v_1) = ... = \partial (v_k), v_1, ..., v_k \in V_i\}$.

The second set is the one of inter-agent constraints C_{inter} that represents the constraints over the variables owned by two or more agents. Obviously, these two subsets are distinct $C_{intra} \cap C_{inter} = \varnothing$ and complementary $C_{intra} \cup C_{inter} = C$.

The variables involved within inter-agent constraints C_{inter} are denoted as *interface variables* $V_{interface}$. Assigning values to a variable in a constraint that belongs to C_{inter} has a direct effect on all the agents, which have variables involved in the same constraint. The interface variables should take values before the rest of the variables in the system in order to satisfy the constraints inside C_{inter} firstly. Then, the satisfaction of internal constraints in C_{intra} becomes an internal problem that can be treated separately inside each agent independently of other agents. If the agent cannot find a solution for its intra-agent constraints, it fails and requests another value proposition for its interface variables. To simplify things, we will assume that there are no intra-agent constraints, i.e. $C_{intra} = \varnothing$. Therefore, all variables in V are interface variables $V = V_{interface}$.

From the functional viewpoint the most common and complete are such solvers as Choco, Gecode and Disolver [9, 12, 17]. But if the last two are closed products, Choco is an open-source product. In addition, Choco supports vectorized syntaxes for formulating the original problem that satisfies representation of constraints as a system of inequalities. Finally, this solver allows to design distributed CSPs and the solving procedure for them in terms of distributed multi-agent systems.

All mentioned solvers need a flexible mechanism to formalize the context of the problem in terms of CSP and to control the process of solution search. When traditional approaches are applied, in a case of the context changes the users have to stop the solving process, modify the source code with constructions responsible for new changes and restart the solving process. Such actions require a lot of time and reduce reactive capabilities of decision support systems. A more comfortable approach is required to modify the context of the problem dynamically, which can allow avoiding terminating the solutions search. Application of DSL seems to be reasonable for that purpose because DSL does not require restarting the solving process.

3 Proposed Framework

We propose a specific software framework, which combines description of the domain problems in terms of DSL, consequent solution of the problems by the methods of DCSP, and presentation of the results in terms of the original DSL. The framework facilitates active end-user participation in the decision process with feedback loops as it is shown in the scheme (Fig. 1). The user formulates an original problem in terms of a DSL scenario, which then is transformed in terms of the semantic model. That semantic model reformulates the input task in mathematical terms (in our case as an instance of the distributed CSP), using commands and constructions of a certain solver. When the solver obtains a solution, our framework represents that solution in the DSL terms and returns it to the user for analysis. Given the results of the analysis, the user can directly change and control the model by special DSL commands.

In our approach a DSL scenario describes not only the way of how-to-solve the problem, but also specifies the constraints which shape the solution. Syntax and semantics of DSL is designed according to the semantic model, which is the tool for the solving process in terms of our specific domain. A syntactic analyzer (or parser) is responsible for translating DSL commands into commands of the semantic model.

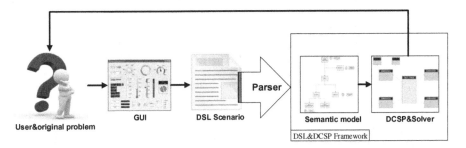

Fig. 1. The scheme of DSL processing in the framework.

As a result, the approach proposed offers an effective tool for management of the context in the semantic model. Users can concretize the context using additional DSL commands at any moment, while the model continues the solution process without needs to restart it. Furthermore, users can manage the process of solution search by filtering found answers by DSL commands. Finally, developers of decision support systems can combine developed DSL with other ways to fix the context changes in the text form. For example, they can use XML-configuration files for this purpose.

4   DSL and DCSP Application in the Railway Domain

4.1   DSL for Railway Allocation Management

The context of the railway allocation problem can change frequently because of arrivals of new trains, or changing the priority of existing services. As a result, a clear and simple way is needed to adapt new changes in terms of the DSL&DCSP framework, responsible for finding the optimal resource allocation. In the process of DSL design for the railway allocation process, it's vital to identify all the types of resources in this domain. There are three general resources for any railway station, each with specific attributes: railways, trains and service brigades.

Trains represent the main resource of the cargo railway station. Each station has different opportunities for servicing different types of trains. The amount of serviced trains defines the effectiveness of the transportation office. Each train has specific set of attributes, which help to service it by an effective and optimal manner. The whole list of these attributes includes such values as train identifier, priority, count of servicing cars, the total number of cars, types of needed services. All attributes are shown in the Fig. 2.

Railways represent the main physical place for servicing trains. Every railway is characterized by an identifier, type, total length, useful length and the list of available equipment. All attributes are shown in the Fig. 2.

Servicing brigades organize the process of servicing in terms of the railway station. The amount of brigades has to be enough to guarantee timely services for all arriving trains. Every brigade has a unique identifier, competence needed to provide services, and amount of people available for this task.

These entities constitute the basic framework of the external DSL. In addition, we need to include into DSL some helper classes to close the syntax of DSL.

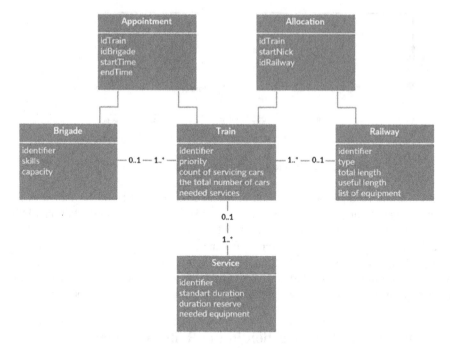

Fig. 2. The structure for DSL: The Object level

In order to work with the designed structure of main and helper classes, the next structure of DSL syntax is developed using ANTLR tool (Fig. 3). The structure of DSL consists of several blocks. The main reason for it is that syntactic analysis of such block structure becomes simple. In addition, such a structure is clear for users, who can see all the structure of the context in terms of DSL. Finally, it can help to control the structure of the model: the DSL blocks correspond to similar blocks in the semantic model and, as a result, can be naturally translated into these structures.

On Fig. 3 the meta-symbol '*' means, that a preceding sequence of objects can be written multiple times. The meta-symbols '[' and ']' specify a list of single-typed entities.

The structure of objects above organizes only the first level of DSL – the level of the objects. In addition, we have to develop the level of functions to manage the objects and their context. In our case this functional level has the next structure (Fig. 4).

Using these commands, we can specify the context for the objects and their management. In addition, such a command structure allows to simplify and accelerate the solving procedure with additional details needed for finding the optimal solutions.

When all objects and functions are designed in terms of the DSL, such DSL scenario is translated into the commands of the semantic model using a syntactic analyzer. In this case we have no opportunities to intervene in the process of solutions search directly. We can only manage it by DSL commands. When the solver found the optimal solution, it translates the solution to the DSL terms using a syntactic analyzer. And then this solution can be checked and filtered by the end user. The main advantage in this case is that the final solution represents not a mathematical view, but a

```
Trains
({id type priority length timeArrival timeDeparture timeReserve
[services] wagonsToService})*
EndTrainsBlock;

Services
   ({name priority mayBeInParallel [skills]
standartDuration timeReserve [equipment]})*
endServiceBlock;

Brigades ({id [ skills ] capacity})* endBrigadeBlock;

Railways
   ({id type totalLength usefulLength [equipment]})*
endRailwayBlock;

Appointments
   ({idBrigade->idTrain timeStart timeEnd})*
endAppointmentBlock;

Allocation
   ({idTrain->idRailway startNick
timeStartOccupation timeEndOccupation})*
endAllocationBlock;
```

Fig. 3. DSL objects

```
Relocate idTrain [from idOldRailway] to idNewRailway;
```
This command allows to move Train with identifier idTrain from railway with identifier idOldRailway to railway idNewRailway.

```
Move forward/back idTrain by countShifts;
```
This command allows to move Train within current railway forward or back by the count of shifts equals to countShifts.

```
Put idTrain on newStartNick;
```
This command places the train with identifier idTrain on start nick with number newStartNick.

```
ChangePriority idTrain/nameService on newPriority;
```
This command allows to change priority of train or service on some new value newPriority

```
Appoint idBrigade on idTrain from startTime [to endTime] perform
nameService;
```
This command allows to appoint brigade with identifier idBrigade for servicing nameService on Train idTrain within the period from startTime to endTime.

```
Get info on brigade/train/service/railway idEntity;
```
This command returns all the attributes for brigade, train, service or railway identified by idEntity.

Fig. 4. DSL functions

domain-oriented description, which contents is clear for the user. In these circumstances we might not to spend time on transforming the solution found in terms of the target domain, but check it immediately and use in practice.

Table 1. Description of model's parameters

Parameter	Description
$1..M$	identifiers of arriving trains
$1..K$	identifiers of railways
L_j	length of j-railway
l_i	length of i-train
N_i	amount of cars for servicing i-train
$Tarr_i$	time arrival i-train
Tsw_i	start time of servicing i-train
Top_i	time for servicing i-train
W_i	identificator of railway for i-train
$C_{i,0}$	start nick i-train
$\delta_{i,t}$	size of shift i-train at the time moment t
T_{cur}	current time moment
$Tshift_{i,t}$	time of shift i-train at the time moment t

4.2   Mathematical Model for Railway Allocation

To formalize the mathematic model of DCSP for solving the railway allocation problem, firstly identify all the set of parameters, based on the above description of entities (Sect. 4.1) (Table 1).

These parameters are needed for solving the railway transportation problem effectively and are not redundant. They have to satisfy the system of constraints (1). The first six constraints are needed to distribute arriving trains in time and protect them against time-conflicts. These constraints assure that trains are serviced in time and no longer and have no conflicts within the timetable. Other constraints control mutual arrangement of trains in space of railways, block trains under the service for shifting.

$$
\left\{
\begin{array}{l}
t \in [0; T_{\max}] \\
Tcur \in [0; T_{\max}] \\
Top_i \geq 0 \\
Tarr_i \in [0, T_{\max}], i = 1..M \\
Tsw_i \in [0, T_{\max}], i = 1..M \\
Tsw_i \geq Tarr_i, i = 1..M \\
1 \leq W_i \leq K, i = 1..M \\
0 \leq C_{i,0} \leq L_{W_i}, i = 1..M \\
\sum_{i:W_i=j} l_i \leq, L_j, i = 1..M, j = 1..K \\
\delta_{i,t} = -\infty, t < Tarr_i, i = 1..M \\
\delta_{i,v} = 0, i = 1..M, v = Tarr_i Tsw_i \leq v \leq Tsw_i + Top_i \\
0 \leq C_{i,0} + \sum_{t=0}^{Tcur} \delta_{i,t} \leq L_{W_i}, i = 1..M \\
0 \leq C_{i,0} + \sum_{t=0}^{Tcur} \delta_{i,t} + l_i \leq L_{W_i}, i = 1..M \\
C_{i,0} + \sum_{t=0}^{Tcur} \delta_{it} + l_i \leq C_{i+1,0} + \sum_{t=0}^{Tcur} \delta_{i+1,t}, i = 1..(M-1)
\end{array}
\right.
\tag{1}
$$

When constrains are formulated, we can identify the goal function for solving procedure. In our case the goal is represented by the next system.

$$\begin{cases} \sum_{i=1}^{M} N_i \rightarrow max \\ \sum_{i=1}^{M} \sum_{t=0}^{Tcur} Tshift_{i,t} \rightarrow min \end{cases} \tag{2}$$

The goal function maximizes the amount of serviced trains, but minimizes the time for their shifting within the operations, which is useless and decreases the effectiveness of transportation.

Given the mathematical model, translation of this model to the terms of Choco solver produces two vectors – for the left and right sides of all constraints and identifying the relations between them, using operators "<, >, =, !=". Then the target function is represented in terms of Choco solver. At the final stage the vectorized view of Choco results is translated to DSL.

4.3 Subject-Oriented GUI

After design of all the constructions for DSL and its DCSP-based mathematical model, we can think over the design of GUI, to simplify the procedure of creating DSL scenarios. First of all, we have to understand, that developing GUI must contain only elements, equivalent to DSL components. No more elements are needed, because no more elements are supported by DSL and, as a result, by the model. In this context GUI should be a graphical equivalent to DSL constructions and therefore is subject-oriented.

The second idea for implementation of GUI is that developed DSL is oriented on the procedure of configuration contexts. As a result, it can be useful to define a first interface element within the main frame of GUI as the working area which reflects the current context status. The second interface area, the panel of objects, contains available objects for defining the context. The GUI prototype is demonstrated in Fig. 5.

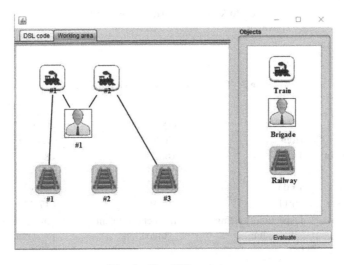

Fig. 5. The GUI prototype

When a user wants to change the context, the user drags the needed element from the panel of objects onto the working area. Then the user has to fill all the attributes for the dragged element in a specific dialog. After the element created, it is added to the context. To include new added elements into the solving process, the button "Evaluate" have to be pressed to start the procedure of finding solutions. If solutions are found, GUI shows them with connections between the objects inside the working area.

To improve the GUI, time scale can be added into the working area. Along this line all the objects are shown at every time of a moment. Such improvement can allow to control the workload for objects at any moment. In addition, we can use this scheme to create a timetable for resource allocation in future outlooks.

5 Evaluation

Let demonstrate using of the DSL&DCSP framework proposed in a real case of the railway resource allocation. Suppose, for servicing trains the station has the next amount of railways (Table 2).

Suppose that three trains arrive at the station, and they have the following characteristics (Table 3).

In terms of DSL we have the following description of that context (Fig. 6).

Table 2. Characteristics of available railways.

Railway identifier	1	2	3
Type	Universal	Universal	Universal
Total length (in cars)	30	24	10
Useful length	28	22	7
Available equipment	Transporter, forklift, conveyor	Transporter, forklift, conveyor	Transporter, forklift

Table 3. Characteristics of arriving trains.

Train identifier	1	2	3
Type	dry cargo	dry cargo	tanks
Priority	High	High	regular
Total length (in cars)	14	16	8
Time arrival	14:03	14:47	15:12
Time departure	16:11	16:19	17:49
Needed services	Inspection, loading, unloading	Inspection, loading, unloading	Inspection, initial service
Cars to service	9	6	1

```
Services
1 1 0,67 0
21 0,450,05 [ 1 3 ]
31 10,5 [ 1 3 ]
endServicesBlock;
Equipment
1 Transporter
2 Forklift
3 Conveyor
endEquipmentBlock;
Railways
1 1 30 28 [ 1 2 3 ]
1 1 24 22 [ 1 2 3 ]

1 1 10 7 [ 1 2 ]
endRailwayBlock;
Trains
1 1 1 14 14:03 16:11 0 [ 1 3 4 ] 9
2 1 1 16 14:47 16:19 1 [ 1 3 4 ] 6
3 2 2 8 15:12 17:49 0 [ 1 2 ] 1
EndTrainsBlock;
```

Fig. 6. DSL scenario (objects)

To simplify the task, we can suppose, that four universal Brigades are available for servicing tasks. Then DSL&DCSP framework translates this DSL specification to the semantic model, which is based on the model of constraint satisfaction (Fig. 7).

Inside the DSL&DCSP framework the Choco solver accepts the constraints model and computes the result in terms of that model. During the final step, the Choco result is translated to the equivalent DSL-based form. The user obtains the result in the following form (Fig. 8).

As we can see, this solution is optimal for our task: services are available for parallel working and the amount of railways is enough for parallel servicing. And finally, trains with identifiers 2 and 3 are placed along the useful length of the second railway and can be located there. The framework provides an optimal solution in terms of effective using of available length of the railways and the factor of service brigades using. Besides, the final solution has ready-to-use domain commands for trains and brigade's allocation. It creates the stable context for future railway resources allocation and allows not only save reserves for changes in the allocation context, but increase the beneficial use of all types the resources.

In comparison, a currently used system, exploited in the railway transportation office, proposes another solution. That system allocates the train 3 on the railway 3 without combination with the train 2. This solution is not optimal, because it does not create a space reserve for the future outlook. Moreover, the currently used system spends more time solving the problem. The statistics is shown in Table 4.

Data in Table 5 show that our proposed DSL&DCSP framework spends on average 2/3 times less than the currently used system. It means that the developed framework is more flexible and is more oriented on the context.

```
Solver solver = new Solver();
IntVar L = VariableFactory.fixed("L", 30, solver);
IntVar deltMin = VariableFactory.fixed("deltMin", 20, solver);
IntVar[] l = VariableFactory.enumerated("l", 10, L.getValue(), solver);
IntVar[] s = VariableFactory.enumerated("s", 10, L.getValue(), solver);
IntVar[] delts = VF.enumerated ("delts", 9, 0, L.getValue(), solver);
solver.post(IntConstraintFactory.sum(new IntVar[]{s,l,delts}, "<=", L));
solver.post(IntConstraintFactory.sum(new
IntVar[]{s,l,VariableFactory.minus(delts)}, "<", s[0]));
```

Fig. 7. Choco DCSP-model view

```
Relocate 1 to 1 from 14:03;
Relocate 2 to 2 from 14:47;
Relocate 3 to 2 from 15:12;
Appoint 1 on 1 from 14:03 perform 1;
Appoint 1 on 1 from 14:03 perform 3;
Appoint 1 on 1 from 14:43 perform 4;
Appoint 2 on 2 from 14:47 perform 1;
Appoint 2 on 3 from 15:17 perform 1;
Appoint 3 on 2 from 14:47 perform 3;
Appoint 3 on 2 from 15:27 perform 4;
Appoint 4 on from 15:17 perform 2;
```

Fig. 8. DSL representation of the solution

Table 4. The comparison statistics

Model	Proposed DSL&DCSP framework	Current system
Time for finding solution (sec.)	17	39
Is solution optimal?	Yes	No

Table 5. Comparison of an existing system and DSL&DCSP Framework: average time for finding the solution (measured in sec.) The results of DSL&DCSP Framework are marked by bold.

		Amount of trains			
		10	25	50	100
Time Reserve (h.)	1	1.96 (**1.78**)	4.66 (**3.33**)	7.29 (**6.08**)	28.61 (**21.84**)
	2	10.38 (**7.41**)	16.23 (**12.48**)	23.47 (**16.77**)	160.27 (**126.19**)
	3	20.93 (**17.44**)	60.60 (**35.64**)	174.38 (**116.25**)	280.19 (**200.13**)

In addition to the time of finding solution, another additional characteristic is used for assessing the quality of the found solution – the utilization rate of a useful length of railways. It shows the quality of using railways and allows to evaluate the load of every railway: the higher the value, the better the quality of the distribution between the railways.

6 Conclusion

In our research we explored an opportunity to organize and simplify decision support during complex resource allocation processes by combining domain specific languages and distributed constraint satisfaction techniques. In the result we have developed DSL&DCSP Framework for decision support in the railway allocation process. That framework includes a domain-oriented external DSL for continuous accounting of changes in the domain, a syntactic analyzer for translating DSL commands into the terms of the semantic model and the DCSP solver Choco inside for solution search. The external DSL uses the concepts, which are equivalent to the main resources of the railway station: trains, railways, brigades and services. The framework translates these concepts into the terms of DCSP, which uses the Choco syntax. We also propose a prototype of GUI, which replaces the textual representation.

In contrast to other examples of using DSL&DCSP inside one framework (like [18]), our solution demonstrates the DSL&DCSP application for one specific domain of railway allocation problem. It facilitates effective specification of varying instances of the same model via different DSL scenarios.

Results of experiments show that the framework solves the allocation problem faster, then an existing system. In addition, the framework facilitates easy user-driven changes of specifications of the underlying model, because the framework uses GUI for this goal instead of the command line interface of the existing system.

According to theory and the case, shown above, we can say that proposed combination of DSL and DCSP becomes a really effective and clear tool for managing the dynamic context in the complex problem solving process. Moreover, we can approve, that proposed DSL&DCSP framework can be extended and applied to other problems. It is vital to outline, that such extension requires only changes in the mechanism of translating an external DSL into the base language. Other parts (a DCSP model, the solving procedure etc.) can be generated automatically. As a result, partial independence from the domain specifics makes the framework flexible and adaptable to different domains.

Playing the central role for the user-oriented context management, designed DSL gives many attractive opportunities for end-users. First of all, our DSL determines the context as well as concretizes it by special commands and objects. DSL also facilitates direct and comprehensive communication between developers and experts in the specific domain. In addition, DSL saves time of decision makers - understanding commands for the context management becomes easy because of their mnemonic nature.

Finally fused with the DCSP-based semantic model DSL offers new features in development new methods for finding solutions in dynamics contexts by providing a flexible mechanism for direct controlling the effectiveness and correctness of the model and its attributes by domain experts.

Our results show that DSL does not require redesign of existing models for solving problems. It can be integrated into current solving methods using XML files, containing information needed for DSL and for the next translation in terms of its semantic model. Such XML files can be used and as an equivalent to DSL, because of their nature, similar to the real language, its semantics and syntax.

All these findings support our initial hypothesis about an important role of DSLs in decision-making process due to significant improving the quality of the whole system and increasing its manageability and flexibility.

Planning further research, we consider such an extension of the proposed DSL&DCSP framework, which provides not only the optimal allocation of trains within one station, but also supports communication of different stakeholders during a complex decision process within different stations, distant from each other. In this case we will face the problem of semantic heterogeneity. We expect that new solutions should be proposed for real-time unification of disparate and heterogeneous DSLs into one single language, allowing precise specification of the interests and preferences of different stakeholders. In this context, we have not to mechanically combine parts of different DSLs, but find the way for communication of different stakeholders with opposite views on the context and its influence on them.

For achieving this goal an approach, described by Pereira, can be used. In [19] Pereira et al. used ontologies and specific grammars to create DSL structures. Starting with ontological specification of the target domain and using automated analyzers for parsing, they end with the DSL scenario, derived from fragmented descriptions of the problem. This approach requires changes in its structure, represented by an ontological analyzer, but allows combine different specifications of the current domain in final DSL language.

References

1. Binmore, K.: Rational decisions. Princeton University Press, Princeton (2009)
2. Hodgson, M.: On the Limits of Rational Choice Theory. Econ. Thought **1**, 94–108 (2012)
3. Fernandez-Lopez, M., Gomez-Perez, A.: Overview and analysis of methodologies for building ontologies. Knowl. Eng. Rev. **17**(2), 129–156 (2002). Cambridge University Press
4. Shcherbina, O.: Nonserial dynamic programming and tree decomposition in discrete optimization. In: Waldmann, K.-H., Stocker, U.M. (eds.) Proceedings of International Conference on Operations Research, pp. 155–160. Springer, Berlin (2007)
5. Martin, F.: Domain Specific Languages. Addison Wesley, Upper Saddle River (2010)
6. Terence, P.: Language Implementation Patterns: Create Your Own Domain-Specific and General Programming Languages. Pragmatic Bookshelf, Frisco (2012)
7. Eric, E.: Domain-Driven Design: Tackling Complexity in the Heart of Software. Addison-Wesley (2013)
8. Makoto, Y.: Distributed Constraint Satisfaction. Springer, Heidelberg (2001)
9. Choco solver. http://choco-solver.org/
10. MetaCase+. http://www.metacase.com/
11. ANother Tool for Language Recognition (ANTLR). http://www.antlr.org/
12. Gecode toolkit. http://www.gecode.org/
13. Barták, R. Constraint programming: in pursuit of the holy grail. In: Proceedings of WDS 1999 (Invited Lecture), pp. 555–564 (1999)
14. Eisenberg, C.: Distributed Constraint Satisfaction for Coordinating and Integrating a Large-Scale, Heterogeneous Enterprise, University of London (2003)

15. Bacchus, F., van Beek, P.: On the conversion between non-binary and binary constraint satisfaction problems. In: Proceedings of the 15th National Conference on Artificial Intelligence (AAAI 1998) and of the 10th Conference on Innovative Applications of Artificial Intelligence (IAAI 1998), pp. 311–318 (1998)
16. Kosar, T., Martınez Lopez, P., Barrientos, P., Mernik, M. A preliminary study on various implementation approaches of domain-specific language. In: Information and Software Technology, pp. 390–405. Elsevier (2008)
17. Disolver. http://research.microsoft.com/apps/pubs/default.aspx?id=64335
18. Prud'homme, C., Lorca, X., Douence, R., Jussien, N.: Propagation engine prototyping with a domain specific language. Constraints **19**(1), 57–77 (2013)
19. Pereira, M., Fonseca, J., Henriques, P.: Ontological approach for DSL development. In: Computer Languages, Systems & Structures, pp. 35–52. Elsevier (2016)

Information Systems Management

A Change Management Review: Extracting Concepts to Preserve Business and IT Alignment

Oscar Avila$^{(\boxtimes)}$, Kelly Garces, and Sebastian Sastoque

Department of Systems and Computing Engineering, School of Engineering,
University of Los Andes, K 1E 19A 40, Bogota, Colombia
{oj.avila,kj.garces971,s.sastoque10}@uniandes.edu.co
http://www.uniandes.edu.co

Abstract. Organisations introduce changes in order to adapt themselves to the extremely changing context. These changes often impact Information Technology (IT) and Business domains. In most of the cases, the scope of the organisational elements in these domains requiring adaptation is not well defined, leaving out elements, this can lead to misalignment. Thus, it is important to know the impact scope with the purpose of performing a full adaptation. When reviewing the literature in the Business-IT alignment research field, we found that there are no works providing support to deal with this aspect. However, there are several works in adjacent areas that have studied change management. In this paper, we report a systematic review of related work in these areas. From the review, we extract a set of clues applicable to the Business-IT alignment field what results in a change analysis framework and a set of rules to estimate impact scope and potential adaptation. Framework elements and rules are illustrated by means of a small example.

Keywords: Change forces · Organisation · Alignment · Information technology · Business-IT alignment · Strategic alignment

1 Introduction

In current competitive context, companies have to adapt themselves as a response to different types of forces and pressures. When adapting, companies introduce organisational changes. In most of cases, these changes have a ripple effect on organisational elements from Business and Information Technology (IT) domains, what is known as change impact [1].

By studying real cases, we found that to adapt the organisation to forces and pressures, IT and Business executive staff make decisions and elaborate action plans. However, because of the complexity of organisations, they may be unaware of the scope of the organisational elements impacted by their decisions and the nature of these elements. In this way, they will suggest only changes to the elements that are in their visibility and well known by them, most of the time the strategic ones, leaving out elements that could be equally impacted. The fact of neglecting change management in these elements may lead to misalignment.

© Springer International Publishing Switzerland 2016
V. Řepa and T. Bruckner (Eds.): BIR 2016, LNBIP 261, pp. 177–192, 2016.
DOI: 10.1007/978-3-319-45321-7_13

When reviewing the literature in the Business-IT alignment research field, we found that there is no works providing with support to forecast impact resulting from changes. What existing approaches do is to provide with support to correct misalignment that is a consequence of impact. Indeed, main research works in this field propose [2,3]: (i) *alignment assessing approaches:* enabling organisations to measure the alignment level between the two domains; (ii) *alignment building approaches:* dealing with the construction of alignment between Business and IT domains.

Therefore the objective of this paper is to review related work about change management in adjacent areas in order to find out clues and apply them in the context of Business-IT alignment. As a result of the application, we contribute a framework that allows the representation of organisational elements subject to change and a set of rules that determines impact scope and potential adaptation. The aim of this contribution is to provide organisations with means to maintain alignment between Business and IT by managing change.

To succeed in, firstly, we present in Sect. 2 a review of the state of the art in change management by following a systematic method and find out clues that help us to understand how change management is undertaken. Section 3 describes our framework and applies it to an illustrating example to ease the explanation of its concepts. Section 4 spells out the types of changes addressed by our approach, a set of rules for leveraging change propagation and illustrates them by using the example. Finally, Sect. 5 concludes the paper, compares our approach to related work and outlines future work.

2   Literature Review

Commonly systematic reviews consist of three phases: planning, conducting and reporting. Within those phases are the following steps [3,4]: (1) Identification of the need for a systematic review. (2) Formulation of a set of review questions. (3) A comprehensive, exhaustive search for primary approaches. (4) Validation and assessment of found approaches with respect to the research questions. (5) Identification and extraction of data needed to describe the approaches and analyse them. (6) Analysis with respect to the review questions and synthesis of the results. (7) Interpretation of the results to determine their applicability. We present the application of these steps to review change management works as follows: Step 1 is described in the Sect. 1. Steps 2 to 4 are described in Sect. 2.1, step 5 is reported in Sect. 2.2 and finally steps 6 and 7 are detailed in Sect. 2.3.

2.1   Review Questions and Approaches Selection

The review goal is to find out clues in adjacent research fields that help us to comprehend the nature of changes and how such changes are propagated in order to apply this understanding to Business-IT alignment. Hence, we conducted a preliminary literature study on change impact and found out a relevant survey [4]. Based on this survey, we formulate the following four research questions to classify the contributions of related work on change management: (1) Why is there a change?. (2) What can be impacted by the change?. (3) What are the type of changes?. (4) How is the propagation of the change?.

In order to search for primary approaches (step 3), we use the Scopus Database by introducing the following criteria: (i) Searching terms: change management, change impact, change propagation, change analysis, impact analysis, change type, and change forces. (ii) Search field type: abstract, title and keywords. (iii) Date range: published from 2006 to 2015.

Given these criteria, the Scopus searching engine gave as a result 650 candidate articles across the subject areas of computer sciences and decision sciences, specifically in the context of the following subareas: information technology, information systems, software engineering, enterprise modelling, software changes, software architecture, object oriented and model driven. To limit the number of papers, firstly, we limited to articles published in journals indexed at Scimago Ranking in quartiles Q1 and Q2 or published at the proceedings of international conferences ranked at Computing Research and Education (CORE) Conference Ranking. This first filter limited the number of works to 110. Secondly, we discarded papers whose title did not mention any of the following subjects: change propagation, impact, analysis and forces, what reduced the number of works to 40. Finally, we read the papers abstract and we eliminated works that did not show evidence of answering any of the raised review questions (step 4). A group of 16 papers were identified and classified in one of the following areas: software engineering, enterprise architecture and requirements engineering.

2.2   Approaches Description

In order to undertake step 5, data was identified, extracted and summarised for selected approaches. A description and classification of them is given below.

Software Engineering. Bohner [5] describe how impact analysis can be addressed through a software change process. This process consists of five activities derived from the software life-cycle process as follows: (i) Manage software change. (ii) Understand Software with respect to the change and determine impact. (iii) Specifying and design the software change. (iv) Implement software change. (v) Retesting the affected software. In this approach, changes are invoked by change requests generated by users (operations staff, system administrators, and end- users). These change requests and the current software system are the key inputs of the change process. The key output of this process is a new software system which is turned over to end users for use.

Jang et al. [6], made a research in the context of object oriented systems. It proposes an approach for analysing change impact in a class hierarchy to reduce retesting efforts. The class hierarchy is described as a graph where the nodes represent methods and attributes and edges represent data dependency and control dependency as well as inheritance. In order to reduce testing effort, the authors propose a set of base cases that relate three aspects: (i) elements of the class hierarchy that can be impacted and change types, (ii) the corresponding ripple effect, and (iii) the specific test needed to verify whether the change broke the functionality.

Chen et al. [7], propose a model-based method to manage software change impact in a holistic approach, i.e., analysing impact on all software products (software components, requirements, documents and data) and not only at code level. This method uses a model and a heuristic rule to identify the impacted products. The proposed model is defined with the following components: Items, that represent the products contents; Attributes, which describe items; Linkage, that connect items and bind attributes; Changes, which affect attributes and are applied on items; and, Impacts, that are generated by a change and have effects on attributes and items. The mechanism that allows propagation of changes through the model is defined by using a heuristic rule, in which an impact is iteratively propagated by the linkages among all the impacted attributes.

Marzullo et al. [8], focuses on the context of Model-Driven Development, specifically on identifying how changes at the requirement level impact the software code and vice-versa. They propose an analysis strategy based on the direct association between the requirements, the software model and the code. This association is established in two steps: first, at the model design phase, tags are added in classes for each fulfilled requirement; and second, at the code generation phase, these tags are transformed into annotations in the code of each class. From the model and the code, the authors propose to create a traceability path using visual graphs, in which each node represents a class or a requirement. The impact analysis is performed by phases in which the nodes are tagged and the impact propagation is performed by transitivity on a graph.

Li et al. [9], propose a technique to calculate impact change in software programs developed with object-oriented paradigm. Specifically, their approach uses Formal Concepts Analysis (FCA) that consists of inferring a concepts hierarchy, by using mathematical techniques, from the relation between entities and their properties. In order to apply FCA, object classes are considered as entities and their methods as properties. The relation between entities and properties are represented using Lattice of Class and Method Dependence (LoCMD). Impact propagation is performed by using the LoCMD and a heuristic impact metric allowing to identify and prioritise the impacted classes and methods. The impact metric is based on the distance between nodes and the identification of joint nodes.

Enterprise Architecture. De Boer et al. [10], proposes a framework for mastering the ripple effects of changes occurring in business strategy and goals within ArchiMate models. Archimate is an enterprise architecture modelling language that focuses on the description of domains within an organisation and the relationships between them. ArchiMate concepts include role, component, process, service and data object, among others. ArchiMate relationships are access, assign, use, realise, trigger, etc. Relationships have their own intended semantics allowing the definition of heuristic rules for calculating direct impact. Three kinds of changes, namely, removing, extending and modifying, are considered.

Kumar et al. [11], presents an enterprise ontology for analysing change impact. The aim of the approach is to support decision making in the architecture management life cycle process. The methodology includes the creation of a logical enterprise model composed of instances of the concepts included in the ontology: business goals, processes, services, infrastructure components and the associations between them. The approach defines rules that allow the change propagation along the enterprise model and helps one to determine the impact on the capacity and availability of services in terms of the attributes composing them.

Diaz et al. [12], propose a change impact analysis technique for Product Line Architectures (PLA) evolution. It proposes to join a traceability-based algorithm and a rule-based inference engine to navigate PLA models via a set of traceability links and propagation rules. The PLA Models are the following: (i) Feature model: specifies the functional and non-functional requirements offered in the product line. (ii) Flexible-PLA Model: describes the PLA structure in terms of components, services, interfaces, aspects and their connections. (iii) PLAK (Product Line Architecture Knowledge) Model: capture variability design rationale, as well as the traceability link between requirements and PLAs. The rules specify how to propagate a change from a model to other through traceability links.

Wang et al. [13], propose a service-oriented business process model to understand the nature of various types of changes that can happen to services and business processes in an organisation and to analyse the change impacts on the entire system. The proposed approach for change impact analysis is based on the study of the dependencies between services and business processes, the identified types of changes, and the change impact patterns. The latter are categorised into impact patterns for service changes and process changes and each one captures a specific type of change effect.

Weidlich et al. [14], made a proposal to analyse change propagation between two semantically overlapping process models that are aligned by correspondences. Their proposal is based on process models representation in the form of Petri Nets, i.e., a directed bipartite graph, which serves to represent a discrete event system in a graphical mode. In this representation, the nodes symbolise transitions (activities or events) and places (conditions), and the arcs describe the position (pre or post) of a place with respect to a transition. The impact propagation between two aligned processes is performed by using the transition relations by using their behavioural profile.

Fdhila et al. [15], propose an approach in the context of choreography processes in which processes are shared between partner enterprises, e.g., cross-organisational manufacturing. The approach uses choreography models to represent interaction between partners processes which are classified in two types: (i) private processes, that are internal operations of each enterprise that are not visible to other partners, and (ii) public processes, that describe views of internal processes making them visible to other partners. Those models are formalised by using Refined Processes Structure Trees (RPST), which are a decomposition of a process model into a set of single-entry/single-exit fragments. The authors propose 4 process change patterns: Insert, Replace, Update and Delete. Impact propagation is performed on the model by defining specific propagation rules for each pattern.

Requirements Engineering. Goknil et al. [16], introduce a metamodel that represent: requirement, requirement relation, requirement property and property constraint. The requirements are defined as a description of a system properties and their constraints, which need to be fulfilled. The relations are given by semantic structures in First Order Logic, i.e., symbolised reasoning where a structure is broken into two parts and one modifies or defines the properties of the other. For each element, three types of changes are proposed: Add, Delete and Update. The impact propagation is done by a change impact function which has as input the change type and the changed requirement and as output a set of decision trees.

Zhang et al. [17], propose a requirements dependency model that defines nine types of dependency relationships: *constrain, precede, be similar to, refine, be exception of, conflict, evolve into, increase/decrease cost* and *increase/decrease value*. The model has two top-level (dependency) and six low-level (source of dependency) categories to represent the requirements. The authors define a change pattern for each dependency and the change propagation is performed by using these patterns and the model structure to identify impacted requirements that affect either the software development process or the final software product features.

2.3   Review Analysis and Interpretation

Table 1 synthesises the contributions of the selected approaches according to the four research questions (step 6). Summarising from the table, it can be concluded the following with respect to each research question:

1. *Why is there a change?* Generally changes are motivated by forces. These forces can have an external source (i.e. regulatory policies, external needs, etc.) [5,12,13,16] or an internal source (software evolution, software maintenance, organisational policies, etc.) [5,9,12,13,16,17].
2. *What can be impacted by the change?* Elements or abstractions that serve to describe an organisational or software system. When regarding the approaches, we see that all of them have elements that can be arranged in a graph whose nodes represent requirements, components, artifacts, entities, etc. and links, in turn, describe relationships among the elements.
3. *What are the types of changes?* Type of changes include add, delete and modify elements/abstractions. Any other type of change can be expressed by means of these three types, for example, a replacement [13,15] is the

Table 1. Answers of related works to research questions

Ref	Why is there a change?	What can be impacted by a change?	What are the types of changes?	How is the propagation of changes?
		Software engineering		
[5]	- User requests	- Software life cycle objects	- No specified	- No specified
[6]	- No specified	- Nodes (i.e., classes, attributes, methods) - Edges (i.e., inheritance relationships)	- Add - Delete - Modify	- Through graph edges - According to base cases
[7]	- Business conditions - Customer demand - Reorganization of business - Budgetary constraints - Scheduling constraints	Software products: - Design documents - Software component - External data - Requirement	- Add, delete or update of software products	- Through linkages - By a heuristic rule
[8]	- No specified	- Requirements - Classes	- Update requirements or classes	- By transitivity rules
[9]	- Software maintenance	- Classes - Methods	- Update classes and methods	- Through relations - By a heuristic metric
		Enterprise architecture		
[10]	- No specified	- ArchiMate concepts	- Delete - Modify - Extend	- By means of ArchiMate relationships - By applying heuristic rules
[11]	- No specified	- Enterprise model elements	- No specified	- According to propagation rules
[12]	- Technical factors - Business factors	- Feature model - PLA artifacts	Changes: addition, deletion, modification	- Through traceability links - According to propagation rules
[13]	- Organisational policies - Regulatory policies	- Service layer - Process layer	- Add, delete, modify, replace	- Through dependencies - By applying impact patterns
[14]	- No specified	- Aligned processes - Relations of behavioural profile	Insert, delete or replace: - Processes - Relations of behavioural profile	- By change process
[15]	- New regulations - New competitors	- Public or private processes on partner enterprises	- Replace, insert, delete, update	- By propagation rules on change patterns
		Requirements engineering		
[16]	- Evolution of business needs	- Requirements - Software architecture - Design documents - Source code	Add, delete or update of Requirements, Properties and Constrains	- By change patterns
[17]	- Software evolution	- Requirements	- Add, delete or update of requirements	- By change patterns

aggregation of a deletion and an addition. Furthermore, in [12], types are classified in terms of structural and behavioural aspects.

4. *How is the propagation of the change?* Propagation is made through relationships and calculated by a formal logic using rules [7, 8, 12], patterns [13, 15–17], process [14] and metrics [9].

From the above analysis, we get the following four clues (step 7): (i) changes are motivated by forces, (ii) impact occurs on components and relationships, (iii) type of changes include add, delete and modify, (iv) impact is propagated through relationships, and a logic is used to determine impact scope.

2.4 Illustrating Example

The example is based on the real case of a world leading company that develops railway equipment (e.g., boogies, motors, traction systems) in a relatively stable market in which it has a comfortable and dominant position. The position of the company was in risk by the arrival of a new entrant having the ability to deliver customised products matching better customers needs. To be able to equal the new entrant offer, the executive committee of the company decided to formulate a new business objective, namely, "to supply customised products to the customer".

Implementing this new business strategy would impact the way in which the products are produced, that is, the design and manufacturing processes. These processes are supported by software applications and IT infrastructures such as a PLM (Product Lifecycle Management) application. This application manages the PBS (Product Breakdown Structure) describing the product hierarchical tree structures (physical, functional or conceptual). Besides this, it was necessary the integration of the PLM application with front office applications allowing customers to configure products.

The IT area of the company assumes the maintenance of the PLM application by following a well defined processes. Sometimes (e.g. in holiday period) they are supported by outsourcing teams. In addition, to modify this application and integrate it with the front office application, a partnership with the PLM supplier was carried out because the company lacks of skills in this subject.

3   Change Management Framework for Business-IT Alignment

In order to to develop the framework, we employed a methodology consisting of three steps: (i) Analysis of concepts proposed by related work concerning the two first clues mentioned above. (ii) Application of the two first clues to Business-IT alignment. To succeed in, we rely on our previous work [18] that explains the rationale behind the found concepts which is supported by related work. (iii) Organisation of concepts to build the framework following the structure element/attribute/value.

3.1   Change Are Motivated by Forces

Forces at the source of organisational change can be classified by their nature into two groups: external and internal.

External sources categories: From a review of main works in the scanning environment area, we suggest the following three external change forces: *External actors:* It deals with complex networks of actors present in the external environment. These networks encompass a large number of interdependent organisations which are interrelated in an intricate way. *External needs:* It represents the demand side of the organisation environment. Actually, changing user needs may require changes into the companies in order to adapt them to these needs. *External issues:* It can be defined as open and debatable questions, events or other forthcoming developments whose realisation can significantly influence the future conditions of the environment.

Internal sources categories: We reviewed the main works in the scanning environment area in [18] and suggested the following three internal change forces: *Internal actors:* Because of their political power, the impact of their decisions and their capacity to lead transformation, internal actors or stakeholders represent an internal force. *Internal needs:* It is defined as the evolution of the internal requirements. It includes evolving needs from internal customers or departments. Therefore, new or modified IT and business services would need to be defined. *Internal issues:* It represents events or other forthcoming developments (e.g., political factors, institutional development and grown, evolutions in organisational culture and governance, etc.) whose realisation can significantly change the future conditions of the organisation.

From the review made in this section, we propose the element *"change source"* as the first element of the framework. This element is structured by three attributes with respective values (see Fig. 1).

3.2   Impact Occurs on Components and Relationships

In order to answer this question, it is proposed to rely on the following definition of Business-IT alignment [2]: Business-IT alignment is considered as the relation between components of the IT domain, including the IT strategy and structure, and components of the Business domain, including business strategy and processes. From this definition, the elements, that can be impacted, are the organisational components of the IT and Business domains as well as the relationships between them. Below we highlight the characteristics of these elements.

Components: Trying to describe Business-IT alignment components in terms of their attributes, to study potential impact on them, can be very difficult and the risk of leaving out some possible attributes can be very high [18]. As a result, it is suggested to characterise Business-IT alignment components by determining their position into the organisation. Thus, we rely on the characterisation made on the Strategic Alignment Model (SAM) [19] that helps one to understand the areas of the organisation involved depending on the position of the component into the SAM sub-domains (i.e. Business strategy, Organisational infrastructure and processes, IT strategy and IS infrastructure and processes). From these concepts, we propose *"component"* as the second element of the framework that is structured by three attributes with respective values as indicated in Fig. 1.

Relationships: In related work, we found that relationship types and components roles (attached to relationships) are used to study change propagation. In addition, relationship type can be impacted and changed. That is why we consider that the attributes *type* and *role* are relevant to relationships. We establish that each relationship has two components playing the next two roles: (i) A component is named the *requester*, i.e., the component that requests for business and IT capabilities. (ii) The other component is so-called the *enabler*, that is, the component that supplies capabilities in order to satisfy the requirement. Relationships are of two possible types [18]: (i) *Necessary*: The necessary relationship links a component B with a component A that realises it, where A is mandatory for B realisation. (ii) *Useful*: The useful relationship describes the relation between a component A that helps to realise a component B, but A is not mandatory. Considering the above exposed concepts, we propose the element *"relationship"* as the third framework element and structure it as shown in Fig. 1.

Element	Attribute	Values	Notation		
Change Source	Source	External	Textual		
		Internal			
	Force	Actors			
		Needs			
		Issues			
	Description	Free	Textual		
Component	Component Name	Free value	Name		
	Domain	Business	External Internal	Business	IT
		Information Technologies (IT)			
	Level	External (strategy)			
		Internal (structure)			
	Id	Set automatically	Textual		
Relationship	Requester	A component	R—		
	Enabler	A component	→E		
	Type	Necessary	——→		
		Useful	- - -→		

Fig. 1. Framework notation and values

3.3 Applying the Framework to Illustrating Example

Change source: The arrival of a new entrant offering customised products is the change source because it was the motivation behind the organisational changes. This change source instantiates the first element of the framework as follows: (i) Source: External, (ii) Force: Actor, (iii) Description: New entrant (see Fig. 2).

Components: The organisational components of the company described by using the notation in Fig. 1 are presented in Fig. 2. To show how we define these components, consider the case of Component A (Value proposition): The decision of "supplying customised products to the customer" will impact, in a first time, the value proposition of the company. This is a typical business strategic element as it defines the positioning of the company in the market. Thus, a first component is instantiated as follows: Component name: Value proposition, Domain: Business, and Level: External.

Relationship: Figure 2 shows the relationships for illustrating example. For instance, relationship R5 is the relationship between component D (PLM maintenance process) and component F (Human Resource HR-outsourcing- for PLM maintenance), where D is the requester and F the enabler. R5 is type of useful because PLM maintenance process normally is carried out by component E (Human Resource HR-internal- for PLM maintenance), however maintenance task may require extra manpower hired in outsourcing in some periods of the year, that is, component F is useful but not mandatory for D realisation.

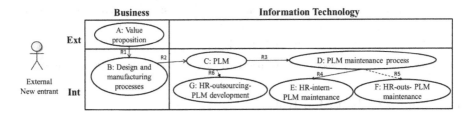

Fig. 2. Application of framework to illustrating example

4 Change Propagation Analysis

In this section, we spell out the types of changes for which our approach performs propagation. After that, we suggest a set of rules that leverages change propagation.

4.1 Type of Changes Include Add, Delete and Modify

Taking into consideration types of changes in related work, types of changes for components and relationships are described as follows:

Components: (i) Introduce a new component to supply capabilities not fully satisfied by the existing components. (ii) Modify an enabler component to add/alter its behaviour in order to satisfy new requirements needed for a requester. Modify a requester component to alter the way in which it accesses enabler capabilities. The modification on requester is motivated by a change force or a prior modification on other component. (iii) Delete component if it is no necessary anymore, i.e., it provides no capabilities to other components and requires no capabilities from other components.

Relationship: (i) Introduce a new relationship from a requester to an enabler. (ii) Modify the type of a relationship from necessary to useful or vice-versa. Modify the enabler or requester of a relationship. (iii) Delete a relationship if enabler is no longer required by requester.

4.2 A Logic Is Used to Determine Impact Scope

We have chosen rules as the underlying logic to propagate changes. The reasons behind this decision are: (i) Their facility of implementation: a rule can be coded as a condition and an action in a representation language. (ii) It is easy to implement an algorithm that in a (semi) automatic way propagates the changes by querying rules. (iii) Rules in a repository makes the algorithm more maintainable, simple and clean than embedded them in the algorithm itself. Each rule consists of:

A condition: Considering the third clue (impact is propagated through relationships), it is defined as an expression that evaluates: (i) the type of change (see last subsection), (ii) the role of the component undergoing the change (enabler or requester) and (iii) the relationship type (necessary or useful).

Actions: the set of possible adaptations needed for avoiding misalignment.

4.3   Impact/Adaptation Rules

Both rules and actions are enumerated to ease their application. In some cases, there is no need for carrying out any adaptation meaning that there is no impact.

Rule I: *Condition*: (i) Change type: modification, (ii) Component role: requester, and (iii) Relationship type: necessary. *Actions*: (1) If there are no new requirements from the modified requester, the enabler does not need to be modified as the requester will be able to use the current services or functions from the enabler. (2) If there are new requirements, a first option is to modify the enabler in order to satisfy the new requirements. In this case, the relationship type remains as "necessary". (3) If there are new requirements, a second option is to introduce or modify a relationship from the requester to another enabler in order to satisfy the new requirements. Concerning the former enabler, two options are possible too: (i) deletion, if it is not necessary anymore, or (ii) modification, if it is necessary to support a part of old requirements or new ones or other requesters. This action will lead to modification or deletion of the respective relationship between the former enabler and the requester.

Rule II: *Condition*: (i) Change type: modification, (ii) Component role: requester, and (iii) Relationship type: useful. *Action*: As the requester was able to fulfil its needs without directly requiring business or IT capabilities from the enabler, it is not necessary to modify the enabler or the relationship between them.

Rule III: *Condition*: (i) Change type: modification, (ii) Component role: enabler, and (iii) Relationship type: necessary. *Actions*: (1) If the reason behind the enabler modification involves new Business or IT possibilities needed for the requester then it is suggested to modify the requester in order to take advantage from these possibilities. (2) If the enabler modification impacts the realisation of the requester then the action is to introduce a new relationship that links the requester to an enabler (a new or an existing one) in order to fully satisfy the requester needs. (3) If the enabler modification does not affect the realisation of the requester then there is no need for modifying the requester.

Rule IV: *Condition*: (i) Change type: modification, (ii) Component role: enabler, and (iii) Relationship type: useful. *Action*: As the enabler just helps to the requester realisation, the modification of the former requires no adaptations on the later.

Rule V: *Condition*: (i) Change type: deletion, (ii) Component role: requester, and (iii) Relationship type: necessary or useful. *Actions*: (1) It is not encouraged to delete or modify the enabler if it is required by other requesters. (2) The enabler and the relationship may be deleted if the enabler is not required by other requesters.

Rule VI: *Condition*: (i) Change type: Deletion, (ii) Component role: enabler, and (iii) Relationship type: necessary. *Action*: It is not necessary to adapt the requester component. What requester needs is a new enabler supplying the capabilities of former enabler no longer available because of deletion. Thus, adaptation actions only imply relationships as follows: (i) to introduce a new relationship between the requester and an enabler component (a new or an existing one), (ii) to delete the old relationship linking the requester and the removed enabler.

Rule VII: *Condition*: (i) Change type: deletion, (ii) Component role: enabler, and (iii) Relationship type: useful. *Action*: No need for adaptation because the deleted enabler is not mandatory for requester realisation.

Rule VIII: *Condition*: (i) Change type: introduction, (ii) Component role: requester, and (iii) Relationship type: necessary or useful. *Actions*: Depending on the requester needs three options are possible: (1) Introduction of a new relationship between the requester and an existing enabler. This enabler may require a few modifications. (2) Introduction of a new enabler to the system because any of the existing components does not fully satisfy the requester needs. In addition, introduction of a new relationship between the requester and the new enabler. (3) Application of both actions mentioned in previous items.

Rule IX: *Condition*: (i) Change type: introduction, (ii) Component role: enabler, and (iii) Relationship type: necessary. *Action*: If a component is introduced as an enabler of a requester then the later needs no adaptations since it is just requiring some capabilities from the enabler in order to achieve its realisation. The only adaptation concerns relationships as follows: introduction of a new relationship between the new enabler and the requester.

Rule X: *Condition*: (i) Change type: introduction, (ii) Component role: enabler, and (iii) Relationship type: useful. *Action*: No need for adapting the requester because the introduced enabler is not mandatory for requester realisation. The only adaptation concerns relationships as follows: introduction of a new relationship between the new enabler and the requester.

4.3.1   Applying Impact/Adaptation Rules to Illustrating Example

Given the decision "supplying customised products to the customer", component A (value proposition) is the first component undergoing a change (it is modified).

From component A, change is propagated to component B through the relationship R1 (see Fig. 2). From there, changes propagation follows the sequence: B R2 C, C R6 G, C R3 D, D R4 E and D R5 F (see Fig. 2). Below we present two steps of the sequence to illustrate the application of the impact/adaptation rules:

A R1 B: Component A is related to B (design and manufacturing processes) via the relationship R1. Given the type of change on component A (modification), the component role (requester) and relationship type between the two components (necessary) the rule to be applied is number I. Now, as this modification involves new design and manufacturing requirements, two set of actions are possible (actions 2 and 3 of rule I). As design and manufacturing process are very complex and strongly coupled to the manufacturing infrastructure, introducing new components (option 3) would be too expensive. That is why the most appropriate option to be applied is number 2.

C R6 G: The company lacks of technical skills required for evolving the functionality of the PLM application (component C) in order to support changes on the design and manufacturing process (component B). To cope with this, the company signs a partnership with the PLM supplier, that is, a new component referred to as G (HR-outsourcing-PLM development) is introduced. In this case, the rule to be applied is number IX and the action 1 which consists of introducing a new relationship (R6) between G and C.

5   Conclusion and Future Work

In this paper, a detailed review in change management was carried out in order to conceptualise how this subject is addressed in adjacent areas and find out clues applicable to the Business-IT alignment field. From these clues, this paper proposes a framework that aims at analysing changes and a set of rules that determines impact scope and suggests potential adaptations. The application of the framework to the illustrating example shows that it helps analysts to: (i) determine change sources; (ii) define impacted elements through placing organisational components into a domain/level model and characterising the relationships between them. In turn, applying the set of rules to the example help analysts to (iii) classify the type of the change; (iv) identify if there was an impact or not and propose a set of adaptations.

When comparing our approach to related work we found the following similarities and differences. The reviewed works aim at maintaining coherence in enterprise models, software systems or requirement specifications. Our approach addresses a similar problem because its main objective is to maintain Business-IT alignment, i.e., preserve coherence between Business and IT elements.

The following are the main differences: (i) the elements of related work are very specialised to specific subareas while the elements of our framework are transversely applicable to different areas; (ii) in contrast to related work in which type of elements are homogeneous, our approach gives the possibility of representing elements that can be heterogeneous; (iii) unlike related work where element simplicity allows the automation of the propagation process, in our approach, propagation must be assisted by the analyst because of the complexity of the involved organisational elements.

As future work, a tool allowing the following is desired: (i) to apply the framework and the rules by using a graphical/textual editor, and (ii) to calculate the actions in a (semi) automatic way.

References

1. Buckley, J., Mens, T., Zenger, M., Rashid, A., Kniesel, G.: Towards a taxonomy of software change. J. Softw. Mainten. Evol. Res. Pract. **17**(5), 309–332 (2005)
2. Avila, O., Goepp, V., Kiefer, F.: Understanding and classifying information system alignment approaches. J. Comput. Inf. Syst. **50**(1), 2–14 (2009)
3. Ullah, A., Lai, R.: A systematic review of business and information technology alignment. ACM Trans. Manag. Inf. Syst. (TMIS) **4**(1), 4 (2013)
4. Williams, B.J., Carver, J.C.: Characterizing software architecture changes: a systematic review. Inf. Softw. Technol. **52**(1), 31–51 (2010)
5. Bohner, S.A.: Impact analysis in the software change process: a year 2000 perspective. In: Conference on Software Maintenance, pp. 42–51 (1996)
6. Jang, Y.K., Chae, H.S., Kwon, Y.R., Bae, D.H.: Change impact analysis for a class hierarchy. In: Proceedings of Asia Pacific Software Engineering Conference, pp. 304–311 (1998)
7. Chen, C., Chen, P.: A holistic approach to managing software change impact. J. Syst. Softw. **82**(12), 2051–2067 (2009)
8. Marzullo, F.P., De Mario, V.F., Da Silva, J.P., Nunes, L.S., De Souza, J.M.: A model-driven development (MDD) approach to change impact analysis. In: ICIS 2010 Proceedings - 31st International Conference on Information Systems (2010)
9. Li, B., Sun, X., Keung, J.: Fca-cia: An approach of using fca to support cross-level change impact analysis for object oriented java programs. Inf. Softw. Technol. **55**(8), 1437–1449 (2013)
10. De Boer, F.S., Bonsangue, M.M., Groenewegen, L.P.J., Stam, A.W., Stevens, S., Van Der Torre, L.: Change impact analysis of enterprise architectures. In: Proceedings of the 2005 IEEE International Conference on IRI, pp. 177–181 (2005)
11. Kumar, A., Raghavan, P., Ramanathan, J., Ramnath, R.: Enterprise interaction ontology for change impact analysis of complex systems. In: Proceedings of the 3rd IEEE Asia-Pacific Services Computing Conference, pp. 303–309 (2008)
12. Díaz, J., Pérez, J., Garbajosa, J., Wolf, A.L.: Change impact analysis in product-line architectures. In: Crnkovic, I., Gruhn, V., Book, M. (eds.) ECSA 2011. LNCS, vol. 6903, pp. 114–129. Springer, Heidelberg (2011)
13. Wang, Y., Yang, J., Zhao, W., Su, J.: Change impact analysis in service-based business processes. Serv. Orient. Comput. Appl. **6**(2), 131–149 (2012)
14. Weidlich, M., Mendling, J., Weske, M.: Propagating changes between aligned process models. J. Syst. Softw. **85**(8), 1885–1898 (2012)
15. Fdhila, W., Indiono, C., Rinderle-Ma, S., Reichert, M.: Dealing with change in process choreographies: design and implementation of propagation algorithms. Inf. Syst. **49**, 1–24 (2015)
16. Goknil, A., Kurtev, I., Berg, K., Spijkerman, W.: Change impact analysis for requirements: a metamodeling approach. Inf. Softw. Technol. **56**(8), 950–972 (2014)

17. Zhang, H., Li, J., Zhu, L., Jeffery, R., Liu, Y., Wang, Q., Li, M.: Investigating dependencies in software requirements for change propagation analysis. Inf. Softw. Technol. **56**(1), 40–53 (2014)
18. Avila, O., Garcés, K.: Change management contributions for business-IT alignment. In: Abramowicz, W., Kokkinaki, A. (eds.) BIS 2014 Workshops. LNBIP, vol. 183, pp. 156–167. Springer, Heidelberg (2014)
19. Henderson, J., Venkatraman, N.: Strategic alignment: leveraging information technology for transforming organizations. IBM Syst. J. **32**(1), 4–17 (1993)

Cloud Computing Governance Reference Model

Soňa Karkošková[1] and George Feuerlicht[1,2,3(✉)]

[1] Department of Information Technologies, Faculty of Informatics and Statistics, University of Economics, Prague, W. Churchill Sq. 4, 130 67 Prague 3, Czech Republic
{xkars05,jiri.feuerlicht}@vse.cz
[2] Unicorn College, V Kapslovně 2767/2, 130 00 Prague 3, Czech Republic
[3] Faculty of Engineering and Information Technology, University of Technology Sydney, Sydney, NSW 2007, Australia

Abstract. Large-scale adoption of cloud computing has resulted in the fragmentation of responsibilities over IT resources between consumers and providers of cloud services, necessitating the re-assessment of governance principles and processes. In this paper we have described a Cloud Computing Governance Reference Model that is an adaptation of the SOA Governance Reference Model with specific extensions to cover the governance requirements of cloud computing environments. The reference model includes definition of guiding principles and specification of governance processes.

Keywords: SOA Governance Reference Model · Cloud Computing Governance Reference Model

1 Introduction

The current rapidly changing business environment necessitates high business agility in order to control costs and to maintain a competitive market position. A key challenge for Information technology (IT) management is aligning IT capabilities to the needs of business while at the same time reducing the risk and optimizing the use of IT resources. To protect their investment, IT organizations must implement governance policies and processes that enable flexible and rapid reaction to a changing business environment.

Cloud computing provides shared, scalable and flexible IT resources in the form of services over the Internet, simplifying and accelerating the implementation of information systems, typically resulting in cost reductions and improved business agility [1]. However, to achieve these benefits, appropriate governance methods that maximize the business value of IT while minimizing associated risks and costs, have to be implemented. At present, widely accepted IT governance frameworks lack focus on cloud computing governance and do not fully address the requirements of cloud computing [2].

SOA Governance Framework [4] is recognized as the international standard [5] for governance of Service-Oriented Architecture (SOA). SOA and cloud computing share key concepts and characteristics presenting an opportunity for a unified service governance framework [6–9]. However, there are also significant differences between SOA and cloud, in particular the assumption that SOA services are designed, developed,

© Springer International Publishing Switzerland 2016
V. Řepa and T. Bruckner (Eds.): BIR 2016, LNBIP 261, pp. 193–203, 2016.
DOI: 10.1007/978-3-319-45321-7_14

provisioned and controlled on-premise by the end-user organization [3]. In the case of public cloud computing services, cloud service providers assume responsibility for the risks associated with the development, provision and maintenance of services typically providing services to a large number of consumers [10]. It follows that cloud service providers cannot take into account the needs of each individual service consumer [9]. The recent shift towards the use of externally provided cloud computing services in enterprise applications has altered the basic premise of SOA governance requiring the re-assessment of governance principles and processes.

In this paper we describe the adaptation of the SOA Governance Reference Model for cloud computing environments taking the service consumer perspective. We describe a Cloud Computing Governance Reference Model (CCGRM) that facilitates the governance of cloud computing in end user organizations. Our approach is based Design Science Research Methodology presented by Peffers [11] starting with literature review, and based on this literature review we have defined the research problem and the objectives of the CCGRM model. We have applied the CCGRM model in an IT organization and observed the impact of using the model on governance processes.

In the next section (Sect. 2) we review related literature. Section 3 introduces the proposed Cloud Computing Governance Reference Model, and Sect. 4 describes how the model was verified. The final section (Sect. 5) gives conclusions and proposals for future work.

2   Literature Review

Dehghani [12] argues that today's organizations need an effective governance framework to determine the requirements of governance and to evaluate the current state of governance in their organization. Over the last decade, a number of IT governance frameworks including COBIT, ITIL, ISO 38500 for Corporate governance of information technology or Service-oriented Architecture (SOA) governance have been developed and deployed in organizations [13]. According to the Open Group [3] effective SOA governance helps to establish decision-making model and organizational structures and to define processes and metrics required to ensure that SOA implementation meets strategic business goals. Numerous SOA governance approaches have been developed [14–18], but there is no widely accepted cloud computing governance standard [19]. Cloud computing has emerged as an evolving approach for delivering shared and configurable IT resources as services over the Internet [22]. As cloud computing shares basic principles of service-oriented computing with SOA [23], cloud computing governance can be considered as a specialized SOA governance system or its extension [24]. Most SOA governance principles can be applied to cloud computing services [19–21], however there is a lack of research that addresses the adaptation of these principles and corresponding processes of SOA governance for cloud computing environments.

The SOA Governance Framework developed by the Open Group covers in detail the governance principles for governing Service-Oriented Architecture environments [14]. SOA Governance Framework was ratified as an international standard ISO/IEC 17998: 2012 Information technology - SOA Governance Framework [22]. SOA Governance

Framework describes SOA Governance Reference Model, which defines aspects of SOA governance including guiding principles, processes, artifacts, roles and responsibilities, and technology [3]. SOA Governance guiding principles define common rules to support business and IT alignment [3]. They assist in the prioritization and decision-making for design, deployment and execution of SOA Governance Reference Model reflecting three governance aspects: people, processes and technology. SOA Governance *governing* processes are constantly executing in an organization and govern *governed* processes that are being controlled, monitored and measured [3].

3   Cloud Computing Governance Reference Model

Large-scale adoption of cloud services causes a fundamental change in the status and position of enterprise IT [25]. In traditional environments enterprise IT is a sole provider of IT services, but following the adoption of cloud services the role of enterprise IT also encompasses facilitation of IT services provided by external third parties. From a governance viewpoint this introduces a number of issues:

- How should the existing (SOA) governance model be modified or extended to ensure that cloud computing services support business processes in accordance to organizational governance principles?
- What changes to (SOA) governance processes are needed to support the adoption and utilization of cloud computing services?

The SOA governance model covers two important areas: People (organizational structure, including roles and responsibilities) and Processes (governed and governing processes). In addition to these areas the cloud computing governance model should also include Enterprise Policies that aim to minimize the risks associated with cloud services. These policies should help to identify services that can be delivered by external cloud providers, identifying data that can be stored in the cloud, and provide guidance for ensuring runtime availability of services. We describe the process of developing the Cloud Computing Governance Reference Model (CCGRM) in the following sections. In Sect. 3.1 we describe the CCGRM conceptual model, in the Sect. 3.2 we define the CCGRM guiding principles, and Sect. 3.3 describes the CCGRM processes.

3.1   CCGRM Conceptual Model

CCGRM is a specialization of SOA Governance framework and forms the basis for the definition of guiding principles and processes that facilitate the development of a consistent governance system. We have used a number of sources for developing this model, including the OASIS Reference Architecture Foundation for SOA [26], integrated conceptual view on governance [27] and conceptual model for governance [28]. Figure 1 shows the CCGRM conceptual model indicating the key entities and relationships.

The central entity of model is the *Process*. Process is defined as a set of *Activities* performed to enable consistent definition, implementation, and enforcement of rules that regulate utilization of cloud computing services. The model defines two types of

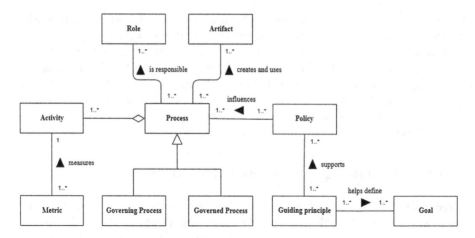

Fig. 1. CCGRM conceptual model

processes: *Governing Processes* and *Governed Processes*. Governing processes control and monitor governed processes; governed processes implement design and operational aspects of cloud computing governance. *Metrics* measures process activity and its performance to ensure effective governance. *Roles* have responsibility for processes that implement governance and authority to define the *Policies*. *Artefacts* are associated with processes and include process description and documentation. *Policy* is the formal characterization of the conditions, constraints and activities that are necessary to achieve governance goals. Policies are defined using *Guiding Principles* that specify rules that a cloud service consumer must follow promote effective use of cloud computing services and also help to define governance goals. *Goals* are the main governance objectives that the organization aims to achieve using the governance processes.

3.2   CCGRM Guiding Principles

The first step in the implementation of CCGRM framework is the definition of governance guiding principles that are used for the design, deployment and operation of the governance model. Cloud computing governance guiding principles focus on the alignment of business and IT and should be compliant with other organizational governance principles and standards, and at the same time reflect the specifics arising from the fact that cloud computing services are provided by third parties external to the organization. Cloud computing governance guiding principles define common rules that enable the application of a consistent approach for the implementation of cloud computing services at all levels of the organization, and provide a reference point for making decisions for the design, deployment and operation of cloud computing governance. The governance guiding principles are defined in accordance with the stakeholders needs and ensure that the policies achieve the strategic objectives of the organization. We have identified the following cloud computing governance principles:

- *Strategic cloud computing initiatives must be aligned with business strategy and must be supported by executive management.* Strategic alignment of business strategy, IT strategy and cloud computing strategy ensures that initiatives in cloud computing are in line with strategic business objectives. Cloud computing initiatives must be supported by executive management and must be based on stakeholders needs.

- *Cloud computing governance must be aligned with enterprise and IT governance.* Cloud computing governance should be developed in alignment with enterprise governance, IT governance and supported by executive management and based on business and stakeholders needs.

- *The expected value derived from cloud computing services must be clearly defined and continuously measured.* The value of a cloud computing service is related to the level to which the service meets stakeholder needs. Estimates of the value of cloud services help to identify implementation priorities; metrics are used to compare the achieved value with the initial estimates.

- *Cloud computing governance should recognize the rights of stakeholders established by law or through mutual contractual agreements.* Approved contractual agreement between cloud service provider and cloud service consumer must meet the needs of services consumers.

- *Cloud computing governance system should maintain metadata about cloud services.* Stakeholders should maintain accessible and transparent information about the purpose of cloud computing services and their role in the context of other services. Cloud computing service metadata includes service description, description of relationships between services, contractual agreements, service level agreements and other service related documentation.

- *Cloud computing governance system should maintain comprehensive information about cloud service providers.* This includes information about service provider selection and information that relates to the management of service provider relationship.

- *Effectiveness and performance of cloud computing governance should be monitored.* The effectiveness and performance of the cloud computing governance system and its compliance with governance principles should be monitored.

- *The risk associated with the use of cloud computing services should be continuously monitored and minimized.* Risk minimization involves identifying, evaluating, and managing the level of risk associated with the use of cloud computing services.

- *Cloud computing governance practices must be in compliance with legal and regulatory requirements.* All cloud computing compliance requirements should be continuously monitored ensuring that cloud computing services are used in accordance with the current legislation.

3.3 CCGRM Processes

SOA Governance Reference Model includes three governing processes and four governed processes [3]. These processes must be redefined, as they are not directly applicable to cloud environments. For Cloud computing governance reference model we use a uniform process description format. Each process has a Process Identifier (ID) and a Name. Other attributes include definition of Process Goals, Process Description, triggering event (Process Trigger), Process Inputs and Outputs, Process Activities and Metrics. Table 1 shows an example of process description for the *Ensure risk management for cloud computing services* process (GdP6).

Table 1. Ensure risk management for cloud computing services process description

Process ID	GdP6
Process name	Ensure risk management system
Process goal	Ensuring managing of risk management system so that risk related to using cloud computing services have been analysed, identified, evaluated and monitored. Measures must be implemented to minimize the level of risk so that the level of risk associated with the use of cloud computing services is acceptable.
Process description	Process ensures that risk management system for cloud computing services is effective and efficient and is an integral part of organizational risk management system. Process coordinates definition and communication of risks associated with the use of cloud computing services. Process ensures that changes in the environment are constantly monitored. The process establishes risk management practices so that risks do not exceed the level of acceptable risk, procedures for continuous monitoring and evaluation of the level of acceptable risk and procedures for the identification, reporting and implementation of measures to reduce risks associated with the use of cloud computing services and procedures for defining roles and responsibilities.
Process trigger	Planning the use of new cloud computing services, planning the use of cloud computing services from a new cloud service provider, information about changing credibility of cloud service provider, changes in security policy, changes in regulatory rules and standards, changes in environment.
Inputs	Cloud computing risk register, internal regulations for cloud computing risk assessment, legislative regulations and standards.
Outputs	Cloud computing risk catalogue, list of measures to reduce risk associated with cloud computing services.
Process activities	Creation, implementation, maintenance, evaluation and improvement of risk management system, changes in strategic business goals, changes in risk management objectives, monitoring and auditing risk management system, setting mechanisms for communication and reporting.
Metrics	The percentage of critical business processes and cloud services covered by risk assessment, frequency of update of risk profile, number of cloud-related incidents that were not identified in risk assessment, number of cloud-related incidents causing financial loss, mean time to detect cloud-related incidents, percentage of cloud-related risk that exceeds enterprise risk tolerance, number of incidents related to non-compliance to policy, reduction in the cost of risk management system activities.

3.4 CCGRM Governing Processes

The CCGRM governing processes are processes that are used for managing governed processes. Our model includes three governing processes:

- GP1: Managing Compliance
- GP2: Managing Exemption
- GP3: Managing Communication

The *Managing Compliance* process (GP1) ensures that the governed process complies with the policies of cloud computing governance. If a governed process does not reach the required compliance level, the managing process generates an *exemption*.

The *Managing Exemption* process (GP2) manages exceptions and determines what action should be taken to rectify the situation. Exceptions indicate violation of governance policies or rules. If the exception is traced to a provider service, then the exception will be escalated to the provider who will be responsible for its resolution. The *Managing Communication* process (GP3) ensures that all necessary and relevant information is communicated to the relevant stakeholders, including the policies, standards and principles of cloud computing governance, and the processes for managing exceptions, including the escalation mechanism.

3.5 CCGRM Governed Processes

The CCGRM governed processes ensure the implementation of cloud computing governance. To ensure conformance with the CCGRM guiding principles, a number of additional process activities need to be defined and implemented:

- GdP1: Ensure governance maintenance
- GdP2: Ensure benefits from cloud computing services
- GdP3: Ensure support for business processes by using cloud computing services
- GdP4: Ensure management of cloud computing services lifecycle
- GdP5: Ensure management of cloud computing solutions lifecycle
- GdP6: Ensure risk management for cloud computing services
- GdP7: Ensure monitoring and management of service levels
- GdP8: Ensure management of service providers

The *Ensure governance maintenance process* (GdP1) provides a consistent approach that together with enterprise governance ensures definition and maintenance of policies, practices, principles, guidelines, processes, organizational structures, roles and responsibilities. The process ensures that cloud services are used in accordance with IT strategy and legal and regulatory requirements.

The process *Ensure benefits from cloud computing services* (GdP2) focuses on ensuring that cloud services will deliver expected benefits to stakeholders while minimizing costs and risks.

The process *Ensure support for business processes by using cloud computing services* (GdP3) defines strategy for identifying business processes that are suitable for implementation using cloud computing services. This process defines criteria and metrics that are used to decide whether a given business process is suitable for implementation using cloud computing services.

The process *Ensure management of cloud computing services lifecycle* (GdP4) manages a response to changing business requirements. In accordance with change management guidelines this process enables timely response to changing requirements.

The process *Ensure management of cloud computing solutions lifecycle* (GdP5) ensures that cloud computing services portfolio is continuously evaluated in terms of the benefits and value delivered to the business. The process ensures that cost of selected portfolio is optimized, detecting situations where the portfolio of services is not fully aligned with the needs of business.

The process *Ensure risk management for cloud computing services* (GdP6) ensures that cloud services risk management is effective and is an integral part of organizational risk management solution. Process coordinates identification and monitoring of risks associated with the use of cloud computing services, and establishes risk management practices, including procedures for defining roles and responsibilities for individual cloud services.

The process *Ensure monitoring and management of service levels* (GdP7) implements monitoring and reporting service levels, comparing the agreed parameters with the observed parameter values. In situations where the agreed service levels are not maintained, the process will notify relevant roles within the organization.

The process *Ensure management of service providers* (GdP8) manages cloud service providers, including the implementation of procedures for the selection of cloud service providers. Process specifies criteria for the selection of cloud service providers based on business and regulatory requirements.

3.6   Cloud Computing Governance Lifecycle

The resulting Cloud Computing Governance Reference Model described in this section consists of ten guiding principles, three governing and eight governed processes. Individual processes are described in generic terms and need to be contextualized before being implemented.

The implementation of the CCGRM model follows a life cycle that consists of four phases: Planning, Definition, Implementation and Monitoring (Fig. 2). The aim of the lifecycle is to continuously improve the governance processes.

The Planning phase involves the analysis of existing governance models and processes, developing a strategy for cloud computing governance, and developing a roadmap for cloud computing governance. The Definition phase involves the specification of the governing and governed processes and the development of transition plans. The following Implementation phase involves the implementation of the governance model, and the final Monitoring phase involves evaluation of metrics to establish the effectiveness of the governance model.

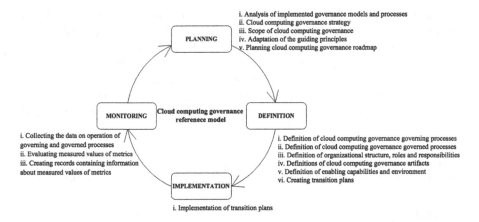

Fig. 2. Cloud Computing Governance Lifecycle

4   Verification of the CCGRM Model

Verification of the applicability of proposed Cloud Computing Governance Reference Model in practice is based on a case study performed in an IT organization which provides IT services to a large retail organization operating within the EU. The case study was performed in accordance with the methodology for the design and implementation of case studies for scientific purposes as defined in publication Case Study Research: Design and Methods [29]. The IT organization decided to utilize a public cloud computing service to support business process for new employees admission. Given that IT organization has not used any cloud computing services so far, this project that includes planning, selection, implementation, operation and monitoring phases is considered as a Proof-of-Concept project. The main objectives of the case study was to adapt the existing IT governance model using CCGRM. The data collected about the applicability of CCGRM included reports and documentation generated during the application of guiding principles, governing processes and governed processes defined in CCGRM, and served as the basis for improving the model to reflect the outcomes of the case study.

5   Conclusions

The trend towards large-scale adoption of cloud computing necessitates the re-assessment of SOA governance principles and processes, and the development of comprehensive guidelines for implementation of governance in cloud computing environments. We have argued in this paper that SOA and cloud computing share key concepts and characteristics presenting an opportunity for a unified service governance framework for cloud computing and SOA. We have also noted significant differences between governance requirements for a traditional SOA and environments that involve cloud computing, in particular the need to extend the governance framework to include services that are controlled by external service providers. Most of the current research efforts in this area focuses on the cloud provider and does not address the needs of end user organizations that are the consumers of cloud services. We have proposed and described a Cloud Computing Governance Reference Model designed to assist organizations to implement a governance framework. The proposed Cloud Computing Governance Reference Model is an adaptation of the SOA Governance Framework and defines guiding principles, governing processes and governed processes suitable for cloud computing environments. Our current efforts are directed towards refining the CCGRM model and verifying its effectiveness in practice.

Acknowledgments. The paper was processed with contribution of long term institutional support of research activities by Faculty of Informatics and Statistics, University of Economics, Prague.

References

1. Buyya, R., Broberg, J., Goscinski, A.M.: Cloud Computing Principles and Paradigms. Wiley Publishing, Hoboken (2011)
2. Feuerlicht, G., Schneider, S., Tranter, L.: Towards enterprise architecture for cloud computing environments. In: Proceedings of the Eleventh Workshop on E-Business (WEB 2012), pp. 412–422. University of North Carolina at Charlote, Orlando (2012)
3. Feuerlicht, G., Thai Tran, H.: Adapting service development life-cycle for cloud. In: Proceedings of the 17th International Conference on Enterprise Information Systems, Barcelona, Spain, pp. 366–371 (2015). ISBN: 978-989-758-098-7
4. The Open Group: SOA Governance Framework. United Kingdom (2009)
5. Kreger, H., Harding, C.: The Open Group SOA Governance Framework Becomes an International Standard (2012). http://blog.opengroup.org/2012/10/12/the-open-group-soa-governance-framework-becomes-an-international-standard/
6. Mircea, M.: SOA, BPM and cloud computing: connected for innovation in higher education. In: International Conference on Education and Management Technology (ICEMT), pp. 456–460. IEEE, Cairo (2010). ISBN 978-1-4244-8616-8
7. Tsai, W.T., Sun, X., Balasooriya, J.: Service-oriented cloud computing architecture. In: Seventh International Conference on Information Technology: New Generations (ITNG), pp. 684–689. IEEE, Las Vegas (2010)
8. Yang, X., Zhang, H.: Cloud computing and SOA convergence research. In: Fifth International Symposium on Computational Intelligence and Design (ISCID), pp. 330–335. IEEE, Hangzhou (2012). ISBN 978-1-4673-2646-9
9. Zhao, J.F., Zhou, J.-T.: Strategies and methods for cloud migration. Int. J. Autom. Comput. **11**(2), 143–152 (2015). Springer-Verlag, ISSN 1751-8520
10. NIST: NIST Cloud Computing Standards Roadmap (2013)
11. Peffers, K., Tuunanen, T., Rothenberger, M.A., Chatterjee, S.: Research methodology for information systems research. J. Manag. Inf. Syst. **24**(3), 45–78 (2008)
12. Dehghani, M., Emadi, S.: Developing a framework for evaluating service oriented architecture governance with approach COBIT. Sci. J. (CSJ) **36**(4) (2015). Special Issue. Cumhuriyet University Faculty of Science, Turkey
13. Jäntti, M., Hotti, V.: Defining the relationships between IT service management and IT service governance. In: Information Technology and Management, pp. 141–150 (2015). ISSN: 1385-951X

14. Javeri, F., Jazi, M.D., Ajoudanian, S., Panah, H.Y., Hojaji, F., Jafari, S., Behrooz, M.: Presenting a model for the deployment of Service-Oriented Architecture Governance (SOA Governance) in Information & Communication Technology Department of Isfahan Municipality. Int. Res. J. Appl. Basic Sci. **5**(11), 1438–1445 (2013)
15. IBM: SOA Governance and Service Lifecycle Management (2009). http://www-01.ibm.com/software/solutions/soa/gov/
16. Niemann, M., Eckert, J., Repp, N., Steinmetz, R.: Towards a generic governance model for service-oriented architectures. In: AMCIS 2008 Proceedings, Toronto, Canada (2008)
17. Oracle: Oracle SOA Governance (2013). http://www.oracle.com/us/products/middleware/soa/governance/overview/index.html
18. Ott, C., Korthaus, A., Böhmann, T., Rosemann, M., Krcmar, H.: Towards a reference model for SOA governance. In: CAiSE Forum 2010, Hammamet, Tunisia (2010)
19. Fortis, T.F., Munteanu, V.I., Negru, V.: Towards an ontology for cloud services. In: Towards an Ontology for Cloud Services Complex, Intelligent and Software Intensive Systems (CISIS), pp. 787–792. IEEE, Palermo (2012). ISBN 978-1-4673-1233-2
20. Rajmohan, B., Balashankar, M.: The CLOUD and SOA - creating the architecture for today and future. Int. J. Res. Eng. Adv. Technol. **1**(6) (2014)
21. Laird, R.: SOA sets the stage for cloud: SOA governance makes it work. Serv. Tech. Mag., Issue LVI (2011). http://www.servicetechmag.com/system/application/views/i56/1111-2.pdf
22. ISO/IEC 17998: ISO/IEC 17998:2012 Information technology – SOA Governance Framework. In ISO (International Organization for Standardization) (2012). http://www.iso.org/iso/iso_catalogue/catalogue_tc/catalogue_detail.htm?csnumber=61240
23. Hui-min, Z., Hai-rong, H., Yang-xia, X., Lu-lu, F.: The Research and design of cloud computing framework model based on SOA. In: Atlantis International Workshop on Cloud Computing and Information Security (2013)
24. Fortis, T.F., Munteanu, V.I.: From cloud management to cloud governance continued rise of the cloud. In: Mahmood, Z. (ed.) Advances and Trends in Cloud Computing. Computer Communications and Networks, pp. 265–287. Springer, London (2014). ISBN: 978-1-4471-6452-4, ISSN: 1617-7975
25. Cisco: Cloud Computing Changing the Role and Relevance of IT Teams (2015)
26. OASIS: OASIS Reference Architecture Foundation for Service Oriented Architecture (SOA-RAF) (2012). http://docs.oasis-open.org/soa-rm/soa-ra/v1.0/cs01/soa-ra-v1.0-cs01.html
27. Janiesch, C., Korthaus, A., Rosemann, M.: Conceptualisation and facilitation of SOA governance. In: Proceedings of: ACIS 2009: 20th Australasian Conference on Information Systems, Monash University, Melbourne, pp. 154–163 (2009)
28. Vicente, P., Mira da Silva, M.: A conceptual model for integrated governance, risk and compliance. In: Mouratidis, H., Rolland, C. (eds.) CAiSE 2011. LNCS, vol. 6741, pp. 199–213. Springer, Heidelberg (2011)
29. Yin, R.K.: Case Study Research: Design and Methods. SAGE Publications, Inc., USA (2009). ISBN 978-1-4129-6099-1

Auditing Security of Information Flows

Dmitrijs Kozlovs and Marite Kirikova[✉]

Department of Artificial Intelligence and Systems Engineering,
Riga Technical University, Riga, Latvia
{dmitrijs.kozlovs,marite.kirikova}@rtu.lv

Abstract. Auditing security of information flows is still considered as one of the challenges in business information systems development. There are different standards and approaches that address information security. However, due to the number of information assets that have to be audited and the frequency of their changes the audit becomes complex and sometimes too subjective. Therefore, to have an opportunity to audit information security at the business process level, we needed to find a method that gives the base structure for the audit activities and supports the choice of information assets for the audit. In this regard, the Security Requirement Elicitation from Business Process approach, which focuses on information security requirements in business processes, provided an idea to ground the audit approach in business processes and information flows in them in order to facilitate integrated consideration of both, business and technology, aspects during the audit.

Keywords: Information flows · Information security · Security audit · Business processes based security engineering

1 Introduction

Haphazard information flows that permeate every business process make the management of information assets complicated. If the management of information assets is considered as complicated, there is a limited possibility that the management of information asset security could provide a simplified straight-forward solution. In order to improve this situation we, by concentrating, in particular, on information security aspects, tried to find the ways how to identify information assets at the business process level and apply certain measures towards the information asset perspective from the audit perspective. The organizational business process level was chosen because it has close relationships to the higher strategic management levels and the information technology infrastructure, and also because, from the audit perspective, the majority of transactions reside at the business process level.

There are different standards and approaches that address information security. However, the vast number of information assets that are audited and the frequency of their change make the audit a very complex and sometimes too subjective endeavor. In order to have an opportunity to audit information security at the business process level we needed to find a method that gives the base structure for the audit activities and supports the choice of information assets for the audit. In this regard, the Security

© Springer International Publishing Switzerland 2016
V. Řepa and T. Bruckner (Eds.): BIR 2016, LNBIP 261, pp. 204–219, 2016.
DOI: 10.1007/978-3-319-45321-7_15

Requirement Elicitation from Business Processes (SREBP) approach [3, 4], that focuses on information security requirements in business processes, provided an idea to focus on business process and information flows in them in order to enhance information security audit.

Thus goal of our research was to answer the question: "What practical method can be used to support the main audit activities if we do the information security audit primarily concentrating on information flows in business processes?"

To answer this question, we used the following steps in our research method:

1. Analysis of related work on information security audit and information technology (IT) audit.
2. Investigation of capacity of the SREBP approach and its related research on Quality Criteria for Information Demand Patterns and Information and Effects Matrix for information flow security audit.
3. Integrating the SREBP approach and the approaches that extend its capability in information flow security audit method.
4. Testing the proposed method on the business processes (procedures) of a small or middle-size company (SME).

In this paper we mainly focus on the background behind the method for auditing security of information flows and on the application example of this method. The paper is organized as follows. In Sect. 2 we briefly discuss the essentials of information security audit. In Sect. 3 we present the audit method and its application. Section 4 consists of brief conclusions.

2 Background

In this section the background material on information security audit is reviewed. The basic concepts are discussed in Subsect. 2.1, the audit perspective is explored in Subsect. 2.2, and the business process role in security auditing is discussed in Subsect. 2.3.

2.1 Data and Information Flows

The usage of data concerns interactions of the data owner, data custodian, and observation of data security principles [5]. In this context, according to Information Security Audit and Control Association's (ISACA) Glossary [2] the main terms are defined as follows:

- Data owner - the individual(s), normally a manager or director, who has a responsibility for the integrity, accurate reporting, and use of computerized data.
- Data custodian - the individual(s) and department(s) responsible for the storage and safeguarding of computerized data.
- Data flow - the flow of data from the input (e.g., in Internet banking, ordinarily user input at his/her desktop) to output (in Internet banking, ordinarily data in a bank's central database). Data flow includes data travel through the communication lines, routers, switches and firewalls as well as its processing through various applications

on servers (e.g., in Internet banking, processing the data from user fingers to the storage in a bank's central database).

- Data security - those controls that seek to maintain confidentiality, integrity, and availability of information.
- Data leakage - siphoning out or leaking information by dumping computer files or stealing computer reports and tapes.

Data security is required, because the vast amount of processed data is transformed into information and information is considered as one of the most valuable business assets, as it permeates each and every activity carried out in the business domain, and, thus, damage done to information leads to material misstatements for the business. Based on this, for further analysis carried out in this paper, it is considered that all criteria and requirements towards data are applicable also to information and all criteria and requirements towards data flows are also applicable to information flows.

The following steps towards ensuring data security are offered by Washington State Standard 141.10 [6]:

- Data classification - classify data into categories, based on the level of sensitivity of this data, whereas the levels of suggested sensitivities are public information, sensitive information, confidential information, or confidential information that requires special handling.
- Data sharing that should comply with local data privacy regulations.
- Secure management and encryption of data.
- Secure data transfer and exchange.

It has to be noted, that data sharing and encryption steps are not in the scope of this paper.

When referring to information security and security of information flows, the following concepts should be taken into consideration [5, 7]:

- Identification of information assets.
- Identification of data owner and data custodian (referring also to information owner and information custodian).
- Classification and labelling of information, based on its significance.
- Use of information demand patterns for reasoning about the use of information for definite users or user groups.

The main threats for data or processed data (information) are disclosure, leak, and unauthorized access [8].

Identification of information assets derives from analysis of data flows with reference to the definition of Infonomics - as the emerging discipline of managing and accounting for information with the same or similar rigor and formality as other traditional assets (e.g., financial, physical, human capital). Infonomics posits that information itself meets all the criteria of formal company assets, and, although not yet recognized by generally accepted accounting practices, increasingly, it is incumbent for organizations to behave as if they were to optimize information's ability to generate business value [9]. The following definition is available from National Archive [10] - an information asset is a body of information, defined and managed as a single unit so it can be understood, shared, and exploited effectively. Information assets have recognizable and manageable value, risk, content, and lifecycles. This definition shows a direct link from information assets to business assets. In the method for auditing security of information flows presented in this paper the flow perspective is taken. It is combined with the view that, first, it is important to map the concept of existing business processes of a particular company by indicating main processes – usually sales, purchase, warehousing, manufacturing, delivery, accounting, personnel, and payroll or any other processes. Then it is important to go through each business process, define activities and check whether any activity can be considered as a sub-process. Breakdown helps to identify process ownership, responsible persons involved, and the hierarchy of accountability as it is recommended by COBIT [11]. To better understand the flow, the information demand patterns can be applied [12], in order to identify what kind of information is required by data custodian. This can be applied to each data custodian group where the data custodians perform similar activities within the business process. The identified information asset can be evaluated from the perspective of the business domain, in order to show to what extent this information asset can influence the business [12]. This approach helps to identify the information assets used by the data/information custodians or groups of data custodians and assess how critical the information asset is in the business domain.

2.2   Information Assurance: Information Security Audit Versus Information Technology Audit

Assurance is divided into three types of services that can be provided to the client: audit services, agreed upon procedures, and control of preliminary assessment services. Each of the services considers a limitation of scope and activities performed during provision of assurance services. Understanding of limitations for each type of assurance services will enhance understanding the differences between Information Security Audit, Information Technology Audit, and IT Security Audit here and further in the text commonly regarded as Audit.

Control preliminary assessment is oriented on finding areas for additional attention and thorough analysis of where higher level risks are present or any critical values of the company are compromised. Agreed upon procedures can be viewed as gaining assurance of the areas of management concerns or management directed audit.

Audit is a complex process initiated by the company or third parties, in order to obtain reasonable assurance that Information Security process and documentation of the company are free of significant misstatements. According to Global Audit Methodology Map [18], any audit should include the following steps: (1) Planning and risk identification, (2) Strategy and risk assessment, (3) Execution, (4) Conclusion and Reporting, and (5) Follow Up. Before the execution of any audit, it is important to determine the auditing strategy by selecting appropriate methodological approaches. There are general concepts that should be taken into consideration as mandatory, nevertheless, the interpretation of certain rules and guidelines could be varied, based on previous issues, current concerns, and future expectations.

According to Campbell and Stamp in [13, 14] there are three types of categories for methodologies: (1) Temporal methodologies that focus on technology systems using actual tests, (2) Comparative methodologies that concentrate on the use of specific standards, and (3) Functional methodologies that apply tests and standards.

The Information Security audit methodology should dictate how to identify security assets and raise audit objectives for security assets, using risk-oriented patterns. The security risk oriented patterns relate to description of a "recurring security problem or potential threat that derives in specific security context as well as presents a scheme for solutions" [4].

Key risk mitigation approaches are offered in each methodology [10, 15]. Different types of risks are defined and the levels of risks are assessed as low, below average, average, above average, and high [8], while the impacts can be assessed as low, moderate, and high [8]. All parts of the risk concept create the formula for Audit Risk (considered as sum of different types of risks mentioned above [8, 10] that are used for Audit purposes in Global Audit Methodology) in the terms of Combined Risk Assessment, where the sum of inherent, control, and detection risks is represented, and then the business risk is added. The Combined Risk Assessment is used for further analysis of Information Security Audit of information flows in business processes and development of audit method, based on audit strategy.

Alternative approach for risk assessment is a twelve-factor model for risk assessment and analysis for the purposes of internal organizational audit [13, 14, 16]. This approach goes through a specific process and ranks the current situation within the process boundaries with an appropriate risk factor point. Each of the risk factor domains has its own weights that in combination with the risk factor point enable to create Entity Level Control Risk Assessment Matrix. Here low risks are considered, if less than 83 points are counted, moderate risks are considered if 84–104 points are counted, high risks are considered, if 105–144 points are counted. This approach will be used in pre-application stage of the method for security audit of information flows, in order to identify the most critical activities that require high level of security protection. Despite the fact that Entity Level Control Risk Assessment Matrix might be assumed as judgmental, it is widely applied due to simplicity and good overview capability of the general business process.

Another alternative methodology – The Operationally Critical Threat, Asset, and Vulnerability Evaluation (OCTAVE) [17] - is described as functional methodology that combines tests and standards. Mainly the approach considers that experts should drive a compromise from the knowledge of methodology, whereas system owners should drive the contextual knowledge. The information obtained from Information Security Risk Assessment (preliminary procedure) is used as the basis for addressing: (1) what assets require protection, (2) what level of protection is required, (3) how might an asset be compromised, and (4) what is the impact on the asset if the protection fails. It is considered expedient to use the options provided by OCTAVE methodology for information security audit of information flows, because it draws the relation between information, security, information flows, and functionality for information security audit.

During analysis of related work, it was noted that available sources differently define specific terms that have similar meaning and therefore could be misused when they are mentioned outside the context. These terms are – Information Security Audit, Information Technology Audit, and Information Technology Security Audit. A brief description of each term is given below, in order to clear the bias of using one or another term.

According to Glossary of Terms introduced by Information Systems Audit and Control Association (ISACA) [2], Information Security encompasses protection of information within the boundary of a company against disclosure to unauthorized users, improper modification, and fact of being unavailable, when required. Hereby the three main information security concepts are indicated, namely, confidentiality, integrity, and availability. Nevertheless, the three main named information security concepts are extended by adding an authentication, authorization, auditability, cryptography, identification, and nonrepudiation. Information Technology, based on Glossary of Terms introduced by Information Systems Audit and Control Association (ISACA) [2], ensures all activities and hardware or software facilities used for data input, processing of data (information considered as processed data), and transmission of information for output purposes. Thus, it indicates the life cycle of data processed into information that is afterwards transformed into knowledge.

Information Technology Security [6] is defined as securing IT environment for IT processing. It is assumed to carry out IT risk management strategy, assess the effectiveness of existing security controls, education, and awareness, IT security assessment, compliance to regulations, audit and maintenance, and data security.

Based on the concepts introduced by German Federal Office for Information Security [23], certain relationships exist between definitions of Information Security Audit and Information Technology Audit (IT Audit). The commonalities and differences of each definition are given in Fig. 1.

	Audit	Focus
IT	securing IT environment for IT processing	Efficiency IT processes and safeguards + Security + Correctness
Information Security	protection of information	Security + (Efficiency & Correctness)

Fig. 1. IT and information security.

IS Audit mainly focuses on Information Security by assessing the current level of Security in the organization, in order to point out gaps and deficiencies. This type of audit takes care of personnel related activities and configuration of systems by using the following criteria in this particular order: (1) Security - set as primary criteria, (2) Efficiency and correctness - set as secondary criteria [23]. In comparison to Information Security Audit, the IT Audit focuses not only on Information Security. It takes into account efficiency, security, and correctness. IT Audit examines the organization by using the same criteria, but in different order and setting where all of the mentioned criteria are primary, based on judgmental proportions led by Audit Strategy: (1) Efficiency of IT related processes, IT organization in the company, and security safeguards; (2) Security; and (3) Correctness by means of completeness, timeliness, reproducibility, and orderliness [23].

According to German Federal Office for Information Security – Information Security Audit and IT Audit are obliged to check IT structure of the organization, get acquainted with existing business processes, applying appropriate tools in order to get an opinion about security, correctness of procedures, as well as orderliness, lawfulness, and usefulness. Both audits use similar techniques. Despite the contextual commonalities of terms Information Security Audit, Information Technology Audit, and Information Technology Security Audit, and the fact that they cover similar backgrounds, these terms should not be used as synonyms and are not interchangeable. Further in the paper the term Information Security Audit is used with the related concepts, considering the methods used by Information Technology Audit and Information Technology Security Audit.

2.3   Use of Business Process Models in the Audit

Global Audit Methodology designed by Ernst and Young [18] considers it expedient to apply business process modelling during certain audit stages, because good understanding of the business helps the participants of the audit domain to apply their knowledge of the audit domain at the business domain. Moreover, as according to risk orient approaches used in Global Audit Methodology [10, 18]; the majority of the assurance activities reside on the transaction and process level. Therefore good understanding of the process level ensures reaching the audit objectives for obtaining reasonable assurance about the operations carried out by the Audit Object. For better understanding of the process, it is advised to apply such additional approaches as M. Porters Value Chain [19] that classifies the processes into core processes, support processes, and management processes. In this perspective, it is possible to distinguish significant classes of transactions (operations) from the non-significant transactions and insignificant transactions. Each process should be assessed at an acceptable level of detail, in order to understand the completeness and quality of the process execution. For this purpose, it is advised to apply Capability Maturity Model Integrated [19] that helps to assess the processes by labeling them with five levels: initial, managed, defined, quantitatively measured, and optimized. As for the third additional technique, it could be considered to compare the existing process to APQC process classification [19] that gives a breakdown for activities that should be covered by certain process domain.

In Accorsi et al. [20] another method that links business processes and Information Security is presented. IT Security audit evaluates the effectiveness of internal controls and detects/analyses outliers. The method described by Accorsi et al. [20] links the concepts of information security to business processes and indicates the use of data flows (processed data considered as information, thus here: information flows) in information security audit. The method considers also business process mining which is out of the scope of this paper. Accorsi *et al.* [20] indicates the following properties to be considered in information security audits: authorization, usage control, separation of duties, binding of duties, conflict of interest, and isolation.

Security Requirement Elicitation from Business Process (SREBP) approach was developed by Naved Ahmed and Matulevicius from Institute of Computer Science, Tartu University, Estonia; afterwards the approach was extended in the international project among Tartu University (Estonia), Riga Technical University (Latvia) and University of Rostock (Germany) [3, 4, 12]. The approach bridges the needs and knowledge of business process analysts and security engineers by transforming the security objectives into security requirements, whereas attracting security engineering and business analysts, in order to determine and lower the intentional harm to valuable assets. Therefore, the key issue of the approach is to identify the security criteria and elicit security requirements from the business process model.

The SREBP approach deals with limitations of the systematic requirement engineering for addressing security in business processes, whereas covering up to 80 % of security requirements, indicated in that research, in comparison to Security Quality Requirements Engineering Method, that covers only 44 % of security requirements [3, 4]. Use of the approach encompasses two phases: the main results that can be expected from the SREBP approach are linking business assets to security criteria, then identifying whether certain security patterns proposed by the authors of [3, 4] can be applied, afterwards proceeding with IT security requirements for the certain business activity or several activities within the scope of the definite business process. The approach is oriented for the use by internal IT auditors or system administrators for providing security requirements to the company. The SREBP approach can be used by external IT auditors, only as guidelines, in the initial phases of IT security audit or within the scope of agreed-upon procedures. The advantage of the SREBP approach is that it directly addresses the issues relevant for information flow security audit. Therefore it was taken into consideration in the method described in the next section.

The Information Security strategy and organization-wide strategy are becoming more coordinated by addressing business processes and value-added capabilities, leveraging the use of applications and technologies through business process re-engineering. Despite any standard auditing approaches used, each audit project is considered as unique due to choice of audit strategy, methodologies, and tools applied.

For the development of method for information flow security audit, it is considered expedient to base the requirements on one of the most important documents that is used in any audit - the Audit Plan. The Audit plan should help to understand all the activities and milestones that should be completed during the audit by breakdown into audit phases [21]. The audit plan that was used in this research is presented in [22].

The following risks should be addresses when information security audit is carried out:

- The system or specific software inaccurately processes data, processes inaccurate data, or both that caused wrong decisions for critical business processes.
- Unauthorized user access to data damaged the data itself or changed the data improperly, or unauthorized or non-existent transactions were processed, or the

transactions were improperly recorded, causing material or immaterial misstatements.

- IT personnel gained advantage of access privileges that exceeded the need to perform their duties that resulted in segregation of duties.
- Users made unauthorized changes in master files that made the data incomparable.
- User made unauthorized changes to systems or software that caused errors in execution of critical operations.
- User failed to make required changes to system or software that resulted in the delay of business operations.
- IT personnel noticed damage of data in backups or were not able to access system data backups as required that resulted in data loss.

On the basis of related work the requirements for information flow security analysis were stated (see Appendix). When evaluating the SREBP approach against these requirements it was estimated that it meets about 27 % of all requirements [22]. Thus the audit method that is presented in the next section included more auditing issues than prescribed by the SREBP approach.

3 The Audit Method and Its Application

For developing the information flows security audit method the SREBP approach [3] was integrated with Octave Allegro Global audit methodology [17], Entity Level Control Risk Preliminary Assessment Matrix [16], and Information demand patterns [12] (Fig. 2). The approaches for integration were chosen to cover all requirements that were derived from different information security and IT security audit approaches (see Appendix). The method assumes that the mapped business processes are available in the company, and it is possible to identify information flows between different activities.

The method itself is the table of items, which have to be considered during the audit, and guidelines of its application. The tabular form of the method has been

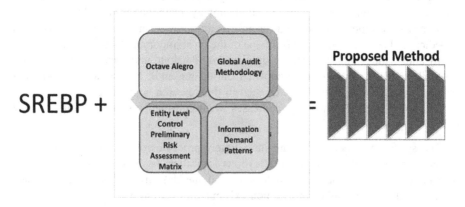

Fig. 2. Constituents of the audit method.

already presented in [22] where the substance of execution of the method is provided with step by step explanation of the rationale. In this paper we focus on the background behind the table and the application results of the method. Therefore we present the method just briefly in Fig. 3. Each slot in Fig. 3 corresponds to the section of the

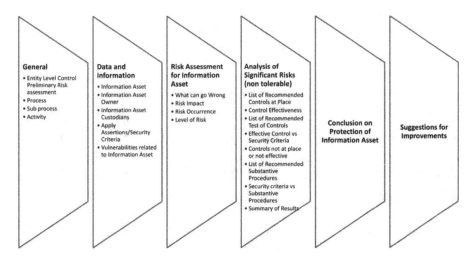

General
• Entity Level Control Preliminary Risk assessment
• Process
• Sub process
• Activity

Data and Information
• Information Asset
• Information Asset Owner
• Information Asset Custodians
• Apply Assertions/Security Criteria
• Vulnerabilities related to Information Asset

Risk Assessment for Information Asset
• What can go Wrong
• Risk Impact
• Risk Occurrence
• Level of Risk

Analysis of Significant Risks (non tolerable)
• List of Recommended Controls at Place
• Control Effectiveness
• List of Recommended Test of Controls
• Effective Control vs Security Criteria
• Controls not at place or not effective
• List of Recommended Substantive Procedures
• Security criteria vs Substantive Procedures
• Summary of Results

Conclusion on Protection of Information Asset

Suggestions for Improvements

Fig. 3. Items to be considered in the audit.

Table 2, and each entry in the slot corresponds to the row in the table. The Table 2 with the empty last column can be used as the base template in the audit.

The method was tested in the IT service company that offers high quality solutions to complex technology and outsourcing services. So the experiment was done in the context of quality processes, business process oriented management, and skilled professionals. Five processes (procedures) of the company were analyzed. The processes were presented in the form of flowcharts and supplementary materials that allowed to identify information flows between activities.

In order to understand the most critical process to be audited in the IT Service Company, Entity Level Control Risk Preliminary Assessment Matrix was carried out for the five processes (procedures) – selection of clients, planning interactions with clients, analysis of customer needs, sales offer, and post warranty support. The results of analysis for one the processes (procedures), titled Process X in the remained of the paper, are presented in Table 1.

Process X totaled 86 points for Entity Level Control Risk Preliminary Assessment, which indicated that it has to be considered for further analysis by the proposed audit method, because of moderate result in Preliminary Risk Assessment. Procedures with low risks were not considered in the audit. Further we illustrate how the audit method was applied to Process X (see the representation of the base table sections in Fig. 3). Process X consisted of several activities. We illustrate only one of them in Table 2. Company confidential information is either deleted or abstracted in the remainder of this section including Table 2.

Table 1. Entity level control risk preliminary assessment matrix - Process X.

No.	Risk factor	Risk factor point and description	Weights	Weighed points
1.	Control assessment	2- not fully implemented or minor lacks indicated	5	10
2.	Changes/Reorganization	3- significant changes of process, procedures, personnel	4	12
3.	Complexity of the process	2- moderate complexity	4	8
4.	Impact on other processes	3- high impact on other processes	3	9
5.	Cost level	1- low	6	6
6.	External or third party Impact	2- moderate	2	4
7.	Time since previous audit	2- one-two years	2	4
8.	Management concern assessment	2- moderate	3	6
9.	Fraud indications	1- low	4	4
10.	Impact on further decision making	3- significant	3	9
11.	Employee experience and qualification	2- experienced and qualified	3	6
12.	Social responsibility and public interest	2- moderate	4	8
Total points: 86 [Moderate risk]				

The application of audit method was time consuming, however, the information available in process models and supplementary materials was sufficient to apply the method. Preliminary assessment gave an opportunity to narrow down the scope of the audit and to concentrate to the most vulnerable issues.

Tables similar to Table 2 were developed for all activities of Process X. The main benefit can be achieved by summarizing the obtained information from each table (each activity in the selected process) by information assets, thus conducting a combined review as it is natural in the SREBP approach. The designed method helps to identify at which process, sub-process or activities the information asset is most exposed to threats and potential misstatements. Furthermore it is possible to verify whether appropriate controls are placed for protecting this information asset. In addition, it is possible to identify all custodians of definite information asset and check whether all information asset custodians are authorized to access this information asset. Moreover, the designed method allows to review whether the information asset is reasonably controlled, controlled not enough, over-controlled without a reasonable basis, or identify overlapping controls that could be limited.

Table 2. Deployment of extension to SREBP for Process X Part 1.

No.	Activities	Work done
1	**General**	
1.1	Entity Level Control Preliminary	Moderate
1.2	Process	Process Name
1.3	Sub process	Sub process Name
1.4	Activity	Activity name
2	**Data and Information**	
2.1	Information Asset	Asset Name
2.2	Information Asset Owner	Head of X line
2.3	Information Asset Custodians	Head of X Dept., Role
2.4	Apply Assertions/Security Criteria	Confidentiality, Accessibility
2.5	Vulnerabilities related to Information Asset	Disclosure or destruction of information; if change of Role, then old manager maintains the access
3	**Risk Assessment for Information Asset**	
3.1	What can go Wrong	List of Y is accessed by unauthorized person with intention to obtain data and disclose it to interested parties harming the Company's reputation. Sensitive Y information is disclosed to non-authorized third parties that results in data leakage of ongoing projects and expected customers or even losing the client
3.2	Risk Impact	High
3.3	Risk Occurrence	Low
3.4	Level of Risk	Moderate
4	**Analysis of Significant Risks (non tolerable)**	
4.1	List of Recommended Controls at Place	Information access rights to each Y or group of Y and the profile files are granted and removed separately on an ad hoc principle by authorization of data/information owner, Taking into consideration the reasoning for the need of this information for execution of daily responsibilities of the employee and which particular information will be used. IT application control works as Software functionality That limits copying and exporting information from Y
4.2	Control Effectiveness	
4.2.1	List of Recommended Test of Controls	Obtain a sampled list of users who have access to the Y, check existence of approval of access rights of data/information Custodian by data/information owner. Obtain the list of daily responsibilities of

(Continued)

Table 2. (*Continued*)

No.	Activities	Work done
		sampled data/information custodian, check the current necessity and purpose of access to particular information from Clients profile
4.2.2	Effective Control vs Security Criteria	Efficient
4.3	Controls not at place or not effective	Not required
4.3.1	List of Recommended Substantive Procedures	n/a
4.3.2	Security criteria vs. Substantive Procedures	n/a
4.4	Summary of Results	Controls are considered to be at place and are efficient
5	**Conclusion on Protection of Information Asset**	**Information asset is protected**
6	**Suggestions for Improvements**	Use Y codification. For processing purposes Y, as well as list of projects may not be identified, showing only total numbers. Apply security roles to users that have access to this information. Ensure the process of granting access rights and removing them, when not necessary for execution of work duties

4 Conclusions

In this paper we shared our knowledge with respect to information flow security audit. We considered different audit methods and, according to the assumption that business process models are available in the company, we integrated knowledge from pattern based security requirements engineering approach and contemporary information technology and security audit approaches to present a dedicated method for information flow security audit.

As mentioned above, the application of the method gave an opportunity to identify vulnerable information assets and perform the security assessment of information flows. However, due to the fact that information flows permeate more than one business process, including several sub processes and vast amount of activities, the application of the method was time consuming. Therefore we can conclude, that while the presented method, which is based on several well known information security and IT security audit and analysis approaches, already now gives means for auditing security of information flows, further research should be aimed at reducing the audit time. This might be achieved by developing IT services for supporting the method with the specific thesaurus, business process analysis tools, and audit visualization techniques.

Appendix: Audit Plan Requirements

1.   Requirements derived from Planning and Risk Identification: 1.1. Complete Entity Level Control Preliminary Risk Assessment Matrix, in order to ensure evaluation of: 1.1.1. Control preliminary assessment of the process; 1.1.2 Changes and reorganization done to the process; 1.1.3 Complexity of the process; 1.1.3 Impact on other processes; 1.1.4 Cost level; 1.1.5 External or third party impact; 1.1.6 Time since previous audit; 1.1.7 Management concern assessment; 1.1.8 Fraud indications; 1.1.9. Impact on further decision making, .1.1.10 Employee (data custodian/information custodian) experience and qualification, 1.1.12 Social responsibility and public interest. 1.2. Ensure ability to design the audit program activities that are aligned with information security management systems intended outcomes and strategic direction of the organization. 1.3. Ensure proper documentation of the results gained during information security audit. 1.4. Be applicable within definite boundaries of information security management system. 1.5. Be capable to identify external and internal vulnerabilities. 1.6. Be capable to check the integration of information security management system requirements in organization's processes.
2.   Requirements derived from Strategy and Risk Assessment 2.1. Map existing business process, mark data input and output, identify information flows/ identify data sources, processing points and end points (information flow). 2.2. Identify information security risk owners. 2.3. Use information flows to identify information assets. 2.4. Identify information demand patterns. 2.5. Apply information security criteria towards activities that involve information flows. 2.6. For activities that involve information flows, identify potential risks, risk impact and risk likelihood. 2.7. Summarize the risk assessment for an activity that involves information flows. 2.8. Support information security risk acceptance criteria state (whether risk is accepted, transferred or mitigated). 2.9. Prioritize analysed risks for treatment based on risk assessment plan and the strategy of the audit – whether to rely on controls or not, by applying substantive procedures for information security audit 2.10. Prepare a list of information that would help to plan the audit activities. 2.11. Specify whether any information, user activity logs are to be observed.
3.   Requirements derived from Execution of Audit Activities 3.1. Determine the match of controls with security assertions. 3.2. Based on the business process mapping, state whether appropriate controls are designed to cover the risks in the concept of security objectives. 3.3. Based on the business process mapping, check whether appropriate controls are effective to cover the risks in the concept of security objectives. 3.4. Define whether additional procedures are required.
4.   Requirements derived from Conclusion and reporting 4.1. Merge all identified issues; 4.2 Compare the indicated issues with risk tolerance; 4.3 Prepare suggestions and improvements; 4.4 Identify if any changes occurred after the audit.
5.   Requirements derived from Follow up 5.1. Mark whether the recommendation towards information security are implemented.

References

1. Schmitt, C., Liggesmeyer, P.: Getting grip on security requirements elicitation by structuring and reusing security requirements sources. In: Complex Systems Informatics and Modeling Quarterly, CSIMQ, 2015, No. 3, pp. 15–34 (2015). http://dx.doi.org/10.7250/csimq.2015-3.02
2. Information Systems Audit and Control Association, Glossary of Terms (2015). [cited Nov 2015]. http://www.isaca.org/Pages/Glossary.aspx
3. Ahmed, N., Matulievičius, R.: A taxonomy for assessing security in business process modelling. In: Research Challenges in Information Science (RCIS), IEEE Seventh International Conference, pp. 1–10 (2013)
4. Ahmed, N., Matulievičius, R.: Securing business processes using security risk-oriented patterns. Comput. Stand. Interfaces 36(4), 723–733 (2013). Elsevier B.V.
5. Wonnemann, C.: Towards information flow auditing in workflows. In: Software Engineering Workshops (2010)
6. Office of the Chief Information Officer, Washington State Standard No. 141.10: Securing Information Technology, Washington D.C., USA, August 2013, p. 29 (2013)
7. U.S. Department of Commerce & National Institute of Standards and Technology. Managing Information Security Risk: Organization, Mission, and Information System View-Information Security, Gaithersburg, p. 88 (2011)
8. Jarockin, V.: Information Security, 5th edn. (2015) (in Russian)
9. Gartner Inc., IT Glossary. (2015) http://www.gartner.com/it-glossary/
10. National Archives, Identifying Information Assets and Business Requirements. http://www.nationalarchives.gov.uk/documents/information-management/identify-information-assets.pdf
11. IT Governance Institute, Control Objectives for Information and related Technology 4.1, p. 213 (2007)
12. Sandkuhl, K., Matulievičius, R., Kirikova, M., Ahmed, N.: Integration of it-security aspects into information demand analysis and patterns. In: Proceedings of the BIR 2015 Workshops and Doctoral Consortium Co-located with 14th International Conference on Perspectives in Business Informatics Research (BIR 2015), Tartu, Estonia, 26–28 August 2015, vol. 1420, pp. 36–47 (2015). Ceur-ws.org
13. ISO/IEC, Common Criteria for Information Technology Security Evaluation. Part 2: Security functional requirements, p. 325 (2005)
14. ISO/IEC, Common Criteria for Information Technology Security Evaluation. Part 3: Security assurance components, p. 233 (2012)
15. Rihtikova, N.: Organizational risk analysis and management, FORUM (2009) (in Russian)
16. Verdina, G.: Possibilities to improve internal control system in educational context, p. 252. Ph.D. Thesis, University of Latvia, Riga, Latvia (2012)
17. Caralli, R.A., Stevens, J.F., Young, L.R., Wilson, W.R.: Introducing OCTAVE Allegro: Improving the Information Security Risk Assessment Process, p. 154. Software Engineering Institute, Hanscom (2007). CMU/SEI-2007-TR-012 ESC-TR-2007-012
18. Nørgaard, H., Kühn, T.: EY Danmark, Presentation: Risikobaseret tilgang til revision (Use of Risk Based Concepts for Financial Statement Assurance), Copenhagen, p. 55 (2013)
19. Dumas, M., La Rosa, M., Mendling, J., Reijers, H.: Fundamentals of Business Process Management. Springer, Heidelberg (2013)
20. Accorsi, R., Stocker, T., Muller, G.: On the exploitation of process mining for security audits: the process discovery case. In: SAC 2013, 18–22 March 2013, Coimbra, Portugal (2013)

21. Information Systems Audit and Control Association. In: IT Standards, Guidelines, and Tools and Techniques for Audit and Assurance and Control (2010). http://www.isaca.org/Knowledge-Center/Standards/Documents/IT-Audit-Assurance-Guidance-1March2010.pdf
22. Kozlovs, D., Cjaputa, K., Kirikova, M.: Towards continuous information security audit. In: Joint Proceedings of REFSQ-2016 Workshops, Doctoral Symposium, Research Method Track, and Poster Track Co-located with the 22nd International Conference on Requirements Engineering: Foundation for Software Quality (REFSQ) (2016)
23. German Federal Office for Information Security, Information Security Audit (IS Audit): A guideline for IS audits based on IT-Grundshutz, Bonn, p. 38 (2008)
24. Information Systems Audit and Control Association. Auditing Global Compliance of Data. Protection Mechanisms. In: ISACA Journal Volume 6 "Emerging and Evolving IT Risk", pp. 46–49 (2011)

Information Security Governance: Valuation of Dependencies Between IT Solution Architectures

Oscar González-Rojas(✉), Lina Ochoa-Venegas, and Guillermo Molina-León

Systems and Computing Engineering Department, School of Engineering,
Universidad de los Andes, Bogotá, Colombia
{o-gonza1,lm.ochoa750,ga.molina28}@uniandes.edu.co

Abstract. Nowadays, information security is a main organizational concern that aims to control and protect business assets from existing threats. However, the lack of mechanisms to direct and control the increasing incorporation of Information Technology (IT) assets to support new security solution architectures creates additional security threats. We created a method to identify the hidden implications that exist after implementing IT assets of different solution architectures. This method comprises two artifacts. The first artifact is a metamodel that characterizes three domains: IT governance, enterprise architecture, and dependencies between IT assets of solution architectures. The second artifact is a model to specify value dependencies, which identify the business impact related to interoperability relations between the aforementioned assets. The application of this method in a Latin American central bank led to rationalize IT assets and to obtain a suitable security solution architecture from two existing architectures.

Keywords: Information security · IT governance · Interoperability · Enterprise architecture · Solution architecture · Value dependency

1 Introduction

The importance of information security has increased in organizational environments, because of the need to minimize the negative impact and the catastrophic consequences of the materialization of security threats [1]. These security threats jeopardize core business processes. Therefore, with the goal of protecting business operation, organizations incorporate heterogeneous and duplicated IT assets into security solution architectures. This behavior entails negative business impacts that result from the extra costs of operating and maintaining new security assets, and from the additional security threats against unprotected assets.

The design of mechanisms for directing and controlling the acquisition and interoperability of IT security assets is a task that must be performed by the Information Security Governance (ISG). Current ISG approaches [2–4] focus on aligning governance elements with business concerns without assessing and

© Springer International Publishing Switzerland 2016
V. Řepa and T. Bruckner (Eds.): BIR 2016, LNBIP 261, pp. 220–235, 2016.
DOI: 10.1007/978-3-319-45321-7_16

quantifying their existing dependencies nor their business impact. Consequently, we aim to identify and asses the interoperability relations between IT and business assets in order to reduce the origin of new security threats.

In this study, we present a governance method created as an operational mechanism to identify the business impact generated by the interoperability relations among IT assets. A core artifact of this method is a metamodel that characterizes (i) the IT Governance (ITG) domain (*e.g.* IT processes, impacts, threats), (ii) a subset of the Enterprise Architecture (EA) domain (*i.e.* relations between business and IT assets), and (iii) value dependencies that represent the business impact (*e.g.* costs, time) of interoperability relations among EA and ITG elements. We created an ISG model that conforms to the aforementioned metamodel to quantify value dependencies with the level at which different IT assets create or destroy value. EA assets are represented using an existing method that quantifies their dependencies [5], whereas the analysis of business impact between value dependencies is performed by using the well-known Object Constraint Language (OCL). The proposed method was used to represent and assess the value dependencies between IT assets of two different security solution architectures of a central bank in Latin America. The identification and quantification of these value dependencies allowed security architects to propose an integrated solution architecture that reduced threats such as the duplication of services and investments, as well as the under-use of IT assets' capacity.

This paper is organized as follows. Section 2 presents the core terminology, a case study of a central bank that uses two solution architectures to illustrate a set of ISG challenges, and the research methodology. Section 3 describes the main components of our ITG and ISG valuation approach. It also presents the instantiation of each component for the case study. Section 4 summarizes the results of assessing the value dependencies identified in the presented solution architectures. Section 5 discusses related work, and Sect. 6 presents our conclusions and future work.

2   Background and Challenges

The concepts of relevance for this research are enterprise and solution architectures, information security, ISG, interoperability, and value dependency. An architecture is defined as "the fundamental organization of a system embodied in its components, their relationships to each other, and to the environment" [6]. Accordingly, an *enterprise architecture* organizes business assets (*e.g.* business processes, goals) and IT assets (*e.g.* software, hardware, services) into an alignment model that highlights their dependencies. A *solution architecture* describes how a set of interrelated IT assets supports a business activity through the translation of requirements into a concrete solution (interrelated IT assets), high-level IT system specifications, and a portfolio of implementation tasks [7].

Information security is the set of actions performed to protect business and IT assets from different threat sources [8]. These threats aim to compromise the confidentiality, integrity, and availability (CIA) of the mentioned assets [1].

Weill and Ross define IT Governance as "specifying the decision rights and accountability framework to encourage desirable behavior in the use of IT" [9]. *ISG* is a system with a multi-dimensional perspective (*e.g.* risks, policies, measurement, organizational management) responsible of guarantying the CIA of the organization's assets [1]. Therefore, the remainder of this paper presents operational mechanisms to control the desirable behaviour of IT assets to protect business assets. *Interoperability* is "the ability of two or more systems or components to exchange information and to use the information that has been exchanged" [10]. A *value dependency* quantifies the positive or negative business impact of an interoperability relation between two IT assets.

2.1 Security Solution Architectures: A Central Bank Case Study

We present two security solution architectures of a central bank in Latin America as a case study. In this company, the information security concern has increased during the last two decades and security has become a core requirement of any organizational solution or service. That is why the organization has 20 different security solution architectures that include more than 500 IT assets such as services, policies, infrastructure, among others. Given the complexity inherited from the wide architectural space, the bank has established a new policy that requires the integration of the two security solution architectures that currently address the same security issue: access control. Figure 1 illustrates both solution architectures through a component-based diagram.

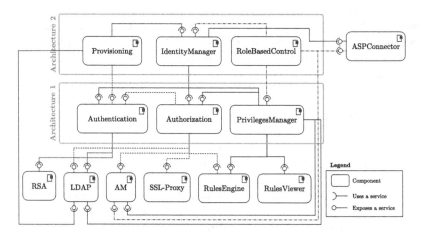

Fig. 1. Two security solution architectures within the central bank.

The first architecture (*cp. Architecture 1* box in Fig. 1) is responsible for delivering authentication, authorization, and privileges management services to the company's web applications. It includes three main components named *Authentication, Authorization,* and *Privileges Manager.* In order to fulfill CIA requirements, the architecture employs external components like the Rivest, Shamir and Adleman (*RSA*) system as an authentication component; the Lightweight Directory Access Protocol (*LDAP*) that works as a user repository asset; the Access Manager (*AM*) component used for authenticating and authorizing users through a cookie-based approach; an *SSL Proxy*, which is a bank legacy component; and finally, authentication and authorization rules are defined and validated in the *Rules Engine* and visualized through the *Rules Viewer*.

The second architecture (*cp. Architecture 2* box in Fig. 1) relates to the security portal employed during the authentication and access control of different applications defined in the corporate portfolio. In general, this architecture delivers identity management services. It has three main components called *Provisioning*, *Identity Manager*, and *Role-based Control*. It also uses the *LDAP* as an external component as well as the *AM* components used in the first architecture; the *ASP Connector* is also employed during the authentication and authorization phases. Each of the three main security portal components uses the services provided by the components that are part of the first architecture.

Both architectures are not exclusive but complementary solutions to provide access control. Despite the dependencies among components being defined, the impact generated by their external components (*e.g.* partial utilization of capabilities) is not evaluated. The bank needs to evaluate dependencies between the involved assets in order to understand their interoperability, and therefore their positive or negative business impacts. To propose a sustainable integrated architecture, negative impacts and consequences must be minimized.

2.2 ISG Challenges

Given the need of direction and control over the IT assets' acquisition that supports information security, we identified the following two main ISG challenges.

C1: **Identifying interoperability relations between IT assets.** There is a lack of mechanisms to identify the interoperability relations between IT assets found within solution architectures. Dependencies among assets are not directed and controlled, nor are the vulnerabilities identified. In the case of information security, new IT assets are incorporated to the security solution architectures in order to mitigate a set of security threats. However, the lack of governance for interoperability relations results in the generation of new business vulnerabilities such as duplication of services (*i.e.* LDAP and AM in Fig. 1), duplication of controls for these services, under-use of assets capacity, un-protected services, among others. The identification of value dependencies is even more critical when organizations incorporate IT assets without aligning them to an enterprise or solution architecture.

C2: **Valuating dependencies between assets.** Once the interoperability relations are identified, there is a need to quantify and classify these dependencies with the goal of analyzing their positive or negative business impact. This allows organizations to simulate or measure the impact (*e.g.* costs, time) assumed by an organization when they evaluate or incorporate different information security assets. For instance, when a service is duplicated in the space of security solution architectures, this supposes a new business vulnerability, and additional costs that should be covered by the organization.

2.3   Methodology

We developed and evaluated the proposed method by following the Design Science Research (DSR) approach. Design science "creates and evaluates IT artifacts intended to solve identified organizational problems" [11]. We focused on the organizational problem of evaluating and adapting IT assets and architectures to changing business activities, through the proposal of IT artifacts such as an ITG metamodel, an ISG model, and instantiations of these artifacts.

First, we analyzed different approaches to align security assets with EA elements and governance mechanisms [1–3, 12, 13], approaches to measure the value delivery of IT investments [14], and approaches to quantify the value of the IT assets that are implemented [4]. Some of these approaches quantify the value of IT assets or IT investments independently. We found that they do not intend to model and assess how the dependencies between IT assets or IT architectures destroy value (*cf.* problem relevance guideline in DSR). Section 5 compares our approach to related work.

Second, we created our own metamodel (an abstract data model) by using the Eclipse Modeling Framework (EMF) as an ecore file to establish relationships between elements of three domains: ITG, EA, and value dependencies. We instantiated the metamodel by creating an ISG model (XMI file) that contains specific elements for each domain. The ISG elements were fed with information (*e.g.* threats, IT processes, metrics, alignment dependencies) taken from frameworks and standards like ISO/IEC 27000 series [15], NIST [16], and COBIT [17]. Then, we selected the OCL due to its ability to read and query EMF models, in order to define queries over the ISG model to quantify value dependencies. A formal specification of artifacts facilitates an unambiguous definition of their structure (*cf.* research rigor guideline in DSR).

Then, we evaluated the designed artifacts by following a qualitative approach based on the case study method (*cf.* observational method guideline in DSR). Two security solution architectures that exist within the aforementioned central bank were selected since both tackle the same concern (control access), which improves comparability. We collected the components and relationships related to these architectures from a set of meetings with an IS expert engineer (one of the authors), a solution architect, a security chief, project managers, and leading engineers who are affiliated to the central bank. Based on this information and additional architecture documents, we modeled the IT assets and dependencies of the two architectures by using an existing IT governance method [5].

Finally, we identified and modeled a set of value dependencies between these assets. The units of analysis for both architectures correspond to the value delivery measured between their EA-specific assets. Certain business criteria were associated to the identified value dependencies (*e.g.* costs of IT assets). We considered the identified artifacts (solution architectures, IT assets, business assets, value dependencies) as a dataset to perform our value quantification approach. The results of the negative impact found in this valuation process were communicated to information security roles of the bank, who designed a new integrated security solution architecture (*cp.* results in Sect. 4).

3   Modeling IT and Business Assets Interoperability

We defined the following artifacts to identify and understand interoperability relations between IT and business assets, and to valuate their dependencies (*cf.* challenges in Sect. 2.2).

3.1   Governance Component of the ITG Metamodel

Figure 2 summarizes the main metamodel entities that represent the ITG governance domain (*cp. Governance* box). The *EA* and *Value Dependency* components are illustrated in Fig. 3.

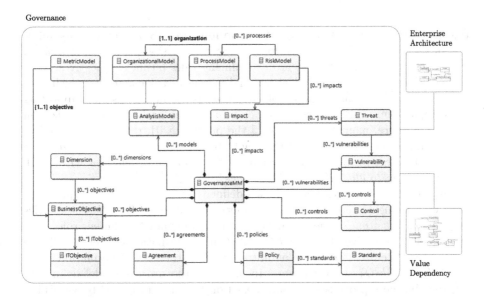

Fig. 2. Governance component of the ITG metamodel.

The *Dimension* entity establishes a governance perspective (*i.e.* risk management, strategic alignment, value delivery, performance measurement). A dimension is aligned to a set of business objectives, which are supported by IT objectives. The *AnalysisModel* entity defines four different analysis models [17]. First, the *MetricModel* allows the measurement of the progress with regard to the objectives. Second, the *OrganizationalModel* defines roles and responsibilities. Third, the *ProcessModel* specifies IT processes while establishing their inputs, activities, and expected outputs. Each process is related to the organizational model through a RACI matrix. Finally, the *RiskModel* manages risks and relates them to certain IT processes. Each risk defines its materialization probability and its possible inception sources as human, natural, physical, technical, or environmental. A risk also has an association to the *Impact* element, which represents the business implication of the materialization of the risk (*e.g.* financial aspect).

Furthermore, the governance component defines a *Threat* entity which represents external or environmental difficulties that directly affect the organization. The threat entity is associated to the *Vulnerability* entity which defines organizational weakness states that can affect the fulfillment of the corporate mission and vision. This is the reason for establishing a *Control* entity that aims to respond to the given threats and vulnerabilities; it also presents safeguards and countermeasures against the exposed weaknesses and it is defined with its corresponding financial cost. Additionally, the *Policy* and *Standard* entities are defined as a framework for guiding organizational acting and operation. Finally, the *Agreement* entity allows the definition of certain quality standards, where responsibilities and warranties are defined. Each agreement has an associated type, importance, and indicators.

Instantiating the Governance Component for ISG. For the instantiation of the ISG model, we defined four different dimensions: *strategic alignment*, which defines how governance is in alignment with business objectives; *risks management*, where risks are identified and managed; *value delivery*, which verifies that the IT systems are accomplishing their predefined goals and supporting the company mission; and *performance measurement*, where the organization aims to measure, monitor, and control the progress with regards to the objectives. These dimensions are related to eight business objectives (*e.g.* to improve processes). These business objectives also establish a set of relations with 14 IT objectives (*e.g.* to align IT with the business strategy).

In the case of analysis models we defined the four proposed types with their own elements. For instance, the metrics model has 26 different metrics (*e.g.* server downtime). The organizational model defines 10 different roles such as the Chief Executive Officer (*CEO*), the Chief Information Officer (*CIO*), the Information Security Steering Committee (*ISSC*), the Chief Information Security Officer (*CISO*), among others. In addition, the process model defines 18 different business processes that are based on the ones proposed by COBIT 5 [17] (*e.g.* to manage EA). Each one of these processes defines their corresponding association to the organizational model while following the RACI approach. Finally, the risk model defines 49 different risks, also contemplated in COBIT 5 for Risk [18] (*e.g.* service agreements breach). The risk model elements are related to six types of impacts, namely, *information disclosure*, *modification*, *loss*, *destruction*, *interruption*, and *strategy*.

Additionally, we defined six threats based on the STRIDE model: *spoofing, tampering, repudiation, information disclosure, denial of service,* and *elevation of privileges.* These threats are related to 24 vulnerabilities (*e.g. nonexistence of access control policies*). In order to mitigate the impact of the threats and of the materialization of vulnerabilities, we specified 27 different controls (*e.g. log generation for auditing*). Finally, the model has three agreements, each one for a different level of importance (*i.e. critic, general,* and *basic*). They are associated to a Service Level Agreement (*SLA*), an Operational Level Agreement (*OLA*), or an Underpinning Contract (*UC*) agreement type.

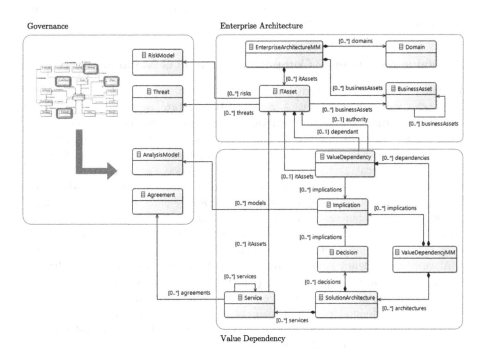

Fig. 3. EA and value dependency components of the ITG metamodel.

3.2   EA Component of the ITG Metamodel

Figure 3 illustrates the subset of EA elements required for modeling value dependencies between assets (*cp. Enterprise Architecture* box) and their relation with governance elements (*cf.* Fig. 2). A *Domain* is associated with an EA perspective (*e.g.* business, application, information, technology) that correlates business and IT assets. A *BusinessAsset* represents a valuable good used during the organization's operation. An *ITAsset* represents a good that supports the IT operation within an organization. As can be seen in Fig. 3, an IT asset has a reference to one or multiple business assets. Similarly, a business asset can have a dependency on one or more business assets. The IT asset also has a reference to the governance risk model and to the threat entity. This means that each IT asset has some associated risks and threats that should be considered by the company.

Instantiating the EA Component for ISG. The created model comprises the four standard architecture domains (*i.e. business, application, information,* and *technology*). On the basis of the case study presented in Sect. 2, we defined a set of business and IT assets. For instance, we specified nine assets: *operating systems, data bases, communication channels, servers, information systems, software, directories, people,* and *file systems*. Additionally, we took into account 13 IT assets that represent the complete set of the architectures' main and external components exposed in Fig. 3 (*e.g. Provisioning, LDAP*).

3.3 Value Dependency Component of the ITG Metamodel

The *Value Dependency* box in Fig. 3 illustrates the main data entities used to represent a value dependency. A *SolutionArchitecture* represents a particular system design that contains a group of architectural decisions and services. The architectural *Decisions* are a set of qualitative considerations taken by the organization with regards to a particular solution architecture. They are related to the *Implication* entity, which represents a consequence associated to an analysis model. A *Service* is considered as a set of functionalities offered by a given system or product, and it is defined by means of an IT asset set. It can also have a dependency on other services, and is related to one or more agreements of the governance component. Furthermore, the metamodel specifies the *ValueDependency* entity that has a reference to the implication entity.

A value dependency is specified in terms of its type (*i.e.* direct or indirect), its impact from a given perspective (*e.g.* financial, strategic perspective), and quantitative business implications (*e.g.* costs, time) related to a given analysis model. A value dependency is of a *direct type* if an IT asset uses the services offered by another asset. The consumer is called *dependent asset* and the consumed element is called *authority asset*. As may be inferred, the absence of the authority asset supposes a threat for the correct operation of the dependent asset. The direct type dependency complies with the following criteria: (*i*) each asset is deployed in a different solution architecture; (*ii*) the dependent asset consumes the services offered by the authority asset. For example, in Fig. 1, the *Authorization* component consumes the services offered by the *SSL Proxy*, which is deployed in a different solution architecture. Then, they share a direct value dependency where the *Authorization* is the dependent asset and the *SSL Proxy* is the authority asset.

Conversely, a value dependency is of an *indirect type* if each asset is deployed in a different solution architecture, and a direct type value dependency does not exist. Moreover, this relation complies with at least one of the following criteria: (*i*) both IT assets offer the same service or functionality; (*ii*) both IT assets aim to solve the same business objective; (*iii*) both IT assets affect the same process or metrics. For example, in Fig. 1, the *Authentication* component and the *SSL Proxy* offer the same authentication service, they do not have a direct value dependency, and they are not part of the same solution architecture. Thus, they present an indirect value dependency.

When specifying a value dependency impact, from a financial perspective, a funding and costs evaluation related to the involved IT assets is required. From a strategic perspective, the objectives that may be affected by the risks related to IT assets should be identified. Finally, the value dependency implication should specify quantitative information in order to identify value creation or destruction. This implication must be related to an analysis model for identifying involved processes, metrics, and risks.

Instantiating the Value Dependency Component for ISG. The created model represents the two security solution architectures described in Sect. 2. Therefore, we created one main service, *access control*, which is dependent on a set of additional services (*e.g. authentication, authorization, privileges management*). Each of these services has a relation to an agreement element, and to one or more IT assets from the governance component. Furthermore, the first architecture has five different architectural decisions, which are qualitative information describing the considerations taken into account by the company (*e.g. RSA and LDAP should be considered as complementary authentication components*), and the second architecture comprises three different decisions (*e.g. all passwords should be managed through the Identity Manager component*).

We specified eight different value dependencies for the case study, to which eight implications are related. For example, we specified a value dependency between the *AM* and the *SSL Proxy* components. This is a direct relation where *AM* is considered the dependent asset, and *SSL Proxy* the authority asset. We defined three different implications that are associated to this relation (*e.g. funding duplication due to the high similarity between components behavior*).

4   Application of the Proposed Method to the Case Study

The bank established a new policy that requires the integration of the two described solution architectures (*cf.* case study in Sect. 2). Therefore, we identified value dependencies to understand and represent the interoperability between IT and business assets. This section summarizes the results obtained when navigating and querying the identified value dependencies. It also presents the integrated solution architecture designed by IT architects.

4.1   Results of Valuating Dependencies Among Solution Architectures

Given this integration need, the company defined seven analytical questions, which were translated into OCL queries that were specified in the value dependencies of the ISG model. These queries are defined according to the concerns and motivations of the company. The answers to these questions, which followed a results analysis on the queries execution, are presented below.

Q1: *Which are the IT assets that offer the authentication, authorization, and privileges management services?* We identified a duplication of services. The *authentication* service is offered by the *AM* external component and by the *Authentication* component of the first architecture. The *authorization* service is offered by the *AM* and *SSL Proxy* external components, and by the *Authorization* component of the first architecture. The *privileges management* service is offered by the *Identity Manager* and the *Privileges Manager* components from the second and first architecture respectively.

Q2: *What value dependencies exist between the aforementioned assets?* For the *authentication* service, we identified one indirect value dependency between the *AM* and the *Authentication* assets. In the case of the *authorization* service there is a direct dependency between the *SSL Proxy* (authority asset) and the *Authorization* (dependent asset) components; and an indirect dependency between the *AM* and the *Authorization* components. Finally, there is an indirect value dependency between the *Identity Manager* and the *Privileges Manager* components in the *privileges management* context.

Q3: *What are the implications of the value dependencies?* In the case of the three identified indirect value dependencies there is a set of negative implications in terms of *integration*, solution architectures are decoupled despite them offering a subset of the same information security services; *complexity*, there is a dependencies redundancy among components offering the same functionality; *support*, the organization needs to support duplicated assets thus having an additional expenditure; and *duplication*, given the existence of different components offering the same services (*i.e.* authentication, authorization, and privileges management).

Q4: *Is there a duplication investment risk related to these IT assets?* The ISG model has an *investment duplication risk* related to the aforementioned IT assets; the *AM* can offer the same services as the *Authentication* and *Authorization* components, and the *Identity Manager* can offer the same service as the *Privileges Manager*.

Q5: *Which are the risk impacts?* The aforementioned risk has *financial* and *strategic* impacts, which consist mainly of additional expenses related to the licensing and maintenance of assets and to the non-alignment of IT assets with a subset of business objectives (*cp.* Q6).

Q6: *Which are the objectives affected by the investment risk?* The aforementioned risk is related to the *IT and business alignment* and to the *IT capacity optimization* objectives.

Q7: *Which are the processes affected by the investment risk?* The processes affected by investment risk are mainly the *EA management* and the *resources optimization* processes.

The analysis performed on the ISG model allowed us to discover that the first architecture was offering three services (*i.e.* authentication, *authorization*, and *privileges management*) that other existing components could offer. The central bank decided to remove these components which were developed in-house, as opposite to the other components provided by a third party. This decision helps avoid service duplication while using the *AM* component for supporting the authentication and authorization services, and the *Identity Manager* for supporting the privileges management service. With regard to the existing direct value dependency between the *Authentication* and the *SSL Proxy*, the bank replaced the first component with the *AM* asset. Figure 4 illustrates the integrated security solution architecture, and highlights the modified components.

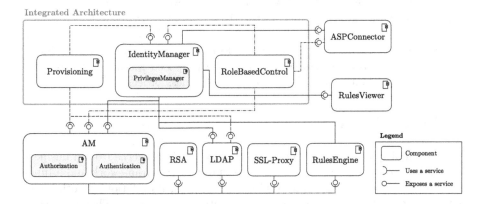

Fig. 4. Integrated solution architecture defined for the central bank.

With further research, the central bank validated that they were exploiting only 5 % and 60 % of the *AM* and *Identity Manager* capacities, respectively. Moreover, the bank reduced by 40 % the maintenance and licensing annual costs related to the authentication, authorization, and privileges management services from more than $500.000 USD to around $300.000 USD. With these decisions, the risks of investment duplication and additional security threats were reduced.

4.2 Threats to Validity and Limitations

The proposed method quantifies and qualifies the negative impact of dependencies between EA assets as a mechanism to support decision-making regarding IT rationalization and re-architecting. However, these decisions are not automated and they have to be made by IT and business experts, who can use additional analysis criteria (*e.g.* financial evaluation, cost-benefit analysis, providers comparison) to create or adjust IT solutions. Therefore, the proposed method must be complemented with capabilities to ease the maintenance of value dependencies according to the natural and continuous evolution of architectures, business, and IT assets. Moreover, additional capabilities are required to keep track of previous decisions, so as to improve control of IT assets. The selection of one subject implies that the obtained results could be valid only for the selected group. Further research is required to apply the proposed method to other enterprises in different domains and with different types of architectures.

The instantiation of the metamodel is a highly time-consuming task, particularly when identifying and modeling value dependencies. The model that we created to analyze the case study contains 247 elements, where 78.13 % correspond to ISG elements, 10.53 % to EA elements, and 11.34 % to value dependency elements. Nevertheless, this effort is required in order to maintain control of the IT assets, and as a mechanism to evaluate the impact of new investments. Further research is required to automate the identification and evaluation of value dependencies. The proposed method quantifies the level at which IT assets create or destroy value without considering the risks generated by dependent business processes. Existing frameworks that govern IT risks [5,19] establish and quantify IT-business dependencies; however, they do not intend to quantify the risk of IT assets. Therefore, we plan to integrate the proposed method with existing approaches for valuating the impact of IT on business processes [20].

5 Related Work

There are multiple research projects that address ISG concerns from a business perspective. For instance, Ohki et al. [2] propose an ISG framework and a functional model that aim to handle ISG characteristics, its relations to other CG elements, and security management and control mechanisms. Therefore, they support decisions while continuously measuring a set of indicators related to business goals. Furthermore, von Solms et al. [1] present an ISG model based on a direct-control cycle. They emphasize the importance of aligning ISG with CG for implementing a holistic governance. Thus, they propose a direct approach combined with a control process, which covers the strategical, tactical, and operational levels of the company. Moreover, Burkett et al. [13] integrates frameworks, models, methods, and processes for addressing security threats and opportunities. These are analyzed at different levels of the IT lifecycle (strategy, design, implementation, and management & operations). We considered these three approaches to integrate ISG elements to governance and EA elements. Additionally, we include concrete solution architectures and their components when modeling dependencies, but also incorporate the quantification of dependencies in terms of their positive or negative business impact.

Kusumah et al. [3] propose a holistic process for implementing ISG in the Center for Financial Transaction Reports and Analysis (INTRAC). The outputs of this research were a tool for defining the scope of the process, a process reference model, and a process assessment model. These outputs were generated from the information provided by COBIT 5 and ITIL. Even though there is a mapping between service management tasks and governance tasks, the approach lacks a further integration with business goals. In addition, Coetzee et al. [12] address the need of supporting ISG in Service Oriented Architectures (SOA) through a more holistic perspective that involves EA. In our approach, we also try to integrate ISG with EA in order to obtain a holistic security view of the business. However, we can represent not only SOA scenarios, but also any type of security solution architectures.

Finally, considering the value measurement related to IT implementation, Davern et al. [14] proposed a theoretical framework for understanding the potential value and payoff from investments in IT, in both, ex-ante project selection and ex-post investment evaluation contexts. They based their approach on the concepts of locus of value and value conversion contingencies, and on the identification of implicated business processes. Nonetheless, these two contributions focus on a performance and financial analysis of independent IT projects without considering other business criteria (*e.g.* risks, time) nor the dependencies among assets. Furthermore, Herrmann et al. [21] addressed the problem of implementing security assets in a cost-effective way. They extend an existing method named RiskREP, and its associated metamodel for aligning business goals, to countermeasure implementations. These countermeasures are considered security requirements with a related cost. From a more general perspective, Tillquist et al. [4] proposed a technique for quantifying value generation according to IT assets implementation. Therefore, they considered roles, goals, activities, and governance controls involved in value generation activities in order to measure a firm's value derived from the usage of certain IT assets. Nonetheless, value dependencies among IT assets are not made explicit nor assessed.

6   Conclusions and Future Work

The materialization of information security related risks has increased the importance of adopting and implementing a proper ISG. These risks jeopardize the CIA of the information employed during core business processes. In order to protect business operation, organizations incorporate IT assets within their own security solution architectures. The lack of mechanisms to govern IT security assets generate extra costs for operation and maintenance. Even more important than controlling costs, ISG must control potential affectations on business operation that may be generated by potential events such as service duplication, heterogeneous platforms, under-use of asset capacity, among others. This behavior can generate undesired security threats on the same assets that are intended to minimize threats on critical business processes. In these scenarios, information security can generate more problems to the business than solutions.

Our approach addresses the mentioned problems by implementing a method that aims to identify and model interoperability relations between IT and business assets considered in solution architectures, and to measure value dependencies that are related to these assets. The proposed method is suitable for scenarios with a high amount of business and IT assets, domain architectures, and solution architectures that are treated in isolation. This approach does not intend to replace an architecture exercise, it is conceived to model and analyze value delivery of dependencies for an IT and architecture portfolio.

This solution was applied to the integration of two information security architectures of a central bank in Latin America, where we identified value dependencies between both architectures. Consequently, the organization identified a set of unsuitable assets that were taken out of the integrated architecture, thus obtaining an appropriate solution that does not destroy value while avoiding service duplication.

We expect to develop new models that represent other components of ITG as future work. Likewise, we want to develop a dashboard that automates the visualization and reading of the given models, thus enhancing and supporting decision-making processes in an organization. The possibility of representing organization solution architectures should also be supported by the developed tool. Lastly, there is a need to relate solution architectures of a particular domain with metamodels and models that represent decision-making scenarios.

References

1. von Solms, R., von Solms, S.B.: Information security governance: a model based on the direct-control cycle. Comput. Secur. **25**, 408–412 (2006)
2. Ohki, E., Harada, Y., Kawaguchi, S., Shiozaki, T., Kagaya, T.: Information security governance framework. In: First ACM Workshop on Information Security Governance, pp. 1–6. ACM, New York (2009)
3. Kusumah, P., Sutikno, S., Rosmansyah, Y.: Model design of information security governance assessment with collaborative integration of COBIT 5 and ITIL (case-study: INTRAC). In: 2nd International Conference on ICT for Smart Society, pp. 1–6. IEEE, Danvers (2014)
4. Tillquist, J., Rodgers, W.: Using asset specificity and asset scope to measure the value of IT. Commun. ACM **48**, 75–80 (2005)
5. González Rojas, O.: Governing IT services for quantifying business impact. In: Matulevičius, R., Dumas, M. (eds.) BIR 2015. LNBIP, vol. 229, pp. 97–112. Springer, Heidelberg (2015)
6. IEEE Architecture Working Group: Std 1471–2000. Recommended Practice for Architectural Description of Software-intensive Systems. Technical report, IEEE (2000)
7. The Open Group: TOGAF Version 9.1 - Enterprise Edition. Van Haren Publishing (2011)
8. Euting, T., Weimert, B.: Information security. In: Bullinger, H.-J. (ed.) Technology Guide: Principles - Applications - Trends, pp. 498–503. Springer, Heidelberg (2009)
9. Weill, P., Ross, J.: IT Governance: How Top Performers Manage IT Decision Rights for Superior Results. Harvard Business School Press, Boston (2004)
10. IEEE Computer Society: IEEE Standard Computer Dictionary: A Compilation of IEEE Standard Computer Glossaries. IEEE Press, Piscataway (1991)
11. Hevner, A.R., March, S.T., Park, J., Ram, S.: Design science in information systems research. MIS Quart. **28**(1), 75–106 (2004)
12. Coetzee, M.: Towards a holistic information security governance framework for SOA. In: 7th International Conference on Availability, Reliability and Security, pp. 155–160. IEEE Computer Society (2012)
13. Burkett, J.S.: Business security architecture: weaving information security into your organization's enterprise architecture through SABSA. Inf. Secur. J. Glob. Perspect. **21**, 47–54 (2012)
14. Davern, M.J., Kauffman, R.J.: Discovering potential and realizing value from information technology investments. J. Manage. Inf. Syst. **16**(4), 121–143 (2000)

15. International Organization for Standardization: ISO/IEC 27000:2016: Information technology - Security techniques - Information security management systems - Overview and vocabulary. Technical report, ISO (2016)
16. Bowen, P., Hash, J., Wilson, M.: Information Security Handbook: A Guide for Managers. Technical report, National Institute of Standards & Technology (2006)
17. ISACA: COBIT 5 for Information Security. Technical report, Information Systems Audit and Control Association (2013)
18. ISACA: COBIT 5 for Risk. Technical report, Information Systems Audit and Control Association (2013)
19. Parent, M., Reich, B.H.: Governing information technology risk. Calif. Manage. Rev. **51**(3), 134–152 (2009)
20. González-Rojas, O., Lesmes, S.: Value at risk within business processes: an automated IT risk governance approach. In: Rosa, M.L., Loos, P., Pastor, O. (eds.) BPM 2016. LNCS, vol. 9850. Springer, Heidelberg (2016, in press)
21. Herrmann, A., Morali, A., Etalle, S., Wieringa, R.: Risk and business goal based security requirement and countermeasure prioritization. In: Niedrite, L., Strazdina, R., Wangler, B. (eds.) BIR Workshops 2011. LNBIP, vol. 106, pp. 64–76. Springer, Heidelberg (2012)

Learning and Capability

Intelligent Tutoring System for Learning Graphics in CAD/CAM

Jānis Dāboliņš[(✉)] and Jānis Grundspeņķis

Faculty of Computer Science and Information Technology,
Riga Technical University, Riga, Latvia
{janis.dabolins,janis.grundspenkis}@rtu.lv

Abstract. In the paper general tendencies of learning graphics in CAD/CAM are described in the aspects of evaluation of performance. The common problems in learning of such systems and tools, in knowledge assessment and in the efficiency and quality of usage of CAD/CAM in graphics are searched. In time when IT technologies and use of automatization is live topic in researches about technology enhanced learning with the aid of intelligent learning systems is necessary to create such tools for fast and accurate result of learning process. Adaptive learning and knowledge assessment principle analysis and description of intellectual tutoring system created are given in the research. The ITS created carries out the compilation of the user's accomplished graphical operations in CAM/CAD system, the analysis of the time spent and data processing. These data help to understand for which operations the user has spent the most time as well as in how many steps the designer has accomplished the task.

Keywords: Graphics in CAD/CAM · Intelligent tutoring system · Knowledge assessment · Adaptive learning · Agent

1 Introduction

Designing is the creation process of an object which most effectively would fulfill its provided functions. Graphics – part of the designing process in which the graphical representation of an object is created – precise drawing for details, plan or their relative position or scale definition [1, 2]. Computer aided designing (CAD/CAM systems) promotes the ensurance of economy, efficiency and quality – it has several advantages: improved product quality, higher productivity, humanization of working conditions, more flexible production, control of the process, the possibility of linking production with customer expectations (quick response) [3]. At any stage of the production design and project (with different amounts and in different areas), CAD/CAM systems are used or can be used [4]. Graphics is the one for the facilitation and automatization of which first automated systems were introduced. Notwithstanding the range of benefits, there are several problems when using these systems – the rapid rhythm of manufacturing requires the design tasks to be done quickly and flexibly, and it outlines the problem of employee training in working with CAD/CAM systems [5]. What is more, the training of employees is made more difficult due to the limited options of diagnostics of employee's operations in the system. It is difficult to determine the level of

V. Řepa and T. Bruckner (Eds.): BIR 2016, LNBIP 261, pp. 239–246, 2016.
DOI: 10.1007/978-3-319-45321-7_17

knowledge of the employees – even if the designer can do his/her job, it may turn out that his/her knowledge of the use of system's tools is too superficial (uses only those tools, which he/she can) for rational and thus quick performance of graphical works (as a result of effective use of tools). Thereby the use of the system is ineffective and thus very expensive. The necessity to understand what exactly the employee knows and how to use it leads to the necessity to accomplish the testing of training results using intelligent tutoring system.

2 Methods

If graphics in CAD/CAM system is as the main designer's requirement in addition to knowledge of the field than it is necessary to create a strategy for the acquisition and testing of that knowledge. It is topical not only in the circumstances of manufacturing and employee training but also in preparation of students for engineering sciences [6].

At present in technical universities CAD/CAM training is included in almost all areas [7], training takes place, but testing of knowledge is possible only with the analysis of input data (task) and output data (student's performance). How rational is the student's performance, what built-in system tools students use in the completion of the task has limited options to determine [8, 9]. This leads to a lack of understanding of the future or existing employee's effectiveness (there are no standards in the field which would specify the speed of job's execution also the accuracy of the work performed can suffer).

The Intelligent Tutoring System (ITS) created (Fig. 1) carries out the compilation of the user's accomplished graphical operations in CAM/CAD system, the analysis of the time spent and data processing. These data help to understand for which operations

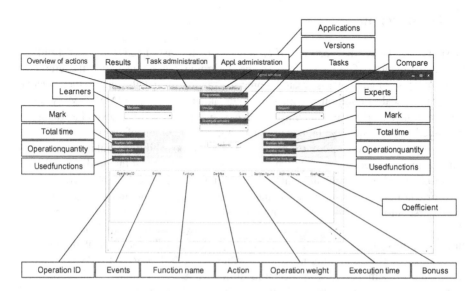

Fig. 1. Intelligent Tutoring System created by author

the user has spent the most time as well as in how many steps (how rational) the designer has accomplished the task. ITS's operation is ensured by the intellectual agent which has the ability to track and process the user's accomplished actions and to learn from these activities. This allows to automate the users knowledge test in CAD/CAM system (each CAD/CAM system as the ITS works as independent tool suited for user needs – can be reorganised for CAD/CAM currently used), easy and quickly understand at which operations the user delayed (was disturbed or had lack of knowledge as well as according to agent's calculation to see which of the operations accomplished could be done faster and/or more precise). The information for the agent is given by the established ITS users tracking system. It is implemented as a transparent window with a customizable function block on it – the amount of its functionalities depends on the used CAD/CAM system and planned graphic design works. This principle ensures that the ITS does not interfere with CAD/CAM operation – there are no problems with licensing and copyright. Also ITS is designed for Windows Platform therefore it works properly for each product that is suitable with Windows.

For the creation of agent's knowledge and launching of the training process, experimentally the period in which the expert (tutor) accomplishes the task is set, where the expert one and the same task carries out ten times (with different parameters in order to exclude routine occurrence, and thus the working run-time reduction). This kind of experiment can be carried out for various tasks the accomplishment of which makes it possible to split each task in notional indivisible operations (units of the work accomplished which repeat in different CAD/CAM works). Such indivisible operation would allow the agent to predict each (also untested) task's execution time.

Similar experiment can be done with the learner – also the learner accomplishes the same tasks (only here at least ten learners, not one learner ten times). By carrying out such a designing work accomplishment it can be determined in how long time the learner does it. By comparing the time of the learner with the time of the expert it is possible to obtain a coefficient that describes the expert time increase by determining the task accomplishment time of the learner.

Here as well it is possible to draw up a forecast of the variables, at which amount of work which coefficient (1) is necessary (Fig. 2). Both forecasts can be tested in control experiments. In addition to the clarification of the time spent, operation and sequence of the use of tools happens, inactivity (idle) time counting takes place and thus balancing of the operation rationalization.

$$Coefficient = \frac{Coefficient_{Max}}{Number\ of\ actions} \tag{1}$$

For example, the step effectiveness coefficient of an equilateral square-drawing is calculated (2).

$$F1 * K + F2 * K + F3 * K + F4 * K = end\ result \tag{2}$$

F- function;
K- operating weight ratio;
Number of operations- 4, but the shortest way- 1. Coefficient = ¼.

$$\text{line} * 0.25 + \text{line} * 0.25 + \text{line} * 0.25 + \text{line} * 0.25 = 1 \tag{3}$$

Learner performance ratio, using a line drawing rectangles (3).

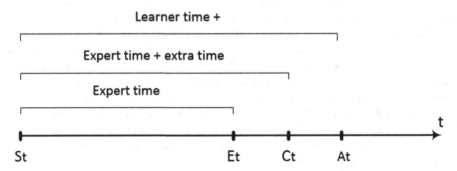

Fig. 2. Time coefficient, taking into account the expert's performance

t- time;

St- task start time;

Expert's time (Et)- time in which the expert accomplishes the task.

Experts time + additional time (Ct)- is the time for expert and learner time weighting.

Weighting is necessary because the learner's operations are not trained in comparison with an expert.

Learner's time + (At)- learner's time that is used when accomplishing the task.

3 Results

The information of the user's operation in CAD/CAM system is perceived through ITS interface, transmitted to agent and analyzed accordingly graphical design task: the use of tools, their number and effectiveness, competence.

The plan of control experiment is shown on the Fig. 3.

The arrival at the result is possible in several variants, it differs with the number of steps (operations) used.

In first example (Fig. 4) until the desired result 10 steps are used, it is, each step is drawn with the command line ("line").

In second example (Fig. 5) a tool polygon is used, which is repeated three times (operation 1–3). Then the transfer of the polygonal to the desired position is accomplished (operation 4) and erasing of the unnecessary lines (operation 5–6). By comparing the 1st and the 2nd example it can be concluded that in the 1st example four extra operations have been done which essentially increases the accomplishment time of the task although the quality and the verifying result does not suffer.

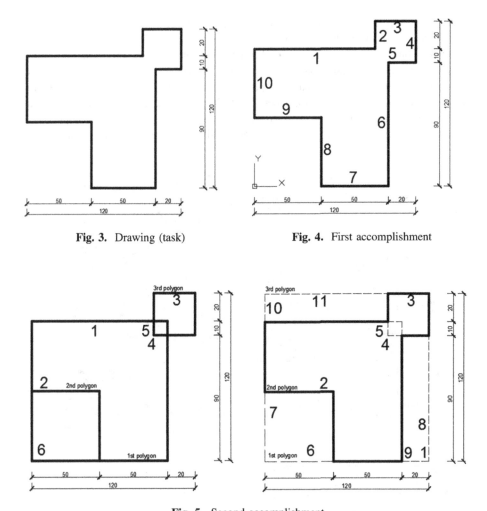

Fig. 3. Drawing (task)   **Fig. 4.** First accomplishment

Fig. 5. Second accomplishment

The processing of the information gained takes place thanks to system operation and the enumeration done, agents training and reaction on user's operations (Fig. 6). When the learner or the expert has logged on, the task window with three menus - programmes, programme versions and tasks are opened. All the menus are displayed one below another in the order named previously. When the user chooses the program, all the program versions from the database that exists for this program are selected. When also the program version has been chosen then all the tasks from the database that have been created for this program and program version implementation in the accomplishment of the tasks have been selected. As soon as the program has been changed, automatically all program versions that exist as well as all the data in task menu have been found. At the moment of opening of this window the username is seen at the top of the system window. The information of the operations carried out is discharged when the user has logged on as expert – the button 'Agents window' is seen. In learner user mode this button is not visible. By default, the very first tab 'Operations output' is selected. In this tab four menus are shown – programs, program versions, existing tasks and users. Program menu data is selected from the database on the opening of the window. If learner's performance review is selected, automatically all the learners who have accomplished the task in previously chosen program, its version are selected and they will be displayed below the menu. The same happens if expert's operation analysis is chosen – experts will be selected from the database.

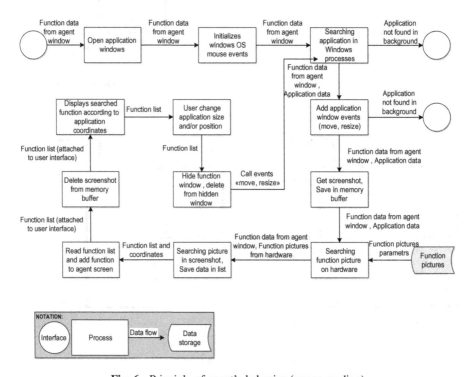

Fig. 6. Principle of agent's behavior (screen reading)

When the button 'see results' is activated, the data of each move that has been made in an accomplishment of the specific task is displayed in tabular form. Conversely, when the user is selected from the menu, on the right detailed information of the user from the menu is shown as well as the result of the task, operations made and achievements.

When the tab 'See results' is opened, the expert is offered five menu programs, versions, tasks as well as learners and experts. The filled data in first three menus and the functionality of menus is identical to the ones in 'operation output. When the task in 'Tasks' menu has been chosen than all the data about learners and experts who have done the tasks is selected and filled in the respective menus.

When the learner or the expert has been chosen, in the below existing units the task execution time, mark, number of operations as well as information of the used functions will be filled in. When both users (learner and expert) are chosen, then when selection a button 'Compare' the results of the task execution time and accuracy as well as time spent on each operation will be compared and displayed in the table below.

All the parameters of the tasks as well as creation of new tasks can be done only in expert's mode. The information of the programs added, their management is also possible only for an expert user. The management of the program includes – name change of the version, adding of functions, correcting and deleting. At the opening of agent's window data about the programs from the database will be selected and shown in program menu. After selecting the program all the existing and registered version for this program are selected. When any of the versions is activated, all the functions that are attached to this program's version are selected. While when activation any of the functions the image of it is seen.

4   Conclusions

Information systems, knowledge based systems, multimedia training techniques and other technologies play ascendingly important role in the dissimilation of knowledge, training and inspection. These technologies characterize interactive learning process that opposed to passive (lectures, reading) process becomes increasingly popular. Therefore, it is important to create intelligent training system specifically for IT and needs of other fields. CAD/CAM system training, understanding and intuitive use is not an easy task – it is complicated not only for the learners but also for an expert because it is necessary to carry out effective transfer of knowledge. Although accomplishment of the learner is obvious – easy to identify whether graphics task has been accomplished or no, a need for quick, rational, qualitative and effective work makes us look for solutions of how to delve into the accomplished. When examining the use of tools in sequence of operations in CAM/CAD systems and the speed of operation it is possible to improve and rationalize user's operations in the system, thus promoting improvement of quality and money saving. The created intelligent training system allows interactively understand graphical designing work performers level of knowledge of CAD/CAM system, thus the acquirement of additional tools, sequence of operations and other problems that can be observed when working with the system are identified. In further work system testing, target group selection and task creation is planned as well as give recommendations for both improvements of the system and the whole training process.

References

1. Xiao, H., Li, Y., Yu, J., Zhang, J.: CAD mesh model simplification with assembly features preservation. In: Science China Information Sciences, vol. 57, pp. 032110:1–032110:11. Springer (2014)
2. Kochan, D.: Techniques of software design for CAD/CAM. In: CAM, pp. 233–239 (1986)

3. Wang, Q.: Research and practice on CAD/CAM highly skilled personnel training based on web. In: Advances in Computer Science, Environment, Ecoinformatics, and Education, pp. 361–367. Springer (2011)
4. Gottschalch, H.: Conception of CAD/CAM training for technical draughtsmen in a model experiment. In: Social Science Research on CAD/CAM, pp. 158–164. Springer (1988)
5. Murthy, S.M., Mani, M.: Design for sustainability: the role of CAD. Renew. Sustainable Energy Rev. **16**(6), 4247–4256 (2012). Elsevier
6. García, R.R., Quirós, J.S., Santos, R.G., Peñín, P.I.Á.: Teaching CAD at the university: specifically written or commercial software? Comput. Educ. **49**(3), 763–780 (2007)
7. Aberšek, B., Popov, V.: Intelligent tutoring system for training in design and manufacturing. Adv. Eng. Softw. **35**(7), 461–471 (2004)
8. Jain, L.C., Howlett, R.J., Ichalkaranje, N.S., Tonfoni, G.: Virtual Environments for Teaching & Learning. Series on Innovative Intelligence, vol. 1. World Scientific Publishing Company, River Edge (2002). eBook, Database: eBook Collection (EBSCOhost)
9. Liu, D., Valdiviezo-Díaz, P., Riofrio, G., Sun, Y-M., Rodrigo Barba, R.: Integration of virtual labs into science E-learning. Procedia Comput. Sci. **75**, 95–102 (2015). Elsevier

Using Alliances to Cut the Learning Curve of ICT

Paul Pierce[(⊠)] and Bo Andersson

Department of Informatics, Lund University, Lund, Sweden
{paul.pierce, bo.andersson}@ics.lu.se

Abstract. Information and Communication Technology (ICT) is arguably an important, emblematic and ubiquitous technology of contemporary society. For many incumbent firms, the infusion of ICT into their industries poses both threats and opportunities. It might drive significant shifts of financial wealth and make firm performance change drastically. It entails managerial challenges of a kind we might not have seen before, but where knowledge of what possibilities and limitations reside in ICT will be a key success factor. One strategy to incorporate ICT-capability is developing the capability in-house; another strategy is to shortcut the learning curve and form alliance with someone having ICT-capability. By applying a design science approach a framework for ICT-capability transfer is put forth, a framework based on 62 interviews from stakeholders with experience of ICT-motivated alliances. By using this framework the risk of failure is reduced.

Keywords: Alliances · Design science · ICT-Capability · ICT competence · Knowledge acquirement · Capability transfer

1 Introduction

Information and Communication Technology (ICT) is arguably an important, emblematic and ubiquitous technology of contemporary society.

For many incumbent firms, the infusion of ICT into their industries poses both threats and opportunities. It might drive significant shifts of financial wealth and make firm performance change drastically. It entails managerial challenges of a kind we might not have seen before, but where knowledge of what possibilities and limitations reside in ICT will be a key success factor [1, 2].

As a response to this we see a range of firms within a variety of industries, ranging from NGO's, the public sector and industries at large setting up alliances in order to tap into the ICT-domain and thereby acquiring ICT-capability to existing products (henceforth ICT-motivated alliances) [3].

However, research shows that ICT-motivated alliances are no straightforward undertaking. Instead, those alliances are error prone and problematic. Where authors such as Baldi [4] discuss how "good" deals go "bad", Steinhilber [5] iterates that fact that out of the more than two thousand alliances that are launched worldwide every year more than half fail, more than one-third report that they have problems with their alliances, Pierce [3] concurs with the number of failed alliances, but also argues that

© Springer International Publishing Switzerland 2016
V. Řepa and T. Bruckner (Eds.): BIR 2016, LNBIP 261, pp. 247–261, 2016.
DOI: 10.1007/978-3-319-45321-7_18

some of the failures can just be a termination of the alliance because they have achieved what they set out to achieve. Yet others who look to alliances specifically crafted in and around ICT capabilities report of hardships when it comes to managing and sustaining alliances e.g. [1, 2, 6, 7].

This paper presents a framework aiding managers whom tries to acquire ICT capabilities. The paper is based on a six year longitudinal study of the alliance between AXIS Communications, Assa Abloy and Stanley Security. A study that resides mainly in the security industry and where Axis represents the ICT-partner and where Assa Abloy and Stanley are representatives for the non-ICT driven industry. Hence – the overarching perspective in the paper will be from the security industry.

The paper is organized as follows. First we present a tentative framework designed as an analytical tool to understand ICT-motivated alliances. This followed by a presentation of the research approach being design science and the applied method. We then present our findings from interviews. This followed by a presentation of the finalized and validated framework. Finally we draw some conclusions.

2   Theoretical Departure

Looking to alliances at large there are a number of different viewpoints. From traditional notions from authors such as Chen et al. [8] and Schilke et al. [9] who argue that the knowledge gained from an alliance is at best short lived and what is really needed is some form of alliance capability that involves continuous learning form the alliance. To others e.g. Kale et al. [10] and Mellat-Parast & Digman [11] who argue that learning from alliances is a capability that managers can acquire and use. Jet another view is voiced by Pierce [3] who argues that we should not focus too much on the transfer of knowledge within an alliance but rather look to how partners use each others knowledge in order to increase value. Haeussler et al. [6] further this notion by showing how technology firms have been successful in acquiring knowledge from alliance, but at the same time left themselves vulnerable to their partners potential opportunistic behavior.

Looking to alliances at large evidence would seem to suggest that while companies often advocate that they have learning motives, they might just really want a shortcut to products and markets where a possible byproduct is to learn about the alliance partner's products. [3] Basole et al. [12] on the other hand argue that we might be seeing a shift from Value exploration to value capturing when it comes to knowledge transfer.

This theoretical work takes its' starting point in the notion that alliances can in fact be used as a substitute to acquiring a specific knowledge.

The aim, as discussed previously, is to build and test a framework that can help managers understand what drives ICT focused Alliances and the first step is the potential overarching ability to absorb, share and transfer knowledge on ICT within alliances. As a first step we adopt Szulanski's [13] framework, and even though he does not label it as transfer capacity, we would argue that it has validity in the context of the alliance framework that will be proposed. Szulanski presents three main factors in his findings, but they are of little interest to us here. What is beneficial for this study are his original four groups of factors for Transfer Capacity, i.e. not only the internal stickiness factors that are the end result of his original study.

2.1   Transfer Capacity

Causal ambiguity describes a situation where a reason for failure, or at least unexpected outcome, is not clear even after the event has taken place. From an alliance perspective this could be a situation where similar or even the same alliance actions give different results for no precise reason. Leischnig et al. [14] argue that Interorganizational Technology Transfer ability is a key component for organizations to achieve innovation and increase the speed at which knowledge can be transferred between firms. This does not go against Szulanski [13] since there can still be ambiguity of value/benefit of what is being transferred. ICT also allows organizations to extend their reach in the world by extracting and combining knowledge from individuals and organizations and structure this knowledge into valuable information that can be traded for other services [15].

Unprovenness, as the name indicates, portrays a situation where it is difficult to motivate action, based on a lack of prior records of usefulness. This also means that if we have empirical evidence showing that a prior alliance was both helpful and contributed to the competitiveness of the company, then it should prove easier to motivate a replication of said alliance. Furthering this discussion Davidson and Olfman [16] have argued that organizations, as well as individuals, can increase the ability to transfer knowledge by trying out a number of alliances or having a high frequency of alliances. A more recognized way of increasing absorptive capacity is to have, or develop, alliance management capabilities, according to among others Kale and Singh [10] as well as Leischnig et al. [14]. Alliance management capabilities would alleviate the unprovenness towards alliances as such but not towards a specific alliance.

ICT, understanding that an organization's absorptive capacity is not only its ability to transfer and assimilate knowledge, but also its ability to exploit this information according to Cohen and Leventhal [17] means that the organization's interface towards both the external world and within the own organization becomes part of the firm's absorptive capacity. We would argue that having an ICT capability will help the company both to get a higher use intensity when it comes to transferring knowledge (due to lower transactions costs within a functioning system) and, more importantly, to accumulate, store and sort prior knowledge. Furthering this notion Davidson and Olfman [16] claim that ICT increases the receptivity of partners, i.e. their ability to absorb knowledge, by providing multiple channels of communication internally as well as externally. Looking to ICT competencies as such, this is one part that has not been thoroughly investigated in ICT research, something that Corvello et al. [15] acknowledge in so much that they argue for a lack of research on technological fit between partners.

2.2   Characteristics of the Source of Knowledge

We can argue that learning takes place in many different ways, and one viable way of learning is to use existing knowledge and experience [18]. This entails that organizations learn by sharing knowledge and experiences, which in itself is a form of knowledge.

In the context of the present study, an alliance learning process helps firms and their managers to learn, accumulate and leverage alliance management know-how and best practices, as claimed by Park and Zhou [19]. One problem with this specific learning process is that the knowledge of alliance building is often tacit; companies need to work on externalizing the knowledge [20–22]. This externalization of the knowledge then would require some specific attributes, or rather a lack of attributes, from the source according to Szulanski [13].

Lack of motivation depicts a situation where the knowledge source might be reluctant to share information based on a fear of both losing it and wasting time and effort. The discussion of lack of motivation could also be compared to a lack of commitment to the alliance, as described by for instance Golonka, Rzadca [23].

Not perceived as reliable is a quite self-explanatory factor that argues a certain need for the knowledge source to be viewed as both knowledgeable and trustworthy in order for any transfer of knowledge to seem meaningful, this would mean that some form of evaluation of risk and trust associated with the source of the knowledge would have to be done [22].

2.3   Characteristics of the Recipient of Knowledge

Lack of motivation, reasons around the potential reluctance to accept outside knowledge. Park and Zhou [19] argue that what corporations should strive for is an alliance learning process which helps firms and their managers to learn, accumulate and leverage alliance management knowhow and best practices. One problem with this is that the knowledge of alliance building is often tacit; companies need to work on externalizing the knowledge in order to not start losing motivation [14, 21].

Lack of absorptive capacity, explores a situation where the recipient is unable to exploit the transferred knowledge. Having a proverbial lack of absorptive capacity occurs when there is a lack of common language between the recipient and the source. Cohen and Levintahl [17] argue that in order to understand an organization's absorptive capacity, we need to understand the individual members of that organization. This means that organizations need to have an ability to build individuals' knowledge richness i.e. teach them to learn how to learn and in this instance this is the ability to learn about alliances, where Simonin [24] maintains that experience alone is not enough to achieve the full benefits of alliance building.

Lack of retentive capacity indicates that transferred knowledge is only effective as long as it is retained within either the recipient or the receiving organization. What Simonin [24] shows is that organizations do learn from prior alliance experiences, but they utilize the experience by transforming it into skills that can be used to identify, manage, monitor and negotiate alliances. The difference compared to Rothaermel and Deeds [25] is that Simonin stresses the fact that experience of any sort is only valuable to the organization if it can be internalized.

2.4   Characteristics of the Context

Knowing how to relate to knowledge is an important factor in learning. Grant and Baden-Fuller [26] argue that we need to have a common language as a basis for interpreting our experiences. By relating the learning to what we already know, we have a greater chance of enhancing our learning, but firms tend to forget that learning is a difficult, frustrating and often misunderstood process according to for instance Pierce [3].

Barren organizational context is an overarching name trying to depict a situation that is inconducive to facilitate knowledge transfers. Having a barren organizational context is for instance a lack of having formal structures and systems in place that can facilitate the coordination of expertise and knowledge.

Arduous relationships is what Szulanski, using work from Nonaka [27], denominates a situation where tacit knowledge causes a need for more exchanges in order for transfer to take place. He argues that ease of communication and familiarity between partners is also of importance. Alliance networks provide firms with access to markets and technologies they would otherwise not have the ability to compete in, but the social capital is needed in order to have the trust needed to transfer knowledge.

Intent. Factors such as motivation and unprovenness show that there is a need for a commitment and intent from management towards the relationship. This also means that we need to understand in what context the alliance is taking place, i.e. if there are divergent interests and/or divergent intents in the sharing of knowledge [28].

2.5   Relationship Governance

Alliances are all about handling relationships, where differences between alliance partners can be both a hindrance and a help according to among others Ho, Wang [22] as well as Pierce [3]. In the following we will look at different aspects that are said to influence relationships starting with Ouchi's [29] model on Markets, Bureaucracies and Clans, which we would argue to be an ideal starting point for discussing relationship governance.

2.6   Juridical Matters and Agency

Proceeding from the framework of Ouchi, it can be argued that you need contracts of different sorts to govern any organization or, more to the point, both contracts and agency or power to take action within a relation. Luo [30], for instance, discusses how in volatile markets a lack of ability to enforce juridical matters will create more opportunistic behavior. Hill and Jones [31] take their starting point from agency theory and discuss how the firm as such is actually constituted of different stakeholders that are in turn part of a nexus of both implicit and explicit contracts.

2.7   Strategic Fit

Grant [32] argues that, since the knowledge that the organization needs resides within the individual, organizations' primary role is to coordinate and organize the knowledge in what he calls "knowledge application". Organizations need to organize themself in respect to both intent and group dynamics, i.e. hierarchy and distribution of decision-making authority. This claim is supported in part by Hamel [33] who argues that there are asymmetries in partners' ability to learn, i.e. discrepancies in strategic fit. Partners might have different competitive and collaborative aims, which might be more important than any potential structure.

2.8   Communication Channels

An intrinsic point of transferring and absorbing any knowledge is to communicate in some fashion. At the most basic level their needs to be at least partial overlap of relevant knowledge to permit effective communication. Davidson and Olfsman [16] show that ICT can increase partners' ability to absorb knowledge in what they call increased receptivity. This is done by ICT's ability to provide multiple channels of communication, internally as well as externally. The study pointed to greater transparency as well as receptivity between alliance partners when using ICT.

2.9   Attitude/Intent

Attitude – in the alliance literature – refers to how companies use resources, commitment and social relations to handle alliances as such. It also encompasses the notion that since there are asymmetries in strategic fit (see above), it is important to understand partners' intent with the alliance according to both Hamel [33] and Grant [32].

2.10   Trust

It can be argued that in order to have and build trusting relations you need to be able to utilize all of the five above-mentioned factors. Ho, Wang [22] argue that companies can increase their market opportunities by using alliances, and by increasing relations capital which is done by repeating the alliance process; this in turn increases the inter-firm trust between the alliance partners. Authors such as Becerra et al. [34] and Judge and Dooley [35] argue that trust as a factor helps to lower transaction costs since trust works as constraining factor on control and coordination needs.

2.11   Cultural Fit

In the following, we refer to culture as the term has been employed by Hofstede [36], who defines culture in the following way:

My favorite definition of "culture" is precisely that its essence is collective mental programming: it is part of our conditioning that we share with other members of our nation, region, or group but not with members of other nations, regions, or groups. (Hofstede, 1983:76)

Hofstede's definition encompasses the group, which can be social, professional, regional, national, and so forth. Given the importance of both regional and national differences in alliances, the definition lends itself well to the present study.

The cultural aspects of why companies choose not to join in an alliance are often overlooked. Great cultural differences create challenges in the communication that, if coupled to no or bad personal relationships, may cause alliance failure. Organizational culture has to be considered when discussing any alliance success and failure according to Golonka, Rzadca [23]. More interesting though is that Sirmon and Lane [37] argue that professional culture cuts through organizational boundaries, which would indicate that it is a stronger influencing factor than organizational culture.

The glue that ties all the different influencing factors together is a capability of some sort; let us call it an alliance capability. Without an alliance capability, or strategy for that matter, the company cannot hope to know how to focus its resources. If a capability exists, then it should have some measurable and tangible benefits. Even though many authors have argued that alliance capabilities exist and have an effect on firms, they have proven hard to measure. As pointed out by Godfrey and Hill [38], many management theories have core constructs that are in fact unobservable, e.g. RBV and Dynamic Capabilities. What is needed is theorizing around what the observable consequences should be when unobservable capabilities are brought to bear, and those consequences should then be observable empirically. By applying design science to the problem we have created a tentative framework to test empirically.

For reasons of clarity, we have created a box matrix built upon the previous theoretical discussion that is illustrated in Table 1 below.

Table 1. Tentative framework for ICT capability transfer

Transfer capacity	Relationship governance	Cultural fit
Characteristics of knowledge transferred	Juridical/Agency	Professional culture
Causal ambiguity	Strategic fit/Steering	Organizational culture
Unprovenness	Communication,	Industrial culture
ICT	ICT augmenting	
Characteristics of the source of knowledge	Attitude/Intent	
Lack of motivation	Trust as a product of the others	
Not perceived as reliable		
Characteristics of the recipient of knowledge		
Lack of motivation		
Lack of absorptive capacity		
Lack of retentive capacity		
Characteristics of the context		
Barren organizational context		
Arduous relationship		
Intent		

3 Research Approach and Applied Method

One branch of IS research addresses real world problems identified by, for example, the target group of the research [39]. This article forms part of an iterative design science research process where the final goal is a design theory for ICT-motivated alliances. We used Carlsson et al.'s [40] IS design theory development approach as our general research framework (depicted in Fig. 1).

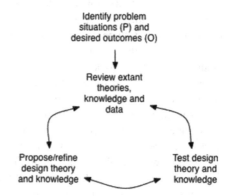

Fig. 1. ICT-design theory development.

The first research activity is identifying problem situations and desired outcomes. As discussed above, a problem for managers pondering the possibilities for ICT-motivated alliances are that the scientific support is weak. The identified problem (P) was the lack of scientific support for ICT-motivated alliances. A logical desired outcome of the research is a design theory for ICT-motivated alliances (O). Design theories and design knowledge aim to support professionals in solving practical problems in such a way that the desired outcomes are reached. A design theory can be presented in the form of a framework or a model [41, 42].

The second research activity is to review extant theories, knowledge and data, and the third research activity is to propose/refine design theory and knowledge. Design theories should be enhanced by being grounded in previous research and knowledge. Hence, a design theory should be enhanced by interacting with what is currently known; that is, grounded in extant theory. This can be called evidence-based or informed design knowledge.

The fourth research activity is the testing of design theory and knowledge. Since the developed theories and the knowledge should be used by managers in their analysis of ICT-motivated alliances, the managers opinion on the theory is vital.

To test the framework applicability and accessibility we interviewed by interviewing managers.

Important is the iterative process between step two, three and four. The data collection, analysis and validation have been conducted iteratively. This approach was possible thanks to the extensive time period of this research project.

3.1 Data Collection

This paper is based on a six years longitudinal study of the alliance between AXIS Communications, Assa Abloy and Stanley Security. In addition a set of other informants from other firms in mainly in the security industry were interviewed and answered surveys.

In all 62 open-ended interviews were conducted. The interviewees, such as CIOs, CTOs, CEOs, CSOs and Alliance managers came from both the security as well as IT industry. Firms participating in the study were, among other, Cisco, General Electric, Intransa, Lenel, RBCS, SIA, Sikyur, Sun Microsystems, Tech Data Corporation, Trans Tech Systems, and Velux. Interviews were conducted in Birmingham UK, Copenhagen DK, Gothenburg SE, Las Vegas US, Lund SE, Norcross US, San Diego US, NYC US and Stockholm SE.

Each interview was analysed (as soon as possible after it was finalized) and categorized accordingly to the tentative framework and saturation was reached after approximate 45 interviews. Analysis was supported by the QDA software HyperResearch. In total 76 h of interviews were conducted.

4   Findings from the Field

Three main themes were supported by the empirical findings, Transfer Capacity, Relationship Governance and Cultural fit. But in each subsection changes have been made. One example being that certain factors have been removed all together, others have changed names to better represent what they actually stand for.

4.1   Transfer Capacity

Characteristics of knowledge transferred. Looking to empirical as well as theoretical material we argue that there is ample evidence showing that ambiguity is a key dimension in complex organizations. The problem, or challenge, that has emerged numerous times during this work is that ICT in itself is ambiguous. Therefore the transfer of knowledge on ICT is ambiguous in nature when it comes to what characteristics of knowledge to transfer. This is not to be confused with unprovenness, which in this instance refers to the different views on unproven knowledge between the recipient and source. They need to be recognized as a potential barrier to knowledge transfer. ICT as a medium of transferring knowledge is also an important factor to take into consideration when looking at the overall characteristics of knowledge transfer.

Characteristics of source of knowledge. This factor illustrates motivation and reliability of the source of knowledge, but it was discovered that the impact from the individuals had on the results was crucial. The reason for this are two-folded, it may be reluctance to stray outside of individual comfort zones, as described by Alvesson, Sveningsson [20] or a mismatch between recipient and source, as discussed by for instance Kalling [43]. The key aspect from the empirical work showed that individuals' commitment to the alliance was instrumental in the success stories, and hence the factor needs to be motivation and not lack of motivation. The issue of non-reliability was such that no alliances were struck outside of what would be considered a reliable partner.

Characteristics of recipient of knowledge. The data shows that on an overall basis motivation (lack of motivation) was somewhat weak since there were few formal commitments towards learning and knowledge sharing. Such commitments are one prerequisite for being able to share knowledge [18]. That being said, we argue that there a number of motivated individuals who could possible receive knowledge. There was a clear lack of formal commitment to learning agendas, but there were other goals attached to the alliance, often sales oriented. One can press this as far as to say that the motivation that was in place was focused towards learning how to use different technology. This leads to absorptive capacity. The fact that there was no indication in the interviews that would suggest knowledge transfer taking place would indicate a lack of absorptive capacity. Retentive capacity is very much connected to absorptive capacity. Teece [44] advocates that firms need to embrace technology change and increase their absorptive capacity by accumulating skills, which translates to increasing the retentive capacity. We argue that the cases pointed towards learning programs being in place. This despite the fact that both absorptive capacity and retentive capacity were shown to be somewhat lacking by the analysis.

Characteristics of the context. The data clearly showed that only the organizational context was of importance. The fact that there was no support for arduous relationships we attest to the second part of the framework, which is focused solely on relationship governance. Much of an arduous relationship falls under or into the barren organizational context. Going back to the organizational context it was visible that large resources were put in place for training on existing products. This in itself should have pointed to what Aral, Weill [45] term senior management championing. This championing did not seem to be evident since it was attested by both theory and empirical work, the hardest sell of all for an alliance can be internally. The interviews showed differences between the companies when it comes to organizational context, but it would seem uncontestable to not include this factor. There is a need to provide employees with a context from which they can both work, grow and learn. One key element derived from the interviews relate to the converging security market where people are worried about their ability to manage outside expectations.

Regarding Intent that was categorized as contextual. Most of the "intent" discussed and described falls under different forms of motivation as described in the entire vertical of Transfer Capacity. More interestingly though is a discussion on situations where the alliance manager typically has to make a range of decisions both on how to enter into an alliance and on how to manage one. In order to do this in an efficient manner, there is a need to be clear on what the intent with said alliance is. Where the key issue is why the organization has an alliance in the first place. Is it to achieve positive outcomes or to avoid negative outcomes? The empirical material shows that there are different intents with the alliances as such, and in fact the intent with the alliance might not be towards learning or knowledge sharing. Instead the firms use alliances as a tool to harvest the potential out of joining different products. This brings the discussion in a full circle since one could argue that this is exactly what is sometimes happening in technology alliances. There the alliance is about getting a product to market in the most efficient way possible, which often means that partners just use other partner's knowledge rather than incorporating it into their own organization. One can claim that it is within this process that capabilities are won and potentially lost. The companies can develop an alliance capability as well as a capability to use partners' technology to their own needs. We further argue that one possible consequence of this is to actually learn and transfer knowledge about the product being used, but that is seldom neither aim nor intent for the alliance.

4.2   Relationship Governance

Alliances are to a great extent about relationships. Starting with Juridical and Agency aspects, we argue that even though there are examples from the interviews that show that alliances can succeed based purely on trust and relationship values as described by for instance Becerra et al. [34] as well as Ho, Wang [22]. There was also evidence that supported the notion that alliances have a better chance of succeeding when legal matters such as contracts have been taken care off. The agency aspect is interesting since it seems to overlap other thoughts on alliance management, where for instance Leischnig et al. [14] argue that managers who have routines for handling alliances tend to get better interaction quality with higher success of technological transfer with lower agency costs. What is clear is that firms suffer less from coordination costs when juridical aspects have been sorted and managers have routines for coordinating alliances. Regrettably coordination is not only hinging on contracts and routines, but also on how well partners intermesh.

The strategic fit or steering of firms has many implications. If the departure is steering of the firm, one could argue that steering should be about resource allocation. However, strategic fit from an absorptive perspective; where for instance Cohen and Levinthal [17] argue that having overlapping knowledge is needed in order to be able to recognize when knowledge and learning is desirable, but at the same time too much overlap will stagnate innovation. What is needed is a strategic fit that implies a sufficient level of overlap of knowledge in order to ensure effective communication, i.e. lower coordination costs. More importantly there is a need for functioning communication interface since:

"an organization's absorptive capacity is not resident in any single individual but depends on the links across a mosaic of individual capabilities, Cohen and Levinthal (1990:133)".

Furthering the discussion around communication and to certain extent agency, it could be argued that dialogue that tries to transvers differences will create a better intercultural understanding, which in turn will facilitates intergroup alliances. This is done through communication and the development of personal agency. Despite the fact that there was not significant data to support the notion, we still argue that it has value. The data showed that ICT is a crucial aspect in alliance work, where ICT can be both a facilitator for communication and, more importantly, a tool for knowledge transfer. Looking to ICT applications they are singularly well suited to help us make sense of complex systems. This would strongly suggest that they should be a key factor in helping firms realize and find potential value in their alliance base.

Attitude and Intent are problematic to measure as such, but never the less intent was mentioned frequently during interviews and was shown to have a significant impact by the survey. Based on the findings we argue that strategic fit in some instances is similar to having similar intent, and not a product of having similar technology or similar knowledge. Pérez et al. [46] argue that by having similar intent, companies with asymmetric technologies, e.g. an IT company and a Security company can still work together.

The word Trust has significant impact on relationship governance. It was ever present within interviews as well as survey and that using trust to overcome potential problems is a good supplement to formal contracts, good communication and intent. Think of Trust as the final safety net for the alliance. Strong trust has been proven to have mitigating qualities in cognitive processes and the potential to be used as a tool to lower risk in alliance building.

4.3   Cultural Fit

Whether culture is viewed as the very problematic concept that is hard to understand and control, or if culture is considered as something that has to be taken seriously in order to understand ICT and organizations this study has showed culture to have far reaching influences for alliance work as well as relationships in general. Findings reveal that two central things have bearing on the cultural fit as well as on the entire framework. First and foremost that professional culture transcends all other cultures as was hypothesized by Sirmon, Lane [37]. The second thing that came to be was that ICT as a tool could be what Cohen and Levinthal [17] discuss as the interface for relationship governance and cultural fit.

Table 2. Validated framework for ICT capability transfer

Transfer capacity	Relationship governance	Cultural fit
Characteristics of knowledge transferred	Juridical/Agency Strategic fit	Professional culture
Causal ambiguity	Communication,	Organizational
Unprovenness	ICT augmenting	culture
ICT	Attitude/Intent	Industrial culture
Purpose of learning	Resource allocations	
Characteristics of the source of knowledge	Trust as a product of the others	
Motivation		
Reliability		
Characteristics of the recipient of knowledge		
Motivation		
Absorptive capacity		
Retentive capacity		
Characteristics of the context		
Barren organizational context		
Arduous relationship		
Intent/measurability		

Despite the expostulated absence of similar organizational cultures, where the two industries could be said to work within their own silos, there was still an awareness of a need to handle both the need to understand the other industry players and the need to eventually adopt products to work together. In essence there was agreement that an organizational culture that could accept change and foster learning was preferable even if the Industrial culture was focused on core values within the silo.

4.4   Final Framework

Based on the findings from empirical data the three main factors are still applicable, but some of the sub factors changed, some fell away and some were added. These factors and underlying concepts are shown in Table 2 below.

5   Conclusions

Alliances with the ambition to tap into another partner ICT-capabilities are a challenge for many managers.

Furthermore, these challenges are problematic to address with existing knowledge on alliances. Hence, supplementary theoretical frameworks are needed. Via a six year longitudinal study aspects important in ICT-motivated alliances were identified and merged into a ICT-capability transfer framework. The aspects identified are Transfer Capacity, Relationship Governance and Cultural Fit. An iterative process develops this framework by using extant theories and a range of interviews from stakeholders working in or close to ICT-motivated alliances.

References

1. Berne, C., Garcia-Gonzalez, M., Mugica, J.: How ICT shifts the power balance of tourism distribution channels. Tourism Manag. **33**(1), 205–214 (2012)
2. Kowalkowski, C., Kindström, D., Gebauer, H.: ICT as a catalyst for service business orientation. J. Bus. Ind. Mark. **28**(6), 506–513 (2013)
3. Pierce, P.: Using Alliances to Increase ICT Capabilities. Lund University, Lund (2013)
4. Baldi, F.: Managing strategic alliances in good and bad times. Options in Alliances. SpringerBriefs in Business, pp. 21–34. Springer, Milan (2013)
5. Steinhilber, S.: Strategic Alliances: Three Ways to Make Them Work. HBS, Boston (2013)
6. Haeussler, C., Patzelt, H., Zahra, S.A.: Strategic alliances and product development in high technology new firms: the moderating effect of technological capabilities. J. Bus. Ventur. **27** (2), 217–233 (2012)
7. Rooks, G., Snijders, C., Duysters, G.: Ties that tear apart: the social embeddedness of strategic alliance termination. Soc. Sci. J. **50**(3), 359–366 (2013)
8. Chen, H.-H., Lee, P.-Y.: The driving drivers of dynamic competitive capabilities: a new perspective on competition. Eur. Bus. Rev. **21**(1), 78–91 (2008)
9. Schilke, O., Goerzen, A.: Alliance management capability: an investigation of the construct and its measurements. J. Manag. **36**(5), 1192–1219 (2010)

10. Kale, P., Singh, H.: Building firm capabilities through learning: the role of the alliance learning process in alliance capability and firm-level alliance success. SMJ **28**(10), 981–1000 (2007)
11. Mellat-Parast, M., Digman, L.A.: Learning: the interface of quality management and strategic alliances. Int. J. Prod. Econ. **114**(2), 820–829 (2008)
12. Basole, R.C., Park, H., Barnett, B.C.: Coopetition and convergence in the ICT ecosystem. Telecommun. Policy **39**(7), 537–552 (2008)
13. Szulanski, G.: Exploring internal stickiness: impediments to the transfer of best practice within the firm. Strateg. Manag. J. **17**, 27–43 (1996)
14. Leischnig, A., Geigenmueller, A., Lohmann, S.: On the role of alliance management capability, organizational compatibility, and interaction quality in interorganizational technology transfer. J. Bus. Res. **67**(6), 1049–1057 (2014)
15. Corvello, V., Gitto, D., Carlsson, S., Migliarese, P.: Using information technolgoy to manage diverse knowledge sources in open innovation processes. In: Eriksson Lundström, J. S.Z., Wiberg, M., Hratinski, S., Edenius, M., Ågerfalk, P.J. (eds.) Managing Open Innovation Technologies, pp. 179–197. Springer, Berlin (2013)
16. Davidson, M., Olfman, L.: The impact of information and communication technology use on interorganizational learning in an IT outsourcing collaboration. In: The 37th Hawaii International Conference on System Sciences, Hawaii, pp. 1–10 (2004)
17. Cohen, W.M., Levinthal, D.A.: Absorptive capacity: a new perspective on learning and innovation. Adm. Sci. Q. **35**(1), 128–152 (1990)
18. Kalling, T., Styhre, A.: Knowledge Sharing in Organizations. Liber, Malmö (2003)
19. Park, S., Zhou, D.: Firm heterogeneity and competitive dynamics in alliance formation. Acad. Manag. Rev. **30**(3), 531–554 (2005)
20. Alvesson, M., Sveningsson, S.: Good visions, bad micro-management and ugly ambiguity: contradictions of (non-)leadership in a knowledge-intensive organization. Organ. Stud. **24** (6), 961–988 (2003)
21. Sveningsson, S., Alvesson, M.: Managerial Work: Leadership & Identity in an Imperfect World. Cambridge University Press, Cambridge (2015)
22. Ho, M.H.-W., Wang, F.: Unpacking knowledge transfer and learning paradoxes in international strategic alliances: contextual differences matter. Int. Bus. Rev. **24**(2), 287–297 (2015)
23. Golonka, M., Rzadca, R.: Does a connection exist among national culture, alliance strategy, and leading ICT firms' performance? J. Bus. Econ. Manag. **14**(sup1), S395–S412 (2013)
24. Simonin, B.L.: The importance of collaborative know-how: an empirical test of the learning organization. Acad. Manag. J. **40**(5), 1150–1174 (1997)
25. Rothaermel, F.T., Deeds, D.L.: Alliance type, alliance experience and alliance management capability in high-technology ventures. J. Bus. Ventur. **21**, 429–460 (2006)
26. Grant, R.M., Baden-Fuller, C.: A knowledge accessing theory of strategic alliances. J. Manag. Stud. **41**(1), 61–84 (2004)
27. Nonaka, I.: A dynamic theory of organizational knowledge creation. Organ. Sci. **5**(1), 14–37 (1994)
28. DeTurk, S.: The power of dialogue: consequences of intergroup dialogue and their implications for agency and alliance building. Commun. Q. **54**(1), 33–51 (2006)
29. Ouchi, W.G.: Markets, bureaucracies, and clans. Adm. Sci. Q. **25**, 129–141 (1980)
30. Luo, Y.: Are joint venture partners more opportunistic in a more volatile environment? Strateg. Manag. J. **28**(1), 39–60 (2006)
31. Hill, C.W.L., Jones, T.M.: Stakeholder-agency theory. J. Manag. Stud. **29**(2), 131–154 (1992)

32. Grant, R.M.: Towards a knowledge-based theory of the firm. Strateg. Manag. J. **17** (Summer), 109–122 (1996)
33. Hamel, G.: Competition for competence and inter-partner learning within international strategic alliances. Strateg. Manag. J. **12**(special issue), 83–103 (1991)
34. Becerra, M., Lunnan, R., Huemer, L.: Trustworthiness, risk, and the transfer of tacit and explicit knowledge between alliance partners. J. Manag. Stud. **45**(4), 691–713 (2008)
35. Judge, W.Q., Dooley, R.: Strategic alliance outcomes: a transaction-cost economics perspective. Br. J. Manag. **17**, 23–37 (2006)
36. Hofstede, G.: The cultural relativity of organizatoinal practices and theories. J. Int. Bus. Stud. **14**(2, Special Issue on Cross Cultural Management), 75–89 (1983)
37. Sirmon, D.G., Lane, P.J.: A model of cultural differences and international alliance performance. J. Int. Bus. Stud. **35**(4), 306–319 (2004)
38. Godfrey, P.C., Hill, C.W.L.: The problem of unobservables in strategic management research. Strateg. Manag. J. **16**, 519–533 (1995)
39. Iivari, J.: A paradigmatic analysis of information systems as a design science. Scand. J. Inf. Syst. **19**(2), 39–64 (2007)
40. Carlsson, S.A., Henningsson, S., Hrastinski, S., Keller, C.: Socio-technical IS design science research: developing design theory for IS integration management. IseB **9**(1), 109–131 (2011)
41. Gregor, S., Jones, D.: The anatomy of a design theory. J. Assoc. Inf. Syst. **8**(5), 312–335 (2007)
42. Hevner, A., Chatterjee, S.: Design Science Research in Information Systems: Theory & Practice. Springer, Berlin (2010)
43. Kalling, T.: The lure of simplicity: learning perspectives on innovation. Eur. J. Innov. Manag. **10**(1), 65–89 (2007)
44. Teece, D.J.: Explicating dynamic capabilities: the nature and microfoundations of (sustainable) enterprise performance. Strateg. Manag. J. **28**, 1319–1350 (2007)
45. Aral, S., Weill, P.: IT assets, organizational capabilities, and firm performance: how resource allocations and organizational differences explain performance variation. Organ. Sci. **18**(5), 763–780 (2007)
46. Pérez, L., Florin, J., Whitelock, J.: Dancing with elephants: the challenges of managing asymmetric technology alliances. J. High Technol. Manag. Res. **23**(2), 142–154 (2012)

Supporting Perspectives of Business Capabilities by Enterprise Modeling, Context, and Patterns

Janis Stirna[✉] and Jelena Zdravkovic

Department of Computer and Systems Sciences,
Stockholm University, Postbox 7003, 164 07 Kista, Sweden
{js,jelenaz}@dsv.su.se

Abstract. Contemporary enterprise information systems (IS) need to be sustainable in order to provision long-lasting functionality in the presence of changes in customers' demand, varying environmental aspects, regulations, and many other factors. A key challenge is the need to adjust according to changes at run-time of the IS because not all of them can be anticipated and elaborates at the design time. Lately, the notion of capability has emerged in IS engineering as an instrument that integrates organizational development with IS development, taking into account changes in the application context of the solution. To this end, a methodology and a development environment have been elaborated with the concept of capability in focus, under the name of Capability Driven Development (CDD). It encompasses three key perspectives of organizational design – Enterprise Modeling, context modeling, and pattern modeling. The objectives of this paper are to present how the key perspectives have been incorporated in the CDD methodology, how the methodology has been supported by the CDD environment, and how the methodology and the environment have been used in practice. The application of the proposed approach is discussed for two business cases – outsourcing of energy management services at SIV AG (Germany), and e-government service portfolio provisioning at Everis (Spain).

Keywords: Enterprise modeling · Capability · Context · Business-IT alignment

1 Introduction

The notion of capability has been gaining much attention in the area of business and IT alignment. For instance, Ulrich and Rosen [1] see capability as the fundamental abstraction to describe what a core business does in the sense of the capacity to achieve a desired outcome. Similarly, the Open Group Standard [2, 3] defines capability as an ability or capacity for a company to deliver value, either to customers or shareholders, right beneath the business strategy.

In essence, capability is seen as originating from competence-based management and military frameworks, further advancing the traditional Enterprise Modeling (EM) approaches by representing organizational designs from a result-based perspective.

© Springer International Publishing Switzerland 2016
V. Řepa and T. Bruckner (Eds.): BIR 2016, LNBIP 261, pp. 262–277, 2016.
DOI: 10.1007/978-3-319-45321-7_19

Thus it is as an abstraction beyond the specifics of the more traditional dimensions of EM, such as *how* (processes), *who* (agents), *what* (concepts), and *why* (goals) by increasing focus on *results*. Capability allows focusing on the aspect of sustainability, i.e. ensuring that the results are delivered and benefits attained even if the initial situation changes. In practice, this requires business capabilities to be adjusted according to the context in which they will be delivered.

To this end a European research project CaaS [4] – "Capability as a Service for Digital Enterprises" was established in order to develop a Capability Driven Development (CDD) approach. It defines capability as *the ability and capacity that enable an enterprise to achieve a business goal in a certain context* [5]. The CDD approach supports a smooth transition from EM to IS design (at design time) and subsequent context monitoring and adjustment of the IS at run time. The CDD approach aims at supporting automation of business activities – by identifying and hence improving how they are currently performed, as well as how they would perform in different contextual situations. CDD supports the development of executable software with built-in contextualization algorithms, which will contribute to reducing the time and resources spent on customization for new business situations. CDD focuses on the following dimensions of design – enterprise modeling, context modeling, reuse and variability modeling, as well as capability modeling.

The objectives of this paper are *(1) to present the requirements for the different perspectives of CDD;* and *(2) to illustrate how the perspectives have been designed and implemented in two industrial use cases of the CaaS project.*

The research approach is based on design science [6] consisting of several design and evaluation cycles. The proposed methodology has been validated in two use case companies of the CaaS project – at SIV (Germany) for business process outsourcing (BPO) in the utility sector and at Everis (Spain) for Service Oriented Architecture (SOA) management in a community of ca 100 municipalities.

The rest of the paper is organized as follows. Section 2 briefly describes EM, context modeling and patterns within IS engineering, on which the CDD approach is based. Section 3 describes the CDD methodology and Environment. Section 4 presents the application of CDD within two industrial use cases. Section 5 provides concluding remarks and directions of future work.

2   Theoretical Foundations and Related Work

In this section briefly presents the topics comprising the main perspectives addressed by the CDD methodology.

2.1   Enterprise Modeling

Enterprise Modeling (EM) is a discipline concerned with the development and use of modeling approaches typically targeting (1) congruent organizational and IS designs; (2) improvement of the quality of business operations; and (3) supporting the problem solving process within organizations in a modeling way [7]. EM methodologies typically address several perspectives of the problem domain such as business goals, processes, concepts, rule, and actors. For an overview of such multi-perspective approaches c.f., for instance, [8].

CDD incorporates components of EM for modeling business goals, KPIs, business processes, as well, process variants.

2.2   Patterns

Pattern-based approaches have established themselves in software programming, software design, data modeling, and in systems analysis, see e.g. [9, 10] with the common objective to capture, store and communicate *reusable solutions to reoccurring problems*, such as fragments of code or diagrams. The pattern concept has been further extended and applied in organizational development and knowledge management under the term *organizational patterns* [11]. In the context of EM, majority of models are created in a design situation and once completed they reflect good solutions and best practices for dealing with a specific business problem or corporate intention, some of which can be captured and represented as organizational patterns.

According to the principles of CDD, capabilities are delivered by existing best practices and reusable model fragments, hence it is practicable to represent them as capability patterns. Their content and the use differ from existing pattern proposals in the way that (a) their scope and structure resembles a business capability, and (b) their life-cycle spans from business context analysis, through design, to run-time when upon monitoring the patterns are replaced or changed.

2.3   Context and Variability

Dey [12] defines context as "*any information that can be used to characterize the situation of an entity*". Several areas, such as artificial intelligence, software development, databases, data integration, machine learning, and knowledge representation fields perceive context mainly as a collection of things associated to some specific situation [13]. Arguing that context is a broad, inaccurate, and non-delimited concept, in [14], Hervas describes the context by identifying users, environment, services and devices, further refined by what, who, where, when and why. More concretely, a user determines a context, by eliciting not only the user itself, but, in addition, what he/she is doing, when he/she is doing, etc. Context categorizations determine the focus to an entity, and often, to a user. In contrast, in our research, there is a need to model the context surrounding the delivery of a business. The context framework of Hervas has been considered as an inspiration when creating the context modeling component of the CDD methodology.

Realizing different contexts in IS engineering is typically done through the concept of *variability defined as ability of a software artifact to be changed so that it fits a context* [15, 16], *Variation point* denotes a particular place in a system where choices are made and which *variant* to use.

3   Capability Driven Development Methodology

The CDD methodology [17, 18] consists of a modeling language and a defined way of working supported by the CDD Environment, which is presented in this section.

3.1   Modeling Language for CDD

The theoretical and methodological foundations for CDD are provided by the conceptual *capability meta-model* (CMM), c.f. for details [17, 18]. CMM was developed on the basis of requirements from the industrial project partners, and related research on capabilities. In brief, it consists of the three main parts of the meta-model:

(a) *Enterprise model* for representing organizational designs with Goals, KPIs, Processes (with concretizations as Process Variants) and Resources;

(b) *Context model* for representing for which context a Capability is designed (represented by Context Set) and Context Situation at runtime that is monitored and according to which the deployed solutions are adjusted; and

(c) *Patterns and variability model* for delivering Capability by reusable solutions for reaching Goals under different Context Situations. Each pattern describes how a certain Capability is to be delivered within a certain Context Situation and what Processes Variants and Resources are needed to support a Context Set.

Note that Fig. 1 is a simplified version of CMM showing the key components of CDD; the full version with definitions of components and associations is available in [18] (Table 1).

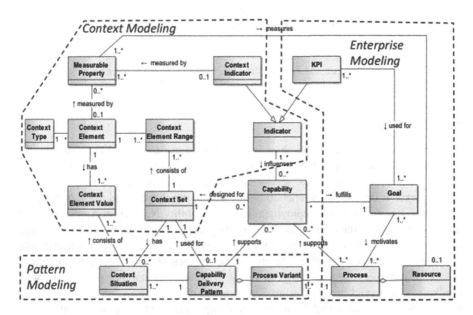

Fig. 1. A conceptual CDD meta-model with dashed lines showing model perspectives [18].

Table 1. Concepts of the core CDD meta-model

Concept	Description
Capability	`Capability` is the ability and capacity that enable an enterprise to achieve a business `Goal` in a certain context (represented by `Context Set`).
KPI	`Key Performance Indicators` (KPIs) are measurable properties that can be seen as targets for achievement of `Goals`.
Context Set	`Context Set` describes the set of `Context Elements` that are relevant for design and delivery of a specific `Capability`.
Context Element Range	`Context Element Range` specifies boundaries of permitted values for a specific `Context Element` and for a specific `Context Set`.
Context Element	A `Context Element` is representing any information that can be used to characterize the situation of an entity.
Measurable Property	`Measurable Property` is any information about the organization's environment that can be measured.
Context Element Value	`Context Element Value` is a value of a specific `Context Element` at a given the runtime situation. It can be calculated from several `Measurable Properties`.
Goal	`Goal` is a desired state of affairs that needs to be attained. `Goals` can be refined into sub-goals forming a goal model. `Goals` should typically be expressed in measurable terms such as `KPIs`.
Process	`Process` is series of actions that are performed in order to achieve particular result. A `Process` supports `Goals` and has input and produces output in terms of information and/or material. When initiated a process is perceived to consume resources.
Pattern	`Patterns` are reusable solutions for reaching business `Goals` under specific situational contexts. The context defined for the `Capability` (`Context Set`) should match the context in which the `Pattern` is applicable.
Process Variant	`Process variant` is a part of the `Process`, which uses the same input and delivers the same outcome as the `Process` in a different way.

3.2 CDD Process

The CDD methodology suggests three interconnected cycles of working – *design, delivery,* and *feedback.* Capability design starts with the configuration of the existing or creation of new enterprise goals, services and processes combined with captured business contexts, followed by the elicitation of required capabilities and relevant patterns. Capability delivery includes deployment of the Capability Navigation Application and run-time monitoring the Capability Delivery Application, for instance, an ERP system. During the execution of the application the changes of context are monitored, and run-time adjustments are used to determine if the changes have become such to require a change of the executing capability, or the consideration of another pattern to apply. Feedback is achieved by monitoring KPIs (measurable properties of goals for monitoring their fulfillment) which facilitates capability refinement and pattern updating.

The CDD methodology is supported by the *CDD environment* consisting of the following key components: *Capability Design Tool (CDT)*, an Eclipse based graphical modeling tool with a complete notation for enterprise modeling and capability design. *Capability Context Platform (CCP)* is an application for aggregating and distributing context information from various kinds of sources, e.g. social networks, application data, and other. *Capability Delivery Application (CDA) is* an application used to deliver capabilities, developed and executed using the engineering process of capability owner/provider. In real case at runtime CDA can, for example, be an ERP system. CDA is monitored by *Capability Navigation Application (CNA)* according to the capability design specified in CDT and based on the real life data received from the CCP. CNA retrieves the stored patterns created in the CDT and according to them configures the CDA used for capability delivery. CNA also selects the run-time capability adjustments by monitoring the capability context. A view of these components is given in Sect. 4.1 for the BPO case at SIV. Currently, technical components are in a prototype stage, i.e. they are functionally complete but still undergo the final stages of customization for the needs of the use case companies.

3.3 Capability Design Process

The CDD methodology recommends starting with capability design from the existing business requirements, enterprise models, and other kinds of organizational design artifacts. The process is iterative and we strongly advocate a participatory approach to stakeholder involvement. Capability design is supported by the CDT.

Capability is a comprehensive concept intersecting elements of EM (goals, KPIs, business processes), context modeling, and modeling of delivery in terms of process variants. Capability design can take several paths depending on what existing organizational designs are taken as a starting point and what the organization intends designing. Hence, several strategies are used, namely, *goal-first, service-first,* and *context-first* elicitation strategies. The concepts used in this discussion are shown the capability meta-model (Fig. 1).

"Goal" first capability elicitation starts by analyzing the intentional perspective of the organization, i.e. its business vision and goals, and how they could be reached in terms of capabilities. The elicitation process includes the steps described in Table 2. The process is not strictly sequential, i.e. each of the steps could be iteratively and incrementally refined until a desired and agreed capability is specified.

"Service" first capability elicitation starts with organization's business services that are in use and are serving customer needs. The business service is improved or optimized by considering context awareness, adaptability, or automation, thus providing a capability to deliver it in varying circumstances with more efficiency.

A new capability is identified supporting a business service that in turn may include a number of underlying actions – processes, software components, and even manual activities. After the actual context of the service is analyzed in detail, the service is re-engineered in terms of the Variation Points related to the context, as well as the variants corresponding to the underlying elements. The Goals and KPIs are related to the service and updated to align with the identified Capability. Using the results of the

Table 2. Goal-first capability elicitation process

Goal-first elicitation steps	CMM perspective	Resulting artifact
A business goal-pathway is elicited from a top goal and completed to leaf goals.	Enterprise Modeling	Goal model
KPIs are defined for the goals, and mandatory for the leaf goals. A goal can be measured by several KPIs; a KPI can be used by a number of goals.	Enterprise Modeling	A set of KPIs with the relations to the goals
For each leaf goal, zero or more capabilities are identified. If for a goal it is concluded that there is no a feasible capability, then the it is left for future work. If a capability already exists, it is related to its goal(s).	Enterprise Modeling, Capability	A set of capabilities with the relations to the goals
Identifying and modeling the context affecting the new capability(ies).	Context Modeling	Context model
Each identified capability is elaborated by analyzing relevant for inclusion of process models, software components, and manual actions, which are then related to the variation point(s) corresponding to the identified context, and the relevant variants.	Enterprise Modeling and Pattern Modeling	Capability structure
Select and adopt an existing capability pattern for the capability design, which in essence means specifying a new capability pattern.	Pattern Modeling	Capability pattern(s)

previous steps, a new Capability Pattern is specified or an existing pattern is adapted and linked to the capability design.

"Context" first elicitation is chosen when the coverage of a wide range of business contexts of an organization (business) is the most important, and where the business change should be driven by a context-aware variability management.

In the elicitation process, the contexts surrounding a business are observed, analyzed in order to identify relevant Context Elements that are subsequently grouped into Context Sets representing relevant situations in the business environment requiring adjustments of capability delivery. Each identified Context Set is then related to a new Capability. E.g., for BPO, one might consider two capabilities – one for heavily regulated business environments, and one for more loosely regulated. The goals of an identified capability are elicited and at least one goal must have a corresponding KPI. Variation Points are set to match the identified Context Sets of the capabilities, and Variants are modeled to include the actions enacting the capability.

3.4 Capability Delivery at Run-Time

The delivery cycle starts with the deployment of a capability design in the form of pattern in a target application environment. This section presents the requirements related to the main activities of the run-time related to relevant concepts in the CMM.

Monitor KPIs: Capture the actual KPI values to present them in the CNA. In some cases the values are fetched from internal, analytical data sources. If a value is acceptable, i.e. within bounds of the KPI specified for the goal that guides the capability (see examples in Sect. 4), then nothing needs to be done. If a KPI Value is not satisfying according to the KPI, then *Capability Delivery Adjustment* shall be invoked.

Capture Context: The context data serves as another input for capability delivery adjustment algorithms and hence it needs to be monitored during run-time. The CCP provides Context Element values to the CNA as they change. If a captured Context Element Value is in the defined Context Element Range of the executing capability, then adjustments are not needed because the change is covered by the designed variation points, variants, actions, and resources. Consequently, if the value exceeds the defined range, then *Capability Delivery Adjustment* shall be invoked.

Capability Delivery Adjustment: It shall be invoked by the CNA when a KPI Value is not satisfying in terms of the designed KPI or when a Context Element Value exceeds its Context Element Range. In the first case, an Adjustment Calculation shall be invoked to execute (automatically or semi-automatically) a planned adjustment to recover the KPI over time. In the second case, to continue delivering the same functionality and the same quality (KPIs) within the newly changed context. If the change is planned then an adjustment calculations may be replaced or extended by another pattern from the repository. Alternatively, a re-design of the internal pattern structure such as adding a new resource or a variant might be performed. If however a needed adjustment is not specified, then a new capability solution needs to be designed.

Update Capability Pattern: If an executing capability based on a pattern is re-designed, then the new solution should be stored in the repository by updating the pattern, or a new pattern should be created. Pattern updating is initiated according capability delivery adjustment, i.e. if a capability structure is changed - additional elements are included, or some are removed or changed (Context Elements, Variation Points, Variants, Actions, Resources, etc.).

4 Application Cases

The CDD methodology and environment have been applied and evaluated for the correctness and the potential for business improvements by three companies in different fields: (1) e-government, (2) compliance management, and (3) business process outsourcing. In this paper we present the results of capability design and deployment at SIV AG, company doing business process outsourcing in the energy sector in Germany (Sect. 4.1), and at Everis, a company managing e-government services for regional municipalities across Spain (Sect. 4.2).

4.1   CDD Application Case at SIV

SIV (Germany) is a business process outsourcing (BPO) provider for the utilities industry – delivery of energy, water supply, waste water disposal, as well as for the management of electricity in the grid. SIV has developed its own ERP platform kVASy® that supports all BPO services offered to SIV's customers - grid access providers, balance suppliers, etc. SIV's role in the market has been stable and kVASy® is well established in the industry. Hence, keeping existing and acquiring new clients in a highly competitive utility market is a top priority. SIV aims to deliver a high efficiency to its customers by combining best practices with compliance to the market rules while allowing for some degree of customization. SIV's business challenges can be summarized as the following:

– frequently changing business contexts affected by new regulations, by laws, and by other circumstances. This leads to a need for the context-aware solutions that will support SIV needs to ensure data exchange for markets with different regulations
– varying load of customers
– different standards of documents
– a high extent of manual routines in clearance of document processes, especially error handling.

According to the SIV's approach, key capabilities are elicited following the principle of the *Goal first* approach (Sect. 3), i.e. the elicitation of the requirements for a capability starts by defining the goals for offering BPO services (Table 3). The reason for choosing this approach lies in the fact that over the years the company's role in the market has been well established and company's vision and its business model are well elaborated. Therefore, addressing the challenge of keeping the existing and acquiring new customers in a highly competitive utility market is a top priority. Performing an enterprise-level analysis with a clear focus on business goals, and linking them to appropriate BPO capabilities is seen as an opportunity to improve the efficiency and increase automation of BPO service processes.

Table 3. A goal path of SIV, with a KPI (excerpt from [19])

Goal no	Goal name
1	To constantly provide value to customers
1.1	To efficiently control grid communication processes
1.1.1	To achieve high process quality
1.1.2	To optimize case throughput
1.1.3	To reduce process cost KPI 1.1.3.1: process cost reduction decreased x% compared to the non-capability solution

From the goal "To reduce process cost", the Capability "Dynamic Data Clearing" is identified and structured as a pattern; the main Action is an existing Clearing Process (Formal Specification) that upon the identification of the context (Table 4) is redesigned to support its variability.

Table 4. Context set for dynamic data clearing capability

Context element	Context element range
Medium	{gas, electricity, water, undefined}
Regulatory document	{GPKE, Geli Gas, WiM}
Message exchange format	{MSCONS, UTILMD}
Message status	{syntax_checked, content_checked}
Meter reading	{manual, automated}

The Context Set is subject to change where the change frequency can be relatively high or low. For example, the German regulation authority biannually issues updated message exchange formats. By contrast, directives how to run intercompany business processes change very infrequently. The main Variation Point of the Clearing Process model concerns different Variants for handling the clearance procedures for different Medium, Regulatory document type, and Message exchange format. The model is re-designed for automatic handling of the documents based on the Concept Elements in Table 4, to be implemented in kVASy®.

Figure 2 shows an architectural view on provisioning BPO services by applying the CDD approach. The capability is distinguished from the conventional BPO service provision as the delivery takes the application context into account, i.e. CNA allows for an adjustment whenever the context of the capability delivery changes or if KPIs drop below acceptable values.

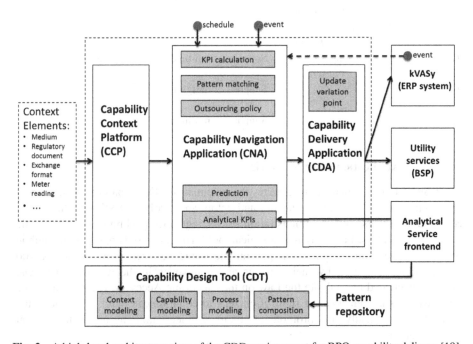

Fig. 2. A high-level architecture view of the CDD environment for BPO capability delivery [19]

In addition to "Dynamic Data Clearing", another analyzed capability pattern was "Urgent Resource Allocation". This pattern supports the provider of a utility service with the allocation of knowledge workers to the faulty clearing cases if the backlog size of the customers (Context Element) exceeds the available knowledge worker capacity (Resource). The solution of the pattern refers acquiring additional resources (Manual Action, with a required Competence); if the effort of allocation is expected to be time-consuming, a better performance could be achieved if a non-controllable size of customers' backlog is predicted, i.e. the activation of the pattern is scheduled.

Table 5 summarizes how components of the CDD environment support the CMM perspectives at design time and run-time. The CDT is only used at design time while at run-time capability monitoring and adjustment is performed by the CNA. The CCP provides available context elements to the CDT for capability design at design time and context element values to the CNA at run-time. Pattern repository is mostly used at design time for selecting existing solutions, while at run-time it can provide suggestions for process variants to the CNA. The role of the CDA is fulfilled by an ERP system kVASy®. It provides measurable property values to the CCP for aggregation into context elements from which the CNA can then calculate capability adjustments.

Table 5. CDD Environment component support of the perspectives of capability design

CDD environment component	Enterprise modeling	Context modeling	Pattern and variability modeling
CDT	Supports at design-time	Supports at design-time	Supports at design-time
Pattern Repository	Supports at design-time		Supports at design-time and at runtime
CNA	Supports at run-time	Supports at run-time	Supports at run-time
CCP		Supports at design-time and at runtime	
CDA		Supports at run-time	

4.2   CDD Application Case at Everis

The case of Everis (Spain) demonstrates the potential of SOA capability management in a community where various factors and actors are involved: SMEs, multinational corporations, diverse public administration's laws, regulations, administrative consortia and calendars, as well as many technological tools. The use case is based on the public sector and the main emphasis is put on electronic services provided to ca 100 municipalities and used by their citizens and companies in the regions. The SOA platform is created to facilitate the Law on the Electronic Access of Citizens to Public Services. This law ensures the right of citizens to communicate with all the administrations electronically to promote a more efficient and a more transparent administration.

Even if the SOA solution for the e-government in municipalities has been implemented, the following challenges are to be considered:

- Update of services is done manually, e.g. if a service of an external provider expires, a technician is responsible to renew it manually. As a consequence, the citizens are not having on-line access to the service.
- Notification service of incidents to the main office is manual. E.g. the SOA technicians receive a notification for an error or an issue. It is a manual task for them to handle all the incidents.
- Municipality infrastructure capacity is a problem when in-person request load is high.
- Service promotion is manual. E.g. once a municipality wants to promote a service, it has to be done manually by a public servant. Considering the large amount of municipalities involved such an approach is inefficient.

Everis aims at delivering several different capabilities – to more effectively maintain the SOA platform, to ensure service execution, and to enhance the usage of electronic services in general. The key capabilities are elicited following the principle of the *Service-first* approach, i.e. where the elicitation of capabilities starts by considering improvements of the organizational business services. This is because the case reflects a dominant service-orientation, and where capabilities are seen as the enablers supporting of variety of customer needs with an efficiency that is monitored and measured by well-defined KPIs.

As an illustrative example, we consider the elaboration of "Service Promotion by Highlighting" capability to enable citizens to see the services easier and to use them more. The limitations of manual promotion are solved by applying the CDD approach and having identified the capability of service promotion automatically based on different contexts. Services will be promoted automatically, so the time needed to highlight them will be reduced and citizens will be able to access them more easily. Moreover, public servants will have more time to perform other tasks. The identified KPIs for the capability are shown in Table 6.

Table 6. KPIs defined for the "Service Promotion by Highlighting" capability

KPI	Expected value
% of citizens consuming the service	25 %
Growth of the number of citizens using the service per year	10 %
% of services in active use from all services provided by municipality	100 %
% of paper submissions (from all submissions where online submission is available)	30 %
% of municipalities starting to use a service after received information	90 %

Service highlighting intends to promote the usage of the services, such as "Marriage Service" or "Swimming Pool Service", or "La Dipu Te Beca" (for obtaining a council grant). Use of a service is dependent on a number of Context Elements that were identified and proven for the influence [20]; they are outlined in Table 7.

Table 7. Context Set defined for the "Service Promotion by Highlighting" capability

Context element	Context element description	Context element range
Number of users per day	If service is highly used, its rank may be increased and service can be highlighted.	[Numeric]
Number of municipalities using the service	If a service is highly used in one municipality, its rank can be increased in another one.	[Numeric]
Number of citizens	Number of citizens in a municipality	[Numeric]
Area	Municipality size in area	[Numeric]
Type of day	Type of the day can affect the usage of the services.	[Working day; Holiday]
Types of events per calendar unit	Calendar events might affect the service usage and the frequency of services ranks recalculation.	[High impact; Neutral impact; Low impact]

At run-time, upon any change of a Context Element Value, a different calculation (Variation Point, Variants) is performed to initiate automatic highlighting of a service to promote it. The KPIs from Table 6 are also enabled for capturing, monitoring and a dashboard-presentation to control improvement and efficiency of the on-line services.

Figure 3 shows a fragment of capability design for Service Promotion with highlighted modeling perspectives for the purpose of illustrating the level of complexity of capability models as well as how capability is linked with other modeling components.

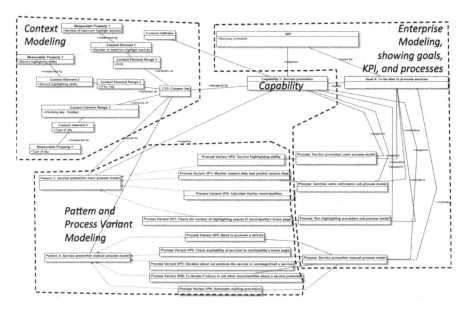

Fig. 3. Overview of the design model for capability service promotion [20]

The complete version of this capability design is available in [20]. This design is supported by architecture of the CDD Environment similar to the one at SIV (Fig. 2) except the role of CDA is performed by Everis SOA platform for municipalities.

5 Conclusions and Future Work

We have presented the CDD constructs with a particular emphasis on the modeling perspectives, such as EM, patterns, and context modeling. The perspectives address the notion of capability that embodies a composite functionality to integrate organizational design with IS development taking into account changes in the organization's business context at both design- and run-time. We have also presented how the capability designs are supported by CDD environments in two industrial cases.

The work reported in this paper has been carried out within the CaaS project and has led to a methodology and an environment for CDD. The key perspectives of capability design are deemed important for approaches using the concept of capability for documenting, managing, and configuring organizational services, business processes, tasks according to delivery context. In summary, the capability relationships to the perspectives are the following:

- Capability should fulfill a business goal. And hence it should be monitored by the same (or a subset of) KPIs as for the business goal it fulfills.
- Capability is context dependent, i.e. for each capability a specific set of permitted contexts is to be specified in which the capability is applicable.
- Capability is delivered by existing best practices. Hence, each capability should be linked to a pattern specifying how it is delivered and what kind of variability is permitted within this capability.

The CaaS project has been elaborating the above requirements into the CDD methodology based on components from the 4EM method [8], BPMN, and newly developed capability and context modeling approach, as presented in [18]. The dedicated CDD environment will always need to be customized for integration with the specific business applications (CDAs) used for capability delivery for the specific company, as well as for integrating the relevant context providers of a specific business case with the CCP. There are however more customizations possible including replacing one context platform with another for the role of CCP. Similarly, one modeling language in the methodology can be replaced with another as long as the links from capability to modeling perspectives are kept in tact.

Amongst plans for future work are elaboration and design of approaches for specifying capability adjustment calculations for various run-time conditions, such as change of KPI(s), context, as well as in relation to predictions of changes. Additional work will also be devoted to including additional model types such as, for instance, business rules, in the CDD meta-model, as well as providing guidance for methodology and environment customization. Currently the CDD Environment is able to collaborate with CDAs that already exist, such as corporate ERPs. The next step of methodological and technological development will target the integration of CDD with Model Driven

Development approaches and tools to be able to develop new CDAs for business cases that do not have prior IT support.

Acknowledgments. This work has been performed as part of the EU-FP7 funded project no: 611351 CaaS - Capability as a Service in Digital Enterprises.

References

1. Ulrich, W., Rosen, M.: The business capability map: Building a foundation for business/it alignment. Cutter Consortium for Business and Enterprise Architecture (2011). https://www.cutter.com/practice-areas/business-enterprise-architecture
2. OPENGROUP: TOGAF - enterprise architecture methodology, version 9.1 (2012). http://www.opengroup.org/togaf/
3. OPENGROUP: Archimate - modelling language for enterprise architecture, v2.0 (2012). https://www2.opengroup.org/ogsys/catalog/c118
4. EU FP7 project no. 61351, CaaS – Capability as a service for digital enterprises, 2013-2016 http://caas-project.eu/
5. Bērziša, S., Bravos, G., Cardona Gonzalez, T., Czubayko, U., España, S., Grabis, J., Henkel, M., Jokste, L., Kampars, J., Koç, H., Kuhr, J., Llorca, C., Loucopoulos, P., Juenes Pascual, R., Pastor, O., Sandkuhl, K., Simic, H., Stirna, J., Valverde, F., Zdravkovic, J.: Capability driven development: an approach to designing digital enterprises. J. Bus. Inf. Syst. Eng. **57** (1), 15–25 (2015). Springer
6. Hevner, A.R., March, S.T., Park, J., Ram, S.: Design science in information systems research. MIS Q. **28**(1), 75–105 (2004)
7. Persson, A., Stirna, J.: Why enterprise modelling? An explorative study into current practice. In: Dittrich, K.R., Geppert, A., Norrie, M. (eds.) CAiSE 2001. LNCS, vol. 2068, pp. 465–468. Springer, Heidelberg (2001)
8. Sandkuhl, K., Stirna, J., Persson, A., Wißotzki, M.: Enterprise Modeling – Tackling Business Challenges with the 4EM Method. Springer, Heidelberg (2014). ISBN 978-3-662-43724-7S
9. Gamma, E., Helm, R., Johnson, R., Vlissides, J.: Design Patterns: Elements of Reusable Object-Oriented Software Architecture. Addison Wesley, Reading (1995)
10. Fowler, M.: Analysis Patterns Reusable Object Models. The Addison-Wesley Series in Object-Oriented Software Engineering. Addison-Wesley, Reading (1997)
11. Rolland, C., Stirna, J., Prekas, N., Loucopoulos, P., Persson, A., Grosz, G.: Evaluating a pattern approach as an aid for the development of organisational knowledge: an empirical study. In: Wangler, B., Bergman, L.D. (eds.) CAiSE 2000. LNCS, vol. 1789, pp. 176–191. Springer, Heidelberg (2000)
12. Dey, A.: Understanding and using context. Pers. Ubiquit. Comput. **5**(1), 4–7 (2001)
13. Zacarias, M., Pinto, H.S., Magalhães, R., Tribolet, J.: A 'context-aware' and agent-centric perspective for the alignment between individuals and organizations. Inf. Syst. **35**(4), 441–466 (2010)
14. Hervas, R., Bravo, J., Fontecha, J.: A context model based on ontological languages; a proposal for information visualisation. J. Univ. Comp. Sci. **16**(12), 1650–1665 (2010)
15. Van Gurp, J., Bosch, J., Svahnberg, M.: On the notion of variability in software product lines. In: Proceedings of IEEE/IFIP Conference on Software Architecture, pp. 45–54 (2001)

16. Pohl, K.: Requirements Engineering: Fundamentals, Principles, and Techniques. Springer, Heidelberg (2011). ISBN 3642125778

17. Bērziša, S., Bravos, G., Gonzalez Cardona, T., Czubayko, U., España, S., Grabis, J., Henkel, M., Jokste, L., Kampars, J., Koc, H., Kuhr, J., Llorca, C., Loucopoulos, P., Juanes Pascual, R., Sandkuhl, K., Simic, H., Stirna, J., Zdravkovic, J.: Deliverable 1.4: Requirements specification for CDD, CaaS – Capability as a Service for Digital Enterprises, FP7 proj. no. 611351 (2014). http://caas-project.eu/deliverables/

18. Bērziša, S., España, S., Grabis, J., Henkel, M., Jokste, L., Kampars, J., Koc, H., Sandkuhl, K., Stirna, J., Valverde, F., Zdravkovic, J.: Deliverable 5.2: The Initial Version of Capability Driven Development Methodology, CaaS – Capability as a Service for Digital Enterprises, FP7 proj. no. 611351 (2015). http://caas-project.eu/deliverables/

19. Czubayko, U., Koc, H., Kuhr, J., Sandkuhl, K.: Deliverable 2.1: Capability Models for BPO, CaaS – Capability as a Service for Digital Enterprises, FP7 proj. no. 611351 (2015). http://caas-project.eu/deliverables/

20. España, S., Garcia, M., Gonzalez Cardona, T., Grabis, J., Hita, G., Henkel, M., Jokste, L., Kampars, J., Koc, H., Kuhr, J., Llorca, C., Juanes Pascual, R., Valverde, F.: Deliverable 4.2: Capability Models for SOA Technological Platforms, CaaS – Capability as a Service for Digital Enterprises, FP7 proj. no. 611351 (2015). http://caas-project.eu/deliverables/

A Method for Situating Capability Viewpoints

Anders W. Tell$^{(\boxtimes)}$, Martin Henkel, and Erik Perjons

Stockholm University, Stockholm, Sweden
{anderswt,martinh,perjons}@dsv.su.se

Abstract. This paper presents a method that is used to enrich existing architecture frameworks or methods by enabling development of situated capability viewpoints. The method addresses the issue that in many cases viewpoint definitions suggest a singular way to consider and model a domain. This issue is particularly prevalent in frameworks developed by one profession, such as IT architects, where general concepts, such as capability and service, may have narrow definitions. The method we suggest is to start with a base capability viewpoint and then tailor that into specific situated capability viewpoints by incorporating situational concerns. Each tailored viewpoint supports a stakeholder's work situation and aims to increase intended and actual use of capability analysis. The method is built upon the ISO 42010 standard, an extendable base capability viewpoint, and concepts from method engineering. The method is demonstrated by applying it to the Strategy Map framework by Kaplan and Norton.

Keywords: Viewpoint · Capability · Capability analysis · Enterprise architecture · Situation · Situational methods engineering · Interweaving

1 Introduction

In the world of enterprise architecture (EA), knowledge about systems and its architecture is commonly organised according to concerns. The concept of viewpoint is used to represent and frame one or more concerns. A viewpoint, its constituent's languages and models kinds are traditionally defined by EA experts or IT architects. Recently the concept of capability has been a popular way of representing, analysing, designing, governing, and managing an enterprise or organization. The concept of capability stems from the field of strategic management where it was used in the 90s to describe resources and core competencies that a company needs in order to compete in a market [1]. Lately the capability concept has been used as a mean to aid in the development of IT systems [2].

It may be tempting to let one profession, such as EA experts or IT architects, to define one single way to represent and analyse capabilities. However, the risk is that such a narrow, single-sided representation may miss to incorporate other essential aspects of an organisation. Thereby, different stakeholders may use the same general capability viewpoint but are in reality interested in different point-of-views and aspects. While EA frameworks try to standardise the capability concept, we can observe from existing use that is has been used from different perspectives, such as the perspectives

© Springer International Publishing Switzerland 2016
V. Řepa and T. Bruckner (Eds.): BIR 2016, LNBIP 261, pp. 278–293, 2016.
DOI: 10.1007/978-3-319-45321-7_20

of functional grouping [3], process orientation [4] and even describing the ability to perform enterprise architecting itself [5]. Furthermore, research have shown that architectural languages tend to favour the perspective of architects and not the perspectives of non-architects [6]. There is clearly a need to adjust the perspective and language according to the situation the concept of capability is used in.

In this paper we present a method that can be used as an instrument to clarify what the different situational perspectives are, why employees have different perspectives, and show how different groups view and use the concept of capability. Through the use of the method the various uses of capabilities can be explored. The method is built upon a base capability viewpoint that can be specialized for stakeholders and their work situations. The method builds upon the international standard ISO 42010 [7] that addresses the creation, analysis and sustainment of architectures of systems through the use of architecture descriptions within architecture frameworks. The main author of this paper participated in the ISO/IEC standardization work through the national delegation.

The method follows the principles of situational method engineering and is expressed as a "method-chunk". It is meant to be combined with an EA framework, or method, such as the Capability Driven Development approach [2] or similar approaches. This means that the method is not aimed to be a complete capability analysis method, it is rather meant as a way to tailor existing frameworks or methods, to allow them to cater for different capability perspectives. The contribution of this paper is the definition of a base capability viewpoint, and the method steps and guidelines to specialize it into situated capability viewpoints.

The structure of the paper is as follows. Related work and the design science research approach taken is described in Sects. 2 and 3, while an overview of the method is given in Sect. 4. Section 5 presents the starting viewpoints: the stakeholder, base capability and situation viewpoints, while Sect. 6 contains a description of the four steps of the method. Sections 7 and 8 concludes the paper.

2 Related Work

The method presented in this paper aims to improve capability analysis. The contribution of the paper is thus related to the definition of capability and its use in analysis. The capability concept, and associated methods of analysis has been described in the field of strategic management and enterprise modelling.

In *strategic management* the notion of dynamic capability [8] has been be used to describe the ability on an organisation to change its capabilities. As pointed out by [9] the definition of the concept of capability itself has fluctuated somewhat in the area of strategic management; however, there is a tendency to associate it with the organisation of resources and their allocation [10]. For example, McKeen and Smiths [11] defines a capability as "the ability to marshal resources to affect a predetermined outcome". In this paper we extend this view of capabilities and elaborate on it, that is, we view resources and their use as an integral part of capabilities while we also honour that the analysis capabilities may cover other aspects as well, such as the capacity of performing tasks. The more elaborated definition of capabilities that we use in this paper allows us to be more precise when tailoring capability analysis to a certain situation.

The concept of capability that is used for the method presented in this paper is further discussed in Sect. 5.

In the area of *enterprise modelling* and *enterprise architecture*, the concept of capability has been used as a way to analyse organisations [12, 13]. It has also been used to describe an organizations ability to use enterprise architecture. This is most notable in the open groups TOGAF framework [5], where capability frequently refers the readiness of an organization to use enterprise architecture. Practitioners has been using *capability maps* [3, 14] to make an overview of the capabilities that an organisation has. Especially [3], the focus has been on capability analysis as a way to functionally break down capabilities into sub-capabilities. While capability maps start with main/large capabilities, there has been other approaches suggested that start the analysis based on processes. Examples of these approaches include [4], which view a capability as a form of process, and the Capability Driven Development approach (CDD) [2], which enable process analysis to be the starting point for capability identification. The method presented in this paper is a compliment to the existing capability analysis approaches. It adds a novel angle to existing approaches in that is uses work situations to frame, adapt, configure, and constrain capability descriptions. Thus, the method can be used to tailor existing approaches, such as CDD.

Besides the contributions related to the work described above, the method is making use of situational method engineering and the ISO 42010 standard for representing viewpoints. Situational method engineering is a major component of method engineering, which encompasses aspects of creating a development method for a specific situation [15]. In this paper we use the method engineering concept of *method chunk* to describe the method. The method, or method chunk, is aligned with the view presented in [16] that a tailored method should include the context of its use.

3   Research Approach

The research methodology used in this paper is design science. Design science is carried out to change the state of affairs by designing and evaluating an innovative artefact. Commonly, the design science process consists of several activities that lead to a designed and evaluated artefact. We use the five activities presented by Peffers [17] to describe our research:

1. *Problem identification and motivation.* The problem addressed in this paper is that the concept of capability may have a narrow, single-sided representation, in existing capability analysis methods, and/or enterprise architecture frameworks or methods, and, thereby, miss to incorporate essential aspects embedded in situations and work people do in an organisation.
2. *Objectives of a solution.* The objectives of a solution are in this paper interpreted as a number of requirements on the artefact. This activity can also be seen as a transformation of the problem into demands on the proposed artefact, which in our case is the method. Based on the authors' consulting experience with capability analysis and international standardisation, we have identified that important requirements on the method should be:

Generally applicable: The method should be generally applicable to different domains, and combinable with existing capability analysis methods. The method should complement existing approaches in domains where a complete analysis of situational concerns is needed, thereby lower the barriers of method application, improving facilitating conditions for, and actual-use of capability analysis.

Compliant with standard: The method should be compliant with the ISO 42010 standard ontology for architecture descriptions. Thereby, enabling effective integration of the method with existing capability analysis methodologies and architecture frameworks.

Efficient result: The method should produce situated capability viewpoints in an efficient way, that is, produce results in a resource efficient way, and by considering situational work factors. This will increase aspects such as job-fit, performance and output expectancy, intentions-to-use, and subsequently actual-use of capability analysis. That is an important prerequisite for organisations to start using the method.

3. *Design and development.* The *solution* presented in this paper that address the problem and fulfil the requirements, is an artefact in form of a method for creating situational capability viewpoints. The artefact is presented in Sects. 4 and 5.
4. *Demonstration.* The artefact, that is, the method, is *demonstrated* by applying it on the Strategy Map framework for strategic analysis, planning and execution by Kaplan and Norton [18], see Sect. 6.
5. *Evaluation.* The *evaluation* is presented in the form of so called informed argument [19], see Sect. 7, where the researchers discuss how the method address the identified problem and fulfil the stated requirements. A more thorough evaluation is planned to be carried out at a later stage.

4   Overview of the Method

The solution (artefact) presented in this paper is a method or, more precisely, a method chunk, that aims at developing situated capability viewpoints by tailoring a base capability viewpoint to address situational work concerns and other use-requirements on the developed viewpoints and their use. The method makes use of three (3) fixed viewpoints (stakeholder, base capability and situation) that govern the creation the methods input and output views and models. These viewpoints are all following ISO 42010 and are further described in Sect. 5. The method contains four (4) steps that may be performed iteratively (Fig. 1):

1. *Situate and focus:* Situate and anchor the tailoring into the situation-of-interest, and what to focus attention on.
2. *Characterize:* Identify affected individuals (stakeholders), categorize them into stakeholders, and identify work situations related to stakeholders.
3. *Tailor:* Develop a set of situated capability viewpoints by tailoring the base capability viewpoint to address situational work concerns and use-requirements.

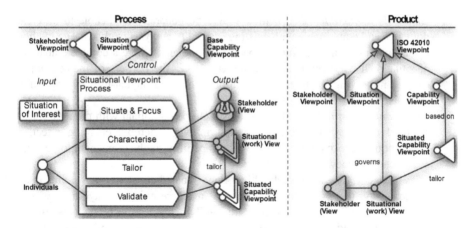

Fig. 1. Overview of process fragment with inputs, controls, outputs, and a product structure.

4. *Validate*: Compare situated capability viewpoints with the perceived real world by evaluating fulfilment of situational work concerns and use-requirements.

The method delivers *results* in form of viewpoints, model kinds, views, and models. A viewpoint frames one or more concerns relevant to stakeholders, and provides conventions, rules, patterns for construction of views of entities of interests, or a system. A view is made up of models, which are governed by a corresponding model kind. A model kind provides conventions for a type of modelling. The results may be used to extend an existing architecture framework or method:

- A *stakeholder view*, which contains a model of the stakeholders.
- A set of *situational work views*, which contains a model of the work situations.
- A set of *situated capability viewpoints*, which frames situational capability concerns and specific situational concern(s).

The four steps in the method, are described using a template that contains the goal, activities, results and guidelines. To demonstrate the method, it is applied to the Kaplan-Norton framework for strategic analysis.

Demonstration example: Strategy Map framework. In their work on strategies, Kaplan and Norton [18] have developed a well-researched and commonly practiced method for understanding, analysis, planning and execution of strategies, called the Strategy Map framework. Essentially, the framework provides four perspectives that aid the analysis and improvement of an organization:

- *Financial*: This perspective concerns long term shareholder value created by addressing productivity (i.e., improve cost structures and asset utilisation), and growth (i.e., new revenue source and increase customer value) strategies, as directed by vision, mission, purpose, and core values.
- *Customer*: This perspective concerns value propositions that describes how the organization will create differentiated, sustainable value to targeted segments in

which the organisation competes, together with measures of performance, such as, customer satisfaction, retention, acquisition, profitability, and market share.

- *Internal processes*: This perspective concerns value that is created through processes that produce and deliver products and services, enhance customer value, created new products and service, and improve communities and the environment.
- *Learning and Growth*: This perspective concerns the organization's assets and their role in strategy: (1) Human capital, i.e., the availability of skills, talent, and know-how, (2) Information capital, i.e., the availability of information systems, networks, and infrastructure, and (3) Organization capital, i.e., the ability of the organization to mobilise and sustain the process of change.

5 The Stakeholder, Capability and Situation Viewpoints

The method makes use of three ISO 42010 compliant viewpoints: stakeholder, situation and base capability. The base capability viewpoint is novel and part of the contribution of this paper, we thus describe it in more detail compared to the stakeholder and situation viewpoints.

An ISO 42010 **Viewpoint** is a "work product establishing the conventions for the construction, interpretation and use of architecture views to frame specific system concerns" [7]. A Viewpoint is documented with references to typical stakeholders and related concerns, one or more model kinds, and its sources such as author, history, and bibliography.

A **Concern** is a "'system' interest in a system relevant to one or more of its stakeholders" [7], including developmental, technological, business, operational, organizational, political, economic, legal, regulatory, ecological and social influences.

A **Model Kind** provides "conventions for a type of modelling" [7] and is documented with the languages, notations, conventions, modelling techniques, analytical methods and/or other operations to be used on models of this kind.

Examples of model kinds include: capability maps, data flow diagrams, class diagrams, Petri nets, balance sheets, organization charts and value streams.

The **stakeholder viewpoint**, is a viewpoint that frames stakeholder concerns, provides model kinds for documenting characteristics of individuals, groups of individual, and stakeholders. Individuals, and groups of individuals may be related to one or more stakeholders, and may be categorized as a stakeholder based on characteristics such as: practice, discipline, profession, organisational job, or position.

The **situation viewpoint**, is a viewpoint that frames situational interests and concerns, provides model kinds for documenting situations, including work situations, and *use-requirements* that is used to *tailor, frame, constrain, contextualise, configure, or regulate the construction and use of other viewpoints, views and model kinds*. In a situation stakeholders may participate in different roles, and a stakeholder may participate in multiple situations. A situation can be characterised in many ways; situational aspects includes:

- *General aspects:* facts, conditions, and events that affect someone or something at a particular time and in a particular place [20, 21].

- *Work oriented aspects:* actual work being conducted, ways of working, tasks, questions asked, goals, objectives, results, outcomes, techniques, tools used, deliverables, work products, professions, organisational jobs or positions [22, 23].

The **base capability viewpoint**, is a viewpoint that frames capability concerns, and that can be tailored into specific situated capability viewpoints. The viewpoint provides view conventions and a *capability model kind* for documenting capabilities. The capability concerns are represented by a general capability definition based on our previous work [24]. A particularity of this capability construct is that it is designed to be general and extendable into specific variants, thus making it suitable for development of situated capability viewpoints through a tailoring process.

In a general sense, a capability can be viewed as a pattern consisting of six (6) essential elements as illustrated in Fig. 2.

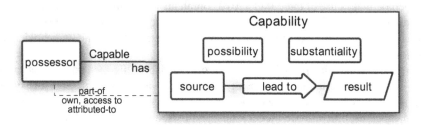

Fig. 2. Illustration of the capability patterns six essential elements.

The essential elements are:

- *Possessor*, is the portion of reality to which the capability is attributed to, owned by, accessed by, or part of.
  Examples: organisational unit, people, machine, enterprise, system.
- *Possibility*, is a possibility for something to come into existence by some source, through a lead-to mechanism.
  Examples: probability, disposition.
- *Source,* is the input factors of a capability.
  Examples: things, assets, facilities, resources, people, knowledge, skills, processes, machines, culture, learning processes, material, information, feedback loops.
- *Result,* is the to-part; the accomplishment, the achievement, effect, consequence, etc. Example: delivered goods, performed service, fulfilment of intended objectives.
- *Lead-to*, is the way source(s) can lead-to the result.
  Examples: natural process, prescribed or described work process, causality.
- *Substantiality*, is the strength of the lead-to mechanism and source factors.
  Examples: capacity of sources, available knowledge of workers, demonstrated achievement of results.

Being *capable* means having access to, owning, or be attributed to capability. If an entity is capable then the source elements must be related the possessor.

A **specific capability viewpoint** can be created by formulating coherent and specific definitions for each of the essential elements of the base capability viewpoint. In the method presented in this paper, we are using the capability pattern to *weave* capability concerns with situational, and work related concerns. The result of the method depends on situational, work related concerns, and the content of the tailored framework, or method. Therefore, we cannot in the method provide a detailed account of the content of produced viewpoints and model kinds in advance.

6 Situation Capability Viewpoint Method Chunk

6.1 Situate and Focus Step

This step provides an essential tool for framing and understanding the general situation-of-interest that surround work situations identified at a later stage, and to allocate attention and effort to the method execution. The step provides an opportunity to identify factors that may influence subsequent steps, such as problems, objectives, challenges, opportunities, motivators, goals, experience, risks, general questions and issues to address, relevant assumptions, constraints, and beliefs system.

Goal
The step aims at situating and anchoring into a situation-of-interest by describing the situation, influencing factors, and what to focus on.

Activities

- Identify, describe, and frame situation-of-interest, and focus of interest.
- Identify, and describe influencing factors.

Result

- A description of the situation-of-interest, and influencing factors.

Guidelines

- Checklands Rich Picture technique may be used to obtain a broader overview [25].

Example
In this example we adopt a standard situation-of-interest for Strategy Map framework, which is a *strategy planning & execution situation* where different organisational units are to be directed, guided, and aligned through the use of Strategy Map framework.

6.2 Characterize Step

The characterize step aims at narrowing down a potentially large set of work situations, originating from each participant own world-view of the situation-of-interest, into a reasonable and practicable set of work situations that can be used as requirements for the tailoring step. One of the most important work situations is framed by the organized work individuals do, such as a job performed in a position or role.

A stakeholder's work situation provides a point-of-reference, value and belief base for analysing and designing the use of a situated capability viewpoint within the frame of the situation-of-interest. The clustering of individuals into stakeholders, based on common characteristics, provides a practical unit of knowledge for subsequent steps.

Goal

The step aims at identifying affected individuals, categorize individuals into stakeholders, and identifying work-situations related to stakeholders, in order to provide use-requirements for the creation of situated capability viewpoints.

Activities

- Identify and describe affected individuals that participate in, are affected by, or perceive themselves as affected by the situation-of-interest.
- Analyse and categorize individuals into stakeholders.
- Identify and describe work-situations and use-requirements.

Result

- Stakeholder view with corresponding model.
- Situational work views including use-requirements, with corresponding model.

General guidelines

- This step can be performed using stakeholder analysis [26].
- Real-world examples should be gathered to provide a pragmatic grounding for discussions, debate, analysis, and evaluations in this and subsequent steps.

Use-requirements guidelines

When identifying a work situation, it is valuable to describe the needs and expectations of stakeholders on what a capability viewpoint should contain. Factors, which has an effect on intention-to-use and actual-use, can be found in the Unified Theory of Acceptance and Use of Technology [23]. The following list summarise their grouping of factors, and provides a single example of a factor; Job-Fit.

- **Performance expectancy:** Individual's beliefs relating to, if the use of a capability viewpoint will help him or her to attain gains in job performance.
    - **Job-fit:** How a capability viewpoint enhances an individual's job performance.
- **Effort expectancy:** Expected ease of use of the capability viewpoint.
- **Social Influence:** Perception of the importance of other people's beliefs that a capability viewpoint should be used.
- **Facilitating conditions:** Perception if a value base, organizational and technical infrastructure exists to support use of the capability viewpoint.

Other factors to consider includes: questions that can be answered through the situated model kinds [7], and factors that affect decision making.

Example

Based on the perspectives of the Strategy Map framework, we have derived the following examples of stakeholders, work situations, and use-requirements (Table 1).

Table 1. Strategy map perspectives, stakeholders, work situations, and use-requirements.

Perspective	Stakeholders	Work situations	Use-requirements
Learning and Growth	Human Resource Management	Competence management	Provide foundation for developing competencies
Internal Process	Operations Managers, Customer Manager, Researcher, Compliance Manager	Operations Management Customer Management Innovation Processes Regulatory & Social Processes	Address understanding of actual performance of processes and contribution to goals.
Customer	Marketing, Service developer	New Product Development	Enable analysis of competiveness
Financial	Top Management, Owners, Business Analyst	Strategy Planning & Execution, Business Analysis	Enable analysis of capabilities contribution to organisational purpose

6.3   Tailoring Step

The tailoring step creates situated capability viewpoints that weave general capability concerns with situational concerns in order to improve qualities such as intention-to-use, actual-use, and to satisfy use-requirements as defined in the characterize step.

Goal

The step aims at developing situated capability viewpoints by tailoring the base capability viewpoint to address situational work concerns and use-requirements.

Activities

For each identified work situation:

- Analyse work situations, use-requirements and their relationships to other situations in order to determine relevant situated viewpoint concerns.
- Develop a situated capability viewpoint by specialising each of the six essential elements of the base capability definition presented in Sect. 5.
- Refine situated capability viewpoint by weaving the capability model kinds and its model elements, with related model kinds in encompassing framework or method.
- Develop view and model examples of each situated capability viewpoints in order to increase understandability as well as comparability in the validation step.

Result

- A set of *situated capability viewpoints* descriptions, with corresponding *situated capability model kinds*, which are ISO 42010 compliant.

Capability element guidelines

- A *possessor* may be determined by identifying units of: inquiry, analysis, design, planning, performance monitoring, organisation, responsibility, and/or production.
- *Possibility* is often not extended since it is well defined. Although modifiers may be included to indicate aspects of enabling, choice, freedom, or potentiality.
- *Substantiality* may be defined based on qualities that determine if a factor has more or less capacity or quantity, level of availability, or repeatability of lead-to process.
- *Source* elements may be identified and selected amongst factors that contribute to the achievement of the result. The choice of inclusion or omission of a particular source element in a capability may have a significant effect on the descriptive, explanatory, or predictive powers of the particular capability.
- *Result* elements can be found amongst phenomenons, in the work situation, which are desired, intended, possible, or must to be accomplished. Examples include work product, outcome, impact, delivered service, realised benefit, and customer value. Note that not all results are desirable, nor intended, such as pollution, and that an actual capability with an desired result may yet lead-to undesirable *side-effects*.
- The *lead-to* element can be found by identification of how the source elements in practice are, or is expected to lead-to the result(s). In an idealistic future situation, the lead-to can be defined as a prescribed business process, or in an analysis of the past situation, the lead-to may be explained by causality, inference, statistical, or mathematical formula argumentation. The lead-to can be instrumental, in the sense that a direct result lead-to or enable a secondary key result.
- In some cases, when substantiality is low, a source factor is missing, and/or the lead-to is weak, a capability may be considered as a *Disability*.

Example

In the previous step, we identified 4 groups of stakeholders and related work situations, and use-requirement. Based on this we can construct four situated capability viewpoints by tailoring the base capability viewpoint, or specializing the underlying capability definition. To illustrate how to do this we make use of existing capability definitions as found in research, books, and industry organisations material. Through this we demonstrate how existing capability definitions may be partitioned into the six essential elements of the base capability viewpoint, and how reasonable situated capability definitions may be defined based on work situation and use-requirements. Note that all capability definitions fit into a language template based on the 6 essential elements:

```
"<substantiality> <possibility> of <possessor> to <result> by
<source> through <lead-to>"
```

The following table provides a summary of the four constructed situated viewpoints for Strategy Map framework:

- *Financial perspective*: To exemplify this perspective we use capability definition by Stephan Haeckel [27] that relates to an organisations purpose: "Capabilities are organizational subsystems with a potential for producing outcomes that contribute to the organization's purpose".

- *Customer value perspective*: The Leinwand/Mainardi capability definition [28] relates to customer values: "Something you do well that customers value and competitors can't beat".
- *Internal Process perspective:* The BABOK capability definition [29] relates to an organisations functions: "A function of an organization that enables it to achieve a business goal or objective".
- *Learning and* Growth *perspective:* The Amartya Sen capability approach [30] relate to a person's real freedoms or opportunities to achieve functioning, and wellbeing

Table 2. Illustration of breakdown of capability definitions into the 6 essential elements.

	Learning and growth perspective: HR	Internal process perspective	Customer value perspective	Financial perspective
Author	Amartya Sen	BABOK	Leinwand/Mainardi	Stephan Haeckel
Authors capability definition	a person's real freedoms or opportunities to achieve functioning, (beings and doings), and well beings	A function of an organization that enables it to achieve a business goal or objective.	Something you do well that customers value and competitors can't beat	organizational subsystems with a potential for producing outcomes that contribute to the organization's purpose
Possessor	person	organisation	you	organisation
Substantiality	real	-	well	potential
Possibility	freedom or opportunity	enable	done it before	potential
Result	functioning or wellbeing	achieve business goal or objective	customer value that competitors can't beat	outcomes that contribute to the organization's purpose
Source	person, knowledge, conversion factors	function	you	organisational sub-system
Lead-to	doing, achieving	achieving, instrumental	doing	producing, instrumental
Related concepts	resource, feasibility, choice, freedom, opportunity, competence	organisation, functional breakdown, goal model	customer value proposition, competitors, market, customer, channel	vision, mission, purpose, values, strategy

where functioning are 'beings and doings', that is, various states of human beings and activities that a person can undertake (Table 2).

Note that all of the above four viewpoints can be combined in a single and integrated enterprise wide capability analysis of an organisation.

6.4   Validate Step

This step provides a real world check of the situated capability viewpoints descriptions, and aims partly at developing insights and possible ideas for improvements, and partly at providing a structured validation. This step offers a space where participation can discuss, deliberate, form intentions and commitment to-use.

Goal
The step aims at comparing situated capability viewpoints with the perceived real world, by evaluating fulfilment of situational concerns and use-requirements.

Activities
- Evaluate fulfilment of situational and capability concerns and use-requirements.
- Record feedback from participants, findings, and ideas for improvement.
- If a situated capability viewpoint is determined to be acceptable by stakeholders then continue, otherwise decide if it is feasible and relevant to reiterate to a previous step, if not then terminate the process.

Result
- Descriptions of evaluation results, findings, conclusions, ideas for improvements.

Guidelines
- Formal validation methods, evidence and data based methods, and assurance case techniques can be used to increase confidence in the results and acceptability.

Example
The descriptions of the developed situated capability viewpoint are presented to the participants, together with situational examples. The participants are presented with a survey aimed at evaluating situational and capability concerns, use-requirement and quality factors such as intention-to-use and actual-use.

7   Discussion and Evaluation

This work has been built upon the authors experience with capability analysis and standardisation work. The method has been partially put to test, but a more thorough evaluation is planned. In this section, we will present so called informed argument for the method. Informed argument, introduced in Hevner et al. [19] is a type of light weight evaluation where the researcher argue for their developed solutions. We will argue for the benefits of the method by revisiting the three requirements as put forward in Sect. 3:

The requirement *general applicability* of the method, states that the method should not be bound to a specific domain or overall capability analysis method. We have ensured this by defining six capability elements that allow us to build capability definitions that fits a domain, and by the explicit construction of a method chunk supporting integration with existing frameworks or methods. Moreover, we have not tied the method to a certain approach to identifying capabilities, such as service, process or goal-based approaches. In the future, the general applicability can be demonstrated and evaluated by weaving the method into existing capability analysis approaches.

The requirement *compliance with standard* is achieved by using the terminology of ISO 42010 standard ontology as a base for defining the base capability viewpoint and as a requirement for situated capability viewpoints.

Finally, we also argue that the method produces situated capability viewpoints in an *efficient* way, due to its considering of situational work aspects and factors such as job-fit, performance and output expectancy, intentions-to-use, and actual-use of capability analysis. These are all concepts within the well-applied theory of technology acceptance model [23]. Furthermore, the requirement is addressed by the inclusion of a separate step for stakeholder and work situation identification, and a validate step that ensures the results are acceptable and applicable for the stakeholders. Finally, the presented guidelines and well-structured descriptions will support the efficiency.

A future evaluation is planned to focus on the last requirement, that is, to ensure that the method produce effective results. This evaluation is intended to be performed in an existing project where capability analysis is performed. After applying the method, the strength of the resulting capability viewpoints to represent stakeholders concerns will be evaluated using semi-structured interviews with the stakeholders.

8   Summary

In this paper we have presented a method for creating situated capability viewpoints. The viewpoints are useful for describing capabilities from different work perspectives and provides a useful complement to existing capability analysis methods. As a starting point for the method a stakeholder analysis should be performed, followed by a description of the work situation that each stakeholder is situated in. The creation of situated capability viewpoints for stakeholder's work perspectives is then done by tailoring a base capability viewpoint. In particular, this entails the specialisation of a six-element capability definition.

The use of the method has been demonstrated by applying it to the Strategy Map framework by Kaplan and Norton. The demonstration shows that four viewpoints can be created based on the Strategy Map framework, each viewpoint addressing a certain stakeholder. The paper applies informed argument as an evaluation, and point towards a future way to perform a formal evaluation.

References

1. Kusunoki, K., Nonaka, I., Nagata, A.: Organizational capabilities in product development of Japanese firms: a conceptual framework and empirical findings. Organ. Sci. **9**, 699–718 (1998)
2. Bērziša, S., Bravos, G., Gonzalez, T.C., Czubayko, U., España, S., Grabis, J., Henkel, M., Jokste, L., Kampars, J., Koç, H., Kuhr, J.-C., Llorca, C., Loucopoulos, P., Pascual, R.J., Pastor, O., Sandkuhl, K., Simic, H., Stirna, J., Valverde, F.G., Zdravkovic, J.: Capability driven development: an approach to designing digital enterprises. Bus. Inf. Syst. Eng. **57**, 15–25 (2015)
3. Ulrich, W., Rosen, M.: The Business Capability Map: The "Rosetta Stone" of Business/IT Alignment. https://www.cutter.com
4. Harmon, P.: Capabilities and Processes. http://www.bptrends.com/publicationfiles/advisor20110712.pdf
5. The Open Group: TOGAF Version 9.1 - The Open Group Architecture Framework (TOGAF) (2011)
6. Malavolta, I., Lago, P., Muccini, H., Pelliccione, P., Tang, A.: What industry needs from architectural languages: a survey. IEEE Trans. Softw. Eng. **39**, 869–891 (2012)
7. ISO/IEC, IEEE: ISO/IEC 42010:2011 Systems and software engineering — Architecture description (2011)
8. Teece, D.J.: Explicating dynamic capabilities: the nature and microfoundations of (sustainable) enterprise performance. Strateg. Manag. J. **28**, 1319–1350 (2007)
9. Dosi, G., Nelson, R., Winter, S.: The Nature and Dynamics of Organizational Capabilities. OUP, Oxford (2001)
10. Schreyögg, G., Kliesch-Eberl, M.: How dynamic can organizational capabilities be? Towards a dual-process model of capability dynamization. Strateg. Manag. J. **28**, 913–933 (2007)
11. McKeen, J.D., Smith, H.: IT Strategy, 2nd edn. Prentice Hall, Upper Saddle River (2011)
12. Henkel, M., Bider, I., Perjons, E.: Capability-based business model transformation. In: Iliadis, L., Papazoglou, M., Pohl, K. (eds.) CAiSE Workshops 2014. LNBIP, vol. 178, pp. 88–99. Springer, Heidelberg (2014)
13. Stirna, J., Grabis, J., Henkel, M., Zdravkovic, J.: Capability driven development – an approach to support evolving organizations. In: Sandkuhl, K., Seigerroth, U., Stirna, J. (eds.) PoEM 2012. LNBIP, vol. 134, pp. 117–131. Springer, Heidelberg (2012)
14. Beimborn, D., Martin, S.F., Homann, U.: Capability-oriented modeling of the firm. Presented at the IPSI-2005, Amalfi (2005)
15. Henderson-Sellers, B., Ralyte, J.: Situational method engineering: state-of-the-art review. J. Comput. Sci. **16**, 424–478 (2010)
16. Ralyte, J., Deneckere, R., Rolland, C.: Towards a generic model for situational method engineering. In: Eder, J., Missikoff, M. (eds.) CAiSE 2003. LNCS, vol. 2681, pp. 95–110. Springer, Heidelberg (2003)
17. Peffers, K., Tuunanen, T., Rothenberger, M., Chatterjee, S.: A design science research methodology for information systems research. J. Manag. Inf. Syst. **24**, 45–77 (2007)
18. Kaplan, R.S., Norton, D.P.: The Execution Premium: Linking Strategy to Operations for Competitive Advantage. Harvard Business School Press, Brighton (2008)
19. Hevner, A.R., March, S.T., Park, J., Ram, S.: Design science in information systems research. Mis Q. **28**, 75–105 (2004)
20. Sowa, J.F., Zachman, J.A.: Extending and formalizing the framework for information systems architecture. IBM Syst. J. **31**, 1–27 (1992)

21. Object Management Group: Semantics of Business Vocabulary and Business Rules (SBVR), v1.0 (2008)
22. ISO/IEC: ISO 24744:2007 Software Engineering - Metamodel for Development Methodologies (2007)
23. Venkatesh, V., Morris, M.G., Davis, G.B., Davis, F.D.: User acceptance of information technology: toward a unified view. MIS Q. **27**, 425–478 (2003)
24. Tell, A.W.: What capability is not. In: Johansson, B., Andersson, B., Holmberg, N. (eds.) BIR 2014. LNBIP, vol. 194, pp. 128–142. Springer, Heidelberg (2014)
25. Checkland, P.: Soft systems methodology: a thirty year retrospective. Syst. Res. Behav. Sci. **17**, S11–S58 (2000)
26. Tools for Institutional, Political, and Social Analysis of Policy Reform. World Bank Publications (2007)
27. Haeckel, S.: Adaptive Enterprise: Creating and Leading Sense-and-Respond Organizations. Harvard Business School Press, Brighton (1999)
28. Leinwand, P., Mainardi, C.: The Essential Advantage: How to Win with a Capabilities-Driven Strategy. Harvard Business Press, Brighton (2013)
29. International Institute of Business Analysis: A Guide to the Business Analysis Body of Knowledge® (BABOK Guide) Version 2.0 (2009)
30. Robeyns, I.: The capability approach: a theoretical survey. J. Hum. Dev. **6**, 93–117 (2005)

Data Analysis

What Role Do Emotions Play for Brands in Online Customer Reviews?

Armin Felbermayr[(✉)] and Alexandros Nanopoulos

Katholische Universität Eichstätt-Ingolstadt, Auf der Schanz 49,
85049 Ingolstadt, Germany
{armin.felbermayr,alexandros.nanopoulos}@ku.de

Abstract. The field of mining unstructured data has been growing
rapidly in business intelligence. An area of application represent online
reviews where customers interact socially to share opinions towards
brands. Thereby, exchanged emotions play a dominant role, which poses
a challenge for brand managers to understand the emotional attitude
in customer's reviews. We develop a text-mining method that extracts
information about emotions from customers' product reviews. We cast
the underlying analysis of emotions as a binary classification problem, by
using features extracted with the help of a psychologically well-grounded
emotion lexicon. Based on this, we identify for various brands, which
emotion features are important in reviews that are perceived as helpful
(and thus more influential) by customers. We have conducted an empirical investigation with a large, publicly available data set from Amazon.
Among other insights, our findings can determine the importance of various emotions for different brands throughout several product categories.

Keywords: Brands · Emotions · Online customer reviews ·
Helpfulness · Text mining · Business intelligence

1 Introduction

Extracting valuable knowledge about customers, which is hidden in large
amounts of unstructured data, such as review texts, has become a major task in
business intelligence. Knowing opinions of customers towards brands is of crucial importance, because customers trust in brands. Research has shown that
brands make consumers willing to pay more for the product, to rely more on the
product's functionalities and to relate more positive emotions to the product.
An established brand loyalty may lead to repurchases and finally to a greater
market share with lower expenses on marketing and more new customers [6].

Emotions that customers feel concerning a brand, have a direct effect on
their perception of a brand's image [21]. Marketers can use that emotional
bond between a customer and a brand for a superior brand performance. Many
social web sites, such as social networks (e.g., Facebook) and e-commerce platforms (e.g., Amazon) enable customers to express their opinions about brands.

© Springer International Publishing Switzerland 2016
V. Řepa and T. Bruckner (Eds.): BIR 2016, LNBIP 261, pp. 297–311, 2016.
DOI: 10.1007/978-3-319-45321-7_21

This way, also much emotional content is created. However, the triangle among emotions, brands and online reviews, as far as we know, has not been studied at all. Therefore, we want to shed more light onto the connection between emotions and their role for brands as expressed through customers in online reviews.

In our study we ask and answer the following research questions:

- What methodology can be used to measure the role of various emotions for different brands within reviews across several product categories?
- In what way can obtained results be analyzed by marketers to gain more insight into their or competitors' brands?

Our approach is valuable to both, practice and theory, because on the one hand it equips practitioners with a methodology to determine the emotional appeal of customers towards brands throughout and within product categories, and on the other hand it provides academia with new insight on the interplay between emotions, brands and reviews.

The remainder of this article is structured as follows: In Sect. 2 we will introduce readers into most related research results about emotions in reviews and brands. A method to extract and measure customers emotions towards brands from reviews is explained in Sect. 3. In Sect. 4 we discuss attained results of our model based on brand management literature, before we conclude our study in Sect. 5 by pointing out further related research questions in the business intelligence domain.

2   Related Work

We split this section into two main literature reviews. The first part introduces into the reasons and the method for extracting emotions from reviews. Additionally, we show in what way our method differs from related work, although, our approach is commonly agreed upon. The second part shows the connection between emotions and brands, and, also pinpoints to the open research question 'what different emotions play a role for different brands in reviews within and across several product categories?' Since, as far as we know, no prior related research has investigated this question, our study closes this existing research gap.

Emotions in Reviews. Research has clarified the need for marketers to participate in the communication of customers through social media. However, managers see themselves confronted with the vastly growing amount of written content in the web. Therefore, text-mining methods from the business intelligence domain can be used to efficiently extract and analyze consumers' sentiment to attain an overall understanding of their opinion.

Several studies have been conducted to extract positive and negative sentiment from online customer reviews, e.g. [15]. With our study, however, we leave this bipolar perspective and follow the suggestion of psychology research, which captures emotions in a multidimensional way. Only very recently scholars from academia and marketing strategists from practice have realized the necessity for more investigation into the multidimensionalities of customers' emotions.

To our knowledge, the study of [10], was the first to prove that emotion dimensions really represent a valuable feature set for online customer reviews. For this reason they created a model to successfully classify reviews as "helpful" or "not helpful" by the help of term extraction, based on an emotion dictionary. Our approach varies from their study in the following main aspects: First, their study was very broad, in the sense that they aimed at enriching the list of functional feature sets with emotion dimensions. On the contrary, we close a more specific research gap by applying a classification model based on emotion vocabulary with a focus towards brands. Second, their study relies on the emotion paradigm of Scherer [19], while we rely on Plutchik's theory of emotion dimensionalities [16]. Their lexicon comprises of 267 stem words distributed across Scherer's 36 emotion dimensions, while we make use of the NRC dictionary [13], which consists of 8,202 terms distributed across Plutchik's eight emotion dimensions.

The well-known and established theory on emotion dimensionalities of Plutchik argues that joy, trust, fear and surprise are the most basic emotions with sadness, disgust, anger and anticipation as their neutralizing counterparts [16]. Also refer to Fig. 1, where all possible emotion combinations of Plutchik are depicted.

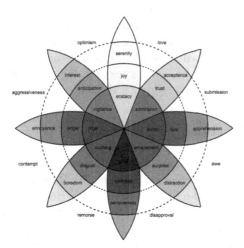

Fig. 1. Plutchik's swung out "Wheel of Emotions" [16], where the inner circle represents strong invisible inherent feelings (e.g., ecstasy, admiration etc.), which lose their intensity vertically to the outer layers (e.g., serenity, acceptance etc.). Combinations are also possible: when someone feels joy and trust this results in love.

Emotions for Brands. The link between emotions and brands is strong. Marketers have developed their own technical terms "Passion Branding" [7] and "Lovemarks" [17] and studies have proven that "emotionally attached consumers are [...] the brand's most profitable customers" [18].

The most related work in the literature, which also aims at having a consumer psychological perspective about the relation between customers and brands is the study of [21], where a so called "emotional attachment scale" was introduced. The researchers had two different groups of students to determine 45 emotion adjectives and to link these words to their favorite brands. The third group, which consisted of non-students validated the test to approve their results and to acknowledge the validity of their findings. According to their analysis "brands in the strong emotional attachment condition tended to be more high involvement and symbolically or hedonically related (e.g., the Body Shop, Hermet Lang, BMW, BeBe, Prada, and Oakley) than low involvement or functionally related (e.g., AT&T, All, Ziploc)".

In demarcation to this research [21], our proposed approach is different in the following main aspects: Firstly, we use an out-of-lab environment, where reviewers do not write texts with the purpose to be scientifically monitored. Secondly, we extract emotional terms from brand related reviews, while they do the opposite by assigning emotion adjectives to brands. Thirdly, with our approach the emotional perception of individual products of a brand can be differentiated from the emotional perception of the whole brand, while their approach only enables conclusions on an aggregated brand level.

In summary, the two perspectives 'emotions in reviews' and 'emotions for brands' have been well-examined in the literature separately. However, we aim at joining these two dimensions to the more specific view of 'emotions for brands in reviews'. So far, according to our knowledge, there is no study that has considered brands' emotions in reviews by using a text-mining tool. Therefore, we propose a method to close this research gap with the following study.

3   Proposed Method

The procedural order of our method is as follows: (a) Emotions are extracted from reviews, based on an emotion lexicon. (b) Reviews are categorized into helpful or not helpful, based on their helpfulness ratings. Finally, (a) and (b) are combined to learn which emotion dimensions influence the helpfulness of reviews for a certain product brand.

This section explains the technicalities of our classification model, which learns to categorize by the help of a feature vector and a target function. To ensure reproducibility of our approach, we introduce into the creation of the feature vector based on an example and explain the target function accordingly. Finally, the underlying classifier will be briefly described.

3.1   Problem Formulation

We aim at identifying the impact of emotion dimensions when used as features that predict the helpfulness-rating of online customer reviews. Therefore we formally define the studied problem as a classification problem, which involves the learning of a classifier γ as follows:

$$\gamma : R \longrightarrow C, \tag{1}$$

where $R = \{r_1, ..., r_n\}$ is the set of reviews and $C = \{c_1, ..., c_J\}$ is an ordered set representing discrete levels (expressed as ranges) of helpfulness-ratings. In our study we focus on two levels, namely of helpful and not helpful reviews. Each review $r_i \in R$ is assigned a helpfulness level $c_j \in C$ and a classifier learns from emotion features, represented by the classification feature vector, to determine the level of helpfulness, represented by the classification target function.

Classification Feature Vector. *The classification feature vector represents the proportional distribution of Plutchik's eight emotion dimensions* (see Fig. 1), *i.e., the classification feature vector is a 8×1 vector, each row representing an emotion dimension.*

In particular we define the feature vector as follows:

$$v_r = \sum_{t \in T_r} \left(\sqrt{f_t^r} \times e_t \right), \tag{2}$$

where T_r is the set of distinct terms in review r and f_t^r is the frequency of term $t \in T_r$ in review r, and the eight-dimensional vector e_t represents Plutchik's eight emotion dimensions "anger", "anticipation", "disgust", "fear", "joy", "sadness", "surprise" and "trust" for each term t. After all, v_r is the sum over the square root of the frequency of emotion terms in a review multiplied by all emotion dimensions for each word, and repeats until all terms of a review are checked.

By taking the square root of the frequency of detected review emotion terms f_t^r the impact of single overused emotion words is regularized. Please note that we choose the square root for simplicity reasons, but any other relativation means may be used. For example, if a review contains the dictionary word "perfect" twice and "love" once, the frequencies of the two terms for the example review would be $\sqrt{2} = 1.41$ and $\sqrt{1} = 1$.

The feature vector v_r incorporates the frequencies and the emotion weights according to Plutchik's eight dimensions as already mentioned above, so that the first item of a vector represents the first dimension ("anger"), the second item the second dimension ("anticipation"), etc. For the given example this yet unnormalized feature vector would look like in Fig. 2, where the first word "perfect" ($t = 1$) contributes to even three emotion dimensions ("anticipation", "joy" and "trust").

$$v_r = 1.41 \times \begin{pmatrix} 0 \\ 1 \\ 0 \\ 0 \\ 1 \\ 0 \\ 0 \\ 1 \end{pmatrix} + 1 \times \begin{pmatrix} 0 \\ 0 \\ 0 \\ 0 \\ 1 \\ 0 \\ 0 \\ 0 \end{pmatrix} = \begin{pmatrix} 0 \\ 1.41 \\ 0 \\ 0 \\ 2.41 \\ 0 \\ 0 \\ 1.41 \end{pmatrix} \qquad (3)$$

Fig. 2. Example for the creation of the unnormalized feature vector v_r

Finally, the normalized feature vector $v'_r = (0, 0.27, 0, 0, 0.46, 0, 0, 0.27)$ is calculated, which cancels the length as a feature, by dividing v_r by its column sum. In other words the underlying review text is represented with 0.27 for anticipation, 0.46 for joy and 0.27 for trust, while anger, disgust, fear, sadness and surprise remain unused in the review example.

These normalized feature vectors are calculated for all reviews and follow the intuition "the higher a feature dimension is valued, the more present is its corresponding proportional emotion intensity in the review".

Helpfulness Score. *The helpfulness score h_r of each review is defined as the logarithm of the ratio between the number of times that the review has been voted as positive (x_r) and negative $(y_r - x_r)$ by other customers.*[1]

$$h_r = log_{10} \frac{x_r + 1}{y_r - x_r + 1} \, for \, x_r \leqq y_r \qquad (4)$$

Note that the higher the h_r score is, the more helpful the review is. The denominator has been extended by $+1$ to avoid division by 0. The same extension has been applied to the numerator as well. As such, reviews that have received no vote regarding their helpfulness (that is, $x_r = y_r = 0$) will be assigned a score $h_r = 0$, which is intuitive.

Based on the h_r scores, that we compute on Amazon's "x of y people found this helpful"-representation, we want to identify two target classes, namely the helpful and not helpful reviews. These two classes comprise the typical 'positive' and 'negative' classes in a binary classification problem. Using the real data from our empirical evaluation (see Sect. 4), all reviews can be ordered increasingly according to their h_r score. Figure 3 illustrates such a case in the left figure (a) for a product category over all brands and in the right figure (b) for only one brand within the same product category. Please note, that all other product categories and brands, that we examined in our discussion, have a similar distribution of h_r.

We distinguish two classes by a threshold at $h_r = 0$ for all product categories and brands based on the logic that for all discussed cases, this threshold

---

[1] We follow the assumption that, as is typical in many e-commerce sites, customers can vote a review as helpful or not helpful.

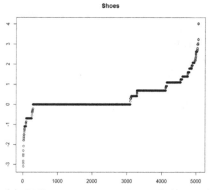
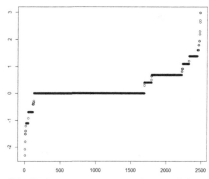

(a) Online customer reviews of the product category "Shoes" are increasingly ordered in terms of their h_r-score.

(b) Online customer reviews of brand "adidas" in product category "Shoes" are increasingly ordered in terms of their h_r-score.

Fig. 3. We use thresholds to differentiate helpful from not helpful reviews according to our helpfulness-rating h_r. The threshold achieves a balanced separation of not helpful reviews ($h_r < 0$) from helpful reviews ($h_r \geq 0$) to improve the classifying power.

effectively balances the amount of helpful ($h_r \geq 0$) and not helpful reviews ($h_r < 0$) in a way which enables the classifier to learn the two classes.

With this possibility to discriminate the positive (helpful reviews) from the negative (not helpful reviews) class, we turn our attention to the classifier, which learns the pictured classes based on the emotion features extracted from the reviews.

3.2 Classifier

We use the popular classification algorithm random forest [3] to classify real-world-reviews as helpful or not helpful according to their emotion content. When comparing this method with other state-of-the-art supervised algorithms, random forest resides among the top approaches in terms of different performance metrics [4]. Thus, we believe that machine learning methods, such as random forests, enable marketers to efficiently analyzing challenging data, such as text of online reviews.

Random forests combine a large collection of decorrelated decision trees in order to reduce the variance of noisy and unbiased models (so called "bagging"). In contrast to standard decision trees, where all variables are taken into account to determine the best split, random forest finds its best split among a subset of randomly chosen predictors. By this inherent randomness of random forests the major problem of overfitting can be addressed.

Moreover, the construction of random forests helps with the differentiation of important from not important variables, by the calculation of errors per permutation. In a sense the error per each step can be probabilistically measured and thus, the variable importance can be determined. This is a great advantage over other popular methods (such as support vector machines), since their decision finding and the interpretation of their variables are not that intuitive and self-explanatory. This is an important characteristic in our study, which focuses on identifying the importance of emotion dimensions. Thus, based on an accurate classification model (measured based on 10-fold cross validation), we can measure the importance of the used features, which reflect the importance of the examined emotion dimensions.

4   Empirical Evaluation

This section shows which data we used to apply our approach. Additionally, in Subsect. 4.1 the F_1-score is introduced as our measure of the classification power of our model. The F_1-score measures precision and recall in a combined and strict manner.

Subsection 4.2 displays results, which we slice into different analytical perspectives in order to get a whole picture of the performance of our approach. For each of these perspectives we discuss the emotion perception by customers according to brand research literature.

4.1   Data and Performance Measure

Our method is used on the Amazon review dataset from [12], where 6.6 Million users wrote 34.6 Million reviews between June 1995 and March 2013. We chose this dataset, because it contains all necessary input (review texts and helpfulness-ratings), it is publicly available, and Amazon is a representative online retailer. Amazon provides the reviewing channel openly to improve customers' decision making. There, reviews present the social interaction from customer to customer (C2C) to help each other to sort out the right reviews. Please look at Table 1 for product examples of our discussed product categories.

Table 1. Product category examples.

Product category	Examples
Shoes	Ballet Shoes, Boots, Sandals, etc.
Sports_Outdoors	Action Cams, Boat Paddles, Pool Sticks, etc.

The validity and quality of review texts of this dataset has been proven by classification experiments, which showed that review texts are in accordance with their product rating (number of "stars"). However, in the process of analyzing emotions expressed for brands, we discovered that reviews in some cases duplicate in the sense that reviews from product category 'Shoes' can be found in 'Sports_Outdoors' and vice versa.

We use the calculation of precision and recall as established measures to evaluate the classification power of our model. In line with this, we use the F_1 score,

$$F_1^{\pm} = 2 \times \frac{Precision \times Recall}{Precision + Recall},\tag{5}$$

which is a strict measure from the information retrieval domain and computes F_1 scores separately for the positive $(+)$ class $(h_r \geq 0)$ and negative $(-)$ class $(h_r < 0)$ per product category and brand. The harmonic mean within the F_1-score in Eq. 5 accounts for the inherent strictness, because both precision and recall need to be high at the same time to yield an overall high F_1-score. Therefore, this score enables to evenly take into account both precision and recall of the positive and negative helpfulness classes in a strict manner.

In order to take into account both values equally and to have a full picture, we calculated a final combined F_1-score, as follows:

$$F_1 = \frac{F_1^+ + F_1^-}{2},\tag{6}$$

which takes into account skewness in the available dataset.

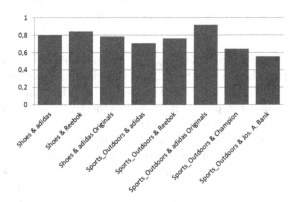

Fig. 4. Measured F_1-scores on average display a good relation between precision and recall.

In Fig. 4, we present all F_1-scores of those product categories and brands, which we discuss in this section. F_1-scores displayed in Fig. 4 indicate that we attained a classification model which adequately discriminates the helpful reviews for the various examined brands.

4.2 Results

Our method enables marketers to analyze emotions expressed towards brands' products through online reviews. In this section we show some results of our approach based on considerable brands to demonstrate several levels of application for brand managers.

Please refer to Fig. 5, where two product categories, i.e., Shoes and Sports-
Outdoors were chosen, to share some insightful observations on emotions towards
the brands of adidas Group: adidas, Reebok (acquired by adidas Group in 2006),
and adidas Originals.

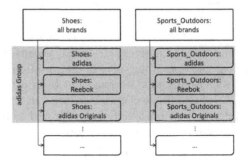

Fig. 5. A multi brand perspective using the example of adidas Group. In the course
of our study emotion expressions of online customer reviews are monitored vertically
(e.g. brand adidas vs. brand Reebok within Shoes) or horizontally (e.g. brand adidas
throughout product categories Shoes and Sports-Outdoors)

Since emotions play a pertinent role in the perception of brands and can
influence customer behavior (see Sect. 2), our method may very well be used to
better understand different emotions expressed towards a whole brand family. In
order to emphasize on a complex multi brand perspective, we demonstrate results
of our model based on the example of the multi brand company adidas Group.
Therefore, we applied our method from Sect. 3 to determine the importance of
each of Plutchik's eight emotion dimensions ("anger", "anticipation", "disgust",
"fear", "joy", "sadness", "surprise" and "trust") for each brand of adidas Group:
adidas, Reebok, and adidas Originals, as indicated by the grey box in Fig. 5.

The results of our model concerning adidas Group are displayed in Fig. 6.
The evaluation of Plutchik's emotions per brand of adidas Group is intuitive,
because the higher a value corresponding to its emotion is, the higher is its bar
chart and rank (indicated by numbers below each bar). For instance, words in
reviews for shoes from adidas are mostly related to "joy", therefore, "joy" is
consequently ranked first. Also, each emotion dimension is expressed in relation
to the other emotion dimensions, i.e., the sum over all eight emotion dimensions
and bars per brand and product category equals one.[2]

Derived from the results of our model (Fig. 6), we present the following marketing applications:

(1) *For a certain product category different brands can become comparable:*
This perspective enables marketers for one product category to directly compare

---

[2] Please note that for a better overview, we have arranged the brands from adidas
Group of Fig. 6 in the same order as displayed in the gray box in Fig. 5.

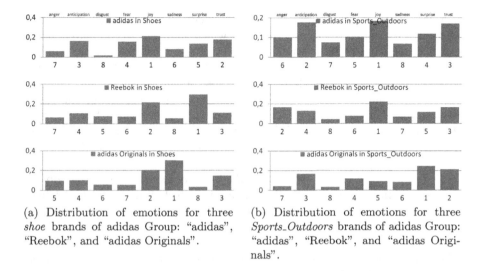

(a) Distribution of emotions for three *shoe* brands of adidas Group: "adidas", "Reebok", and "adidas Originals".

(b) Distribution of emotions for three *Sports_Outdoors* brands of adidas Group: "adidas", "Reebok", and "adidas Originals".

Fig. 6. Emotion distributions can be compared horizontally and vertically, i.e., adidas in Shoes might be compared with adidas in Sports_Outdoors (horizontally) or to Reebok in Shoes (vertically). Numbers below bars indicate the ranking of an emotion dimension within one brand and product category.

a brand from their own brand family against brands from the same or other brand families. Results of this perspective within adidas Group is displayed by Fig. 6a for product category Shoes and by Fig. 6b for product category Sports_Outdoors.

For adidas shoes, the joy dimension wins over all other emotions, directly followed by 'trust' and 'anticipation'. Reebok shoes, however, display an unusual outlier for the surprise emotion dimension (rank one), which in the case of other brands of shoes is usually residing among the least important emotion dimensions. Further investigation into reasons for this characteristic could be developed by looking closer at the actually used 'surprise'-related emotion words of Reebok's reviews: "birthday", "expect", "gift", "hope", "luck", etc. These example terms indicate, that Reebok's shoes are commonly received or made as gifts.

Although joy seems to play a decisive role in reviews for shoes of adidas Originals (rank two), still customers express even more sadness (rank one). Brand managers should early detect, if their customers are unhappy, because the satisfaction level plays a role in the willingness to buy products [8] and higher customer satisfaction results in more profit [1]. A straight way to encounter reviews with much sadness content, would be to contact such reviewers directly and to provide explanations or further offerings. According to [5] such reactions should be triggered very soon and product category related.

Figure 6b subsequently proceeds with the same brands of adidas Group, however, within the Sports_Outdoors domain. The brand adidas unites joy, anticipation and trust among the first three most frequently used emotions in online customer reviews for Sports_Outdoors. Reebok, although in most emotion dimensions comparable to adidas, trades anticipation with anger as its second mostly expressed customer emotion, which indicates accumulated needs to reduce anger and at the same time to increase trust for products of the Sports_Outdoors segment of this brand. Brand managers must take such results very seriously, because research has proven that "anger is a significant predictor of switching, complaint behavior, negative WOM [Word of Mouth], and third-party complaining" [2]. From a service perspective, direct contact to the respective customers is advised, but if the service staff is not well-trained enough to satisfy these customers, then customers will most certainly switch and will never recover [20].

(2) *For a certain brand, different product categories can become comparable:* For this reason, we compare the brands adidas, Reebok and adidas Originals of adidas Group *across* their product categories 'Shoes' and 'Sports_Outdoors'. Please note that this perspective is also visibly accessible through a horizontal comparison between Fig. 6a and b.

For the brand adidas the distribution of emotion expressions of customers seems to be almost identical, which indicates the power of this brand in the sense that joy, trust and anticipation dominate, although different product categories are scrutinized. This picture impressively reflects a strong corporate strategy for multiple brands, because different products show the same customer perception of brands in terms of emotion content.

The most deviating brand of adidas Group in terms of emotion expressions in online customer reviews across product categories 'Shoes' and 'Sports_Outdoors' is adidas Originals. Only trust is almost equally ranked (rank three for shoes and rank two for Sports_Outdoors). Thus, in contrast to the brand adidas, brand management has not yet succeeded in establishing an identical emotional appeal of adidas Originals to customers throughout various product categories. However, an authentic perception of a brand should be achieved, because with the existing competition in developed markets "it is no longer sufficient to be known. One must also consistently evoke a set of values and stimulate emotional resonance" [9], which is not facilitated when evoked emotions vary across different product categories of the same brand.

(3) *Descriptive evaluation of targeted emotion dimensions:* This perspective enables campaign managers to detect best, average, and worst brands of a selected emotion dimension based on relative occurrences of emotion dimensions within online customer reviews. The reason for such a descriptive perspective per emotion dimension is straightforward: analysts see their brand in relation to other competitors who sell articles of the same product category. Therefore, this examination adds to the perspectives from above another analytical instrument for a more complete picture of a targeted emotion dimension of a brand.

For instance, the brand family of adidas Group (adidas, Reebok, and adidas Originals) received 18.4 % of trust-related terms among Plutchik's eight emotion dimensions in online customer reviews. Descriptive statistics, as depicted in Fig. 7, allow for assessing this value more properly in the light of other brands.

Fig. 7. In order to create a full picture of a brand's emotion dimension, its respective minimum and maximum representations, along with the average across all products of the concerned product category are considered.

Accordingly adidas Group with 18.4 % resides close to the average of 26.1 % of trust-related terms in online reviews for articles of the Sports_Outdoors segment. Customers of the brand 'Champion' express the least trust-related words (only 7.7 %), while for the brand Jos. A. Bank the most trust is expressed in reviews (85.9 %). Based on the consideration of this comparison, brand managers can put their results into relative perspective and derive necessary steps to change the way their brand is perceived by customers.

5   Conclusions

The amount of unstructured data is constantly growing. Managers can make use of advanced business intelligence methodologies to make use of such data. Customer reviews belong to the set of unstructured data and as such also contain valuable emotional information of customers towards brands. However, to the best of our knowledge, we are the first to present a model which measures customer reviews' emotions related to brands from a single and multi brand perspective.

Based on our model, emotional terms related to brands throughout different product categories can be extracted in order to learn to what extent Plutchik's eight emotion dimensions ("anger", "anticipation", "disgust", "fear", "joy", "sadness", "surprise" and "trust") influence the helpfulness rating of customer reviews. This consideration improves the understanding of marketers of their own brand and the way customers perceive their brand. According to [11], such improved understanding of target groups' emotions "would allow more effective ad-targeting and knowledge about actual trends".

With our presented marketing applications in Sect. 4.2, managers can create and improve products and services according to their understanding of the emotional and social perception of customers [14]. Additionally, these applications serve brand managers as an opportunity to detect interesting coherences within their (multi) brand company and can help to improve the perception of their brand products and services accordingly, e.g., to increase the promotion of trust and security through CRM campaigns, etc., whenever trust is not expressed very often through consumers' posts.

Future work may include the investigation of dynamics of brands emotions over time. Another interesting research direction would be the establishment of product category related dictionaries in cooperation with linguists to improve the entire classification model. And lastly, researchers can use textual content from different social media channels to enrich their dataset and to compare their intermediate role.

References

1. Anderson, E.W., Fornell, C., Lehmann, D.R.: Customer satisfaction, market share, profitability: findings from Sweden. J. Market. **58**, 53–66 (1994)
2. Bougie, R., Pieters, R., Zeelenberg, M.: Angry customers don't come back, they get back: The experience and behavioral implications of anger and dissatisfaction in services. J. Acad. Mark. Sci. **31**(4), 377–393 (2003)
3. Breiman, L.: Random forests. Mach. Learn. **45**(1), 5–32 (2001)
4. Caruana, R., Niculescu-Mizil, A.: An empirical comparison of supervised learning algorithms. In: Proceedings of the 23rd International Conference on Machine Learning, pp. 161–168. ACM (2006)
5. Cho, Y., Im, I., Hiltz, R., Fjermestad, J.: An analysis of online customer complaints: implications for web complaint management. In: Proceedings of the 35th Annual Hawaii International Conference on System Sciences, HICSS, pp. 2308–2317. IEEE (2002)
6. Dick, A.S.: Customer loyalty: toward an integrated conceptual framework. J. Acad. Market. Sci. **22**(2), 99–113 (1994)
7. Duffy, N., Hooper, J.: Passion Branding: Harnessing the Power of Emotion to Build Strong Brands. Wiley, New York (2004)
8. Ittner, C.D., Larcker, D.F.: Are nonfinancial measures leading indicators of financial performance? An analysis of customer satisfaction. J. Account. Res. **36**, 1–35 (1998)
9. Kapferer, J.-N.: The New Strategic Brand Management: Advanced Insights and Strategic Thinking. Kogan page publishers, London (2012)
10. Martin, L., Sintsova, V., Pearl, P.: Are influential writers more objective? An analysis of emotionality in review comments. In: Proceedings of the Companion Publication of the 23rd International Conference on World Wide Web Companion, pp. 799–804. International World Wide Web Conferences Steering Committee (2014)
11. Maynard, D., Bontcheva, K., Rout, D.: Challenges in developing opinion mining tools for social media. In: Proceedings of the@ NLP can u tag #usergeneratedcontent, pp. 15–22 (2012)
12. McAuley, J., Leskovec, J.: Hidden factors and hidden topics: understanding rating dimensions with review text. In: Proceedings of the 7th ACM Conference on Recommender Systems, pp. 165–172. ACM (2013)
13. Saif, M.M., Peter, D.T.: Crowdsourcing a word-emotion association lexicon. Comput. Intell. **29**(3), 436–465 (2013)
14. David, W.N., Jeffrey, F.D., VanDe Velde, J.: Producing customer happiness: the job to do for brand innovation. Des. Manage. Rev. **21**(3), 6–15 (2010)
15. Pang, B., Lee, L.: A sentimental education: sentiment analysis using subjectivity summarization based on minimum cuts. In: Proceedings of the 42nd Annual Meeting on Association for Computational Linguistics, p. 271. Association for Computational Linguistics (2004)
16. Plutchik, R.: A general psychoevolutionary theory of emotion. In: Theories of Emotion, vol. 1 (1980)

17. Roberts, K.: Lovemarks: the future beyond brands. LA COMUNICACIÓN DE LAS MARCAS, p. 35 (2005)
18. Rossiter, J., Bellman, S.: Emotional branding pays off: how brands meet share of requirements through bonding, companionship, and love. Faculty of Commerce-Papers (Archive), pp. 291–296 (2012)
19. Klaus, R.: What are emotions? And how can they be measured? Soc. Sci. Inf. **44**(4), 695–729 (2005)
20. Amy, K., Ruth, N.B.: The effect of customers' emotional responses to service failures on their recovery effort evaluations and satisfaction judgments. J. Acad. Mark. Sci. **30**(1), 5–23 (2002)
21. Thomson, M., Deborah, J.M., Whan Park, C.: The ties that bind: measuring the strength of consumers emotional attachments to brands. J. Consum. Psychol. **15**(1), 77–91 (2005)

Associations Rules Between Sector Indices on the Warsaw Stock Exchange

Krzysztof Karpio[(⊠)], Piotr Łukasiewicz, and Arkadiusz Orłowski

Faculty of Applied Informatics and Mathematics, Department of Informatics,
Warsaw University of Life Sciences – SGGW, Warsaw, Poland
{krzysztof_karpio,piotr_lukasiewicz,
arkadiusz_orlowski}@sggw.pl

Abstract. In this paper an Association Rules data mining technique is adopted to explore the co-movement between sector indices listed on the Warsaw Stock Exchange. The sector indices describe various parts of the Polish economy as well as Ukrainian companies and are not as sensitive to individual random events as single companies are. The measures describing discovered rules are calculated and strong rules are selected. Based on the strong rules the relations between parts of the Polish economy are presented. The interesting mutual interrelations between parts of Polish and Ukrainian economies are also observed.

Keywords: Data mining · Association rules · Sector indices

1 Introduction

Identification of patterns in the stock markets has been an important research subject for many years. More and more advanced statistical methods have been applied to analyze market data. In the recent years, data mining methods have been used as well. Association Rules (AR) is one of the more interesting and frequently used data mining techniques. The aim of studying the associations is to find interesting dependences in big data sets. Origin of this method dates back to the problem of discovering dependencies in the context of the so-called analysis of the shopping cart (MBA - Market Basket Analysis). In the classical MBA problem the method yields the results in the form: "when product A is purchased then product B is also purchased" called association rules. AR is used in the wide range of branches of science where big data sets are analyzed, from natural sciences to management, economy and business [1, 2]. This method was applied to study the interdependences between financial time series [3–5]. In [4] the authors were forecasting changes in the Korea Composite Stock Price Index based on its relations to various worlds' stocks indices. The relations between main stocks indices in Europe, USA, Brazil and Japan have been investigated in [5]. Our previous papers [6–8] are devoted to analysis of stock indices too. In the latter one we used AR to study the relations between return rates of the assets on the Warsaw Stock Exchange (WSE).

The aim of this work is to use AR method to discover relations between various sectors of Polish economy. Those sectors are represented on the Warsaw Stock

© Springer International Publishing Switzerland 2016
V. Řepa and T. Bruckner (Eds.): BIR 2016, LNBIP 261, pp. 312–321, 2016.
DOI: 10.1007/978-3-319-45321-7_22

Exchange by their respective indices. Some relations between various sectors of economy can be expected. However, those relations are usually determined qualitatively without measuring their relative strength.

Our analysis consists of three steps. The first one is a selection of data in order to simultaneously have long history of return rates and possibly big number of sector indices. Referring to the classical MBA we define baskets in the second step. Our baskets are constructed on the daily basis and contain sector indices that meet defined conditions. The third step is a determination of association rules between indices, evaluation of their qualities and a selection of the strongest rules. In order to perform the last step we use two key measures: support and confidence.

This paper is organized as follows. The Sect. 2 contains definitions of rules and measures. The data used in this paper are described in the Sect. 3. The results and their discussion are in the Sect. 4. The Sect. 5 is the summary of this paper.

2 Association Rules and Their Measures

The association rules are defined as in [9]. Let $I = \{i_1, i_2, \ldots, i_m\}$ be a set of binary attributes called items. By transaction T we understand every non-empty subset of I ($T \subset I$ and $T \neq \emptyset$). A set of all transactions is called the database and is denoted by D. An association rule is any relation of the form $X \rightarrow Y$, where $X \subset I$, $Y \subset I$ and $X \cap Y = \emptyset$. A support value of the set $A \subset I$ is the ratio of number of transactions T such as $A \subset T$ to the number of all transactions in the database D. A support of the set A will be denoted by $Supp(A, D)$. We define support and confidence of the rule $X \rightarrow Y$ in the following manner

$$Supp(X \rightarrow Y) = Supp(X \cup Y, D) \tag{1}$$

$$Conf(X \rightarrow Y) = Supp(X \cup Y, D) \,/\, Supp(X, D) \tag{2}$$

Values of support and confidence are usually expressed in per cents. Support of the rule $X \rightarrow Y$ is the proportion of the transactions containing $X \cup Y$ in the database D. Confidence is an estimate of $P(Y \mid X)$ that is the probability of observing Y given X. Support is a frequency the rule occurs and it reflects a usefulness of the rule. Confidence measures strength and reliability of the rule. A number of discovered rules might be very big so it is crucial to select those which are the most interesting. The selection is usually done based on the minimum support *minSupp* and the minimum confidence *minConf*. Their values will be set and discussed in the next chapter.

There are cases when rules with high supports and confidences are not useful [10]. That is why the selected rules are also checked for satisfying the inequity: *Lift* > 1, where *Lift* of the rule: $X \rightarrow Y$ is defined as:

$$Lift(X \rightarrow Y) = Supp(X \cup Y, D) \,/\, (Supp(X, D) \cdot Supp(Y, D)) \tag{3}$$

We used the Apriori algorithm [9, 11] built in Oracle Data Miner 11.2.

3 Data Characteristic and Selections

The analyzed data have been downloaded from the Bank for Environmental Protection website [12]. The full data set consisted of daily return rates of sector indices since 1997-12-31. However, there were only five sector indices during the first years. Afterwards other indices were introduced on the regular basis. Therefore we face the dilemma between analyzing either longer period of time or greater number of indices. Figure 1 shows the number of sector indices vs date.

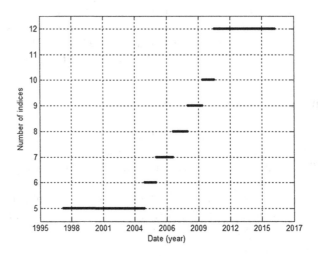

Fig. 1. Number of sector indices traded each day on the WSE vs date

We decided to analyze the greatest possible number of indices by taking into account data since 2010-12-31. That allowed us to search for coincidences between 12 sectors of economy and still having 1311 trading days and 15732 return rates. The analysis of the whole period of time would require modifications of the Apriori algorithm but this is not the subject of this work.

For the purpose of the analysis, special attention has been focused on defining positive and negative return rates. Distributions of the return rates are concentrated around zero, so the most probable values are also close to zero. One shall also remember about statistical fluctuations. Those two factors together could lead to the situation when random statistical fluctuations change the sign of the return rate. Moreover, excluded return rates have minimum or no practical meaning because of the trading costs. We set the limits on the return rates in order they could be taken into account as positive or negative. Distributions of the return rates of the indices are similar to each other. The distribution of all return rates is presented in Fig. 2 (left plot). We set the common values of limits for all indices equal to about one third of standard deviation of that distribution (±0.005).

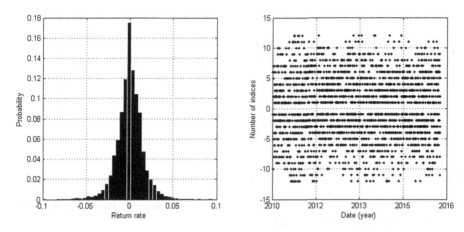

Fig. 2. Distribution of the daily return rates for all sector indices (left plot) and number of indices having daily positive and negative (negative numbers) return rates vs date (right plot)

Number of indices with positive/negative return rates each day is distributed uniformly across all the trading days, Fig. 2 (right plot). We also calculated numbers of days every index earned positive/negative return rate. The analyzed sector indices are summarized in Table 1 together with the percentage of days each index grew up or declined. We do not observe significant differences between indices.

Table 1. Analyzed sector indices with the percentage of daily return rates.

Index	Positive daily returns [%]	Negative daily returns [%]
WIG-BANKING	33.7	32.5
WIG-CHEMICALS	38.8	34.0
WIG-CONSTRUCTION	31.2	29.7
WIG-DEVELOPERS	29.8	30.4
WIG-ENERGY	31.7	32.1
WIG-IT	30.9	28.2
WIG-MEDIA	34.5	33.4
WIG-OIL&GAS	35.4	34.9
WIG-FOOD	33.6	34.3
WIG-BASIC MATERIALS	37.8	36.8
WIG-TELEKOM	31.7	32.3
WIG-UKRAINE	34.0	36.2

The name of each index reflects its content. A remark is required in the case of WIG-UKRAINE index. It contains companies with their headquarters in Ukraine as well as the companies which operate mainly in Ukraine. Every analyzed index also participates in the main WSE index WIG.

4 Results

The goal of our analysis is to find strong associations between the parts of Polish economy. We try to find relations between pairs of stock indices both having positive or negative return rates. Discovered rules undergo further selection based on support and confidence. We select the strong rules based on the values of 90-th percentiles of both measures. Based on those values we set *minSupp* and *minConf*. Additionally we require *Lift* of each strong rule to be greater than unity.

4.1 Analyzing Positive Return Rates

Values of the measures for discovered association rules between indices having positive daily return rates are presented in Fig. 3.

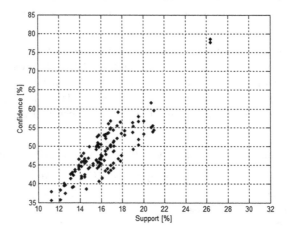

Fig. 3. Confidence vs support of association rules between indices with positive return rates

The values of supports indicate that the best two rules are present in about 26 % of all days. The remaining rules have support between 11 % and 22 %. On the other hand, the strength of the rule is described in terms of confidence. The two rules mentioned above have confidence about 78 %. The confidences of remaining rules are between 35 % and 62 %. We calculated limit values of measures: *minSupp* = 19.48 % and *minConf* = 55.35 % as the 90-th percentiles of their distributions. The strong rules are presented in Table 2 along with their measures. They are sorted by their confidence. All the listed rules have *Lift* greater than 1.42 thus being significant.

We selected twelve association rules. The first two rules show mutual strong relationship between Polish food sector and Ukrainian companies. The remaining rules concern mainly the banking, basic materials, chemical, oil&gas and energy sectors.

Table 2. The strong rules between increasing indices sorted by the confidence.

Rule	Supp [%]	Conf [%]	Lift
WIG-FOOD → WIG-UKRAINE	26.39	78.46	2.31
WIG-UKRAINE → WIG-FOOD	26.39	77.58	2.31
WIG-BANKING → WIG-BASIC MATERIALS	20.75	61.54	1.63
WIG-OIL&GAS → WIG-CHEMICALS	21.05	59.48	1.53
WIG-DEVELOPERS → WIG-BASIC MATERIALS	17.62	59.08	1.57
WIG-BANKING → WIG-CHEMICALS	19.53	57.92	1.49
WIG-OIL&GAS → WIG-BASIC MATERIALS	20.06	56.68	1.50
WIG-MEDIA → WIG-BASIC MATERIALS	19.53	56.64	1.50
WIG-ENERGY → WIG-CHEMICALS	17.85	56.39	1.45
WIG-BANKING → WIG-OIL&GAS	18.99	56.34	1.59
WIG-ENERGY → WIG-BANKING	17.54	55.42	1.64
WIG-BASIC MATERIALS → WIG-CHEMICALS	20.90	55.35	1.43

4.2 Analyzing Negative Return Rates

In this step we investigate coincidences between indices earning negative daily return rates. All the discovered association rules are localized in Fig. 4 based on their support and confidence.

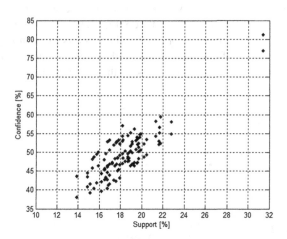

Fig. 4. Confidence vs support for association rules between indices with negative return rates

We observe the same two rules with the highest values of the measures. Their supports are about 31 % but their confidences are different and are about 81 % and 77 %. As previously the remaining rules have significantly smaller values of both measures. They are located between 12 % < *Supp* < 23 % and 37 % < *Conf* < 60 %. The limit values of measures in this case are *minSupp* = 20.47 % and *minConf* = 54.61 %. The strong rules are listed in Table 3.

Table 3. The strong rules between indices with negative daily return rates.

Rule	Supp [%]	Conf [%]	Lift
WIG-FOOD → WIG-UKRAINE	31.43	81.11	1.98
WIG-UKRAINE → WIG-FOOD	31.43	76.84	1.98
WIG-BANKING → WIG-BASIC MATERIALS	21.78	59.39	1.43
WIG-BANKING → WIG-OIL&GAS	21.35	58.22	1.48
WIG-OIL&GAS → WIG-BASIC MATERIALS	22.82	57.99	1.39
WIG-CHEMICALS → WIG-OIL&GAS	21.70	56.50	1.44
WIG-OIL&GAS → WIG-CHEMICALS	21.70	55.14	1.44
WIG-BASIC MATERIALS → WIG-OIL&GAS	22.82	54.87	1.39

The strongest rules are, as previously, between WIG-FOOD and WIG-UKRAINE. Therefore strong correlations between values of those indices exist when they are growing up as well as declining. However, when they decrease the influence of Polish food companies onto the Ukrainian ones is bigger than the other way round. The remaining rules concern similar sectors as previously: banking, basic materials, chemical and oil&gas.

4.3   Discussion

We observe the strongest relations between Polish food sector and Ukrainian companies in the case of both positive and negative return rates. The observed relations are mutual and there are no strong relations with other sectors of economy. They can be explained by the content of the WIG-UKRAINE index, which is composed of the companies operating also on the food market, though they are not included in the

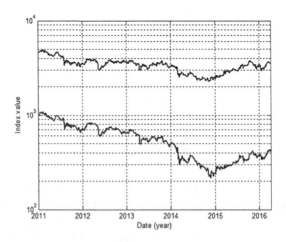

Fig. 5. Values of WIG-FOOD (upper curve) and WIG-UKRAINE (lower curve). Horizontal axis indicates day number between 2010-12-31 and 2016-04-05. Vertical axis has logarithmic scale

WIG-FOOD index. That means the financial condition of the food sector companies does not depend on their location. The similar overall behavior of those two indices is visible on the graph containing their historical values (Fig. 5).

Both curves have similar shapes in the long scale as well as in the short one when we can observe sharp drops or rises. However, when return rates are negative we have stronger influence of WIG-FOOD on WIG-UKRAINE than in the opposite direction. This asymmetry can be justified by the fact that Polish food sector index consists of 26 companies with total capitalization of 4×10^9 PLN. On the other hand the WIG-UKRINE consists of only 7 companies and its capitalization is 10^9 PLN. The remaining strong rules have similar values of supports and confidences. One can notice the special role of the banking sector (Fig. 6). Increasing index of this sector influences basic materials, chemical and oil&gas sectors. Two of them: basic materials and oil&gas, are also influenced by the banking sector during the decrease of the indices. On the other hand the banking sector is influenced only by energy sector when they both are increasing.

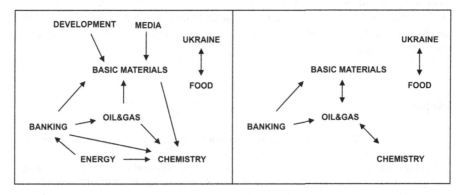

Fig. 6. The strong rules between indices increasing (left plot) and decreasing (right plot) indices

Another sector which is commonly present in many rules is the chemical sector. However this sector participates in the strong upstream rules exclusively as consequent, being influenced by energy, oil&gas, basic materials and banking sectors. We also observe mutual relation between chemical and oil&gas sectors when indices decrease.

The basic materials sector is another sector which is influenced by other sectors. Good conditions of the oil&gas, banking, development or media sectors imply the increase of their value. In the case of decreasing of indices we observe only a mutual relation with the oil&gas sector as well as influence of banking.

The discovered association rules are justified from the economic point of view. One observes strong and durable relations between: mining and fuel industry, energy distribution, chemical and banking sectors. All of them are economically and financially interdependent. The origin of the influence of the media sector on the basic materials sector is not clear.

5 Summary

We analyzed values of the sector indices listed on Warsaw Stock Exchange from 2010-12-31 to 2016-04-05. Using AR technique we discovered strong relations between sector indices. We studied simultaneous growths and declines of the indices. The rules of the types: *up → up* and *down → down* have been presented. The strongest relations are present in the food sector. There is strong mutual interaction between WIG-FOOD and WIG-UKRAINE indices. At the same time there is no relation between those two indices and remaining sectors. The other strong rules exhibit relations mainly between the basic materials, chemical, oil&gas and banking sectors. Mutual interactions exist between declines of the following index pairs: WIG-CHEMICAL ↔ WIG-OIL&GAS and WIG-BASIC MATERIALS ↔ WIG-OIL&GAS. The rules: WIG-OIL&GAS → WIG-BASIC MATERIALS, WIG-OIL&GAS → WIG-CHEMICAL, WIG-BANKING → WIG-OIL&GAS, WIG-BANKING → WIG-BASIC MATERIALS are present between both positive and negative return rates.

We plan to further investigate relations between sector indices in other developing as well as mature markets. It would be interesting to study coincidences between prices of indices in different days. The other issue, what to be investigated, is the existence of possible rules of type *up → down* and *down → up* which are used by many investment diversification methods.

References

1. Huang, Z., Lu, X., Duan, H.: Mining association rules to support resource allocation in business process management. Expert Syst. Appl. **38**(8), 9483–9490 (2011)
2. Kamsu-Foguem, B., Rigal, F., Mauget, F.: Mining association rules for the quality improvement of the production process. Expert Syst. Appl. **40**(4), 1034–1045 (2013)
3. Srisawat, A.: An application of association rule mining based on stock market. In: 3rd International Conference on Data Mining and Intelligent Information Technology Applications, pp. 259–262 (2011)
4. Na, S.H., Sohn, S.Y.: Forecasting changes in Korea composite stock price index (KOSPI) using association rules. Expert Syst. Appl. **38**, 9046–9049 (2011)
5. Pan, Y., Haran, E., Manago, S., Hu, Y.: Co-movement of European stock markets based on association rule mining. In: Third International Conference on Data Analytics, pp. 54–58 (2014). ISBN: 978-1-61208-358-2
6. Karpio, K., Łukasiewicz, P., Orłowski, A.: Price-volume relationship in polish stock market. Acta Phys. Pol. A **121**(2-B), B61–B66 (2012)
7. Karpio, K., Łukasiewicz, P., Orłowski, A.: Stock indices for emerging markets. Acta Phys. Pol., A **117**(4), 619–622l (2010)
8. Karpio, K., Łukasiewicz, P., Orłowski, A., Ząbkowski, T.: Mining associations on the warsaw stock exchange. Acta Phys. Pol., A **123**(3), 553–559 (2013)
9. Agrawal, R., Imielinski, T., Swami, A.: Mining association rules between sets of items in large databases. In: International Conference on Management of Data. ACM SIGMOD, pp. 207–216 (1993)

10. Azevedo, P.J., Jorge, A.M.: Comparing rule measures for predictive association rules. In: Kok, J.N., Koronacki, J., Lopez de Mantaras, R., Matwin, S., Mladenič, D., Skowron, A. (eds.) ECML 2007. LNCS (LNAI), vol. 4701, pp. 510–517. Springer, Heidelberg (2007)
11. Agrawal, R., Shafer, J.: Parallel mining of association rules. IEEE Trans. Knowl. Data Eng. **8**(6), 962–969 (1996)
12. http://bassa.pl. (last access 10 May 2016)

Algorithms for Database Keys
Discovery Assistance

Christian Mancas[(✉)]

Mathematics and Computer Science Department,
Ovidius University, Constanta, Romania
christian.mancas@gmail.com

Abstract. Only humans may decide whether a column or a set of columns of a table should store minimally unique values. Not adding to a table any existing constraint (business rule), which includes keys, allows for storing implausible instances in it. Unfortunately, 2^n possibilities should be considered in the worst case for a table with n columns in order to discover all of its keys. This paper presents and discusses contrastively three as efficient as possible, sound, and complete algorithms that assist database designers in discovering all existing keys in the corresponding subuniverse of discourse.

Keywords: Key · Superkey · Candidate key · Non-prime attribute · Prime attribute · Keys discovery · Surrogate key · Primary key

1 Introduction

1.1 Constraints

The Relational Data Model (RDM, e.g. [2, 6, 15]) has three major contributions: the querying formalism, the inter-related tables simplicity and naturalness, and the introduction and formalization of constraints (business rules): logic formulas that are added to database (db) schemas (and enforced by Relational Database Management Systems (RDBMS)) in order to reject attempts to store undesired data in their instances.

All business rules of any data subuniverse to be modeled, be them explicit or implicit, should be discovered, in order to be able to guarantee that only plausible data is stored in the corresponding dbs. In order to do it, it is simpler to first search for those of the types provided by the vast majority of the available RDBMSes, which are:

- *Attribute ranges* (or *allowable/permitted values* or *(co-)domain constraints*);
- *Compulsory attributes* (*data*) (or *mandatory values*, or *not null constraints*);
- *Minimal uniqueness* (or *key*) *constraints*.

Next, we should add a fourth type for *other business rules*, whenever needed. For example, a table *COUNTRIES* having a column *CapitalCity* also needs the constraint "the capital of any country should be a city of that country".

For other simpler business rules (i.e. only involving columns of a same table and one universally quantified variable, which allows for declaring them as propositional calculus ones), RDBMSes also provide a fourth relational constraint type, namely the

V. Řepa and T. Bruckner (Eds.): BIR 2016, LNBIP 261, pp. 322–338, 2016.
DOI: 10.1007/978-3-319-45321-7_23

tuple (or *check*) ones; for example: *BirthDate* $\leq$ *HireDate* $-365 * 18$, *HireDate* $\leq$ *PassedAwayDate*, etc. Not even terminology is unfortunately standardized for this constraint type: for example, Oracle calls check constraints both range, not null, and tuple ones.

Finally, a fifth type of constraints, called *referential integrity* (theoretically known as *typed inclusion dependency*), is provided too by all RDBMSes, but, as proved in [15], this is not related to conceptual data modeling, but rather to RDM implementation of foreign keys (i.e. columns linking tables and/or table instances).

Domain, not null, and even tuple constraints are very easy to understand and detect: for example, *BirthDate* for *EMPLOYEES* should be both not null and taking values only between e.g. *SysDate* $-365 * 65$ and *SysDate* $-365 * 18$ (assuming that employment is legal only for those having at least 18 and at most 65 years old) and not in the whole DATE datatype. Uniqueness constraints are much more complicated to detect.

1.2 Keys and Superkeys

Just like for (algebraic) sets, db tables should not allow for duplicates: it does not make sense to store more than once same data. A *key constraint* is a statement of the type "C_1 • ... • C_n *key*", where $n > 0$ is a natural, C_i are columns of a table T, "•" denotes concatenation of these columns (i.e. mapping (Cartesian) product: $f • g : D \rightarrow$ codom $(f) \times$ codom(g); in RDM $f • g$ is abbreviated as $f g$) and *key* means *minimally unique*, i.e. is unique and it does not include any other key. When $n = 1$, the key is called *simple*; when $n > 1$ it is called *concatenated*; if a unique column concatenation properly contains a key, then it is a *superkey*. Superkeys are of no actual, but only theoretical interest: enforcing only superkeys allows for storing implausible data, while also enforcing superkeys results in useless waste of storage space and processing time.

Keys are extremely useful for providing: better selectivity estimates in cost-based query optimization; query optimizers with access paths that might lead to substantial query processing speedups; deeper insights into application data; db administrators with opportunities to improve the efficiency of data access via physical design techniques (e.g. data partitioning, creation of indexes, materialized views, etc.); data-integration process automation.

1.2.1 Primary and Surrogate (Syntactic) Keys

Although RDM does not require it, it is a best practice to declare for each fundamental table a primary key. Conventionally, its name is underlined. The best solution for primary keys is the surrogate (syntactic) type one: numeric, with no other semantics than unique identification, and preferably having their values automatically generated by RDBMSes. Surrogate keys are generally denoted by "ID", used as such or as a prefix/suffix of the table name; we are using x for them, as they play this mathematic role for all other columns thought of as functions.

1.2.2 Semantic (Candidate) Keys

All non-surrogate keys are called semantic (or candidate) keys. There are only a couple of exception types among object sets that might not have associated semantic key constraints: subsets and poultry/rabbit cages type sets.

For example, the subset *TOURISTS* of *PEOPLE* does not have any key. For subsets, unique identification may be done through the keys of the corresponding supersets. Subsets may have their keys too; for example, the subset *DRIVERS* of *EMPLOYEES* (that we might abstract in order to store only for them the otherwise inapplicable properties *LicenseType, LicenseDate, LicenseNo, LicenceIssuingAuthority*, etc.) has *LicenseNo • LicenceIssuingAuthority* as its key.

Poultry/rabbit/etc. *CAGES* in a (farming) db might not need any other uniqueness than the one provided by surrogate keys too: you can use their system generated numbers also as cage labels (surrogate keys thus exceptionally getting semantics too).

For example, let us consider the table from Fig. 1, where keys are enclosed in the parenthesis after the table name, the primary key is underlined, and domain and not null constraints are written on second and third header lines, respectively.

COUNTIES (x)

x	County	County Code	State	Seat	Popula- tion	Created	Area (km^2)
AutoN umber(8)	ASCII (128)	ASCII (3)	STATES .x	CITIES .x	$[10^5, 10^8]$	[1000, Year(Sys Date)]	$[1, 10^5]$
NOT NULL	NOT NULL	NOT NULL	NOT NULL	NOT NULL			
1	Rensse- laer	083	5	1	159,429	1791	1,722
2	Sche- nectady	093	5	2	154,727	1809	541
3	Albany	001	5	6	304,204	1683	1,380
4	New York	061	5	5	1,636,268	1683	87
5	Bronx	005	5	5	1,438,159	1914	150
6	Queens	081	5	5	2,321,580	1683	460

Fig. 1. An rdb table example

For foreign keys the second row contains their referential integrity constraints, from where corresponding domain constraints may be inferred too. For example, in column *Seat*, *CITIES.x* contained by the corresponding cell is an abbreviation of the referential integrity constraint *COUNTIES.Seat* ⊆ *CITIES.x* (an abbreviation of the math inclusion *Im(COUNTIES.Seat)* ⊆ *Im(CITIES.x)* [15], where the image of a mapping $f : D \rightarrow C$ is the set $Im(f) = \{y \in C \mid \exists x \in D, y = f(x)\}$), and if, for example, *CITIES.x* ⊆ AutoNumber (16), it can be inferred that *COUNTIES.Seat* ⊆ AutoNumber(16) too.

Any table should have all keys existing in the corresponding subuniverse: a table lacking an existing constraint allows for implausible data storage in its instances. For example, in the table from Fig. 1 it is possible that users enter 061 (instead of 083) in column *CountyCode* for the first row too, storing the implausible fact that Rensselaer and New York counties have same codes.

1.2.3   Minimal Uniqueness Relativity

Uniqueness is not an absolute, but a relative property: in some contexts a column or concatenation of columns are unique, while in others (even in a same subuniverse) they are not. For example, for computer file names everybody knows that "there may not be two files having same name and extension in a folder", i.e. the triple *FileName • FileExtension • Folder* is a key; in fact, OSes enforce a supplementary constraint too: "there may not be two files in a same folder having null (no) extensions and same names", i.e. for the subset of files without extension *FileName • Folder* is a key.

Consequently, semantic keys may only be discovered by humans: there may not ever be any tools able to do such a job, but only to assist it.

1.2.4   Implausible Constraints

Dually, again just like for any other constraint type, you should never assert keys that do not exist in the corresponding subuniverse: were you doing it, you would aberrantly prevent users to store plausible data. For example, if in the table from Fig. 1 you were declaring *Population* as a key too, then no two counties having same population figures could be stored simultaneously.

1.2.5   Prime and Nonprime Attributes

RDM also introduced the concepts of prime and nonprime attributes: if it is part of at least one (unique) key, a column is said to be prime (essential) and otherwise nonprime (nonessential). As they are applied only *after* the set of table keys is established, they are purely syntactic. We need in fact slightly different semantic definitions for them, to be applied *before* the set of all keys for a table is established: in the (Elementary) Mathematical Data Model ((E)MDM, [14–18]) a mapping is said to be prime if it is either a key or might be part of a key and nonprime otherwise. Consequently, in particular, this semantic definition of nonprimeness of a column is: "not only it is not a single key, but it cannot be part of any concatenated one either" (in that particular subuniverse).

For example, in Fig. 1 columns *Population*, *Created*, and *Area* are nonprime, while *County* and *Seat* are prime too in (E)MDM. Generally, except for very few particular contexts (e.g., tables for time zones or colors), very many other numeric properties, like population, area, temperature, pressure, altitude and their dual (rivers, lakes, seas, oceans, etc.) depth, length, width, GDP, rating, probabilities, percentages, time zones, etc., some text ones like color, notes, even some calendar dates (like, for example, discovery, national dates, etc.), etc., as well as most of the Boolean ones (for example *Married? Divorced? Widow? Author? Holiday?* etc.) are nonprime.

Algorithm *A7-8/3* from Sect. 3.6 of [15], which is assisting validation of the keys declared for any table and discovery of any other existing ones, proves that correctly declaring of all nonprime mappings is crucial in significantly reducing the otherwise huge number of possible cases to analyze. This is why we are using the semantic concept of nonprimeness, instead of the RDM syntactic one.

1.3   Paper Outline

The following three sections of this paper introduce and contrastively discuss three new algorithms for assisting keys discovery; all of them have as input the set of prime and not one-to-one columns of a table and output the corresponding set of keys. *A1*, the simplest possible, is purely bottom-up, starting with individual columns and ending, in the worst case, with the product of all of them. *A2*, the most sophisticated one alternates in each step the bottom-up and the top-down approaches. Finally, *A3*, the best one in our opinion, starts with a first top-down step and then, if needed, continues bottom-up. The paper ends with a case study, conclusion, and references.

1.4   Related Work

Two dual types of approaches are used for discovering keys: syntactic and semantic. All attempts to discover keys within the RDM framework are purely syntactic: for example, starting with a set of functional dependencies, algorithms were devised to infer corresponding keys (e.g. [8, 13]). As such, for example, [2] –that most of us consider to be the RDM "bible"– does not even mention keys discovery. It is true that in the meantime algorithms for assisting discovery of functional dependencies were designed too (e.g. [11, 12]). However, keys are central to RDM as well: the highest relational normal form is the Domain-Key (DKNF) one [9], solely based on domain and, especially, key type constraints.

Even recent approaches based on data mining are purely syntactic: keys are searched for in db instances (e.g. GORDIAN [18], HCA [1], DUCC [10]). Obviously, any such method might yield both false negatives and false positives: on one hand, due to stored implausible (duplicate) data (which may happen anytime when corresponding keys are not enforced) not all existing keys may be discovered and, on the other, they may discover implausible keys only because, by chance, at the moment when such algorithms are run against a db instance, a particular product of a table columns does not store any duplicates.

For example, if any such algorithm were run on the instance from Fig. 1, it would not discover any correct key, but only the implausible ones *County*, *CountyCode*, *Population*, *Area*, and *Seat • Created*. Note that both false positives and negatives are possible anytime: when there are few rows, false positives abound, but false negatives are also possible, as you may duplicate data even with only two rows; when there are very many rows, false negatives abound, but false positives are still possible too: e.g. both *Area* and *Population* are very unlikely to store duplicates even in the worldwide context (or, even worse, their product is almost surely containing no duplicates even if both of them might store some).

To conclude with, generally, data mining approaches may find all keys (but false positives too) if and only if the users of that db did not make any duplication mistake while entering/updating corresponding table instances. This is just another example that [4] is right: on one hand, very large dbs have to contain arbitrary correlations, which in this case mean that false both negatives and positives are always possible; on the other, the Big Data "philosophy" "with enough data, numbers speak for themselves" (implying "the end of science") is wrong: understanding and guided prediction and action should not be replaced by computer-discovered correlations; as they put it, "too much information tends to behave like too little information". As a consequence, it is crystal clear that data mining may enrich scientific methods, but never replace them.

For example, [20] introduced the concept of almost keys in the framework of RDF resources, according to OWL2 semantics (but also applicable in dbs for columns or column products that have almost all values unique, with a settable threshold for accepted duplicates) and a fast algorithm for detecting them; in a final step, experts may or may not validate them individually as keys.

All three algorithms presented in this paper are of the semantic type. A similar to algorithm $A1$ was proposed in the framework of the (E)MDM, first for relationship structural keys (i.e. keys made up only of canonical Cartesian projections) [17] and then for all other possible keys [16]. $A7$-$8/3$ from [15] is much more complicated than $A1$, as it is designed for legacy rdbs, hence includes validation of already enforced table keys, as well as of nonprimeness of all attributes, which also makes it run much slower. For all three of them, the following Theorem was also proved:

Theorem (*Keys Discovery Algorithm Characterization*). The algorithm has the following properties:

  (i)   its complexity is $O(2^n)$;
 (ii)   it is complete (i.e. it is generating all possible keys);
(iii)   it is sound (i.e. it is generating only possible keys);
 (iv)   it is relatively optimal (i.e. it generates the minimum possible number of questions relative to its strategy and it is doing its job with minimum number of statement executions).

However, none of them is absolutely minimal: for example, $A3$ from this paper is bringing significant improvement in the case when the only semantic key is the concatenation of all of its n input columns (see the fourth section below). Moreover, $A7$-$8/3$ is too complicated when there are no semantic keys defined or when existing keys were already validated and new columns are added to a table. When most keys have arity either 1 or $n - 1$ and $n > 4$, $A2$ is better suited than not only $A7$-$8/3$, but also $A1$.

Algorithm $A3$ extended with the validation part of $A7$-$8/3$ from [15] (which may optionally be skipped if you consider all existing keys to be correct) is implemented in *MatBase* (see, e.g., [18, 15]), a prototype Knowledge and DBMS based on both the Entity-Relationship Data Model (E-RDM) (see, for example, [5, 15, 21]), (E)MDM, RDM, and *Datalog¬* (see, for example, [2, 18]). Consequently, its users do not need to bother with either missing combinations or detecting superkeys.

All such algorithms, be them syntactic or semantic, should stop when they discover the maximum possible number of keys for any set of n columns, which is $C(n, [n/2])$ ([7, 14, 22]).

2   A1: An Algorithm for Assisting Initial Discovery of Keys

Each time when for a fundamental table all non-prime columns have been identified
and set apart, and there are either no semantic keys at all or there are only some
validated single ones (which can thus be set apart too), and we are left with a non-void
subset of prime columns that are not keys, we propose to apply the much simpler and
faster algorithm $A1$ presented in Fig. 2, in order to be assisted in discovering all other
semantic keys that exist for that set in that particular subuniverse of interest.

2.1   Applying $A1$ Example

Let us apply, for example, Algorithm $A1$ to the *COUNTIES* table from Fig. 1 (only
"actual" statements being numbered: *repeat for, else, end,* etc. are not): $T =$
COUNTIES, $n = 4$, $C_1 = County$, $C_2 = CountyCode$, $C_3 = State$, $C_4 = Seat$, $K = \{\underline{x}\}$,
$k = 1$.

01. $K' = \{\underline{x}\}$;
02. $l = 1$;
03. as $4 > 0$:
04. $k_{max} = C(4, 2) = 4!/(2! * 2!) = 6$;
05. $i = 1$; $(C(4, 1) = 4)$
06. *allSuperkeys = false*;
07. as $1 \leq 4$ *and* $1 < 6$ *and true*:
08. *allSuperkeys = true*;
09. as *County* is not a superkey:
10. *allSuperkeys = false*;
11. as *County* is not unique (there may be two counties having same names in different states):
11. as *CountyCode* is not unique (there may be two counties having same codes in different states):
11. as *State* is not unique (states generally have several counties):
11. as *Seat* is not unique (there may be two counties having same seat: for example, all New York City counties have it as seat):
14. $i = 2$; $(C(4, 2) = 6)$
07. as $2 \leq 4$ *and* $1 < 6$ *and true*:
08. *allSuperkeys = true*;
09. *County* • *CountyCode* is not a superkey:
10. *allSuperkeys = false*;
11. as *County* • *CountyCode* is not a key (as there may be two counties having same codes and names, but in different states):
11. as **County** • **State** is a key (there may not be two counties of a same state having same names):
12. $K' = \{\underline{x}, County • State\}$;
13. $l = 2$;

ALGORITHM A1. Keys Initial Discovery Assistance

Input: a set of n prime not key columns $S = \{c_1, ..., c_n\}$ of a same table T and a set of associated keys K, card(K) = k, k and n naturals.

Output: K', card(K') = l, l natural, the set of all the keys of T.

01. $K' = K$;

02. $l = k$;

03. **if** $n > 0$ **then**   // for all mappings, if any, look for keys

04. $k_{max} = C(n, [n/2])$;   // maximum possible numbers of keys

05. $i = 1$;   // starting column products arity

06.   *allSuperkeys = false*;   // initially, no superkeys possible for $i = 1$

07.   **while** $i \leq n$ **and** $l < k_{max}$ **and** *not allSuperkeys* **do**

08.   *allSuperkeys = true*;   // all $C(n, i)$ combinations might be superkeys

          repeat *for all* $C(n, i)$ mapping products p made out of i elements

09.   **if** p is not a superkey **then**   // at least one no superkey was

10.   *allSuperkeys = false*;   // discovered on the current level i

11.   **if** p is minimally unique (in the given context) **then**

12. $K' = K' \cup \{ p \}$;   // add newly found key

13. $l = l + 1$;   // correspondingly increase K' cardinal

            end if;

          end if;   // (of 09.: *if* p is not a superkey)

        end repeat;

14. $i = i + 1$;   // increment level (mapping products arity)

      end while;

    end if;   // (of 03.: *if* $n > 0$ ...)

15. s = "add a surrogate primary key to T, according to best practices!";

16. **if** $l = 0$ **then**   // T does not even have a surrogate primary key!

17.   *display s*;

18. **elseif** $l = 1$ **then**

19.   **if** the only key of T is not a surrogate primary one **then**

20.   **display** s;

      else   // the only key of T is the surrogate primary one

21.   **if** T does not correspond to a subset **then**

22.   **display** "is T corresponding to an object set of type poultry cages?";

23.   **if** answer is *no* **then display**   // T needs at least one semantic key

24.   "T needs at least one more mapping in order to have semantic keys too!";

        end if;

      end if;   // (of 21.: *if* T is not a subset)

    end if;   // (of 19.: *if* the only key of T is ...)

  end if;   // (of 16.: *if* $l = 0$)

End ALGORITHM A1;

Fig. 2. Algorithm A1 (keys initial discovery assistance)

11. as *County • Seat* is a key (**there may not be two counties having same names and same seat, which implies that they belong to a same state**):
12. $K' = \{\underline{x}, County • State, County • Seat\}$;
13. $l = 3$;
11. as *CountyCode • State* is a key (**there may not be two counties of a same state having same codes**):
12. $K' = \{\underline{x}, County • State, County • Seat, CountyCode • State\}$;
13. $l = 4$;
11. as *CountyCode • Seat* is a key (**there may not be two counties having same codes and seat, which implies that they belong to a same state**)
12. $K' = \{\underline{x}, County • State, County • Seat, CountyCode • State, CountyCode • Seat\}$;
13. $l = 5$;
11. as *State • Seat* is not a key (there may be two counties of a same state having same seat, e.g. boroughs of a same big city, like it is the case of New York City):
14. $i = 3$; ($C(4, 3) = 4$)
07. as $3 \leq 4$ *and* $3 < 6$ *and true*:
08. *allSuperkeys = true*;
09. as *County • CountyCode • State* is a superkey:
09. as *County • CountyCode • Seat* is a superkey:
09. as *County • State • Seat* is a superkey:
09. as *CountyCode • State • Seat* is a superkey:
14. $i = 4$; ($C(4, 4) = 1$)
18. as $4 \leq 4$ *and* $5 < 6$ *and false* (because *allSuperkeys = true*), the *while* loop is exited
15. $s = $ "add a surrogate primary key to *T*, according to best practices!";
16. as $5 \neq 0$:
18. as $5 \neq 1$, execution of A1 ends.

Corresponding output is $K' = \{\underline{x}, County • State, County • Seat, CountyCode • State, CountyCode • Seat\} \supseteq \{\underline{x}\} = K, l = 5 \geq 1 = k$ that is, when correctly applying A1, to table *COUNTIES* from Fig. 1 four semantic keys have to be added as well: *County • State*, *County • Seat*, *CountyCode • State*, and *CountyCode • Seat*.

2.2   Reasoning Techniques for Discovering Keys

Proving that a given combination is not a key in the corresponding subuniverse may use the *ad absurdum* type technique, assuming that the current combination is a key: consider any combination $c_1 • ... • c_m$, $1 < m \leq n$; you should build a corresponding subtable with two identical lines in it, except for the surrogate key, and with distinct values for all of the rest of the columns, e.g.:

x	c_1	...	c_m	c_{m+1}	...	c_n
1	1	1	1	1	1	1
2	1	1	1	2	2	2

Then, you should ask yourselves whether or not the second may correspond to an actual object in that subuniverse of discourse; if the answer is *no*, this means that no such duplicates are allowed, so you just discovered a new key (and its proof is of the type: "there may not be two elements of this set having same values for $c_1, ..., c_m$"); if it is *yes*, then the proof that it is not a key should be based not only on $c_1, ..., c_m$, but also on at least another column from $\{c_{m+1}, ..., c_n\}$ whose different values for the two lines make them correspond to different possible objects in that particular object set (and be of the type: "there may be two elements of this set having same values for $c_1, ..., c_m$, but having different values for ...").

For example, let us consider the above combinations *County • Seat* and *County • CountyCode*. For the first one, the table should like this:

x	County	CountyCode	State	Seat
1	1	1	1	1
2	1	2	2	1

The corresponding question is: "may there be two distinct counties having same name and seat (but possibly in different states and/or having different codes)?"; the answer being negative (because the fact that they have same seat implies that they belong to a same state and there may not be two counties of a same state having same names), that's how the second semantic key of *COUNTIES* is found.

County • CountyCode is not a key (as there may be two counties having same codes and names, but in different states)

For the second one, the table should like this:

x	County	CountyCode	State	Seat
1	1	1	1	1
2	1	1	2	2

The corresponding question is: "may there be two distinct counties having same name and code (but possibly in different states and/or having different seats)?"; obviously, the answer is positive (because, even if a country is coding its counties uniquely across it, there still may be counties of different countries having same name and code), so this combination is not a key.

Writing down (in parenthesis) the reasons for which column products are or are not minimally unique is not a must only for documentation purposes: they are the proofs of the values assigned to the corresponding logic propositions.

Obviously, the first important step when manually running algorithm $A1$ is not to miss any of the $2^n - 1$ combinations; there are two crucial "secrets" for it:

1. on any level $1 \leq i \leq n$, first compute $C(n, i)$, in order to know in advance the maximum total number of cases (combinations) that you have to analyze on that level;
2. orderly generate then combinations from left to right; for example, for $n = 5, i = 3$ (for which there are $C(5,3) = 5!/(3! * 2!) = 10$ combinations), this order yields: $c_1 • c_2 • c_3, c_1 • c_2 • c_4, c_1 • c_2 • c_5, c_1 • c_3 • c_4, c_1 • c_3 • c_5, c_1 • c_4 • c_5, c_2 • c_3 • c_4, c_2 • c_3 • c_5, c_2 • c_4 • c_5, c_3 • c_4 • c_5$.

Semantically, both discovering keys and rejecting non-keys with the help of this algorithm does not always require experts in the corresponding subuniverse of discourse: on one hand, in very many cases, common sense is enough (e.g. nobody/nothing may simultaneously be present in several locations, no space "slot" may simultaneously accommodate several persons/objects, there is no need whatsoever to store same data twice, there is no "supreme" body in the world that could force states not to use same names as other ones for their states or cities, there is no person/country that would baptize alike two of their children/states, etc.) and, on the other, always thinking dually as well helps a lot (e.g. as soon as you discover that $MD \bullet ConsultStart$ is a key, the dual $MD \bullet ConsultEnd$ is also a key, etc.).

Obviously, for highly specialized subuniverses (e.g. computational biology) consulting corresponding experts is a must. Trivially, this is the case also for most syntactic approaches (be them data mining based or not), either in their initial (for validating functional dependencies) or final steps (for validating found keys).

2.3   Algorithm A1 Characterization

All considerations from [15] on Algorithm $A7$-$8/3$ keys discovery portion also apply to $A1$, with the following particularizations:

✓ In the worst case (happening when K' contains at most the surrogate key and no key is discovered, so $l < 2$), all possible $2^n - 1$ combinations are considered (as there are $2^n - 1$ questions on existing keys, all answered with *no*), which means that the complexity of the algorithm is 2^n. Consequently, in average, this algorithm needs some $2^{n-1} - 1/2$ steps (i.e. half of the worst case one).

✓ $A1$ cannot ever loop indefinitely:
  (i)   input n and k, as well as n, i, l, k_{max}, and $C(n, i)$ are always finite (being naturals);
  (ii) the *repeat* loop, the one inside *while*, is always executed $C(n, i)$ times;
  (iii) the *while* loop is executed at most n times, as i starts with 1 and is incremented by 1 in each such execution.

✓ $A1$ is optimal relatively to its strategy: it asks the minimum number of questions in each possible case and it is doing its job with minimum number of statements.

✓ $A1$ is not absolutely minimal, as proven by the above example: in order to detect the *COUNTIES*' keys, as they are only discovered when $i = 2$, only 4 superkeys are then found and the user has to analyze 11 out of the total of 15 possible combinations.

✓ A purely top down approach is not desirable, as it could not skip superkeys. It is true that this would be somewhat compensated by the fact that, dually, once a key of arity m is found none of its subproducts may be keys.

✓ Obviously, a similar to the above characterization Theorem holds for $A1$ too.

3 A2: An Improved Algorithm for Assisting Keys Discovery

Theoretically, in average, the best strategy possible would be to combine both approaches (bottom-up and top-down) into a single, alternating one: start with $i = n$ and then continue with $i = 1, n - 1, 2, n - 2, 3$, etc., and stop in the worst case with $[n/2]$, as proposed by the algorithm A2 presented in Fig. 3. The last steps (from 15 to 24) of A1 are not shown any more for saving paper space, as they are identical.

ALGORITHM A2. Improved Keys Discovery Assistance
Input: a set of n prime not key columns $S = \{c_1, ..., c_n\}$ of a same table T and a set of associated keys K, card$(K) = k$, k and n naturals.
Output: K', card$(K') = l$, l natural, the set of all the keys of T.
01. $K' = K$;
02. $l = k$;
03. **if** $n > 1$ **then**   // for all mappings, if any, look for keys
04. $k_{max} = C(n, [n/2])$;   // maximum possible numbers of keys
05. $top = true$; $itop = n$; $ibottom = 1$; $i = n$; // starting top down
06. $allSuperkeys = false$;   // initially, no superkeys possible for $i = n$
07.   **while** $ibottom \leq itop + 1$ **and** $l < k_{max}$ **and** not $allSuperkeys$ **do**
08. $allSuperkeys = true$;   // all $C(n, i)$ combinations might be superkeys
          repeat *for all* $C(n, i)$ mapping products p made out of i elements
09.   **if** there is no $x \in K'$ such that p is a subproduct of x **then**
10.   **if** p is not a superkey **then**   // at least one no superkey discovered
11. $allSuperkeys = false$;   // on the current level i
12.   **if** p is minimally unique (in the given context) **then**
13. $K' = K' \cup \{ p \}$;   // add newly found key
14. $l = l + 1$;   // correspondingly increase K' cardinal
                end if;
             end if;   // (of 10.: *if p is not a superkey*)
          end if;   // (of 09.: *if there is no $x \in K'$...*)
          end repeat;
15.   **if** top **then** $i = ibottom$; $ibottom = ibottom + 1$; $itop = itop - 1$;
16.   **else if** $i = itop$ **then** $ibottom = itop + 2$ **else** $i = itop$; **end if**; **end if**;   // next arity
17. $top =$ **not** top;   // swap between top-down and bottom-up
       end while;
    end if;   // (of 03.: *if n > 1 ...*)
End ALGORITHM A2;

Fig. 3. Algorithm A2 (improved keys discovery assistance)

Here Is $A2$'s Characterization:

✓ The worst case remains the same as for $A1$. Only the best case is sensibly improved, as it could take only the first step in order to discover the only key. Sensible improvements are also obtained when keys have high arities (e.g. $n - 1$, with $n > 3$).

✓ However, this syntactic improvement is, from the semantic point of view, potentially risky, especially when n is high: it is increasingly dangerous to "invite" users to consider this generally superkey as being a key.

✓ $A2$ is asking for Fig. 1 all 15 questions, as neither superkeys nor subsets of keys are detected, so $A1$ is faster and more convenient to use in this case. This should not be surprising, as both keys have arity 2 of 4 and $i = 2$ is the last step in $A2$.

✓ $A2$ requires two types of thinking when answering to its questions, although the proving technique is common to both of them: besides the bottom-up type one required by $A1$, you also need a top-down one (in which, essentially, you should analyze whether or not data stored by the current mapping product image is *more than* enough in order to uniquely *and minimally* identify the objects from the corresponding set).

✓ For the top-down reasoning you have to also apply the definition of the minimal uniqueness, by discarding one by one each member of the current product in order to analyze whether or not at least one of the corresponding subproducts is also uniquely identifying the elements of the corresponding object set, which is not easy. $A1$ is fully leveraging this task, by automatically detecting superkeys in every step and not only in every one out of two.

✓ Obviously, a similar to the above characterization Theorem holds for $A2$ too.

4   A3: The Best Algorithm for Assisting Keys Discovery

We strongly believe that the best strategy to assist key discovery is algorithm $A3$ from Fig. 4, which is like $A1$, but the worst case ($i = n$) is considered first, instead of being the last one. Just like for $A2$, the last steps (from 15 to 24) of $A1$ are not shown any more for saving paper space. For the *COUNTIES* example above $A3$ is asking 12 questions, one more than $A1$, but three less than $A2$, as it discovers four superkeys too.

$A3$ has same complexity, worst, and average cases as $A1$ and $A2$, same best case as $A2$, and requires only once the top-down reasoning type. Trivially, a similar to the above characterization Theorem holds for $A3$ too.

ALGORITHM *A*3. Best Practical Keys Discovery Assistance

Input: a set of *n* prime not key columns $S = \{c_1, \ldots, c_n\}$ of a same table *T* and a set of associated keys *K*, card(*K*) = *k*, *k* and *n* naturals.

Output: *K'*, card(*K'*) = *l*, *l* natural, the set of all the keys of *T*.

01. $K' = K$;

02. $l = k$;

03. **if** $n > 0$ **and** $c_1 \bullet \ldots \bullet c_n$ is unique **then**   // for all mappings, if any, look for keys

04.   **if** $c_1 \bullet \ldots \bullet c_n$ is minimally unique (in the given context) **then**

05. $K' = K' \cup \{ c_1 \bullet \ldots \bullet c_n \}$;   // add newly found key

06. $l = l + 1$;   // correspondingly increase *K'* cardinal

      else

07. $kmax = C(n, [n/2])$;   // maximum possible numbers of keys

08. $i = 1$;   // starting column products arity

09. $allSuperkeys = false$;   // initially, no superkeys possible for $i =$ 1

10.   **while** $i < n$ **and** $l < k_{max}$ **and** *not allSuperkeys* **do**

11. $allSuperkeys = true$;   //all   C(*n*,   *i*)   combinations   might   be superkeys

            repeat *for all* C(*n*, *i*) mapping products *p* made out of *i* elements

12.   **if** *p* is not a superkey **then**   // at least one no superkey

13. $allSuperkeys = false$;   // discovered on the current level *i*

14.   **if** *p* is minimally unique (in the given context) **then**

15. $K' = K' \cup \{ p \}$;   // add newly found key

16. $l = l + 1$;   // correspondingly increase *K'* cardinal

              end if;

            end if;   // (of 12.: *if p* is not a superkey)

          end repeat;

17. $i = i + 1$;   // increment level (mapping products arity)

        end while;

      end if;   // (of 04.: *if* $c_1 \bullet \ldots \bullet c_n$ is minimally unique)

    end if;   // (of 03.: *if* $n > 0$ and $c_1 \bullet \ldots \bullet c_n$ unique)

End ALGORITHM *A*3;

Fig. 4. Algorithm *A*3 (best practical keys discovery assistance)

5 Case Study

Dozens of case studies were conducted using the *A*3 implementation of *MatBase*. The most complex one was on an expense management application db having 521 fundamental tables with a total of 8621 columns. The first step was identifying the 6421 nonprime columns, which took some 430 work hours (i.e. 14 days for a team of four). The next one was discovering all 550 existing keys, which took some 55 work hours. Finally, enforcing these keys took some 300 work hours, as for many of them the db instance contained duplicates that had to be analyzed and correctly removed. The maximum number of prime columns in a table was 6. The maximum key arity was 4.

6 Conclusion and Further Work

All constraints (business rules) that are governing the subuniverses modeled by dbs should be enforced in the corresponding dbs' schemas: otherwise, their instances might be implausible. Among them, key (i.e. minimal uniqueness) type ones play a corner-stone role both practically and theoretically.

As [3] puts it in its 10th rule (Data Integrity Is Its Own Reward) "each 1 % data integrity failures will double the amount of time you spend troubleshooting them" and 11th rule (The Data Integrity Tipping Point) "any database which contains 20 % or more untrustworthy data is useless and will cost less to replace from source data than to fix". In our opinion, today's business cannot be really successful if their data is not almost 100 % trustworthy. For example, lack of keys may result in not paying invoices on due dates or paying them twice…

Unfortunately, minimal uniqueness is both relative, highly dependent on the context, semantic, hence only discoverable by humans, and not that easy to fully detect, as the complexity of this process is exponential in the number of involved table prime columns.

Consequently, it is our firm belief that any purely syntactic approach to inferring keys may not be successful. However, math and computer science may assist db designers in both validating existing enforced keys and discovering all those that are possibly missing, by algorithmically guiding them not to miss any possible key, not to waste time with either non-prime attributes or superkeys, and when to safely stop looking for them, as none others might be discovered afterwards.

This paper provides not only an overview of constraints and, especially, keys, but also three such algorithms designed in the framework of the Relational Data Model, applied on a real life interesting example, as well as a convincing case study.

In our opinion, $A3$ is the best suited of them for most practical cases of keys discovery. For validating existing keys, the first part of $A7$-$8/3$ from [15] is enough, as its bottom-up approach is the best possible in any context. $A1$ is faster and simpler than $A7$-$8/3$. $A2$ performs better than $A1$ and $A3$ when keys have high arities, exactly the same as $A3$ when there is only one key of the highest arity possible, but worse than $A1$ and $A3$ when arities are small. Moreover, $A2$ intensively requires both types of reasoning, bottom-up and top-down, which is much more difficult and prone to errors.

Our approach is semantical, just like keys are. All other existing approaches for keys discovery are purely syntactical; in particular, those based on data mining might yield lot of both false negative and false positive results.

Consequently, it is our firm belief that any RDBMS should implement at least $A3$ in order to assist its users in discovering all keys in any subuniverse modeled by an rdb, as keys discovery is a crucially important task in many areas of data management, including conceptual data modeling, query optimization, indexing, anomaly detection, and data integration.

Moreover, data mining approaches to keys discovery could also benefit from eliminating nonprime columns from their input, as well as, when validating their findings, from the reasoning techniques proposed in this paper.

Further work is intended towards at least partially automating the process of keys discovery by using ontologies and/or knowledge bases that would capture required expertise for various subuniverses of interest, starting with sets of non-prime properties and ending with sets of known keys.

References

1. Abedjan, Z., Naumann, F.: Advancing the discovery of unique column combinations. In: ACM CIKM 2011 International Conference on Information and Knowledge Management, Glasgow, UK, pp. 1565–1570. ACM Press, New York (2011)
2. Abiteboul, S., Hull, R., Vianu, V.: Foundations of Databases. Addison-Wesley, Reading (1995)
3. Berkus, J.: Josh's Rules (of Database Contracting). http://it.toolbox.com/blogs/database-soup/joshs-rules-of-database-contracting-17253
4. Calude, C.S., Longo, G.: The deluge of spurious correlations in big data. CDMTSC Report Series, CDMTSC-488. University of Auckland, New Zealand (2016)
5. Chen, P.P.: The entity-relationship model: toward a unified view of data. ACM Trans. Database Syst. 1(1), 9–36 (1976)
6. Codd, E.F.: A relational model for large shared data banks. CACM 13(6), 377–387 (1970)
7. Demetrovics, J.: On the equivalence of candidate keys with Sperner systems. Acta Cybernetica 4(3), 247–252 (1979)
8. Fadous, R., Forsyth, J.: Finding candidate keys for relational data bases. In: Proceedings ACMSIGMOD International Conference on Management of Data, pp 203–210. ACM Press, New York (1975)
9. Fagin, R.: A normal form for relational databases that is based on domains and keys. ACM Trans. Database Syst. 6(3), 387–415 (1981)
10. Heise, A., Quiane-Ruiz, J.-A., Abedjan, Z., Jentzsch, A., Naumann, F.: Scalable discovery of unique column combinations. Proc. VLDB 7(4), 301–312 (2013)
11. Huhtala, Y., Kärkkainen, J., Porkka, P., Toivonen, H.: TANE: an efficient algorithm for discovering functional and approximate dependencies. Comput. J. 42(2), 100–111 (1999)
12. Ilyas, I.F., Markl, V., Haas, P., Brown, P., Aboulnaga, A.: CORDS: automatic discovery of correlations and soft functional dependencies. In: Proceedings of the 2004 ACM SIGMOD International Conference on Management of Data, pp. 647–658. ACM, New York (2004)
13. Lucchesi, C.L., Osborn, S.L.: Candidate keys for relations. J. Comput. Syst. Sci. 17(2), 26–279 (1978)
14. Mancas, C.: A deeper insight into the mathematical data model. In: Proceedings of 13th ISDBMS International Seminar on DBMS, pp. 122–134. ICI Bucharest, Romania (1990)
15. Mancas, C.: Conceptual Data Modeling and Database Design: A Com-pletely Algorithmic Approach. Volume I: The Shortest Advisable Path. Apple Aca-de-mic Press/CRC Press, Waretown (2015)
16. Mancas, C., Crasovschi, L.: An optimal algorithm for computer-aided design of key type constraints. In: Proceedings of 1st Balkan BIT 2003 Information Technology Conference, pp. 574–584. Aristotle University Press, Thessaloniki, Greece (2003)

17. Mancas, C., Dragomir, S.: An optimal algorithm for structural keys design. In: Proceedings of SEA 2003 IASTED Conference on Software Engineering and Applications, pp. 328–334. Acta Press, Calgary (2003)
18. Mancas, C., Dragomir, S.: *MatBase Datalog¬* subsystem metacatalog conceptual design. In: Proceedingsof IASTED DBA 2004 Conference on Software Engineering and Applications, pp. 34–41. Acta Press, Calgary (2004)
19. Sismanis, Y., Brown, P., Haas, P.J., Reinwald, B.: GORDIAN: efficient and scalable discovery of composite keys. In: Proceedings of VLDB 06 Conference, pp. 691–702. VLDB Endowment (2006)
20. Symeonidou, D., Armant, V., Pernelle, N., Saïs, F.: SAKey: scalable almost key discovery in RDF data. In: Mika, P., Tudorache, T., Bernstein, A., Welty, C., Knoblock, C., Vrandečić, D., Groth, P., Noy, N., Janowicz, K., Goble, C. (eds.) ISWC 2014, Part I. LNCS, vol. 8796, pp. 33–49. Springer, Heidelberg (2014)
21. Thalheim, B.: The number of keys in relational and nested relational databases. Discrete Appl. Math. **40**, 265–282 (1992)
22. Thalheim, B.: Fundamentals of Entity-Relationship Modeling. Springer-Verlag, Berlin (2000)

A Classifier to Determine Whether a Document is Professionally or Machine Translated

Michael Luckert[1], Mortiz Schaefer-Kehnert[1], Welf Löwe[2], Morgan Ericsson[2], and Anna Wingkvist[2(✉)]

[1] Department of Computer Science, Linnaeus University, Växjö, Sweden
{ml223vs,ms224fw}@student.lnu.se
[2] Department of Computer Science, Linnaeus University, Växjö, Sweden
{welf.lowe,morgan.ericsson,anna.wingkvist}@lnu.se

Abstract. In an increasingly networked world, the availability of high quality translations is critical for success, especially in the context of international competition. International companies need to provide well translated, high quality technical documentation not only to be successful in the market but also to meet legal regulations. We seek to evaluate translation quality, specifically concerning technical documentation, and formulate a method to evaluate the translation quality of technical documents both when we do have access to the original documents and when we do not. We rely on state-of-the-art machine learning algorithms and translation evaluation metrics in the context of a knowledge discovery process. Our evaluation is performed on a sentence level where each sentence is classified as either *professionally translated* or *machine translated*. The results for each sentence is then combined to evaluate the full document. The research is based on a database that contains 22,327 sentences and 32 translation evaluation attributes, which are used to optimize Decision Trees that are used to evaluate translation quality. Our method achieves an accuracy of 70.48 % on sentence level for texts in the database and can accurately classify documents with at least 100 sentences.

Keywords: Information quality · Machine learning · Translation quality

1 Introduction

Machine translations are not perfect; it is for example difficult to ensure that the meaning of a sentence is preserved across translations. For certain texts, e.g., technical documentation, the quality of the text is critical since several product-specific standards must be met to be compliant with laws and regulations, and avoid possible compensations claims. Within the EU, multiple binding directives are adopted into national law and are often complemented by common industry standards [5, p. 5 et seq]. Hence, it is essential to be able to rank the quality of a given translation as part of the process to ensure that a document is correct.

© Springer International Publishing Switzerland 2016
V. Řepa and T. Bruckner (Eds.): BIR 2016, LNBIP 261, pp. 339–353, 2016.
DOI: 10.1007/978-3-319-45321-7_24

Machine translations need to be approved by people to ensure quality, so when it is used, the time and cost is shifted from document creation to evaluation and correction. Consequently, the evaluation of translated technical documentation provides an opportunity where companies can reduce time and costs as well as to create an effective way of translating documents. This is in a sense similar to the problem of outsourcing the translation task to external translators and then judging their work.

The difficulty of evaluating translation quality is due to the subjective nature and different aspects concerning the term quality, such as grammatical correctness, style improvements, or semantic correctness. It is also possible that the person requesting the translations does not speak the targeted language.

As a first step to ensure that a translation has been done properly and professionally as ordered, and not (only) by a machine translation system, we aim to use machine learning to produce a classifier that can determine whether a document has been translated by a human or a machine. The machine learning technique will be used in a knowledge discovery process [13] to classify documents by their translation type (i.e., *professional translation, machine translation*). Further, an approach on how to evaluate the quality of translated technical documents will be proposed. Concerning this issue, we address two main research questions:

1. How can the translation quality of technical documents be evaluated when the original document is available?
2. How can the translation quality of technical documents be evaluated when the original document is not available?

We answer these questions by providing a machine learning algorithm with optimal prediction quality for identifying professional and automated translations of technical documents with and without access to the original document.

Our focus on technical documentation has the potential to implicitly generate knowledge during the machine learning process, due to a smaller sized vocabulary compared to having no limitations on the text domain. Other domains, such as news stories will not be included. The classification and evaluation will focus on syntactic aspects of technical documentation, while the semantic parts will be left out.

We limit ourselves to translations between German and English. Since the examined technical documents did not provide multiple professional translations, there will be no human references used to evaluate the technical documents. We instead rely on pseudo references to circumvent the lack of human translations.

Finally, our work focuses on evaluations based on the results of machine learning approaches. Other techniques, such as the creation of a new metrics comparable to the BLEU or METEOR metric will not be taken into account.

2   Background

The idea of automatically rating machine translations is not new. One of the basic methods discussed in literature is the "round-trip translation", which works by translating a text fragment into a foreign language and back. Afterwards, the original text and the newly generated text are compared [16]. The "BiLingual Evaluation Understudy" (BLEU) algorithm, developed and presented by Papineni et al. in 2002, is based on comparison. BLEU defines document quality as a strong correlation between machine translations and the work of professional human translators. It is based on the idea that the length of a translated text is important, in addition to word-accuracy. According to Papineni et al., human translations have the tendency to be of higher quality and shorter than automated translations [9]. This idea was further developed in *NIST algorithm for machine translation evaluation* by the National Institute of Standards and Technology. This algorithm weights matching words according to their frequency in the respective reference translation [3]. A second evolution of the BLEU metric, *Metric for Evaluation of Translation with Explicit ORdering* (METEOR) was developed by Lavie et al. in 2005. The main difference is METEOR's ability to detect synonyms of words, which results in potentially fewer erroneous translations [7]. Furthermore, Kulesza and Shieber (2004) propose the use of Support Vector Machines to classify machine translations on a sentence level [6].

The use of human-produced reference translations is a costly way to evaluate machine translation systems. Popović et al. propose to use the IBM1 lexicon probabilities as a metric that does not rely on reference translations [10]. Gamon et al. propose a metric where a learned model is used to evaluate an input rather than a comparison with a reference. The model relies primarily on linguistic indicators and language features that are derived from the input. Furthermore, Albrecht and Hwa successfully use regression learning in combination with pseudo references [1,2]. These pseudo reference are generated by other machine translation systems rather than by human translators.

However, the focus on a specific domain of documents in order to gain implicit additional knowledge by using machine learning techniques is not sufficiently addressed and neither is the comparison of different machine learning approaches in order to classify whether documents have been translated professionally or automatically.

3 Method

The aim of this research is to train a binary classifier to classify a *candidate* translation as either *professionally* or *automatically* translated. Many of the methods to evaluate translation quality require a *reference* translation of high quality.

It is beyond the scope of this research to professionally translate documents, so we used 14 documents from an existing technical documentation available in both English and German[1]. We first extract text from these technical documents to form sentences. The sentence extraction resulted in 30,000 lines of

---

[1] Documentation for VMware's vSphere, available at https://pubs.vmware.com/vsphere-51/index.jsp?topic=%2Fcom.vmware.vsphere.doc%2FGUID-1B959D6B-41CA-4E23-A7DB-E9165D5A0E80.html (last accessed: January 19, 2016).

text that contained text fragments. Sentence extraction is not a straightforward task; 8,000 of the lines of text were not extracted correctly and resulted in fragments that did not form valid sentences. The final data sets that were used to train and test the machine learning algorithms each consisted of 22,327 sentences per translation system. To ensure an even distribution between the labels *professional translation* and *machine translation*, each data set was combined from two sets of sentences, one professionally translated and one automatically translated. So, each data set contained a total of 44,654 sentences.

To further examine the validity on different lengths of technical documents, we created documents with lengths that varied from 5 to 3,000 sentences per documentation by randomly combining sentences from the original 14 documents. Note that the creation of larger documents was more challenging, due to the limited amount of sentences and the needed amount of training data to generate a meaningful classification model. However, the information gained from the smaller documents is most likely more valuable, since we expect to need about 60 to 300 sentences to correctly classify a document.

Many of the evaluation metrics require high quality reference translations, e.g., the BLEU Score calculates a similarity value that indicates how similar the candidate and a reference are. Since we only have access to a single professional translation, we need to generate additional reference translations.

When we have access to the original text, we use it to generate three independent machine translations and use these as references. Since these references are not necessarily of high quality; we use them in two different ways to avoid the problem:

1. We use one of the machine translations as a reference. We know that this is not necessarily a high quality reference, but we are not interested in the quality of the translation, but rather if it is professional or automated. Since we use automatically translated references, it is reasonable to expect that these will be more similar to automatically translated candidates.
2. Albrecht and Hwa [1] show that multiple automatically translated references, *pseudo references*, can be combined to form a single high quality reference that is as good as a professionally translated reference. We rely on this result and combine two automatically translated references. We expect this combined reference to be more similar to a professionally translated candidate.

When we do not have access to the original text, we use a round-trip translation (from English to a foreign language and back to English) of the candidate as a reference. It is widely acknowledged, e.g., Somers [16], that it is not appropriate to use round-trip translation to evaluate translation quality, but it is again reasonable to expect the round-trip reference to be more similar to an automatically translated reference than a professional translated reference.

To reduce possible dependencies from the chosen machine translation systems, we use nine data combinations (cf. Table 1), where each system is used as candidate with one or two others as references. We used Freetranslation for all round-trip translations so all combinations that also used it as a candidate were removed. In addition to these, we used similar combinations for each professional translation, with one or two references selected from the three machine translation systems.

Table 1. Combinations of the various machine translation systems to create candidates and references. Note that a similar system is used to create references the professional candidate translations.

Candidate	Reference 1	Reference 2	Round-trip reference
Google Translate	Bing	—	via Freetranslation
Google Translate	Freetranslation	—	via Freetranslation
Google Translate	Bing	Freetranslation	via Freetranslation
Bing Translator	Google	—	via Freetranslation
Bing Translator	Freetranslation	—	via Freetranslation
Bing Translator	Google	Freetranslation	via Freetranslation
Freetranslation	Google	—	—
Freetranslation	Bing	—	—
Freetranslation	Google	Bing	—

We selected nine measurements from existing methods to evaluate machine translation quality as features.

1. Modified Unigram, Bigram, and Trigram BLEU Score
2. METEOR Score
3. METEOR Precision
4. METEOR Recall
5. METEOR F_1
6. METEOR Mean
7. METEOR Chunks
8. METEOR Fragmentation Penalty
9. METEOR Total Matches

The BLUE algorithm is a fast and inexpensive method to evaluating the quality of machine translations in a fully automated manner, by calculating a value between 0 and 1 depending on "closeness" of reference and candidate. To examine the difference between single word BLEU scores and word sequence *BLEU Scores* for the given data set, we added BLEU scores for 2-grams and 3-grams as features.

The *METEOR Score* is a version of the BLEU score that has been optimized to work on sentence level.

The *METEOR Precision and Recall* scores describes the amount of similar unigrams in candidate and reference translation, relative to the unigram count in the candidate fragment. The *METEOR F_1* score calculates the harmonic mean between Precision and Recall. The *METEOR Mean* is similar to the F_1 score, but Recall is weighted as nine times more important than Precision.

The *METEOR Chunk* score counts the minimum number of chunks required for each sentence and *Fragmentation Penalty* calculates penalties to give more weight to longer n-gram matches. A sentence with many longer n-grams in the candidate and reference translations requires fewer chunks, which in turn results in a lower penalty score.

The *METEOR Total Matches* score counts the total matches found between reference and candidate translation on a unigram basis. The grammatical correctness of a sentence or text can be validated or evaluated. Rule-based programs that check the sentence on violations of these rules and report the corresponding errors normally do this.

Overall correctness is harder to evaluate than the grammatical correctness in our case. The focus on technical documentation results in some properties of the documents that complicate these evaluations. The used language is highly technical by nature and contains many words that are not in common dictionaries. Since technical documentation often focuses on a specific product by a company, it will probably contain many proper nouns that would not even be in dictionaries that are specialized for technical documentation.

The style of a sentence is in general not applicable to detecting false sentences. However, metrics, such as readability can be used to determine document quality. We used the following additional six measurements as features.

1. Reference Length
2. Translation Edit Rate (TER)
3. Parts of Speech
4. Flesch Reading Ease
5. Used References
6. Mistake Count

The *Reference Length* score is the difference between the candidate translation length and the reference translation length. The *Translation Edit Rate* [14,15] score measures the amount of required edits to transform the candidate text to the reference translation, relative to the text length. We also use the absolute number of edits, the TER Total Edits.

Table 2. Overview over the parameter optimization ranges.

Parameter	Minimum	Maximum
Maximal Depth	1	50
Minimal Gain	0.01	0.3
Minimal Leaf Size	50	500
Number of Prepruning Alternatives	0	100
Minimal Size for Split	50	5,000
Confidence	0.001	0.5

The *Parts of Speech* score is a boolean value that signifies whether the candidate translation matches a given minimal pattern of required parts of speech tags to form a grammatically correct sentence in English. *Mistake Count* is the number of style and grammar mistakes according to Language Tool. Language Tool groups mistakes into 94 different categories. The numbers of mistakes in each of these categories were also used as features.

The *Flesch Reading Ease* algorithm calculates a score that measures the readability of sentences and documents.

Table 3. Overview over the best Decision Tree results on a sentence level.

Candidate	Reference 1	Reference 2	Accuracy	F_1-professional	F_1-machine
Google	Bing	—	69.09 %	0.649	0.724
Google	Freetranslation	—	67.91 %	0.646	0.706
Google	Bing	Freetranslation	70.48 %	0.651	0.744
Bing	Google	—	70.18 %	0.698	0.706
Bing	Freetranslation	—	68.75 %	0.683	0.692
Bing	Google	Freetranslation	70.23 %	0.689	0.715
Freetranslation	Bing	—	66.22 %	0.629	0.689
Freetranslation	Google	—	67.85 %	0.669	0.687
Freetranslation	Bing	Google	67.52 %	0.675	0.676

Table 4. Results from the classifications of the 14 original documents professionally and machine translated. The two columns with prediction results show the percentage of sentences classified as either professionally or machine translated for the two translations. All documents are correctly classified.

Document	Length	Predicted professional	Predicted machine
1	213	65.73 %	62.05 %
2	360	66.94 %	68.89 %
3	722	67.87 %	75.67 %
4	790	65.32 %	72.93 %
5	903	71.10 %	73.71 %
6	1,081	66.05 %	72.72 %
7	1,175	66.30 %	75.13 %
8	1,387	59.63 %	74.53 %
9	1,607	72.56 %	66.15 %
10	1,973	69.54 %	71.91 %
11	2,461	63.71 %	66.74 %
12	3,065	59.38 %	72.15 %
13	3,076	69.15 %	71.80 %
14	3,514	73.76 %	67.69 %

Multiple reference translations were used to provide a more standardized reference. Most metrics, such as the METEOR and BLEU score are able to cope with multiple reference translations, by calculating scores for all references and choosing the best score. The *Used References* is the reference translations that were used. We monitor which references that were used more often during the calculation of all metrics to generate additional knowledge that could ease the classification process for the given machine learning algorithm.

We used Decision Tree Learning to create a classifier. The main advantage of Decision Trees is that they are transparent; the model and the relevance of features can easily be inspected. Decision Trees are robust when it comes to outliers and missing values, which is a huge benefit for mining tasks. We used the C4.5 [11,12] Decision Tree Learning algorithm. The parameters in Table 2 were used to optimize the Decision Trees and the holdout set was randomly selected as 30 % of the data set.

The values for each of the metrics were post-processed to remove outliers and duplicated values, normalize the values, and finally remove features that are correlated. We used Class Outlier Factors to detect outliers and remove the 5 %

Table 5. Results from the classification of randomly created documents. The two sets of documents contained a majority of professionally and machine translated sentences, respectively.

Document length	Number of documents	Predicted correctly (Avg.)	Misclassification
5	5,000	67.45 %	969 (19.38 %)
10	2,500	68.15 %	153 (6.12 %)
20	1,250	68.66 %	23 (1.84 %)
50	500	68.12 %	4 (0.80 %)
100	250	68.22 %	0 (0.00 %)
250	50	68.38 %	0 (0.00 %)
500	25	68.25 %	0 (0.00 %)
1,000	10	68.70 %	0 (0.00 %)
3,000	10	68.88 %	0 (0.00 %)
5	5,000	71.04 %	1,345 (26.90 %)
10	2,500	69.92 %	404 (16.16 %)
20	1,250	69.98 %	63 (5.04 %)
50	500	70.56 %	1 (0.20 %)
100	250	71.01 %	0 (0.00 %)
250	50	70.20 %	0 (0.00 %)
500	25	70.70 %	0 (0.00 %)
1,000	10	70.45 %	0 (0.00 %)
3,000	10	69.57 %	0 (0.00 %)

most deviating values. To reduce the training and computation time, we remove attributes that correlate by more than 90 %.

4   Results

Research Question 1 focuses on the evaluation of translations when we have the original document. We achieved an average accuracy of 68.69 % and a standard deviation of 0.014 for the nine combinations of candidates and references. Table 3 shows the results with the highest accuracies for sentence predictions including the respective F_1 scores. We built and evaluated 50,000 Decision Trees for each candidate-reference combination.

To evaluate not only sentences but entire documents, we applied the sentence-based approach to documents by classifying each sentence as either professionally or machine translated. The full document was then classified according to the majority of the sentences. Table 4 shows how the professionally and machine translated versions of each of the 14 original documents were classified. For example, the 65.73 % of the sentences in the professionally translated version of Document 1 were classified as professionally translated and thus the entire document was considered as such.

The more generalized approach, based on randomly created documents used for the evaluations, supports our initial findings (cf. Table 5). The evaluation uses

Table 6. Results from the classifications of the 14 original documents professionally and machine translated without knowledge of the original document. Note that predictions below 50 % indicate a bad prediction, so the professionally translated Document 1 was misclassified as machine translated, for example.

Document	Length	Predicted professional	Predicted machine
1	213	49.30 %	62.44 %
2	360	66.94 %	56.39 %
3	722	49.31 %	54.02 %
4	790	53.92 %	61.39 %
5	903	64.23 %	56.37 %
6	1,081	58.09 %	60.41 %
7	1,175	64.17 %	56.77 %
8	1,387	60.27 %	51.12 %
9	1,607	59.61 %	60.61 %
10	1,973	56.61 %	60.52 %
11	2,461	52.95 %	59.37 %
12	3,065	58.30 %	51.48 %
13	3,076	61.35 %	58.06 %
14	3,514	69.24 %	50.88 %

a separately optimized Decision Tree model for each document length. Every used model is the optimal from a set of 729 tested trees.

Research Question 2 focuses on evaluation of translations without the original document. If we only consider features that do not require a reference translation, the accuracy is about 51–54 % on sentence-level, which is about as classifying on random. If we add a reference generated from round-trip translation, the accuracy becomes about 60 %. If we use Google as a candidate, the accuracy is 56.79 % and F_1 scores for Professional and Machine are 0.562 and 0.574, respectively. If we instead use Bing as a candidate, the accuracy rises to 60.50 %, with F_1 scores 0.593 and 0.612.

Tables 6 and 7 show the results of the classification on document-level. We optimize the Decision Trees in the same way as Research Question 1. As expected, the classifications are on average worse than those for Research Question 1.

Table 7. Results from the classification of randomly created documents without knowledge of the original documents. The two sets of documents contained a majority of professionally and machine translated sentences, respectively.

Document length	Number of documents	Predicted correctly (Avg.)	Misclassification
5	5,000	60.46 %	1,561 (31.22 %)
10	2,500	62.05 %	765 (30.60 %)
20	1,250	60.11 %	316 (25.28 %)
50	500	62.55 %	55 (11.00 %)
100	250	62.00 %	7 (2.80 %)
250	50	64.14 %	0 (0.00 %)
500	25	63.01 %	0 (0.00 %)
1,000	10	60.37 %	0 (0.00 %)
3,000	10	59.64 %	0 (0.00 %)
5	5,000	58.66 %	1,720 (34.40 %)
10	2,500	57.23 %	534 (21.36 %)
20	1,250	58.43 %	216 (17.28 %)
50	500	56.54 %	72 (14.40 %)
100	250	56.81 %	13 (5.20 %)
250	50	55.47 %	0 (0.00 %)
500	25	56.77 %	0 (0.00 %)
1,000	10	58.54 %	0 (0.00 %)
3,000	10	58.43 %	0 (0.00 %)

5   Discussion

Our method makes a number of assumptions, e.g., that multiple references that are combined add value, that round-trip translation references add value, and that we can generate additional documents from sentences from the 14 original documents. The validity of these assumptions has an impact on how our results should be interpreted.

Table 3 shows that the accuracy is generally improved when we use two references. We speculate that one reason for this is the machine learning task. In contrast to many evaluation approaches concerning machine translation systems, we aim to classify the given sentences into two classes instead of rating its quality. Therefore, the use of a single or multiple pseudo reference serves a different goal. Many of the used attributes calculate similarity scores between the reference and the candidate translation; a machine translated reference can be used to identify automated translations due to high similarities with the given reference, while professional translations might deviate from it. In contrast, the use of multiple pseudo references aims to generate a high quality translation reference by combining the given machine translation systems [1, 2, 4]. The use of multiple references seems to increase the accuracy slightly, e.g., the addition of Freetranslation as a second reference to a data set that uses Google as candidate and Bing as a reference tends to improve accuracy.

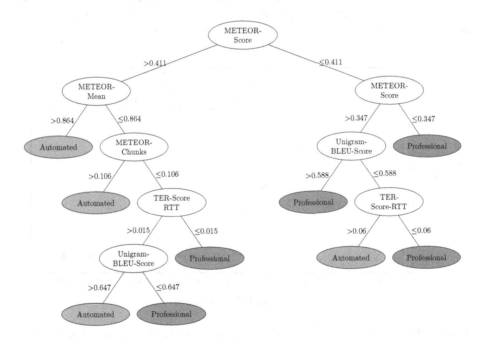

Fig. 1. An example of a created Decision Tree

The improved accuracy from multiple references suggests that features that rely on references are more important. To verify this, we analyzed the Decision Trees. Decision Trees place the most influential attribute at every splitting point and the most significant attribute is always placed as the root node. Figure 1 depicts an optimized Decision Tree for a combination with Google Translate as the candidate translation and Freetranslation as a reference. The most used attributes by a substantial margin were the METEOR Score and its intermediate results, such as METEOR Mean and METEOR Chunks. The next most important attributes, showing the most frequently in the top levels of the Decision Tree, were the BLEU Score and the difference in translation lengths. It is clear that features that rely on reference translations are more influential than metrics that only use the candidate.

The addition of a round-trip translation to be used as an additional reference further improved the accuracy for both research questions. We decided to use Freetranslation for round-trip translations since it achieved the worst results when used as a candidate. However, it always improved accuracy when it was used as a second reference. This suggests that combinations of different translations, but not necessarily better ones, improve accuracy.

As expected, a longer document (measured in number of sentences) are not misclassified as often as shorter. In our experiment, we observe up to a 34.40 % misclassification rate for documents with five sentences. This drops to 5.20 % when we increase to 100 sentences. If we have the original document, 100 sentences is enough to always classify documents in our dataset correctly, while we need at least 250 sentences when we do not have the original.

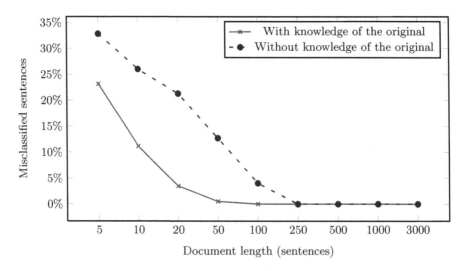

Fig. 2. The misclassification rates are strictly lower for every document length when using the classified developed for Research Question 1. Furthermore, the required document length to avoid any misclassification is lower.

There are clearly visible differences in prediction distributions between the 14 original documents, e.g., if we have the original between 59.38 % and 75.13 % are correctly classified. This suggests that certain documents are easier to classify than others. If we instead consider the documents that are constructed by randomly generating sentences from the original documents, there is a much smaller difference (3.59 compared to 15.75 % points). So, our generated documents are more even than the original, which might have an impact on our results. Furthermore, the misclassification rate is clearly higher for Research Question 2, with 5,259 misclassified documents for the complete data set of 19,190 documents, while the classifier for Research Question 1 classifies 2,962 documents falsely. This results in a total accuracy of 72.59 % for the classifier with no knowledge of the original document and an accuracy of 84.56 % for the classifier with knowledge of the original document. This accuracy should be taken with caution, since the results are highly dependent on the length of the given document; documents with five sentences have misclassification rates of 19 % to 34 % and documents with 250 sentences or more are not misclassified at all. Figure 2 compares the misclassification rates based on the respective document lengths for both classifiers.

6   Conclusions

We investigated how well we can identify professionally and machine translations with and without the original document. We relied on Decision Tree Learning to create a number of optimized binary classifiers. We achieved an average accuracy of 68.69 % when we have access to the original document and 58,65 % when we do not. We are able to correctly classify all of the 14 documents when we have access to the original document, but fail to classify two when we do not have access to the original.

To further validate the document-based results, we created a set of 19,190 documents by randomly combining sentences to fictive documents of lengths varying from 5 to 3,000 sentences. When we used a classifier trained without knowledge of the original document, we observed a misclassification rate of 34.40 % for the smallest documents to no misclassification for documents containing 250. A classifier trained with knowledge of the original document achieved a misclassification rate of 26.90 % for the smallest documents and no misclassification for documents with 100 or more sentences.

The work presented here only considers Decision Tree Learning. We have conducted preliminary studies using other learning algorithms, e.g., k-Nearest Neighbor but need to perform further optimization steps to report on it.

There are many opportunities to improve the features used and how we evaluate documents. We can, for example, improve the Mistake Count measurement. In areas of highly technical vocabulary, attempts to, e.g., use neutral nouns as a replacement for technical terms or proper nouns have been introduced. Additionally, we could study the different mistake categories more closely to further elaborate their influences on text quality and correctness.

Our current approach classifies a document based on what the majority of the sentences are classified as, no matter the confidence. We could potentially improve our approach by considering confidences for each sentence and aggregate these to document-level. This approach would result in a more fine-grained document classification, since the algorithm's certainty for the sentence-based classifications is taken into account.

Acknowledgements. We are grateful for Andreas Kerren's and Ola Peterson's valuable feedback on the Master's thesis project [8] that this research is based on.

References

1. Albrecht, J., Hwa, R.: Regression for sentence-level MT evaluation with pseudo references. In: Proceedings of the 45th Annual Meeting of the Association of Computational Linguistics, pp. 296–303 (2007)
2. Albrecht, J.S., Hwa, R.: The role of pseudo references in MT evaluation. In: Proceedings of the Third Workshop on Statistical Machine Translation, pp. 187–190. Association for Computational Linguistics (2008)
3. Doddington, G.: Automatic evaluation of machine translation quality using n-gram co-occurrence statistics. In: Proceedings of the Second International Conference on Human Language Technology Research, pp. 138–145. Morgan Kaufmann Publishers Inc. (2002)
4. Gamon, M., Aue, A., Smets, M.: Sentence-level MT evaluation without reference translations: beyond language modeling. In: Proceedings of the 10th Annual Conference of the European Association for Machine Translation (EAMT), pp. 103–111 (2005)
5. Kothes, L.: Grundlagen der Technischen Dokumentation: Anleitungen verständlich und normgerecht erstellen. Springer, Heidelberg (2010)
6. Kulesza, A., Shieber, S.M.: A learning approach to improving sentence-level MT evaluation. In: Proceedings of the 10th International Conference on Theoretical and Methodological Issues in Machine Translation, pp. 75–84 (2004)
7. Lavie, A., Agarwal, A.: METEOR: an automatic metric for MT evaluation with high levels of correlation with human judgments. In: Proceedings of the Second Workshop on Statistical Machine Translation, pp. 228–231. Association for Computational Linguistics (2007)
8. Luckert, M., Schaefer-Kehnert, M.: Using machine learning methods for evaluating the quality of technical documents. Master's thesis, Linnaeus University, Sweden (2016). http://urn.kb.se/resolve?urn=urn:nbn:se:lnu:diva-52087
9. Papineni, K., Roukos, S., Ward, T., Zhu, W.J.: BLEU: a method for automatic evaluation of machine translation. In: Proceedings of the 40th Annual Meeting on Association for Computational Linguistics, pp. 311–318. Association for Computational Linguistics (2002)
10. Popović, M., Vilar, D., Avramidis, E., Burchardt, A.: Evaluation without references: IBM1 scores as evaluation metrics. In: Proceedings of the Sixth Workshop on Statistical Machine Translation, pp. 99–103. Association for Computational Linguistics (2011)
11. Quinlan, J.R.: Induction of decision trees. Mach. Learn. **1**(1), 81–106 (1986)
12. Quinlan, J.R.: C4.5: Programs for Machine Learning. Morgan Kaufmann Publishers Inc., San Francisco (1993)

13. Rokach, L., Maimon, O.: Data Mining with Decision Trees: Theory and Applications. World Scientific, River Edge (2014)

14. Shapira, D., Storer, J.A.: Edit distance with move operations. In: Apostolico, A., Takeda, M. (eds.) CPM 2002. LNCS, vol. 2373, pp. 85–98. Springer, Heidelberg (2002)

15. Snover, M., Dorr, B., Schwartz, R., Micciulla, L., Makhoul, J.: A study of translation edit rate with targeted human annotation. In: Proceedings of Association for Machine Translation in the Americas, pp. 223–231 (2006)

16. Somers, H.: Round-trip translation: what is it good for? In: Proceedings of the Australasian Language Technology Workshop, pp. 127–133 (2005)

Author Index

Printed in the United States
By Bookmasters